"These are essential documents pertaining to one of the most important theological debates in American history. They remain of great interest today for not only deepening how Reformed churches might understand the Lord's Supper in accord with Calvin, but also for the possibility of Reformed ecumenical convergence with churches from which they have long been divided. . . . The editors have performed a great service to theology and the church."

—GEORGE HUNSINGER
Princeton Theological Seminary

"No theological debate in nineteenth-century America displayed more erudition, logical acumen, and knowledge of European scholarship than the clash between Hodge and Nevin over the sacraments. The editors of this volume not only provide stunningly good introductions, but they also arrange the material in an ingenious way that deepens our insights into the issues and enables us to easily follow the discussion."

—E. BROOKS HOLIFIELD
Emory University

Coena Mystica

The Mercersburg Theology Study Series
Volume 2

The Mercersburg Theology Study Series is an attempt to make available for the first time, in attractive, readable, and scholarly modern editions, the key writings of the 19th-century movement known as the Mercersburg Theology. We believe this will be an important contribution to the scholarly community and to the broader reading public, who can at last be properly introduced to this unique blend of American and European, Reformed and catholic theology.

PLANNED VOLUMES IN THE SERIES (TITLES SUBJECT TO CHANGE):

The Mystical Presence, and the Doctrine of the Reformed Church on the Lord's Supper
Edited by Linden J. DeBie

Coena Mystica: The Eucharistic Debate of Nevin and Hodge
Edited by Linden J. DeBie

Principles of Church History: Selected Writings of Philip Schaff
Edited by Theodore Trost and David Bains

The Incarnate Word: Selected Writings on Christology
Edited by William B. Evans

"One, Holy, Catholic, and Apostolic": Nevin's Writings on Ecclesiology
Edited by Sam Hamstra

Miscellaneous Writings on the Sacraments
Edited by David Layman

Essays in Church History
Edited by Nick Needham

The Early Creeds
Edited by Charles Yrigoyen

The Heidelberg Catechism
Edited by Lee Barrett

The Mercersburg Liturgy
Edited by Michael Farley

Schaff's America and Related Writings
Edited by Stephen Graham

Philosophy and the Contemporary World
Edited by Adam S. Borneman

Mercersburg and Its Critics
Edited by Darryl G. Hart

See www.mercersburgtheology.org for more about the series, as well as a treasury of resources for Mercersburg research.

Coena Mystica

Debating Reformed Eucharistic Theology

Edited by LINDEN J. DeBIE

General Editor, W. BRADFORD LITTLEJOHN

WIPF & STOCK · Eugene, Oregon

COENA MYSTICA
Debating Reformed Eucharistic Theology

The Mercersburg Theology Study Series 2

Wipf & Stock
An Imprint of Wipf and Stock Publishers
199 W. 8th Ave., Suite 3
Eugene, OR 97401

www.wipfandstock.com

ISBN 13: 978-1-62032-767-8

Manufactured in the U.S.A.

Contents

Foreword

T HE MERCERSBURG THEOLOGY STUDY Series is a welcome addition to the treasury of primary historical theological sources available to scholars and students of American Protestantism, Reformed theology and ecumenical sacramentology. The present volume is a natural companion to the first volume in the series, John Williamson Nevin's *The Mystical Presence and The Doctrine of the Reformed Church on the Lord's Supper*. Two years after Nevin published *The Mystical Presence*, Charles Hodge, arguably the most important Old School Reformed theologian, published a review of the book in the *Biblical Repertory and Princeton Review*. Largely critical, Hodge accused Nevin of Romanist leanings and a host of enduring heresies. While Nevin could not publish his response to Hodge in such a prestigious journal, he published a series of articles in *The Weekly Messenger*, reprinting sections of Hodge's long essay along with commentary defending his own work and criticizing the positions inherent in Hodge's review.

Why should this extended critique of a book review warrant republication today? Perhaps the most important reason is the key theological question underlying the debate—as Nevin states it, "What think ye of Christ?" The debate over Nevin's treatment of the Lord's Supper underscores the interconnections among key Christian doctrines. One cannot talk about the Eucharist without also talking about the person and work of Christ, the nature and role of the church, sanctification, or even how doctrines develop over time. Also important is the key historical question guiding this debate, "What was the real doctrine of the Reformed church on the Lord's Supper?" Toward the end, Nevin apologizes for the length of his series of articles, yet claims that it is warranted by "the importance of the subject discussed, and the character of the occasion requiring it." He recognized in Hodge "a respectable argument against it, based on some knowledge of the subject, and paying some proper tribute of respect to its intrinsic importance." (171)

Substantial debates help illuminate deep questions. The trinitarian and christological debates of the 4th and 5th centuries could not be brought to rapid conclusions because the issues they addressed were so fundamental to Christian worship, self-understanding, and salvation. Their progress clarified what was at stake, what was enduring, what was less than sufficient. Nevin and Hodge themselves often refer to these debates, recognizing similar stakes in their own disagreements, even though they disagree on how doctrinal clarity comes about. Hodge distinguishes between what was "an uncongenial foreign element" and what was "a genuine portion of [the church's] faith," while Nevin seeks to recognize the "product of [the church's] general life, starting forth at various points from the fermenting process which had gone before."

The church in the early centuries found it difficult to find precise language that was culturally intelligible; a similar challenge is evident here. What do such important terms as "nature," "presence," "life," and "union" mean? The 19th-century debate over the Eucharist presented in this volume, while less ecumenical in scope, sheds light on issues involved in historical and contemporary questions concerning the Eucharist. Also helpful is the interplay between historical and theological questions which serves as a window onto the burgeoning historical sensibility of 19th century American scholars. This dynamic continues to apply to a variety of contemporary theological debates.

The volume editor, Linden DeBie, has provided a helpful biographical essay, indicating the shared theological formation of Nevin and Hodge as well as their divergent paths. The Introduction provides an overview of the debate which orients the reader to the structure of the series of *Weekly Messenger* articles. Throughout, the footnotes guide the reader via background information and evaluations by contemporary scholars of the historical arguments made by Nevin and Hodge, indicating both arguments that have withstood historical scrutiny and those that overreached their sources.

This debate over the Reformed understanding of the Eucharist deserves more attention than it has generally received. Hodge and Nevin each have their theological descendants in the church today. While Hodge's have often had the more prominent voice, those of Nevin are enjoying a renewed evaluation in light of recent ecumenical, theological and ecclesiological developments. This volume smoothes the way for those seeking to understand the historical and theological heritage of Reformed Protestantism.

Anne T. Thayer
Paul and Minnie Diefenderfer Professor of Mercersburg and Ecumenical
Theology and Church History
Lancaster Theological Seminary

Editorial Approach and Acknowledgments

THE PURPOSE OF THIS series is to reprint the key writings of the Mercersburg theologians in a way that is both fully faithful to the original and yet easily accessible to non-specialist modern readers. These twin goals, often in conflict, have determined our editorial approach throughout. We have sought to do justice to both by being very hesitant to make any alterations to the original, but being very free with additions to the original in the form of annotations.

The entirety of Nevin's twelve *Weekly Messenger* articles, which contained the entire text of Hodge's review of *The Mystical Presence*, are republished here, without significant alterations. We have decided to leave spelling, capitalization, and emphasis exactly as in the original (including Nevin's somewhat idiosyncratic indulgence of all-caps), except in cases of clear typographical errors, which have been silently corrected. We have, however, taken a few liberties in altering punctuation (essentially just comma usage, with which Nevin is exceedingly prodigal) and abbreviations for clarity, consistency, and ease of reading, as well as adopting standard modern conventions such as the italicization of book titles and foreign-language words. The entirety of the text has been re-typeset and re-formatted to render it as clear and accessible as possible; pagination, of course, has accordingly been changed. Original section headings have been retained, although to make it easier for the reader to follow the back-and-forth of the debate, we have clearly noted which sections are Nevin's and which are Hodge's, which has occasionally required additional headings. Chapter headings are not original and have been supplied by us.

Original footnotes are retained, though for ease of typesetting, they have been subsumed within the series of numbered footnotes which includes the annotations we have added to this edition. Footnotes in the original came from one of three sources: Hodge (notes appearing in his original review), Nevin (notes he appended to his critique of Hodge, or which he occasionally added to sections of Hodge's text by way of response), or the Editor of the *Weekly Messenger*. In each case, we have indicated the source of the footnote in brackets at the beginning of each note. Our own annotations and additions, which comprise the majority of the footnotes, are wholly enclosed in brackets, whether that be within a footnote that was original, or around an entire footnote when it is one that we have added, and are marked with the ascription "—ed."

Source citations in the original have been retained in their original form, but where necessary, we have provided expanded citation information in brackets or numerated footnotes, and have sought to direct the reader toward modern editions of these works, where they exist. Where citations are lacking in the original, we have tried as much as possible to provide them in our footnotes.

In the annotations we have added (almost entirely in the footnotes, though very occasionally in the form of brackets in the body text), we have attempted to be comprehensive without becoming cumbersome. In addition to offering citations for works referenced in the original, these additions fall under three further headings:

1) Translation

2) Unfamiliar terms and historical figures

3) Additional source material

4) Commentary

We have attempted to be comprehensive in providing translations of any untranslated foreign-language quotations in these works (a number of passages were translated already by the editor of the *Weekly Messenger*, and we have not attempted to revise these translations), and have wherever possible made use of existing translations in standard modern editions, to which the reader is referred. Ryan Handermann served as an indefatigable research assistant in tracking down these translations, and, where they were unavailable, used his own extensive knowledge of Latin to provide a translation. We are deeply grateful to him for his assistance.

Additional annotations serve to elucidate any unfamiliar words, concepts, or (especially) historical figures to which Nevin refers, and where applicable, to provide references to sources where the reader may pursue further information (for these additional sources, only abbreviated citations are provided in the footnotes; for full bibliographical information, see the bibliography). Interestingly, one of our chief aids in compiling this information was the *New Schaff-Herzog Encyclopedia of Religious Knowledge* (Grand Rapids, MI: Baker, 1949–50), the descendant of Philip Schaff's original celebrated reference work. Other reference works include *The Oxford Dictionary of the Christian Church*, edited by F. L. Cross, Second Edition (Oxford: OUP, 1993) and *The Encyclopedia of Philosophy*, edited by Paul Edwards (London: Macmillan, 1967).

Note that whenever the disputants refer to or quote from Nevin's *Mystical Presence*, we have provided in the footnotes the page number from the edition just published in this Mercersburg Theology Study Series (abbreviated "MTSS edition").

As for commentary, we have sought to resist the temptation to play referee in this dispute any more than strictly necessary. Although some readers, when Nevin and Hodge are tossing back and forth contradictory historical claims, may desire to hear a quick verdict on who was right and who was wrong, based on the insights of modern historical scholarship, many others no doubt would rather be left the freedom to consult the sources and judge for themselves. And indeed, any verdict we might offer on such complex questions would be partial and contentious. Accordingly, we have sought to make it as easy as possible for readers to find the relevant primary and secondary sources to adjudicate this debate. However, to that end, we have taken advantage of a few opportunities when a particularly unjustified claim may be flagged as a way of pointing toward a more nuanced discussion in the secondary literature, particularly the magisterial work of Brian Gerrish in this field. Other annotations will serve to elucidate the nature of Hodge and Nevin's disagreement at key points. Much more extensive commentary of both sorts, critical and elucidatory, may be found in the Introduction below.

ACKNOWLEDGMENTS

As the general editor, I would like to thank Linden DeBie for his willingness to add this volume, which had been a pet project of his already for a few years before I proposed the Mercersburg Theology Study Series, to our project. Adapting the volume for the series required a great deal of extra work and reformatting, all of which he undertook immediately after having completed the editorship of the first volume in the series. No other contributor has committed to edit more than one volume, so Linden's willingness to undertake two in a row has been an immense gift, without which it might have taken this series much longer to get off the ground. Moreover, I would again like to thank Christian Amondson at Wipf and Stock and Deborah Clemens of the Mercersburg Society for their support of this project, and the whole Mercersburg Society for lending it generous financial support. Ryan Handermann has, as with volume 1, taken time away from a grueling teaching schedule to chase down footnotes and provide translations. And thanks also to Keith Mathison for taking the time to read through draft chapters of this volume to flag any omissions or errors.

* * * * *

As volume editor, I want thank the editorial team for their superb support and counsel. I would especially like to thank our general editor Bradford Littlejohn "who saved me from a world of sin." I have come to fully understand the value of gifted and committed colleagues without whom a volume of this quality would not be possible. He has already become a leading light in the cause to bring the Mercersburg movement to the attention of a wider audience. The Mercersburg Theology Study Series will open up a virtually overlooked corpus of theological and historical material of monumental importance to the history of American theology. Bradford Littlejohn will be a significant factor in that effort insuring the highest quality in the material produced. As I take my leave of the series I do so in full confidence of the series' leadership. On a personal note I want to thank my wife Mary and my daughter Cailyn for their patience with me in this long process. Finally, I want thank Charles Yrigoyen Jr. for reading the early draft and making many helpful comments.

Biographical Essay

Parallel Lives, Antagonistic Aims

CHARLES HODGE WAS BORN in Philadelphia on the 28th or 29th of December, 1797, at midnight. His great-grandparents were Irish immigrants who joined the European exodus and found economic stability in the New World. As successful merchants, they embraced the promised security of higher education for their children and access to otherwise closed doors of opportunity. Charles's father, Hugh, born August 20, 1755, took full advantage of the family's new prosperity and graduated from the College of New Jersey[1] in the field of medicine in 1773. But reading, writing, and arithmetic, indeed education itself, had as its first goal the indoctrination of Protestant young men and women into the evangelical faith. Biblical texts and stories were the materials of learning, and for Presbyterians the world of the Westminster Catechism[2] was the context of that learning. Such was the world of Charles and his four older siblings.

John Williamson Nevin was born just seven years later on Sunday, February 20, far outside of Philadelphia into a Presbyterian, Scots-Irish family. His birthplace was Herron's Branch, near Shippensburg, Pennsylvania, a modest Franklin County farming community. Yet the area was less sleepy than today. Shippensburg was an important port on the Susquehanna River and a bustling center of commerce and trade. Nevin's family had accumulated considerable wealth in farming, and Nevin's father was a prominent and well-educated pillar of the community.

Like Hodge, Nevin was reared on the Westminster Catechism, but also in the same culturally conditioned way of reading the Catechism. By then Presbyterian communities reflected the domination of *New Light*[3] piety. The hinge of the system was

---

1. The College of New Jersey became Princeton University.

2. In 1647 the General Assembly of the Presbyterian Church ratified the Westminster Confession. It became the definitive statement of Presbyterian doctrine, and was the work of the Westminster Assembly. Based on that confession, the assembly provided the church with handbooks of questions and answers. Called "the Larger" and "the Shorter" Catechisms, they were finished in 1647.

3. The New Light perspective had become universal among American Calvinists by the time of Hodge and Nevin. The division over *Old Side* and *New Side* goes back to pre-colonial times, having as much to do with questioning European habits as anything, and had virtually disappeared. The New Light challenge dates as far back as the late 1600s, but is most commonly associated with the Great Awakening. It

the family, where intimate Christian nurture insured that family members received a thorough background in the Westminster tradition. Children began their training with simple Bible questions, followed by the Mother's Catechism, then the Assembly's Shorter Catechism, and finally, the Assembly's Larger Catechism. Likewise, the church was fundamental to the young person's incorporation into the faith. Preaching was central to the Reformed, and the sacraments played a vital role in establishing the community's identity. Preparation and celebration of the Lord's Supper could last as many as four days and preoccupy the entire community. Congregates were expected to fast and pray throughout the festival season.[4]

In 1810, Charles along with his brother Hugh attended the Classical Academy in Somerville, New Jersey. Two years later Charles entered Princeton Academy. It was the same year that Princeton Theological Seminary was founded. The beloved Dr. Archibald Alexander, Hodge's future lifelong friend and confidant, was its first professor. Hodge entered the academy as a sophomore and faced the rigors of classical education. A glance at the required texts provides a first insight into how philosophic realism became the foundation of Hodge's theological system. Hodge read Blair's Lectures for moral philosophy; *Andrew's Logic* provided skill in reasoning, and Witherspoon's Lectures were the basis of sound theology.[5]

is broadly described as a form of Pietism having both European and American characteristics. The New Light revolution began as early as 1690 among the Dutch Reformed, and centered around identification with certain leaders' particular interpretations of Calvin, and spilled over into social practices including, among Old Siders, long hair as preferred to short, more personal freedom, especially on Sunday, and an obvious class distinction, with Old Siders being the wealthier class. Old Siders kept closer ties to Europe and were generally less progressive and less willing to follow the latest fashions. As time went on, gifted preachers supported the New Light cause as typified in enthusiastic preaching, an emphasis on inner conversion, and rigid standards for admission to the Lord's Table. Such preaching became the hallmark of the Great Awakening and can be most closely identified with Theodorus Jacobus Frelinghuysen c. 1726 among the Dutch, Jonathan Edwards and George Whitefield c. 1746 in New England, and Samuel Davies c. 1748 in the South. A second, great religious movement began at the end of the eighteenth century. Its roots are in New England, but it spread throughout American Protestantism. It was this second awakening that influenced Hodge and Nevin while they were in college.

4. See Leigh Eric Schmidt, *Holy Fairs*.

5. Hodge provides a valuable insight into his practical orientation when he reflected on that early period in the study of logic that "the excessive study how to reason often impairs the ability to reason." See Archibald Alexander Hodge, *The Life of Charles Hodge*, 24. It was Witherspoon who first imported Scottish commonsense realism to Princeton. See John Witherspoon, *Lectures on Moral Philosophy*, 1768. Sydney Ahlstrom was one of the first to identify Witherspoon as an early source of Scottish realism in America. Ahlstrom calls Witherspoon the "first real ambassador" of Reid and the Scottish school. Under Witherspoon, Berkeley fell to the Scottish school with the rest of American institutions following suit. Of course, Witherspoon had his own way of reading the Scottish philosophy. Says Ahlstrom, Witherspoon's "common sense" was mediated by his "Evangelical bias." See Sydney E. Ahlstrom, "The Scottish Philosophy and American Theology," 261. See also Mark Noll, ed., *The Princeton Theology; 1812–1921*, and David Hoeveler, *James McCosh and the Scottish Intellectual Tradition*. Witherspoon's first dependence in moral philosophy was Francis Hutcheson (1694–1746). Thomas Reid's impact was only recently felt by Witherspoon, who includes him in his bibliography, and Stewart would have a major influence on Hodge. Witherspoon wrote that, in opposition to Hume, "Some late writers [referring to Reid and James Beattie] have advanced, with great apparent reason, that there are certain *first principles* or dictates of *common sense*, which are either simple perceptions, or seen with intuitive evidence. These

On January 13, 1815, Hodge made his public profession of faith.[6] Not coincidentally, there was, in Princeton, during the first part of the year, a conflagration of the spiritual sort. Students at the academy were experiencing religious "crisis," and a revival of religion was claiming many of them. Such was the heat of this revival, that "personal religion—the salvation of the soul, became the absorbing subject of attention."[7] Hodge threw himself into his work with an eye to ministry and graduated second in his class. However, the effort left him exhausted, and he required respite at home in Philadelphia before he returned to Princeton to begin his theological studies (late 1816).

During the first year of Hodge's theological study, the students at Princeton met in the homes of the professors until the following year when the main edifice was opened. Undoubtedly this fostered the intimacy evident in the letters and notes written by alumni. Alexander read to them from Turretin,[8] but warmed the cold Scholasticism with his own insights into personal faith and spiritual pilgrimage. Turretin would remain Princeton's theological text even under Hodge, for lack of something better in English. (Records indicate that John Dick's *Lectures on Theology*[9] were also in use.) Throughout their lives, Alexander and Hodge remained convinced Calvinists, but they harbored serious differences with Turretin.

The year that Hodge and his classmates occupied the first seminary building in Princeton, Nevin began his academic career at Union College in Schenectady, New York. Union was at the height of its fame under the outstanding leadership of Dr. Eliphalet Nott. Nott built on the "plan of Union" developed by the son of the legendary preacher Jonathan Edwards. As president, Jonathan Edwards Jr. established a course for the college that would take it into the nineteenth century. Soon it would prove to be one of America's finest institutions of higher education. Nott was as much a gifted educator as he was an able administrator (and fund-raiser). He increased Union's reputation and attracted bright students and well-qualified teachers. There were few colleges in America at the time that could rival Union, and the education provided was first rate. That reputation convinced the Nevin family to enroll their son in spite of his chronic dyspepsia. Nevin was weak both physically and emotionally and feared an early death, even as an undergraduate at Union. His disposition to depression and ill health plagued him all his life.

Nor was Nevin's health aided by his conscience and study habits. He was a perfectionist and stern by constitution. His expectations of himself were high, and he

---

are the foundation of all reasoning, and without them, to *reason* is a word without meaning" (*Moral Philosophy*, 50).

6. In the Reformed tradition, young men and women make a public profession of their faith. This ritual of affirmation makes them communicant members (today sometimes referred to as "confessing members") of the congregation where the profession takes place.

7. A. A. Hodge, *Life*, 30. Of course, this would have an impact on the seminary and in many ways was a reason why the seminary came into existence. It was a product of the Second Great Awakening, which occurred at the end of the eighteenth century and the beginning of the nineteenth century.

8. Francois Turretini, *Institutio Theologiae Elencticae*.

9. John Dick, *Lectures On Theology by the Late Rev. John Dick, 2 vols.*

worked all the harder thinking that diligence might relieve him of his sad disposition. Like Hodge, the rumblings of the Second Great Awakening surrounded him, and the daunting conviction of sin ultimately drove him to a religious decision during his junior year (1819–20). It also drove him to nervous exhaustion. After all, what chance might an impressionable youth have against the enormous pressure exerted by Asahel Nettleton, "the most noted Congregational revivalist of the day"?[10] Nettleton was conducting revivals in the area, and many students at his meetings experienced newfound conviction in their religious attitudes. Broken and unsure of himself, it seemed to Nevin the only course was to pursue a religious vocation, and so he returned home for the summer to ponder his prospects.

As Nevin contemplated his future and struggled with the question of assurance, Hodge was being invited to accept a position at Princeton Seminary by Alexander. While he considered his friend and teacher's generous offer, he graduated from the seminary, learned Hebrew, and received his license to preach from the Presbytery of Philadelphia. In June, Hodge accepted Alexander's offer and was appointed "teacher of oriental languages." Later that month he "came under care" of the Presbytery of New Brunswick.[11] The year 1822 was a significant one for Hodge. He married Sarah Bache, organized a student society for the promotion of the study of biblical literature,[12] and was elected professor of oriental and biblical language and literature by the General Assembly. All this just three years after graduation!

Hodge had been a professor at Princeton only a year when he met the bright and sickly student from central Pennsylvania. Nevin entered the seminary fully expecting not to live through the three years of graduate study. Yet he found Princeton delightful. It was a safe haven, and his brightness made it congenial to his tastes and abilities. Secure in the care of the beloved Alexander, the influential Miller, and the young Hodge, Nevin drew knowledge and inspiration from two of America's greatest educators at a time when they were at the height of their combined powers. (Hodge would soon blossom as well as the promising new star of the Princeton faculty.)

It was then that an event occurred in Nevin's life that would shape his future. Despairing of his slow progress in Hebrew, he thought he might drop it altogether, having no faith in its usefulness. But his roommate, a young man whose name was Matthew Fullerton, advised him to stick with it. The encouragement was such that Nevin became "the best Hebrew scholar in the institution" and given the title "assistant

---

10. Nichols, *Romanticism*, 5. Nichols makes the valid point that the revivalism of this period placed less emphasis on conversion than did the revivalism of such noted nineteenth-century preachers as Charles Finney. Finney would become a central target of Nevin's later attack on the system of revivals as most clearly spelled out in his *Anxious Bench: A Tract for the Times*. This allows us to distinguish between the terms "revivals," which were universally popular among Protestants (including Nevin), and "new measures revivalism," which became a target of Nevin's attacks.

11. In the Reformed system of government "coming under care" occurs prior to ordination. Care is administered by a regional judiciary made up of pastors and elders that oversees the candidate's session or consistory (consequently named from the Presbyterian and Reformed systems of governance) and congregation.

12. This society was the inspiration behind the *Biblical Repertory and Princeton Review*.

teacher." Along with the title came the offer to remain at the seminary an additional two years. Nevin had nowhere else to go (but home) and few places he loved better, so he stayed. It was during those years that he wrote his *Biblical Antiquities*, a short and popular history based on the work by Jahn.[13]

History was not studied as a science in America. Mosheim's text[14] was preferred in church history, but even as they read Murdock's translation of the German rationalist, a new spirit was defining the study of history. The scientific study of church history was being pioneered by the German Mediating school of scholars who followed in the wake of the revelations of Hegel and Schleiermacher. Neander would eventually surface as, perhaps, the best of the lot, the man whom Nevin credits with awakening him from his "dogmatic slumber," but in 1822 America, history was merely the dispensations of the biblical narrative. Still, history seemed important and both Hodge and Nevin took in what they could of it. Ironically, it would be as "authorities" on church history that they would eventually clash.

As Nevin concluded his seminary studies, Hodge founded the *Biblical Repertory and Princeton Review*. From the beginning this popular and influential journal was under his editorship and stayed that way for forty-three years (except the short time that Hodge was in Germany). Originally the title was *Biblical Repertory, a Collection of Tracts in Biblical Literature*. Hodge was the principal "translator," along with R. Patton and J. W. and J. A. Alexander. The journal's advertisement described the editorial board as an "Association of Gentlemen in Princeton," including Archibald Alexander, Samuel Miller, President Carnahan, and Professors Maclean and Dod. In 1837 the title was changed to the *Biblical Repertory and Princeton Review*. Much later, in 1868, Hodge wrote a telling description of the *Princeton Review*'s publication philosophy, providing us with a revealing insight into what would represent an insurmountable obstacle preventing Nevin's introducing German idealism to American Protestantism. Hodge wrote,

> The conductors of the *Princeton Review*, however, were Presbyterians. They firmly believed that the system of doctrine contained in the Westminster Confession of Faith, the system of the Reformed Church and of Augustinians in all ages, is the truth of God revealed for His glory and the salvation of men. They believed that the upholding of that system in its integrity, bearing witness to it as the truth of God, and its extension through the world, was the great duty of all those who had experienced its power. *They believed also that that organization of the Presbyterian Church, its form of government and discipline, was more conformed than any other to the Scriptural model, and the best adapted for preserving the purity and developing the life of the Church.* It was, therefore, the vindication of that system of truth and of the principles of that ecclesiastical polity,

---

13. Appel, *Life*, 49–50. See also Johann Jahn (1750–1816), progressive Roman Catholic scholar. Published the popular *Biblische Archäologie* from 1797 to 1805.

14. Johann Lorenz von Mosheim (1694–1755) introduced objectivity (some suggested extensive rationalism) to the study of history with his *Institutiones historiae ecclesiasticae* (1726). Mosheim pioneered the field of church history, but he did not match Neander in piety, nor was he equipped with the concept of historical development that made Neander's work so revolutionary.

the conductors of this Journal, from first to last, had constantly in view. . . . It is with unfeigned and humble gratitude to God that the conductors of the *Biblical Repertory and Princeton Review* can look over the comparatively long period of its existence with the conviction that from first to last it has been devoted to the vindication of that system of doctrine contained in our standards, and which, as all Presbyterians believe, is taught in the word of God. *No article opposed to that system has ever appeared in its pages.* It has been the honest endeavor of the conductors to exhibit and defend the doctrines of our standards under the abiding conviction that *they are the doctrines of the word of God. They have advanced no new theories, and have never aimed at originality. Whether it be a ground of reproach or of approbation, it is believed to be true that an original idea in theology is not to be found in the pages of the Biblical Repertory and Princeton Review from the beginning until now. The phrase "Princeton Theology," therefore, is without distinctive meaning.*[15]

That Hodge distinguished himself as America's patron of orthodoxy has long been a widely known fact. The bold statement above demonstrates just how seriously, how long, and how successfully Hodge commanded that patronage. Less well known is the fact that Hodge inherited the role from his teachers, certainly Alexander, but even more from Miller. Miller was the faculty historian; Miller established Princeton's reputation as a besieged bastion of orthodoxy and the last home of Scholastic theology; and Miller initiated the contest with New England.[16] Miller's role would pass to Hodge: historian, defender, crusader; and he would gain the greater reputation in the role.

Meanwhile, even as the mantle was being passed to Hodge, the seminary of the German Reformed Church was moving from Carlisle, Pennsylvania, to York. The seminary was established by an act of the Synod at Bedford, September 1824, and began operations in May 1825 with five students. After moving to York, an academy (high school) was founded to prepare students for seminary learning. The denomination appointed Frederick Augustus Rauch as principal of the academy (also called the classical school). Its next move would be to Mercersburg, Pennsylvania, in 1836. Lewis Mayer would soon resign as seminary president and Frederick Augustus Rauch, the first American Hegelian and an exemplary representative of Germany's Mediating philosophy and theology,[17] would take command of both the seminary and the acad-

---

15. Italics are mine for emphasis. A. A. Hodge, *Life*, 257. The *British Quarterly*, the oldest quarterly in the United States at the time (1871), wrote of the *Biblical Repertory and Princeton Review*, calling it the "greatest purely theological Review that has ever been published in the English tongue." At the same time, Dr. Lyman Beecher called the *Biblical Repertory* "the most powerful organ in the Land."

16. Nichols, *Romanticism*, 16.

17. See DeBie, "Frederick Augustus Rauch: First American Hegelian," 70–77. Lloyd Easton might take issue with this. Easton looks to Ohio for original North America Hegelianism. If to be a Hegelian is to accept without modification the philosophy of Hegel, Easton is correct. However, Rauch was a Hegelian of the Mediating branch of theologians and philosophers. He was a student of Daub, who was a disciple of Hegel, and Rauch's philosophy (*Psychology*) duplicated the third part of Hegel's system, i.e., Hegel's Philosophy of Mind. In the British philosophical tradition, Rauch's book would come under the heading or title of "mental philosophy." However, according to Easton, Rauch's churchmanship and deviation from Hegel's strict triadic model of historical development disqualify him from being America's first Hegelian. See Easton, *Hegel's First American Followers*. This is in contrast to Howard J. B.

emy. Later Rauch would encourage Nevin in the Mediating thought, but in 1826 Nevin remained a modern Calvinist of the Princeton stamp, indeed, so much so that he was a trusted instructor of Hebrew and a likely candidate for leadership in the proposed Presbyterian sister seminary in Pittsburgh.

From November 1826 to November 1828 Hodge confronted Princeton's foreign antagonists, the German idealists, on their own turf. His reason for going to Germany was clear, if threatening. Europe was far beyond America in the scientific study of Christianity, especially in the languages where Hodge felt particularly deficient. He was keenly aware that he had not had the time to master the Greek and to read enough in the field. His plan was to spend half his time in Gottingen and half in Paris. The responsibility to find his replacement was his own: "Mr. John W. Nevin, a member of the class just graduating, was appointed the substitute for Mr. Hodge during his absence, and he fulfilled the office for the following two years with eminent ability."[18]

Hodge sailed from New York for Le Havre in October 1826. From there he went on to Paris where he stayed from November 1 to February 15. He studied with de Sacy, then with Stapfer.[19] It was while in Paris that he was referred to Friedrich August Gottreu Tholuck (1799–1877) of Halle, "of which is not to be found elsewhere" (referring to both his learning and to his piety). He was also advised of the importance of Johann August Wilhelm Neander (1789–1850). Hodge then left for Halle and arrived there February 28, 1827. The very next day he was introduced to Heinrich Friedrich Wilhelm Gesenius, the leading Hebrew scholar in the world, and to Tholuck. Tholuck and Hodge were the same age and became immediate friends. Tholuck took Hodge under his wing and provided him with the current affairs of German intellectual life. It was a friendship that would last a lifetime.[20]

Ziegler who shared with me the belief that Rauch was the first Hegelian teaching in America. See Ziegler, *Frederick Augustus Rauch, American Hegelian*. It is worthy to note that in Germany, virtually no one, including Hegel's students, simply duplicated Hegel's philosophy. Rather they took it in three distinctive directions.

18. A. A. Hodge, *Life*, 103.

19. Philipp Albert Stapfer (1766–1840), a member of a large and influential family of theologians, Philipp being perhaps the most distinguished. From 1800 to 1803 he was the Prussian ambassador to France. In 1806 he moved to Paris to live the rest of his life. Antoine Isaac Silvestre de Sacy (1758–1838), a French orientalist, Roman Catholic, and a major influence on the future of biblical criticism.

20. Prussian cultural life was tightly entwined in the eighteenth and nineteenth centuries, and blended the arts, education, politics, and religion. Until about 1740 the Pietists had controlled German religious and academic life. But after 1740 rationalism took control, only to lose it again to Romanticism at the turn of the century. On the heels of Romanticism came the comprehensive systems of the idealist philosophers and theologians. In 1827 Hegel was the dominant intellectual figure, but even then a new challenge, in the form of neo-Pietism, was seeking to dominate. At the head of this new movement was E. W. Hengstenberg. Hengstenberg was a vocal critic of liberalism and rationalism (often gaining sympathy from those who feared the revolutions in France). By 1815 Prussia's ecclesiastical affairs minister adopted neo-Pietism over Hegelianism, and by 1820 Hengstenberg's political maneuvering had gained his conservative neo-Pietist party control of the state-run church. He secured Olshausen the theological chair at Königsberg, got Otto von Gerlach a position at Berlin, and Tholuck his chair in Halle (1826). With Tholuck entrenched, if embattled, in Halle, the neo-Pietists were able to isolate Hegel in Berlin. See Robert M. Bigler, *The Politics of German Protestantism*. Tholuck studied oriental languages, but through Pietist influence, turned to theology, and later became one of Germany's leading theologians.

Under the watchful eye of Tholuck, Hodge began his tour of Germany. His examination of the German educational system led to the remark, "The great superiority of German learning (and the superiority is great) arises not from the mode of instruction in the universities, but from the excellence of their primary schools."[21] From early March until September Tholuck was Hodge's best friend, confidant, and intellectual guide. It was from the conversations with Tholuck that we first learned of Hodge's deep suspicion of German theology and where we gained remarkable insight into Princeton's loathing of German philosophy. In reaction to that suspicion and loathing we discovered the earliest evidence of an antagonism that would split former friends and solidify Princeton's commitment to commonsense realism and the philosophical dualism that supported it.

Early in March, Tholuck asked Hodge if he feared "Neology."[22] Hodge said that he did not. Tholuck then asked Hodge his view of inspiration. Hodge's reply amounted to a theory of divine dictation that was very popular in America, called the "high" or "strict" view of inspiration. It was accompanied by a view of inerrancy in the original autographs. Hearing this Tholuck responded, "No wonder [you do not fear neology]." Thanks to the recent changes in German thought, Hodge had even less to fear of rationalism and the demystifying of sacred texts. Kant was universally abolished in Germany, along with Fichte. The same was the case with Schelling (although in his later period he would experience a revival). But neology still held sway. The leading philosopher in Germany was still Hegel. Of course, Schleiermacher had his own system, but Tholuck charged that in spite of their popularity, their systems were both "pantheistic." Hodge recorded Tholuck's conclusions as follows (these will weigh heavily in Hodge's future criticism of Nevin's Mediating position):

> Hegel and Schleiermacher both deny the personality of the Deity and the individuality of the soul of man. The universal principle with them is God, and, according to Hegel, the world itself is the *Realitat* of Deity, and all it contains, the different races of men, and the animals in their various order, are all modes of existence on this one universal principle. This, at least is the idea I got from Tholuck's description.[23]

Hodge's personal reflections are most interesting. It is clear that he was straining to objectively report the words and ideas of Tholuck. Yet they seemed to him utterly foreign, and when he spoke from his own practical, realist, or commonsense perspective, he found Tholuck's position heavily dependent on Hegel. He feared that Tholuck was himself filled with Hegel's "philosophizing spirit." He wrote of his suspicions, commenting with obvious chagrin that Tholuck, with Hegel, believed that matter was simply a different form of spirit, while the essence of each was identical. Hodge was

---

21. A. A. Hodge, *Life*, 117. This part of Alexander Hodge's biography comes directly from Charles's own journal, transcribed and kept while he was in Europe.

22. Tholuck means the speculative methodology of the "new German learning," i.e., the schools of Schleiermacher and Hegel and, ultimately, their offshoot in the Mediating school that attempted to harmonize the insights of phenomenology with traditional faith in virtually every field of the humanities.

23. A. A. Hodge, *Life*, 119.

shocked to hear his friend praise Hegel and Schleiermacher and at the same time acknowledge them to be "pantheistic." Tholuck told Hodge that great good had come from Hegel and Schleiermacher because it was they who reawakened "vital religion."

Throughout the middle of March Hodge and Tholuck had a series of conversations about German religious science. Tholuck told Hodge that in Germany Reid and Hume were the most esteemed of the English philosophers. Stewart was less so and Locke not at all. But for Hodge it was a great shame and pity that Germans mixed philosophy and religion. Such confusion

> gives so abstruse and mystical a character to explanations of important truths that there is little reason to be surprised that the term Mystics has been applied to the advocates of piety. Thus, for instance, they make faith to be the development of the life of God in the soul—that is—the divine essence everywhere diffused and the universal agent unfolding itself in the heart.

To help Hodge understand his meaning here Tholuck read to him several passages from Schleiermacher's "*Dogmatick*,"[24] but Hodge confessed "they seemed to me to darken counsel by words without wisdom."[25]

In spite of Tholuck's allegiance to the grammatical-historical school of interpretation, he was an earnest and sensitive evangelical and a pious churchman. Indeed, he shared with Hodge his extreme anxiety over his struggles with rationalism at Halle. Tholuck was identified with Hengstenberg and the politically conservative von Gerlach brothers who were committed monarchists of Prussian nobility. Tholuck's enemies were determined to remove him from his post in Halle and he was all too aware of his unpopularity and precarious situation. Hodge described how his friend's anxiety grew to near paranoia and depression such that he required a stay in the country to recuperate.

On April 18, Hodge attended a "high" Lutheran service and commented that "I felt like a stranger here and longed for the time when again, in the simple Scriptural manner of our Church, I could partake of the memorials of our dying Savior's love." Later that day he met with Schleiermacher. In a subsequent conversation with Krummacher and Sanders, Tholuck revealed to Hodge his understanding of the essence of idealist thinking. Once again, Hodge sought to represent Tholuck honestly, yet with an incredulousness that cannot be hidden.

> What *actually* is, is all that is *possible*. That the world cannot possibly be other than it is. He bases this opinion on the attribute of God. He urges the idea that attributes and essence are the same in the divine Being. That beauty, holiness, knowledge are in God essential, that is, that God is essential beauty, holiness and knowledge, etc., and that all the beauty, holiness and knowledge in the universe is not only derived from God, but is the beauty, holiness, etc., of God, so that

24. Friedrich Daniel Ernst Schleiermacher (1768–1834), *Der christlich Glaube nach den Grundsätzen der evangelischen Kirche im Zusammenhang dargestellt* (1821–22).

25. A. A. Hodge, *Life*, 122–23.

God is not only the most perfect being, but is all that is good or beautiful in the universe.[26]

Tholuck concluded that man's consciousness and all his moral and religious powers are the essence of God. For, said Tholuck, "God cannot be only the partaker of good, but must be all that is good."

When Hodge objected that as much as the abstract "proportion" cannot be conceived as an essence, neither can we conceive of beauty as "an essence or seyn (esse)," Tholuck argued that proportion is, indeed, an essence, such that even the proportion or relation of say, eight to sixteen is an essence. Likewise, proximity is an essence and to support his ideas Tholuck cited Augustine.

To this, Hodge was as much confused as opposed. It seemed to him that Tholuck, like "all Germans," make *Anschauung* (intuition) the test of all truth regarding invisible things. The ability to form a distinct image of the subject in the mind through intuition becomes, for them, the litmus test for "feeling" its truth. But, said Hodge, it is impossible to form such a *bild* (image) for God or the soul or, for that matter, of any spiritual subject. Tholuck would not relent: All clear ideas of these spiritual objects must conform to the test and so assume this form in order to be correctly understood. Later, in another discussion, Tholuck argued that everything in nature is endowed with consciousness, including animals, plants, even stones. This consciousness is a sense of life.

After hearing Tholuck's views, Hodge concluded that while Tholuck abjures pantheism, he sounds the pantheist. Soon after that conversation Hodge met with Neander, another German scholar attempting to harmonize neology and traditional faith. Hodge wrote, "Neander is beyond competition the first man in his department in Germany, and is as much distinguished for his piety." Still, Hodge was not convinced by the erudition of the German idealist, and he continued to hold back on the concern that Neander's ideas were often "peculiar" and "arbitrary" and he wondered if the rumor that Neander was "really a Sabellian and Patripassian" was true.[27]

During September and October Hodge traveled throughout Germany, meeting some of its most prominent educators. But the most interesting meeting was with Ludwig and Otto von Gerlach in Berlin on October 12. Hodge formed an unlikely friendship with Ludwig that would broaden, in spite of great differences of opinion, into the same durable love and esteem he had for Tholuck. Of Ludwig von Gerlach Hodge wrote,

> A man who has excited more love and respect in me than almost any other I have seen here . . . I was surprised to find how much that was unchristian mingled in

---

26. Ibid., 137–38.

27. Johann August Wilhelm Neander (1789–1850) was the gifted church historian responsible for bringing science to bear on the study of history by focusing on the original sources. Neander differed from Mosheim in his concentration on people rather than on institutions. He was born a Jew, David Mendel by name, but converted to Christianity under the influence of Schleiermacher. Here the epithet Sabellian suggests that Neander denied that the Spirit was a distinct divine person. Patripassianism denotes the heresy that the Father suffered together with the Son on the cross.

all my feelings on this subject. With this dear man I cannot agree in his opinions, yet I felt that he was much more a free-man in his heart (with all his strong ideas of the divine right of kings) than I.[28]

What begins to emerge, as a most revealing insight into the formative shaping of Hodge's conservative position, is his pattern of skepticism. Truly he was struggling to understand the Germans in their language, idiom, and ideas. But it is also clear that he was effectively comprehending the sense of what they represented and not liking it. Moreover, Hodge was under tremendous pressure from Princeton not to be influenced by the German "new thinking." While he was away in Europe he received correspondence reminding him of his orthodoxy and importance to Princeton. On March 27, he received a letter from Alexander that included the words, "Remember that you breathe a poisoned atmosphere." And, again later in July, this word from Alexander, "The air which you breathe in Germany will either have a deleterious effect on your moral constitution, or else . . . your spiritual health will be confirmed."

Later in that same letter, Hodge was warned of the "poison of *Neology!*" and admonished to "come home enriched with Biblical learning, but abhorring German philosophy and theology." Alexander confessed that in his anxiety over Hodge he had begun to read Kant, "but it confounds and astonishes me." Finally, in a letter dated August 16, Alexander wrote, "But it will be worthwhile to have gone to Germany to know that there is but little worth going for." Each letter begged haste to return.[29]

As the year 1828 commenced, Hodge was busy taking in German culture. In the first month he attended the Royal Academy of Sciences to hear Schleiermacher speak, where he also met with geologists as well as theologians. In February he had the opportunity to visit with students and discovered that they were wonderfully versed in philosophy, "but amazingly deficient in plain, healthy good sense." In March he met again with Ludwig von Gerlach who reported to him the upheaval at the faculty in Berlin. Von Gerlach told Hodge that "The Hegelians are working strongly against the Evangelical party." Tensions were high as the two parties traded insults. At the meeting of the Senatus Academicus, Marheineke[30] called Neander "ignorant" because "he knows nothing of philosophy," which, of course, noted Hodge, meant "Hegel's system." Hodge dismissed the comment as partisan and sought out Neander. In conversation with Neander, Hodge was shown letters from Jacobi[31] warning of the dangers of the German speculative philosophy. Neander confided in Hodge that he hated the character of men who make "themselves God" and who reduce "God to an idea (*Begriff*)—so that Hegel says that *Nichts ist die allerhochste Realität.*" Hodge then asked Neander whether something of Hegel's "Pantheistical system" passed into Germany's current

---

28. A. A. Hodge, *Life*, 158.

29. Ibid., 160–61.

30. Philipp Konrad Marheineke (1780–1846) was professor of theology at Berlin and an ardent Hegelian. He led the battle against Pietist theologians and those who followed Schleiermacher, identifying himself as a theologian of the "idea."

31. Most likely, Friedrich Heinrich Jacobi (1743–1819), prominent German philosopher and anti-Kantian.

evangelical writings? "By no means," Neander responded.[32] Of course, by now Hodge was convinced otherwise.

In April of that year Hodge met again with Neander who told him that Hegel's system "makes God but an idea—nullity the origin of everything—and the universe a mere phantom." Neander concluded with this insightful, if not original, stereotype: There are contrasting characters among the English and Germans. Germans are marked by the speculative spirit and the English by practical common sense.

Neander remained an unforgettable friend to Hodge. After six months in Germany Hodge closed his journal, reflecting on the people he had met. He wrote:

> The kindness, the Christian love, the warm-hearted conduct of those with whom
> I have passed this winter so happily, will remain deeply impressed on my heart
> as long as I live. When I bid my friends farewell I cried like a child. Neander's
> farewell I shall never forget.

Hodge made an attempt to study in England, but it being the summer with most professors away, he returned home on September 18, 1828. In spite of having met and found friendships with some of the greatest minds of Europe, Hodge was unchanged in his commonsense realism and in the orthodoxy of Princeton. Alexander's anxious letters and Hodge's own conservative disposition had safely inoculated him from "neology." Nor could he anticipate that the man with whom he had entrusted his students would become a willing convert to neology, without benefit of a personal visit, but by reading Neander, Hodge's newest friend.

That is not to say Hodge learned nothing in Germany. Indeed, as soon as he returned to Princeton he began building on what he had gained. His earliest lectures reflected the foundation upon which he would secure Protestant orthodoxy in America. The three-tiered platform included the importance of civil liberty, the concept of German education in its thoroughness, and "the intimate connection between speculative opinion and moral character." His sojourn in Germany convinced him that wherever one finds speculative opinion above "vital piety," one will find faithlessness and moral corruption. On the other hand, where one finds moral character as the gift of vital piety one will find a penitential and devotional spirit, along with "the doctrines of the fall, of depravity, of regeneration, of atonement, and of the deity of Jesus Christ."[33]

Nevin joined the Princeton faculty in welcoming home their friend and colleague, undoubtedly relieved he had returned untainted. He could afford to be pleased because he had been approached that year by Dr. Herron concerning the new seminary to be opened "west of the mountains." Dr. Herron wondered if he might be interested in teaching there. Meanwhile, he was licensed to preach by the Presbytery of Carlisle and he preached often, getting a reputation for being quite a crusader for temperance. In

---

32. A. A. Hodge, *Life*, 181.

33. Ibid., 207.

1829 he took responsibility for the congregation in Big Spring, supplying their pulpit while they sought a new minister. He lost his father during the interim.[34]

At the end of the year, in December, Nevin joined Dr. Halsey at Western Seminary, taking the chair in biblical literature. He would remain at Western for ten years. While in Pittsburgh, Nevin wrote for the *Friend (of the American Anti-Slavery Society Organized in Philadelphia)*, a small literary and morals weekly. He became its editor on behalf of the Young Men's Christian Society, which was an interdenominational organization meant to promote evangelical faith in the Pittsburgh area. Like his teachers at Princeton, little of Nevin would change during his time in Pittsburgh, although he began to read authors that Hodge would consider rationalistic and above all pantheistic. But in stark contrast to Hodge, Nevin was on the verge of shedding his realist perspective. Still, in so many ways, while in Pittsburgh, Nevin remained a modern American Puritan; an evangelical of the Princeton stamp, eager to promote the cause of Christianity by joining hands with other Christians. He passionately believed in minimizing confessional differences (he himself being upset by the divisions among Presbyterians), and he tried to focus on the pragmatic aims of ridding the world of immorality and injustice. The *Friend's* manifesto reveals this spirit in Nevin:

> The paper was to be decidedly religious in character; and this on the high platform of the Gospel, the only true basis of morality; but all in such a way as to avoid the incidental belligerent discords of the different evangelical denominations, and to move only in the supposed far wider and deeper sphere—something hypothetical—in which they are lovingly concordant—that mighty domain of doctrine and life, which has never yet been made the scene of Christian controversy at all, and over which our spirits may freely expatiate, in fellowship with all who belong to Christ, in the midst of the most magnificent and endearing forms of truth.[35]

Still it was Pittsburgh where Nevin began his transformation to idealism and to evangelical catholicism. So significant was the change that later in life he regretted the words of the *Friend's* manifesto. He called them "naive" and "pseudo-catholic." To him they betrayed a stand entirely outside of the "authentic pale" of Christianity. But these so-called "naive" words were Nevin's just out of Princeton. Theologically the Bible was the one and only indispensable means of grace. Like Hodge he believed that, armed with Scripture, any man, woman, or child could find his or her way to heaven.

Clearly, in the early years (before 1830), there is little theological difference between Hodge and Nevin. Of course, they each had their particular interests. Nevin was rabid about his pet causes. (Interesting how we might admire his zeal on the issue of slavery, but chuckle at his bluster about alcohol.) On the other hand, Hodge, while in every way a vocal opponent of slavery, was less controversial an activist and more consumed with academic matters. But in these early years there was no evidence of

34. Nichols, *Romanticism*, 18.

35. Appel, *The Life and Work of John Williamson Nevin*, 68. Nevin used the *Friend* to blast away at Christ's "real" enemies: intemperance and slavery, with the issue of temperance being by far the paper's central focus. Later, Nevin added a two-penny sheet called the *Temperance Register* as a companion to the *Friend*.

the issues that would separate them in the future. The only trait that might suggest that Nevin would embrace German idealism was that, unlike Hodge, Nevin was less suspicious of European ideas. (The exception, of course, was and continued to be European rationalism, but even there he confesses that early on he was nearly taken in by rationalism.) Indeed, at Western, Nevin greatly appreciated Romantic poetry and he admired Coleridge, although he condemned his drug addiction. He read Wordsworth and the other Romantics, and devotionally, he was enthusiastic about the neo-Platonists and Puritan mystics. Finally, his enthusiasm for the Scottish commonsense philosophy was thoroughgoing. (This would soon change.)

So, one might speculate that deep within the men there was a fundamental psychological difference. Hodge was by nature a practical man who admired plain speaking, plain reasoning, and common sense. In contrast, Nevin had a romantic bent and longed for a mystical glimpse of the infinite. Throughout the thirties this romantic bent manifested as intense social activism led Nevin to seek the ideal in social reform and in the prodigal nation's divine errand. After Western it took an altogether different direction toward the idealism latent in the Mediating thought of Germany, the home of his adoptive denomination.

Hodge had begun to sense that Princeton's solitary role as guardian of orthodoxy was growing, and so he began to keep a watchful eye on Europe. He had inherited from Miller a suspicion and distance from New England. But as he came into his own he realized that the greater threat might lie overseas. Virtually everyone in America felt threatened by the revolutions in France. Deism was an obvious import that had powerful allies in America, and Hodge's trip to Europe had convinced him that, while an able defense was being attempted by the pious and faithful, the upheavals were bound to overwhelm them. In a letter to Tholuck dated February 9, 1831, Hodge voiced his concern and recommended a remarkable solution:

> The wonderful changes that have occurred in the political state of Europe since you wrote, are full of interest for the Christian. I fear troublous times are at hand for your poor Prussians; with Poland convulsed on the east, and intoxicated France on the west, it seems scarcely possible that peace can long be maintained. *Will you not be tempted to seek asylum on our peaceful shores, far from the struggles of the dying systems of feudal Europe?* I have profited much from the lesson of Ludwig von Gerlach, and though I rejoice in the progress of liberty as much as ever, I am rather cautious to see that what is just, as well as what is desirable, should be kept in view.[36]

Hodge's and Nevin's concerns about Europe in the decades of the thirties were matched by concerns at home. Nevin's stand against slavery had gotten him into serious trouble in Pittsburgh. In 1833 he published the "Declaration" in the *Friend* arguing that slavery is a "sin" and that full emancipation was a moral imperative. Public reaction was frightful. Pittsburgh had extensive slave interests, and Nevin was perceived as a threat to its economic standing. Two years later, the same year that Nevin married Martha Jenkins (New Year's Day, 1835), the pressure on Nevin to resign from

36. A. A. Hodge, *Life*, 217. Italics are mine for emphasis.

the *Friend* had reached a climax. It would appear that the last stroke came in Nevin's reference to slavery as a sin. It brought such an offense that Nevin was publicly referred to as "the most dangerous man in Pittsburgh."

For years Nevin had wrestled with the question of colonization versus full emancipation. For a time Nevin favored some idea of colonization. In the end, finding himself a leader in the debate over slavery's abolition, availing himself of the full spectrum of arguments, and listening to leaders from the black and white communities, Nevin called for full emancipation. He believed it a biblical mandate and wrote that he had been blinded in the past, but he now recognized that sympathy for colonization was a smoke screen for what was obviously no solution.[37]

The result of his journalistic jeremiads was not only unpopularity among the citizens of Pittsburgh, but disharmony and problems at the seminary. Of course, Nevin's politics were not the cause of the seminary's financial trouble, but his unpopularity certainly exacerbated the distress. The conditions were serious enough for Nevin to consider resigning. Sadly, as much as Nevin spent his life battling poor health, he spent equal time considering resigning from whatever position he held due to controversy.

Personal disharmony was not all that the young scholar had to deal with. Like Hodge and the faculty at Princeton, Nevin was shaken by the divisions within the Presbyterian Church in America. The year 1835 marked the famous trial of Albert Barnes. Barnes was a leader of the New School movement in the Presbyterian Church. The trial pitted the Scholastic tradition of theology against Presbyterians who were looking for a simpler, more biblically literal theology.[38]

Princeton tended to be slightly right of center in the conflict, displaying its conservative stripe. But all those at Princeton, including Nevin, disapproved of the mean-spirited inflexibility of many of the Old School leaders. At every juncture the Princeton professors worked to mediate between the parties and to reconcile their differences. When the suggestion was made that the denomination be split all were dismayed—Nevin so much so that he would not participate in the debates that raged.

Two years after the trial the Presbyterians were, indeed, divided. Rather than involve himself in the theological divisions within the denomination, Nevin lost himself in the study of the church. From 1837 to 1840 Nevin immersed himself in the study of history, such that he called it his period of "historical awakening." Later he reflected that the experience reminded him of Kant's critical awakening at the hands of Hume. Of course, the prerequisite of this new discovery was mastering the German language, which Nevin did. This enabled him to read Neander in the original. Nevin believed that Neander was the antidote to Mosheim, who was too coldly rationalistic if brilliant. But the price was critical maturity. Nevin would never again read history uncritically,

37. Appel, *Life*, 71. The "solution" to the problem of slavery was varied. Some argued for recolonizing former slaves in Africa. Emancipators argued for liberty in America. Of course, there were many other "solutions" and a host of variations.

38. Albert Barnes (1797–1870), tried by the Presbytery of Philadelphia on ten specific charges of heresy. He was acquitted, convicted on appeal, then acquitted again on another appeal. The affair brought the denomination's divisions to a head.

although he never abandoned the confessional censor. Still, he committed himself to read the historic authors in their own time and on their own terms.

Neander provided Nevin with an introduction to Schleiermacher. (It seems that, as Nevin was reading Neander, Tholuck was writing to Hodge that Neander had been won back by Schleiermacher.)[39] He remained in debt to Gieseler[40] for a first glimpse at the original material and to Ernesti,[41] whose text was a valuable if controversial source at Western. Providentially, just as Nevin was becoming competent in the German language and historical science he was approached by Samuel Fischer of the German Reformed Church. The Germans were looking for a professor to help their new president, Frederick Augustus Rauch, lead the seminary and academy, which had moved from York to Mercersburg. Rauch had taken control in 1837 and initiated a thoroughgoing German orientation complete with a Goethe Society.

Nevin's disappointment with the experiment at Western Seminary left him desperate. By 1839 the prospects of a career in Pittsburgh were doubtful. His despair led him to resign from Western just as Fischer was making his offer. Yet Nevin must have guessed that for the Germans to approach a Scots-Irishman, their prospects for the future were as sad as his own. He declined the offer, but he could not resist a sigh of regret, commenting that not only was he well qualified, but having "a dash of transcendentalism" about him, he might have fit right in with the Germans.[42]

That year Nevin published his prophetic *Party Spirit*,[43] a reflection on America's (as well as the Presbyterian Church's) "dreadful" but growing political pluralism. Philosophical in nature, it was an early sign that Nevin would continue as the nation's Jeremiah. As exemplified in his sacrificial assault on slavery in Pittsburgh, he would always be controversial (no matter where his career took him), because underlying his practical solutions to ecclesiastical problems and the divisions that both frustrated and identified the American Church was his burgeoning philosophical idealism and speculative approach. In true idealistic and post-Enlightenment fashion, Nevin would seek to capture the historical moment of human experience and say whether it was good or evil. Skeptical as one might be at the success of such an undertaking, *Party Spirit* (although undertaken before his full exposure to speculative theology) was remarkable, to say the least, in anticipating the political pluralism that we take for granted today.

The year 1840 was a watershed for both Hodge and Nevin. Although Nevin declined Fischer's offer, his name was brought before the Synod of the German Reformed Church meeting in Chambersburg. The synod knew of his reluctance and resolved

---

39. A. A. Hodge, *Life*, letter entry from Hodge's biography dated February 28, 1834.

40. Johann Karl Ludwig Gieseler (1792–1854), noted church historian, educated at Halle and professor of theology at Bonn (1819), and Göttingen (1831), where he lectured in church history. The work so admired by Nevin was his *Ecclesiastical History* published from the first quarter to the first half of the nineteenth century. Gieseler provided the original texts to students of history.

41. Johann August Ernesti (1707–81), professor of theology at Leipzig (from 1759). Ernesti employed philology and critical thinking to include a historical quality to theological inquiry, benefiting from Wetstein and so popularizing the *grammatico-historical* method of hermeneutics.

42. Appel, *Life*, 94.

43. Nevin, *Party Spirit*.

that he would be prevailed upon only if he was convinced that it was his "duty" to serve the German Church. On March 5, Nevin wrote his acceptance. He was inducted into the office of professor of theology at the college and seminary on May 20 and soon joined the denomination by way of the Classis of Maryland. His work with Rauch developed into admiration, friendship, and an appreciation for all things German. However, Rauch fell ill and was forced to resign his position that same year.

So it was, in the year 1840, as if by providence, Hodge and Nevin assumed control of their respective institutions. Alexander had become ill as well, and Hodge was transferred to the chair of exegetical and didactic theology. Meanwhile, in Mercersburg, Rauch's health continued to deteriorate after the publication of his major work, *Psychology; or, A View of the Human Soul Including Anthropology*. Nevin served in his place taking over his course in ethics, carefully following Rauch's lecture notes. What this meant was that theology was now in the hands of Hodge and Nevin as the leaders of Princeton and Mercersburg, respectively.

Hodge taught theology at Princeton until his death in 1878. During those thirty-eight years he met with both the second-year students and with the seniors twice a week, assigning a topic along with the corresponding text. The text remained the Latin edition of Turretin's *Institutes of Theology* until 1848 when he began using his own outline and lecture notes. These would eventually become his *Systematic Theology*.

As the intellectual leader of the German Reformed, Nevin felt likewise obligated to represent his new confession. He steeped himself in the Heidelberg Catechism and Van Alpen's commentary on the same. This remarkable confession added a new dimension to Nevin's theology. In many ways it reshaped his thinking because he discovered a symbol of historic interest yet timeless relevance. In practical terms, he thought it might be an antidote to the denomination's ills.[44] Given his admiration for the Catechism, his feelings of responsibility for representing the Reformed, and the potential it held for revitalizing the denomination, it is little wonder that he launched into a series on the Catechism in the *Weekly Messenger* beginning on December 9, 1840.[45]

Likewise, Hodge was in full command of his institution's intellectual direction, and his influence in the Presbyterian Church was unsurpassed. As did Nevin, Hodge sensed the mantle about his shoulders. Neither man was shy about leadership, nor about his role as representative of his denomination's orthodoxy. Nevin set about to communicate the German Reformed position and likewise his position, by means of his research into the Heidelberg Catechism. Hodge would articulate Presbyterian orthodoxy through his enormously popular The Way of Life, published in 1841. The *New England Puritan* called it "the best work on doctrine yet," eminently scriptural and demonstrative of the fact that "in his field Dr. Hodge is *Primus inter pares*."

44. The German Reformed Church was troubled by disunity, economic instability, confessional ignorance, and difficulty in supplying pulpits.

45. The April 7, 1842, installment of the series was most significant. It presented the outline of the conclusions that would form the main argument of *The Mystical Presence*.

Hodge's work received international acclaim. Ludwig von Gerlach, Hodge's life-long friend and a man he greatly admired, gave it highest praise speaking twenty years later! But, most helpful for the illumination of the debate that ensued, von Gerlach's reservations are precious insight. The quality and reserve of his remarks deserve the full, if lengthy, citation.

> There is something in your book I must take exception to. For this very minor difference is shedding a brighter light on the essential unity, which our blessed Savior, by His grace, His word, and His Spirit, has established between us; and which, I trust, He will maintain through time and eternity. The development of Germany, in a religious and in a political respect, makes the Christians of our country to long after catholicity, and perhaps after the essential truth of what you would call "sacramental religion." It is not the way of salvation, which is now the prominent subject of our minds, but rather the high articles of the Divine Majesty, which occupied so much the primitive Church, and about which there was no difference of opinion between the contending parties of the 16th century. Being surrounded by Atheists and Pantheists, we strive to establish a consciousness of the essential unity of all Christians, Romanists not excepted; and the great fact of the *whole* Church being the body of Christ is foremost in our minds. . . . And we cannot suppose, as you perhaps are entitled to do, that our inquiries are standing vis-à-vis of this book, and examining it as a whole. They oblige us to take higher ground, and to develop the ideas of authority and of inspiration, etc., in order to establish on firm ground the, for us, all important doctrine of the Church. But all this shall only give you an idea of the feelings with which I have thankfully perused your excellent tract, which exhibits in a very clear way and with great force those blessed doctrines, which constitute the true Way of Life.

Finally von Gerlach brought his criticism to bear on what, for him, was the most important difference between the two. "The chapter of your tract on baptism and the Lord's Supper is the only one from which I must dissent on any essential point." He reports to Hodge that his doctrine of the Supper does not "quite" do justice to the "objective content and import" of these ordinances, "but leaves them to the state of mind of the recipient." Von Gerlach concluded, "I cannot see why you do not reject pedobaptism . . . I hold the sacraments to be in their nature, the actual means, not only signs and seals of grace."[46]

In March of 1841 Rauch died. He was only thirty-five years old. That spring the second edition of his *Psychology* was published with Nevin contributing the foreword. Nevin assumed the presidency of Marshall College, *pro tempore*. He was offered the presidency but refused, fully aware that they could not pay his salary. He took over Rauch's responsibilities as an act of duty, and he continued as acting president until 1853. His most difficult, yet pressing responsibility, was fund-raising. In typical fashion he dedicated himself to the pursuit. The idea was to celebrate the centennial of the denomination with a promotional program tied to the historical theme.

46. Hodge, *Life*, 328–30. It would be fascinating to ponder the question how this letter might have influenced Hodge had he received it when his book appeared twenty years earlier and seven years prior to publishing his review of *The Mystical Presence*. Still, Hodge was well aware of von Gerlach's views and felt no sympathy on that score.

Earlier the idea that the German Reformed Church should be studied as far back as its origins in Switzerland and Germany had motivated Nevin to write on the Heidelberg Catechism. The resurgence of interest in the old symbol became a boon to Nevin's fund-raising efforts. Yet in spite of the new interest and improved funding, Nevin's worries over the seminary, college, and denomination continued. His concern was clearly financial, but he also worried about the soundness of American theology. His unspectacular success on behalf of the Reformed was in stark contrast to the numerous inroads forged by revivalists. Their meetings, revivals, and self-promotion were changing the face of American religion.

But to Nevin, modern revivals not only threatened orthodox theology by making its institutions redundant, they produced a trite and fickle faith. Thus Nevin found himself battling on two fronts. His first beachhead was established to raise money for the support of traditional faith; his second was the battle to revive and save institutions that "new measures" sought to replace.

It is little wonder that in 1842 at Nevin's recommendation, when the Reverend William Ramsey of Philadelphia (a former missionary)[47] preached as a candidate for the vacant pulpit in Mercersburg and proceeded in the style of a revivalist, Nevin was adversarial. The style of revivalist methods frequently included setting aside a section of the church or chairs for those who in repentance found themselves converted or recommitted. That section was called by various names. Nevin referred to it as "The Anxious Bench," but it was also "The Mourner's Bench" or "The Anxious Seat." Ramsey embraced the idea of what today we refer to as an "altar call."

In the meeting that followed to decide whether to call the Reverend Ramsey, Nevin launched into a spirited invective against revival methods as a replacement to the sound system of the Catechism. Understandably, here was a desperate president of a struggling religious institution exhausting himself to breathe life into an ancient system, a system dependent on paid faculty, sacred buildings, highly developed programs, and an educational approach that required years of study. Along came "new methods," requiring little more than a camp, an inspired speaker, and the simple message of sin and conversion. But the obvious personal and practical dislike for new measures revivalism was clearly second to Nevin's intellectual and philosophical suspicions. Nevin believed that the revivalist theology would promote the sectarian spirit of American Protestant Christianity and lead to a further proliferation of sects, as well as the instability and disunity of the one church.

In spite of Nevin's remarks, Ramsey had the approval of the consistory and students, and so the church called him. Satisfied that his caveat would be taken seriously, Nevin gave his support to Ramsey. However, he took it upon himself to write Ramsey that should he accept the call he must abandon his "new measures" and adopt the system of the Catechism. Ramsey wisely refused the call, writing the consistory that Nevin's letter was the reason. This infuriated many and spilled over into scandal in the seminary. Nevin was intractable. He launched into a series of lectures in his course on

47. The source of Mercersburg's most virulent criticism was Philadelphia, not without reason. Philadelphia was a bastion of revivalist practices.

pastoral theology, specifying the subject of "new measures." Ramsey had captured the students' imaginations with something novel and popular. Nevin pressed in on them with history and tradition.[48] Of course, Nevin was not naive about the broader embrace of "new measures." His lectures led to a remarkable tract with a wide circulation and enormous interest, called *The Anxious Bench—A Tract for the Times* (fall, 1843). That year Hodge favorably reviewed Nevin's *The German Language*.[49] But behind the review was a Hodge slowly turning against Nevin.

Earlier, in 1841, Nevin had written a eulogy of his colleague Dr. Rauch.[50] He spoke of Rauch's unparalleled learning in the field of German philosophy. That year Hodge reviewed the work and displayed great anxiety about Nevin's philosophical direction. He was blunt that Nevin's embrace of German neology or speculative science was leading him on the path of heresy.[51]

Nevin desperately needed help at the seminary. In January of 1843, at a special meeting of the General Synod held at Nevin's request, the synod voted to call the Reverend Dr. Krummacher of Germany. A delegation was sent to convince Krummacher of the call. But Krummacher was hard at work promoting the cause of Pietism in Germany and was unwilling to move to America. At the recommendation of some of Germany's leading evangelicals, for example, Neander, Tholuck, Hengstenberg, and Mueller, Philip Schaff was suggested as an excellent candidate. Schaff's qualifications were presented to the synod's delegation and the call was issued. Dr. Schaff was in agreement, and in the fall of that year he was elected to fill the chair of church history and biblical literature.

In the summer of 1844 Schaff arrived in Mercersburg. The first thing he did was prepare his inaugural address. It was called *The Principle of Protestantism as Related to the Present State of the Church* and, perhaps unconsciously, he cast himself in the role of controversialist. A part of that address was delivered in German in October at Schaff's installation in Reading, Pennsylvania. However, little notice was taken of this first reading. Rather, the focus was on Hodge's favorable review of Nevin's *The Anxious Bench*. The only question raised by Hodge was his confusion about Nevin's idea of the church. Other than that, Hodge took the side of Nevin against the excesses of "new measures revivalism."[52]

The following year saw Hodge and Nevin united in protest of the Presbyterian Church's decision to annul Roman Catholic baptism. Hodge wrote of his dismay and Nevin followed suit, supporting at great length the position of Princeton. That spring

48. Appel, *Life*, 161.

49. John W. Nevin, "*The German Language*," *Weekly Messenger of the German Reformed Church*, New Series, vol. 8, no. 1 (1842); Charles Hodge, "Review of *The German Language: An Address Delivered Before the Goethean Literary Society of Marshall College* by John W. Nevin," *Biblical Repertory and Princeton Review* 15 (1843): 172–73.

50. John W. Nevin, "Eulogy on Doctor Rauch," *Weekly Messenger of the German Reformed Church* 5 (1859): 441–67.

51. Charles Hodge, *Biblical Repertory and Princeton Review* 13 (1841): 464.

52. Charles Hodge, "Review of *The Anxious Bench*, by John W. Nevin," *Biblical Repertory and Princeton Review* 16 (1844): 137–38.

Nevin finished translating Schaff's *The Principle of Protestantism*. The author chose to include Nevin's introduction and his sermon on *Catholic Unity* as an appendix (since it was quoted extensively). Nevin had preached his sermon on unity at the Triennial Convention of the Dutch and German Reformed Churches in Harrisburg the previous year. Interestingly, it contained the same militant language of catholicity that was found in *The Anxious Bench*—the language that was puzzlement to Hodge—but here Nevin is even more clear and direct. Given that fact, it is curious that the sermon was "sanctioned by the full approbation of the worthy representatives of both Churches at the time." The sermon itself provides the only plausible explanation of why so controversial a position was endorsed. As oratory, the sermon's terse positions certainly passed without close scrutiny. It is fair speculation that the delegates simply did not grasp Nevin's full intent, nor did they hear a defense of Roman Catholicism.[53] The scandal would wait for the publication of Schaff's *The Principle of Protestantism* where the sermon could be studied and identified with the controversial positions of Schaff.

The author of the seething scandal was a leading German divine named Joseph Berg. Two issues infuriated him. Berg had shared the podium with Schaff in Reading, but in direct contrast to the theories of Schaff who saw a continuous line of development for the church through the Middle Ages right into the Reformation, Berg held to the popular and more recent theory of evangelical history: that Protestants were the *true* descendants of original Christianity; that a band of refugees from Rome escaped with Polycarp to the Alps, circa AD 122, and remained hidden until the Reformation when they reemerged under the leadership of Peter Waldo; and that the Roman Catholic Church represented a perversion and abomination of original Christianity. Schaff's statements to the contrary antagonized Berg. In addition, Berg, who was a revivalist and anti-Catholic crusader in Philadelphia, heard from a former monk and convert of his whom he sent to Mercersburg Seminary for an evangelical education, that the professors at the seminary were teaching things favorable to Rome, specifically that Rome is "of the church" and that Christ is present in the Holy Supper.

These issues launched Berg into a diatribe against Nevin (as well as Schaff) published in his Protestant Banner. As editor, Berg used the *Banner* as a tool against Roman Catholicism. In this particular issue Berg challenged Nevin's orthodoxy and commitment to the Heidelberg Catechism and concluded with a call for the impeachment of Nevin and Schaff. Nevin responded with three articles in the *Messenger* titled "Pseudo-Protestantism" (August 1845). It was here that Nevin fully articulates the astonishing fact that Calvin held the doctrine of the real presence of Christ in the Eucharist.[54]

---

53. Nevin later wrote in his letter to the Rev. Dr. Harbaugh that some objection had been raised concerning his sermon to his use of the term "mystical union" (*The Personal Papers of the Rev. Amos Seldomridge*, n.d. Published in *Reformed and Catholic: Selected Writings*, 1).

54. Appel, *Life*, 242. There had been a considerable drift toward the sacramental theology of Zwingli among evangelicals of the nineteenth century. Although Nevin had previously said as much in his articles on the Heidelberg Catechism, little notice was taken.

A week after the last installment of "Pseudo-Protestantism" appeared in the *Messenger*, the Classis of Philadelphia met to consider Schaff's *Principle of Protestantism* with Joseph Berg as clerk. The Classis approved several anti-Catholic resolutions and then included two judicial resolutions asking that the synod call *The Principle of Protestantism* into question and that it brand that the papal system there represented an apostasy.

The synod met to consider the complaint. However, it was observed that protocol had been violated when the Classis failed to bring the matter first before the seminary's Board of Visitors. This would have been the proper procedure. An appeal of the board's ruling could then be brought before the synod. But the seminary professors were anxious to proceed to a public hearing of the accusations and prevailed upon the synod to take up the matter directly. It was referred to committee. The committee returned with the finding that the charges were false and irrelevant to the material of the book. The complaint's conjecture was not germane, thus the complaint was irresponsible. The committee's conclusion was unanimous. With the committee's recommendation before them, the synod debated the matter for two days (including evenings!). When the vote was finally taken, all agreed with the professors except three: Berg and two elders. A single delegate abstained.

Still, there hung the cloud of uncertainty, especially over the comments made by Nevin in "Pseudo-Protestantism." It was lingering doubt that led Nevin to publish his most important work, *The Mystical Presence*. But Mercersburg was now prepared to begin an offensive against the anti-churchly direction of American Protestantism. Nevin included as his introduction an essay by Ullmann, a member of the Mediating school and a leader among the majority in Germany who considered Nevin and Hodge "the greatest theologians that North America had produced."[55] Nevin thought that *The Mystical Presence* would silence his critics and satisfy the denomination that his position was utterly orthodox and in keeping with modern historical and theological science. He was sadly mistaken. And although Nevin sought vindication and ostensibly peace, his book rang with an air of militancy that he must have known would antagonize many evangelicals. Moreover, with the inclusion of Ullmann's essay he was declaring war on Princeton's philosophic embrace of commonsense realism. The total eclipse of Locke and all he represented for an empirically based theology was sure to infuriate Hodge.

That year, 1846, Hodge reviewed Schaff's *Anglogermanismus*. He remained an ally although the review betrayed a growing sense of caution.[56] Hodge made it clear to his readers that Schaff was wrong to suggest that German idealism had advanced the cause of Christianity. His 1847 review of Nevin's sermon on *The Church* offered the same respectful, if cool, treatment.[57]

---

55. Ibid., 280.

56. Charles Hodge, "Review of *Der Anglogermanismus, eine Rede u. s. w.* by Philip Schaf [sic]," *Biblical Repertory and Princeton Review* 18 (1846): 482–83.

57. Charles Hodge, "Review of *The Church: A Sermon Preached on the Opening of the Synod of the German Reformed Church at Carlisle, October 15, 1846,* by John W. Nevin," *Biblical Repertory and*

Hodge allowed his copy of Nevin's *Mystical Presence* to sit on his desk for two years. In fact, Hodge could not bring himself to read the book on his own, but was prevailed upon by those who wished to know the authentic doctrine of the Reformed on the Lord's Supper. It would appear that a group of advocates sought Hodge's help in stopping any influence the book might have in promoting the doctrine of the real presence of Christ in the Eucharist. Hodge published his "Doctrine of the Reformed Church on the Lord's Supper" as a review of *The Mystical Presence* by John W. Nevin in the *Biblical Repertory and Princeton Review*, no. 20 (1848), occupying pages 227–78.

What was to follow would take the question of the Reformed position on the sacrament of Holy Communion beyond the historical reach of *The Mystical Presence*. From the Wednesday, May 24, 1848, edition of the Messenger to the Wednesday, August 6, 1848, issue, the small denominational weekly ran both the arguments of Hodge as taken directly and without omission by Nevin from the *Biblical Repertory* and Nevin's counterarguments, such that the style was in a broad sense, that of a debate. Nevin structured his articles in such a way that Hodge's position was quoted verbatim in sections roughly resembling topics. Below these Nevin wrote addressing the topics and refuting Hodge's conclusions.

There is little question, given the purpose of the Messenger, that a good number of readers were taken far beyond their theological depth and historical interest. It has even been suggested that complaints of the space taken up by the debate pressed on Nevin and led him to look for another vehicle in which to debate Hodge.[58] However, the letters section of the Messenger paints the opposite picture, revealing not only great interest in the topic of debate, but clear theological sophistication on the part of these bright and well-educated German farmers. Undoubtedly, however, in the end there was earnest desire expressed for a wider audience, so the alumni of Mercersburg Seminary created the *Mercersburg Review* with Nevin as editor with instructions to include Nevin's revised version of the debate "in as early an issue as possible."

The same year that the debate appeared in the *Messenger* Nevin published two of his most fascinating philosophical works. These two essays, *Human Freedom* and *A Plea for Philosophy*, were manifest testimony to his conversion to the idealism of speculative theology. In January of the following year, 1849, the first issue of the *Mercersburg Review* appeared. Later that year, at the synod meeting in Norristown, Nevin was made a member and chairman of the committee to begin work on a new liturgy for the denomination. This too became a controversial undertaking for Nevin and certainly his last and greatest in terms of interdenominational strife.

From January to November 1850, Hodge was "absorbed" in grief over the death of his wife. He had also lost Dr. Miller that year and would lose his beloved friend and teacher Archibald Alexander in October 1851. Nevin was suffering as well. Yet his was an internal struggle, something on the level of a nervous breakdown. Criticism of his positions, that he was soft on Rome and that he was a pantheist, weighed on him. He

---

Princeton Review 19 (1847) 301–4.

58. Thompson and Bricker, 12.

submitted the resignation of his chair in theology to the synod, ostensibly for the simple reason that he wasn't being paid, but he clearly felt he had lost their support. The synod asked him to remain, but he resigned nonetheless. He also resigned as chairman of the liturgical committee, feeling it imprudent to proceed. It was during the tumult of 1850 that Nevin published his revised reply to Hodge in the *Mercersburg Review*. It was an article of 128 pages constituting the final draft of one of America's first original and comprehensive contributions to historical science in the area of sacramental theology. Hodge did not reply directly to the article, and although he continued his criticism of the Mercersburg theology, he wisely avoided further contention over the issues of debate.

From 1851 to 1852 Nevin was convinced that he would soon die. But, just as much as in his youth, it appears his health problems were psychological. Although a leader in a denomination with conservative American, evangelical habits, Nevin had become a lonely Protestant voice on behalf of the hated Roman Catholic tradition and the feared philosophical methods of Germany. In 1852 Nevin published a series of articles on St. Cyprian, perceived by many to be the defense of his anticipated defection to Rome. Nevin did not defect, but he seriously considered it. Several of his students became Roman Catholics, and the articles on St. Cyprian cannot be read without sensing that Nevin was in crisis. As far as Nevin was concerned his articles on St. Cyprian concluded his case for evangelical catholicism, resting it firmly on the historic, Catholic faith, acknowledging Roman Catholic weaknesses in terms of the place of Scripture and scriptural authority and anticipating a new synthesis in the union of Protestants and Roman Catholics in a future age. With that he proposed the closing of the *Mercersburg Review*.

Nevin's anxiety was understandable. The number of critics within the denomination had grown significantly, and he was attacked in the *Messenger* for his articles on St. Cyprian. Defections within the denomination were growing as well. In 1852 Berg withdrew to the Dutch Reformed Church. Berg was followed by the Reverend Jacob Helfenstein along with his entire congregation going over to the Presbyterians.

In spring of 1853 the college was moved to Lancaster with the seminary remaining in Mercersburg. The move brought on Nevin's retirement, lasting more or less until 1861. In 1854 he moved his family to Carlisle, but in 1855 he returned to Lancaster. He continued to write and supply vacant pulpits in the area. In 1857 the liturgical committee published a "Provisional Liturgy." A storm of controversy arose around it. Two years later, in 1859, Nevin considered critically the theories of the celebrated Horace Bushnell in the pages of the *Mercersburg Review*.[59]

In January 1860, Hodge lost his best friend, J. A. Alexander. His grief was made complete when the country split itself in war. Hodge was an old Federalist at heart, but joined the Whig Party and finally identified with the conservative wing of the Republican Party by the end of the Civil War. Nevin was equally distraught by the

---

59. Horace Bushnell (1802–76), a leading Congregationalist and author of *Christian Nurture* (1847). Bushnell was a prominent figure in the expansion of the liberal theology of New England. His contribution to the field of Christian education was exceptional.

prospect of war. At its outbreak he felt that perhaps the South should be allowed to go its own way. But after two of his sons joined the Union he gave his support to the North. In 1862 the area around the seminary was raided by Confederate troops. By 1863 the fierce fighting in the area forced the closing of the seminary. Nevin gave up most of his denominational duties.

From 1861 to 1872 Hodge wrote his *Systematic Theology*. This was effectively the material of his lectures to the students of Princeton over the course of years, but it also represented his response to the liberalization of theology and the eclipse of what he believed was the God-inspired tradition of Locke and Edwards. Long before, Hodge had dreamed of a new Calvinistic system able to address a legion of threats to "American Protestant orthodoxy." The various theologies of New England, deism, the Unitarian "heresy," pantheism, and Roman Catholicism all had taken on new meaning in the years preceding the war. Hodge felt a sense of urgency and spoke, as early as 1839, of a system that he was contemplating called "realistic dualism." The same year that Hodge began his work on his *Systematic Theology*, Nevin became the close personal friend and spiritual advisor of president James Buchanan, ultimately preaching his funeral oration in 1868.

In 1862 (until 1866) Nevin became a lecturer at the college primarily in the department of history. Three years later, Franklin and Marshall College opened its college church. Nevin became its pastor. Buchanan was frequently in attendance. With the college once again in dire financial straits, Nevin assumed the role of provisional president. The war had nearly ruined the college in terms of enrollment. For a short time the college did well, but soon it was again steeped in financial trouble. Ultimately Nevin resigned in frustration in 1876. That year Hodge published his *Systematic Theology* to wide acclaim. In 1877 Tholuck died. In April of the following year President Lincoln was assassinated, and in June Hodge died. Eight years later, in 1886, Nevin died, peaceful at last.

Introduction

It is a matter of some perplexity to students of American religious history why certain literary debates and exchanges gain national recognition while others do not. This is especially curious, since some debates of unremarkable content are frequently cited and seem to live forever in our corporate memory, while others of significant originality and erudition find themselves in volumes that gather dust on library shelves. Such volumes are missed as potential classics whose quality is easily appreciated for the way they not only disclose the historic moment and its issues, but anticipate so much of what follows as the current state of North American religion. Naturally, the challenge and obligation to dust off these lost but classic works and offer them in a more readable and accessible format are irresistible. Once recovered, these debates become literary archeological sites, able to provide valuable information about how we got where we are.

Such is the case with the 1848 literary debate between Charles Hodge of Princeton Seminary and John W. Nevin of Mercersburg Seminary.[60] Not only did the debate feature two of America's preeminent theologians, but two leaders with burgeoning international reputations—at a time when America was still in the early stages of developing the reputations of native-born thinkers. Their influence over their students and readers was unsurpassed. It was a debate that introduced scholarship never before seen on the American continent, in a method of critical research that would revolutionize the study of history. It featured a summary of evangelical faith and practice that would adjust Protestant orthodoxy, and articulate a system popular and resilient enough to remain, to this day, a blueprint of evangelical theology. It raised questions of ecclesial practice; questions still unresolved and echoed by contemporary ecumenical leaders. It laid bare the fundamental differences between catholic and evangelical Christians in a novel and controversial way; such that, for the first time, Protestants could objectively, historically, and comprehensively consider the character of their faith. In effect, it captured the spirit of middle-nineteenth-century American religion with its rabid suspicion of European liberalism and violent opposition to the Roman Catholic Church and dramatically displayed it for what it was, while predicting with

---

60. Now Lancaster Seminary of the United Church of Christ, located on the campus of Franklin and Marshall College in Lancaster, PA.

uncanny accuracy much of what would follow as America considered to whom it would turn for its idea of the church.

THE OCCASION OF THE DEBATE AND ITS PUBLICATION HISTORY

The literary debate originally appeared during the summer of 1848 in an all but invisible series printed on the pages of the *Weekly Messenger of the German Reformed Church*.[61] The occasion of the debate was Hodge's belated review of Nevin's book, *The Mystical Presence*,[62] and one might say that the debate really began with *The Mystical Presence*. Hodge had undertaken the review only reluctantly, so dismayed was he at the contents of the book. But his followers believed he alone could effectively refute the book's incredible conclusions: that American Protestant practice descended directly from the Roman Catholic Church, and the historic confession of Reformed Protestantism and its eucharistic theology is essentially catholic in character, sustaining the real presence of Christ in the Holy Communion. So Hodge was pressed into service.

Published in 1848 in the internationally recognized and revered journal the *Biblical Repertory and Princeton Review*, Hodge's review aggressively challenged Nevin's conclusions in lengthy detail. Step by step, Hodge attacked the historic research undertaken by Nevin and replaced it with his own, inductive[63] conclusions which amounted to the Princeton model of evangelical faith and practice. It was a defense, in his and his readers' minds, of the "old faith": the faith of the Reformation and of the Reformation's "last stronghold" in America at Princeton.

In effect, the article was not a review at all. Indeed, Hodge clearly stated his real purpose for the rebuttal, which was to answer the question, "What is the true doctrine of the Reformed Church on the Lord's Supper?" So, what appeared as a review became instead an argument,[64] which was reproduced by Nevin later, with Nevin's responses inserted in the appropriate places. Effectively, what Nevin created from Hodge's material was a literary debate over the question of the Reformed Church's view of the Lord's Supper, and while Hodge never volunteered to debate Nevin on the subject, his subsequent response left the impression that what had occurred was in fact a debate. Likewise, scholars to this day refer to the exchange as a literary "debate."

It was simply not in Nevin's nature to allow such a review to go unanswered. The problem was that the *Princeton Review* would not (could not, in principle) publish Nevin's reply. This was their rule and long-standing policy. Nor did Nevin have adequate access to Hodge's readership, nor, indeed, to a religious public of significant size and quality. He was confined to the pages of the *Weekly Messenger*, which was the

---

61. John W. Nevin, "Dr. Hodge on the *Mystical Presence*."

62. Charles Hodge, "Doctrine of the Reformed Church on the Lord's Supper, Rev. of *The Mystical Presence* by John W. Nevin."

63. Hodge called his method "inductive theological science." See his *Systematic Theology*, 1:9.

64. Nevin referred to his reply as "notes or observations." As we will see, it was considerably more than that.

humble (yet admirably learned) newsletter of the German Reformed Church.[65] It was specifically for that reason in 1849 that the seminary alumni launched the *Mercersburg Review* with Nevin acting as editor and supplying most of the articles. And although it reached a greater and more diverse audience, it simply could not equal the impact and range of the *Princeton Review*. Moreover, it was extremely naive to believe that Nevin could convince American evangelicals that Hodge was wrong, and so the debate was doomed to obscurity from the beginning.[66]

After all, Nevin's reputation was fledgling, and while his fierce and eloquent defense of Protestant catholicity would add to his recognition it certainly would not increase his popularity. Just the contrary, it is likely that Nevin's position made his future prominence impossible. In his edifying volume on Calvin, the historical theologian Brian Gerrish wrote of Nevin and called his most important work, *The Mystical Presence*, "The most intriguing discussion of Calvin's Eucharistic thought in English." But he added, "First published in Philadelphia in 1846, it has never been as widely known, even in America, as it should be; on the whole, it has been seen as something of a curiosity."[67]

The "curiosity" amounts to a small mystery. However, our curiosity might be assuaged by noting that the debate revealed an unpopular truth that had been routinely ignored by American Protestants in general. Moreover, Nevin served the small German Reformed denomination and often held views that were unacceptable to the majority of American Protestants. That was true from the very beginning when he fought slavery in Pittsburgh and pleaded the case of temperance, and it did not change later in life when he led the cause of evangelical catholicism, battled revivalism, opposed Jacksonian democracy, defended the Roman Catholic Church, and argued that Americans should abandon the preeminent philosophy of commonsense realism for German idealism.

The opposite was the case with Charles Hodge. Rarely a crusader, Hodge was the very embodiment of the establishment. He was a leader in the large and well-established Presbyterian Church, and as Princeton's champion and preeminent theologian he mustered enormous power and influence throughout the country. Had the debate appeared in his journal, the *Princeton Review*, it is likely that this book would

65. Nevin tried to get his reply published in a theological journal but was turned down.

66. *The Mystical Presence* and his later article, containing a revision of much of the material from this debate, "The Doctrine of the Reformed Church on the Lord's Supper," were published together in 1966 in an edited work by Bard Thompson and George Bricker Jr. It appeared under the title *The Mystical Presence and Other Writings on the Eucharist*. (They have been published together again, with extensive new notes, introduction, and bibliography, in vol. 1 of this series, *The Mystical Presence and the Doctrine of the Reformed Church on the Lord's Supper*.) However, the original debate, which included the brilliant work of both Nevin and Hodge, set in its proper sequence, has never been published or given the attention it deserves. All of the subsequent work on the debate of Hodge and Nevin, with the exception of James Hastings Nichols, came from the "Doctrine of the Reformed on the Lord's Supper," and many scholars either ignored or were unaware of the existence of the earlier debate. Thus they benefited from the expanded historical section of Nevin's later work but missed the fascinating philosophical intrigue of the original debate.

67. Gerrish, *Grace and Gratitude*, 3.

be unnecessary. Indeed, that Hodge was indisposed to continue the debate after it appeared in the *Weekly Messenger* or the *Mercersburg Review* sheds further light on why the debate was all but lost. Most readers had subscriptions to the *Princeton Review* but not the *Weekly Messenger*, and so their only access was to Hodge's review. They never knew of Nevin's meticulous response. They assumed that the famous Charles Hodge had dispatched the lesser theologian with his review of *The Mystical Presence* and that the matter was closed.[68]

The publication of Nevin's argument in the *Mercersburg Review*, with the expanded historical section, revisions, and further notes (dropping a good deal of the philosophic material), did not change most readers' minds. They were convinced that Hodge's was the authentic history and doctrine of the Reformed in America. Notwithstanding, the elegance, scholarship, and insight of the debate were unprecedented in America. The outstanding historian of Mercersburg, James Hastings Nichols, wrote of this debate (specifically Nevin's revised article, which appeared in the *Mercersburg Review*) that it was "one of the first significant American contributions to the history of theology."[69] Dr. Nichols was characteristically demure. There simply was no work of similar historical scholarship that preceded *The Mystical Presence* and the subsequent debate, other than Nevin's colleague Philip Schaff's *The Principle of Protestantism* in 1845, which Nevin translated and was clearly the work of a Swiss German and not an American. Indeed, Brian Gerrish wrote in his *Tradition and the Modern World*, commenting on Nichols's statement (of "The Doctrine of the Reformed on the Lord's Supper") that as a "historical monograph, it remained without rival in English until the twentieth century." Gerrish continues and wonders what twentieth-century work might come up

---

68. In a delightful exchange in the "Letters to the editor" section of the *Weekly Messenger* (June 14, 1848, vol. 13, no. 40), a correspondence between Edward and Henry appeared (no mention of surnames). Edward was writing to Henry expressing what most readers expected would be the outcome of Hodge's review and any attempt on the part of Nevin to defend himself. Edward confessed his and his father's deep foreboding concerning the harsh review, and of Hodge's tanning of "the Dr." (Nevin). "We were not prepared for such an assault." Edward's father was upset and saw no avenue of escape "for [his] friend Dr. Nevin." "The old gentleman" repined, "Imagine the Dr. a rationalist, a denier of the Trinity, a Eutychian, and ten times further from Calvin." Henry concluded that Nevin could not afford to take this lying down, but that it was likely "no life raft will appear." The father thought Nevin ventured too deep into the ocean—but now he feared he would "drown." A second letter appeared from Edward (June 21, 1848, vol. 13, no. 41) in which he wrote to Henry that his father hopes that Dr. Nevin will deport himself favorably against the assault of Dr. Hodge. He went on: "The undismayed tone in which the 'criticisms' are written has weakened some of the old gentleman's fears, and given him new confidence. The impression had been that the charges of Dr. Hodge were unanswerable, and that Presbyterians simply take it that 'Dr. Hodge must be right.'" In the last letter on the subject of the debate, Edward wrote to Henry saying, "The old gentleman" had just read number 5 of Nevin's reply to Hodge and expressed regret that he rued the day Hodge had come against the Dr.; now he is utterly pleased with the debate. He said that it had "drawn out Nevin" and one gets full measure of his argument, even more convincing than what one had before, "and he puts more hay down low in the rack, that such short scholars as I am, can reach a good deal of it." It is a bit of a wonder that subsequent scholars have described the debate as so overwhelming to the readers of the *Messenger* that they were "heartily sick of the true Calvinist doctrine" (Gerrish, *Tradition and the Modern World*, 64). I suspect in contrast it provided them great drama, worthy of the surprising erudition of these gentleman and lady farmers.

69. Nichols, *Romanticism in American Theology*, 89.

against it? Certainly not Barclay's *The Protestant Doctrine of the Lord's Supper*, which borrowed heavily from Nevin without proper credit.[70]

In the critical summary that follows, we offer an bird's-eye overview of the sometimes dizzying back-and-forth of Nevin's and Hodge's arguments, and seek to offer insight into the critical issues at stake both then and for contemporary scholarship, especially those having to do with philosophy and Reformed theology. Since Nevin got both the first and the final word in the debate, it seems appropriate to offer a few thoughts in this section about points where Hodge may have had a legitimate case to make, or where recent historical scholarship has suggested a somewhat more nuanced narrative than Nevin provides. (Of course, despite failing to answer Nevin's arguments, Hodge emerged the de facto victor, as his view won the day with the vast majority of Reformed congregations in the United States. While his influence is certainly not what it once was, it is fair to say that his theology provided a blueprint for much of contemporary evangelical theology.)[71] Nonetheless, on the particular historical point at issue, Nevin's confidence in his position has been largely vindicated, and it is high time for his achievement to be recognized by a wider audience.

The question may nonetheless be asked whether the publication of this material is genuinely worthwhile, given that a great deal of it has already been made available by the republication of the expanded and revised material that appeared in "The Doctrine of the Reformed Church on the Lord's Supper." Four considerations justify this new edition: First, although the main substance of the debate does reappear in the later text, much of the character and nuance of the debate consists in the juxtaposition between American and European ideas, which is displayed so vividly here, but is largely hidden from view in the later historical essay. Second, the debate, although somewhat one-sided, allows Princeton's view (which will be that of many evangelicals today) to speak for itself, whereas Hodge appears merely as a silent adversary in "The Doctrine of the Reformed Church on the Lord's Supper." Third, the debate includes a great deal of material highlighting the contesting philosophical systems. Nevin was an idealist and Hodge a commonsense realist. This difference plays an enormous role in the debate but does not appear prominently in Nevin's "Doctrine of the Reformed on the Lord's Supper," which focused squarely on the historical issues. Finally, recently a welcome spate of books, on Nevin and his eucharistic theology, have given prominent attention to the clash between Nevin and Hodge, but without making any use of this crucial, heretofore largely unseen, material.[72] We hope that its appearance now

---

70. Gerrish, *Tradition and the Modern World*, 66.

71. This has been admirably argued by Mark Noll in *The Princeton Theology, 1812–1921*.

72. Some notable examples: Keith Mathison, *Given for You: Reclaiming Calvin's Doctrine of the Lord's Supper* (2002); D. G. Hart, *John Williamson Nevin: High Church Calvinist* (2005); William B. Evans, *Imputation and Impartation* (2008); W. Bradford Littlejohn, *The Mercersburg Theology and the Quest for Reformed Catholicity* (2009). And perhaps the best example for a researcher's need for this edition is Jonathan Bonomo's *Incarnation and Sacrament: The Eucharistic Controversy between Charles Hodge and John Williamson Nevin* (2010); a good overview of the debate, but the author seemed unaware that Nevin's original reply to Hodge appeared first in the *Weekly Messenger* of 1848. Bonomo worked

will prove timely in fostering a fresh wave of research and reflection in the recent Mercersburg renaissance.

CRITICAL OVERVIEW OF THE DEBATE

Chapter 1

Nevin betrays his reason for writing in the opening sentences of the literary debate. Charles Hodge's 1848 review of his Mystical Presence was not only unfavorable, it sought to replace Nevin's account of the true doctrine of the Reformed Church on the Lord's Supper with one that bore the imprimatur of Hodge and Princeton. Princeton had been wary of the general theological direction of Mercersburg for some time, no doubt concerned over what would be frequently described as their "Romanizing tendencies." In a period dominated by strong anti-Catholic passions in the United States (Philadelphia had seen anti-Catholic riots in 1844), this was the criticism of Mercersburg that loomed largest. So along with replacing Nevin's theory of sixteenth-century Reformed eucharistic theology, Hodge sought to stem the tide of Mercersburg's more catholic and high-church perspective. Hodge was also eager to contest Mercersburg's decidedly German philosophical and theological mind-set. Nevin and his colleague Philip Schaff were especially influenced by the most recent evolution in German theology, the Mediating school, which followed in the wake of Hegel and Schleiermacher. Princeton had repeatedly warned against the speculative approach and published multiple criticisms in the *Biblical Repertory and Princeton Review*.

Having introduced the debate as a way of setting the record straight (as to who held the true doctrine of the Reformed on the Lord's Supper), Nevin allows us to hear Hodge's general concerns and his summary of his argument. Hodge begins by expressing his reservations about the subject matter in general. The subject of the Eucharist is one shrouded in mystery, and its history even more so. This arises particularly from attempts at compromise among the Reformers, all straining to bring about consensus and more importantly peace, so that it is hard to pin down their actual convictions. Nevin denies, however, that their attempts at compromise were such as to confuse or distort their teachings. Hodge also raises the question of authority: Who can speak for the entire body of the Reformed, and which creeds and confessions should be accorded the greatest weight, since they do not appear to agree with one another? Accordingly, Hodge looks to the later seventeenth-century dogmatists such as Turretin and Pictet for a source of clarity as to what the earlier era was striving for and to set the doctrines in their right sense, although he has the gall to describe them as "contemporaries or immediate successors of Beza," a stretch that Nevin will call him on. Nor will he bow to Nevin's granting Calvin chief authority, insisting that alongside confessions that bear Calvin's stamp we find others, equally important, that present the Swiss view. A third

---

exclusively from the Thompson and Bricker material originally printed in the *Mercersburg Review*, 1850.

class, most credible and representative of all, says Hodge, are confessions "in which both parties concurred."

In his response to this section, Nevin solemnly protests against this slice-and-dice approach to history as an attempt to set aside the actual historical relations of the confessions in favor of predetermined theological criteria. This charge of being "unhistorical" is one that we will find Nevin repeating throughout the debate.

Chapter 2: The Views of Zwingli and Calvin

The second chapter comprises Hodge's summary, by means of extensive extracts, of the three different classes of Reformed confessions he has identified. Most important for him is the *Consensus Tigurinus*, a statement that not only fairly represents the Reformed of the sixteenth century but also, he deems, the Reformed churches of modern-day Protestant America. Of course, the *Consensus* was that very symbol that Nevin intentionally left out of *The Mystical Presence*, and he declares here that it was of no authority at the time. For Hodge, however, this document unified the Calvinists and the Swiss over the essential point: the rejection of any transference of the essence of Christ's flesh from heaven in the sacrament. Indeed, there is in these articles, "not a word, which any of the evangelical Church of the present day would desire to alter. We should like to print them all as the confession of our own faith on this whole subject." Hodge offers also the Heidelberg Catechism and the Second Helvetic Confession as further support of this same consensus position.

Nevin responds by stating rather bluntly that Hodge has simply borrowed the quotations from *The Mystical Presence* and not bothered with any original research on his own. The exception, as previously mentioned, was the *Consensus Tigurinus*, which Nevin maintains is the "Procrustean bed" that all the Reformed symbols must fit. However, although Nevin may not admit it, it is undeniable that Calvin's desire to find a middle path between the Swiss and Lutherans was the source of some confusion about his meaning, and some doubt about his loyalties.[73]

Chapter 3: In What Sense Is Christ Present in the Sacrament?

The next chapter begins with Hodge's answer to the question, "In what sense is Christ present in the Lord's Supper?" That Christ is present, says Hodge, cannot be denied by any Reformed, who opposed the Lutheran caricature that for them, Christ is no more present in the Supper than a god is present in his statue. The question, then, must revolve around the mode of that presence. To answer this question Hodge resorts to the faculty psychology (mental philosophy) popular at the time at Princeton to argue that things are made "present" to the mind either by the object being locally perceived by the senses or apprehended by the intelligence subjectively. It is in this latter sense, says Hodge, that the Reformed understood the presence of Christ in the Supper.

---

73. It was a mistake for Calvin to have thought he provided a solution to the "eucharistic impasse." There remained a difference between "*est*" and "*significat*." See Gerrish, *Grace and Gratitude*, 182.

In response, Nevin repeatedly begs "caution!" None of the Reformed, including he, teach a local presence in the flesh, as Hodge seems to imply. But when Hodge applies his faculty psychology to Calvin, Nevin believes he fails to take into account that there is a third alternative to local presence and to "presence to the intelligence." Calvin, says Nevin, would have rejected both as being found in the sphere of nature. But the mystical transaction exists exclusively in the sphere of spirit.

Because of his reductionist account of eucharistic presence, Hodge can see no reason for Calvin's distinction between eating and believing, which he takes to be mere semantic quibbling about a matter in which all the Reformed were united—to have faith was the same as to feed on Christ, and thus the sacrament offered no unique grace that was not elsewhere available to the believer. Nevin takes Hodge's easy dismissal of the question as proof that he has not really understood the doctrine of the sixteenth century, and insists on the contrary that Calvin's distinction of faith and eating, and stress on the unique grace available in the sacrament, was essential to Reformed eucharistic doctrine.

It now appears clear that Nevin wants more from the sacred meal than Hodge will give. For Hodge, the Lord's Supper sets forth what Calvary accomplished in terms of the atonement and what faith receives by that atonement, and no more. But Nevin sees something more transpiring—the power of Christ's life made present, not merely the benefits of his death—and he believes so did the Reformers. Hodge argues that the carnal language of the Reformers was not meant to be taken literally; it is not so much Christ in the meal that we should be looking to, but Christ on the cross and what he accomplished. However, the result of such language was that, in addition to the understanding that stressed our reception of the atoning force of the sacrifice at Calvary in the Supper, some such as Calvin conceived in addition a unifying force in the Supper that through the Holy Spirit could make us one with Christ, sharers in his life. Hodge acknowledges the presence of both concepts in the tradition, but says that if one view predominated it was the former view, of sacrificial efficacy. The second view was, in fact, an uncongenial intrusion of Lutheran theology into the Reformed camp, which was purged out in the seventeenth century.

Nevin is unconvinced, and finds it telling that Princeton finds the language of eating and drinking primitive, even superstitious. The prominence of this strong language in the Reformers clearly suggests that they saw something more in the sacrament than the "good thoughts and pious feelings" the "modern Puritan system of Princeton" will allow—for Hodge's view reduces in his judgment to little more than that. To shed sufficient clarity on the sixteenth-century teachings that Hodge finds so ambiguous, Nevin interrupts the back-and-forth debate to provide a long historical excursus, most of which will appear in little-altered form in his 1850 "The Doctrine of the Reformed Church on the Lord's Supper."

Chapter 4: The Ancient Creeds

In his historical excursus, Nevin has frequent recourse to the concurring views of August Ebrard, as given in the second volume of his monumental *Dogma of the Holy Communion*, which Nevin did not have access to when he wrote *The Mystical Presence*.[74] This, says Nevin, was in fact an advantage, as the resulting convergence of views supports the findings as arrived at independently. However, today it is generally agreed that although Nevin and Ebrard did arrive at the same conclusions, they both failed to fully appreciate the complexity of the confessions with regard to the many sources that led to their development, and further that they assumed a degree of uniformity among those confessions that did not exist. This gives weight to Hodge's argument that a wider range of views than Nevin appreciated existed among the Reformed of the sixteenth century.

Moreover, while today we recognize the truth of Nevin's view, which attributes to Calvin the lion's share of influence, recent scholarship has found many more creative and important streams feeding the confessions than were appreciated by Nevin.[75] In any case, though, while Hodge is right that the earlier confessions display the sacrificial interest more strongly, the later confessions of the sixteenth century do show an emphasis on participation in the "life" of Christ. Indeed, Nevin argues that the two hang together and depend on each other. The merit achieved by the sacrifice of Christ is to be had in union with Christ, and not sundered from it in a merely extrinsic doctrine of imputation. Nevin's summary of Calvin's doctrine on this point is "Christ first, then the merits."

In the first part of his historical overview, under the heading of "Ancient Creeds," he outlines the old Reformed creeds and distinguishes himself from Hodge with the historical and developmental approach alluded to earlier in the debate—one that culminates in the "architectonic agency of Calvin" as the end product of the confessions' theology. In contrast, says Nevin, Hodge analyzes the confessions as a single mass without paying attention to the progressive emergence of ideas seeking ever more satisfactory expression in a final, authoritative form. Nevin describes this approach as "mechanical," and in contrast describes a process in which theologians become conscious of the fuller implications of the doctrine, such that the weaker elements of older doctrine would be overcome or sublimated (*aufheben*) as the sounder doctrine supplanted it. While Hodge allows some kind of doctrinal development, it is a mere weeding out of wrong ideas, not, as for Nevin, a synthesizing of those ideas, in which a less mature idea transforms itself into a purer form. In the case of the Reformed doctrine

---

74. In introducing Ebrard, Nevin takes a swipe at Hodge, saying that some would question Ebrard's credentials since he is German. Princeton, and particularly Hodge, had a congenital paranoia of German scholarship and was often ruthless in attacking it. Nevin would complain, however, that being the German Reformed Church in the United States, he could hardly be expected to avoid cultivating a familiarity with these doctrines. And indeed, cognizant of the superiority of German scholarship, Mercersburg could be equally severe in condemning Princeton and indeed mainstream American Protestantism for being antiquated and irrelevant in its inattention to "the church question" that occupied Europe.

75. Indeed, Calvin himself said that "the whole [doctrine of the Eucharist] was crowned by Peter Martyr, who left nothing more to be done" (quoted in Hunsinger, *Eucharist and Ecumenism*, 39).

of the Eucharist, contends Nevin, this meant the gradual deference of the confessions to the superior concepts and terminology of Calvin, so that Hodge is wrong to play down the importance of Calvin.

Of course, Nevin will not admit that the later ascendancy of what he calls "modern Puritanism" and its unsacramental tendencies are a legitimate form of development; rather, they are an apostasy from the original Reformed ideas. Hodge, on the other hand, while he might have been well served by a theory of "non-originalism," arguing that later Reformed developments legitimately superseded earlier errors, cannot bring himself to embrace such a method. Rather he strains to make the doctrine of the atoning sacrifice to be the historical and therefore the one true doctrine of the Reformed on the Lord's Supper.

Nevin does not leave his theory of development, however, at the level of philosophical fancy, but seeks to demonstrate such development through a careful narrative of the progress of the sixteenth-century controversies. In chapter 4, this narrative takes him from the early Zwingli, whom he grants, on the basis of Ebrard's evidence, to have been perhaps less baldly memorialist than often assumed, to the emergence of Calvin upon the scene in the later half of the 1530s. In this narrative, which gives particular attention to the Colloquy of Marburg and to Bucer's attempts to find a mediating doctrine in its aftermath, Nevin suggests that amid the seemingly intractable disagreement, the seeds of the true doctrine lay hidden, waiting for the opportunity to come to full development through the "medium" of Calvin.

Chapters 5 and 6: Sacramental Doctrine of Calvin and the Reformed Confessions

Nevin begins his examination by setting the stage, which previously had Luther and Zwingli in opposition to each other as the chief actors. Zwingli did not live to see the maturing of his memorialist view, but in Zwingli's sad departure the leading role would go to Calvin who could be said to have been "providentially placed" at the right time and place to bring the doctrine into it fullest and most meaningful sense. Nor was Calvin's banishment from Geneva a disaster, since it brought him into close contact with Bucer in Strasbourg. In signing the Augsburg Confession there he showed that he felt himself on the same ground as Bucer and Melanchthon. But, says Nevin, this does not mean he had defected to "the Lutheran side," for at this time, the reigning Melanchthonian understanding of the Confession was substantially the same as his own.

In tracing the historical development further, Nevin must now turn his attention to the *Consensus Tigurinus*, which was Hodge's main weapon in his review. He briefly discusses passages from the *Consensus* but more importantly (as he sees it), from Calvin's exposition of the *Consensus*. This, Nevin argues, is needed to bring the sense Calvin intended by the document, a sense that can be in no way squared with Hodge's reading of the document. Here resides the familiar Calvin, but it is clear that he is speaking to reticent Lutherans and those in his party that might find the *Consensus* weak on the real presence. Indeed, Calvin goes so far as to say that nothing in the

Consensus would not square with the Augsburg Confession, although he admits its language had no interest in placating papists. In any case, however, Nevin insists that the *Consensus* cannot be considered the final and definitive word on the subject, as Hodge would have it; on the contrary, it merely set the stage for the outbreak of a second, great sacramental war in which the issues would be hammered out with much greater precision.

This conflict, of course, was ironic given the *Consensus*'s irenic intent, and it owes largely to the agency of Joachim Westphal, an extreme Lutheran who in the wake of the *Consensus* became a vociferous adversary of Calvin, painting him as insincere, having thrown in his lot with the Swiss while merely toying with the authentic Lutheran position. Nevin notes that this accusation of hypocritical conciliating is precisely the same charge we find Hodge leveling at Calvin. To answer this, Nevin compresses the lengthy engagement between Calvin and Westphal into an ingenious dialogue between Calvin and Westphal, which succeeds in helping clarify the issues at stake, even if the acrimonious language of the disputants distracts from the issues at hand. It is no surprise that the exchange dramatically supports Nevin's interpretation of Calvin: that he was in sympathy with the best of Lutheran sacramental theology, and hostile only to its crass and extreme form defended by Westphal and later Lutherans.

In the following chapter, Nevin convincingly argues that the essence of Calvin's teaching passed into the authoritative confessions of the Reformed including the Gallic, Old Scotch, Belgic, and Second Helvetic Confessions, together with the Heidelberg Catechism. The last of these, penned to help resolve the Second Sacramental War in the Palatinate, is particularly useful for Nevin's purposes, since its chief author Zacharias Ursinus wrote a lengthy explanation and defense of its sacramental doctrine. Nevin's extracts from this text, which Hodge had not consulted, decisively overthrow Hodge's attempt to enlist the Catechism as a fair representation of his own view.

This whole historical rebuttal went without comment from Hodge, even after its republication in "The Doctrine of the Reformed Church on the Lord's Supper." Nevin no doubt took this as vindication for his reading, which he believed was simply stating the historical facts as they were and without spin. As he ends the historical excursus and returns to the debate, he impresses upon us the central theological issue at stake—that what we have as the result of Hodge's view is the sundering of Christ's life from his sacrifice.

Chapter 7: What It Means to Receive the Body and Blood of Christ

Before again allowing Hodge to have the floor, Nevin reiterates this last point, insisting there is no reason that we must reject participation in Christ's triumphal life when affirming the memorial force of Christ's atoning death. Behind Hodge's denial of participation in the life of Christ, says Nevin, is the virus of rationalism and it infects all of Princeton's theology—so much so that it would reduce the sacramental mystery to a phenomenon of thought or feeling, as opposed to recognizing that behind this mystery stands "the power in truth of a new real creation in the world, embracing an objective and substantial life of its own."

Hodge is now allowed to return to where he left off, asserting that participating in Christ means believing in Christ, which again means that the benefits of Christ are received in the Holy Supper as the participant believes in Christ and his benefits. Hodge accordingly lines up his confessional witnesses so as to emphasize that participation is the result of faith, and cites Calvin that anyone who believes that our souls are intermingled with the substance of Christ's physical body is harboring fantasies. But now Hodge must face the outstanding question that Nevin insisted on: Is there any participation in Christ's human nature? To this question, says Hodge, the Reformed unequivocally answer "no!" Just as there is no room for a carnal reception of Christ, so neither is there room for a union of Christ by way of the imputation of his physical life or nature. Not in body, life, or nature, says Hodge, will the Reformed permit union with Christ, but only by the Holy Spirit through faith.

Nevin complains that what this amounts to is leaving the entire transaction to the work of the Holy Spirit, in abstraction from the second person of the Trinity whom he represents. Thus it removes Christ from direct contact with the believer, substituting a surrogate in his place. Moreover and perhaps more seriously, he charges, this idea of Hodge severs Christ's human nature from his divine nature and it is thus Nestorian in flavor.

In any case, Nevin contends, none of Hodge's claims pass the test of historical scrutiny, so much so that he will suggest, in a barb sure to rankle his opponent, that Hodge's system is like the philosopher Hegel's as "it makes the ideal the mistress of the fact." Nevin thinks that Hodge has fashioned the sixteenth-century doctrines into a self-fulfilling scheme which subordinates the "factual" historical case enshrined in the ancient confessions to the modern Princeton view. Hodge's view was that not just Calvin but the period itself left enough ambiguity that a more biblically scientific system would need to be found to put the material in its right sense. Princeton believed itself to be both inheritor and refiner of that system.

Chapter 8: *The Sacramental Efficacy of the Lord's Supper*

To the charge that Calvin was obscure in his teaching on the Holy Eucharist, Nevin retorts that it is rather modern divinity that is obscure and Calvin's teachings flow like a clear running stream. And yet in this last section of historical exposition, neither Hodge nor Nevin are altogether clear on the question of how the sacramental elements do and do not convey grace. Hodge distinguishes the Reformed doctrine by contrasting it with the Roman, in which the medium itself conveys the power or grace of the sacrament, and the Lutheran view, in which the power flows from Christ through the medium. The Reformed view, says Hodge, recognizes no medium but Christ (of course by way of the Holy Spirit), whose use of physical symbols is accidental to the power that flows directly from him into the believer. Nevin does not in the end really differ from this formulation, but he staunchly resists the implication Hodge draws—that the grace provided by the sacrament requires only Christ and so can be equally found elsewhere. For Nevin, the Supper confers a unique grace.

The difference lies in the very different concept of reality held by the two men. Hodge's dualism gives the elements no role beyond that of physical object and mere accident in the mystical transaction. Nevin's more monistic idealism sees a dialectic in the spiritual transaction that allows it a physical dimension. The elements do not contain or convey the grace, but the transaction clearly does. The physical aspects of the transaction are therefore integral to the transaction. Nevin draws on Calvin's example of the dove in the baptism of Jesus, which he compared to the elements in the Holy Supper. The dove represented the outward or physical side, which corresponded to the inward spiritual reality. Thus the elements like the dove are not merely "accidents," but a necessary part of the hierophany. It was not the Holy Ghost, but it was the sign and seal of the Holy Ghost's presence—the spiritual reality depicted in a natural phenomenon:

> but the presence of the one was bound to that of the other really and truly, as inward and outward sides simply of one and the same mysterious fact. And thus it is, that inward and outward go together also, not by identification or physical conjunction of any sort, but sacramentally and mystically, in the holy Eucharist.

Like an icon in Eastern Orthodoxy, the spiritual reality is depicted in the icon; the reality is joined with the sign. Not in an outward way, but inwardly and in the way of mystery.

For Nevin, then, while the elements themselves do not contain grace (they are not literally Jesus' body), they are so tied to the transaction in which Jesus' body and blood are conveyed that they are essential to the sacrament and by no means mere accidents. They show the reality that is being conveyed spiritually. Hodge, in contrast, allows the elements to be only legitimate symbols and signs of the grace conveyed; their purpose is historical, symbolic, and noetic, bringing the benefits of Christ's sacrifice to mind. The spiritual transaction is an utterly invisible phenomenon.

Of course, Nevin says he understands why Hodge was confused over Calvin's language being that he was at the mercy of Calvin's primitive psychology and the erroneous faculty psychology practiced at Princeton.[76] Nevin believed that Calvin's metaphysics would have benefited from modern psychology, where the organic unity of all things is fully understood and renders the idea of a dynamic relationship between outward and inward, physical and material, the reasonable explanation of how the elements fit into the sacramental mystery.

---

76. In *The Mystical Presence* Nevin was more adamant about this than in the debate. He softened his view because of Ebrard's work, which made him reconsider the degree of Calvin's alleged faulty psychology. Although Nevin became convinced by Ebrard that Calvin was not as naive about the workings of the mind or of philosophy in general, as he had first assumed, he still believed that modern idealist psychology provided the better theory. It is likely that Leibniz first pointed out Calvin's more mature understanding, and this was discovered by Nevin in Ebrard. Leibniz thought that Calvin's view might lead to a resolution of the impasse created by confusion over the question of Christ's substance in the sacrament, which divided Protestants and Catholics alike.

Likely Hodge's distortion of the Reformed doctrine, says Nevin, is "unwitting"; Hodge simply did not take the time to study the subject thoroughly and with the benefit of modern historical theory. But is Nevin fair to treat it as a matter of simple historical fact that Hodge has thus replaced of the old Reformed view with the modern Puritan system? Has Nevin added nothing to what was said in the sixteenth century? All along Nevin has included with the material of Calvin and the rest, interpretations reflecting his own Mediating position, which is evident as much in the work of Dorner (which he previously cited) as it is in his own conclusions. Nevin has indeed labored to allow Calvin and the Reformers to speak for themselves, yet he has been eager to identify that higher mode of confessional development both in the later sixteenth-century confessions and in the modern conceptions represented by Ullmann, Ebrard, Neander, and Dorner, among others. Nevin's own theory of historical development required that he no more than Hodge could speak without the influence (or taint) of his own era.

Gerrish notes in his *Tradition and the Modern World* that Nevin was convinced by the modern German historical method, and its influence is apparent throughout *The Mystical Presence*.[77] Moreover, Gerrish draws attention to the fact, as noted above, that Nevin believed the Reformed doctrine of the sixteenth century "labors under serious difficulties, and he proposes a revision of Calvin's psychology to resolve at least some of them" (though Nevin moderated this judgment somewhat after his reading of Ebrard)—this by way of replacing Calvin's idea of identity as constituted by "the material volume of a body" with identity as constituted according to "the organic law." This Nevin believed would repair Calvin's more primitive attempt "to bring Christ and believer together."

Not only that, but, says Gerrish, we might recognize "some special pleading and occasionally a slight shift of Calvin's own emphasis" in Nevin's summary of Calvin's doctrine. For instance, Hodge in fact follows Calvin in his preference for the term "communication" when speaking of our participation with Christ's body and blood over that of "presence." Likewise, Calvin was "more emphatic than Nevin in defining 'spiritual' as effected by the Holy Spirit," an emphasis that of course Hodge shares. Still, Gerrish has no hesitation in saying that in general, "the position advocated [by Nevin] is firmly based on the pronouncements of the Reformer [Calvin]."[78]

---

77. Gerrish does not appear to have had access to the debate, though he knew about it probably through Nichols. Instead he relied on the Thompson/Bricker edition of *The Mystical Presence* (which included "The Doctrine of the Reformed Church on the Lord's Supper," later published in the *Mercersburg Review*). With others he concluded that the DRCLS was an expansion of the *Messenger* material. However, it was an expansion and reworking of the historical material with a great deal of the philosophical issues jettisoned. Gerrish speaks of Nevin's being "fully conversant" in German theology (*Tradition and the Modern World*, 51), and had he seen the debate he would have been even more impressed by the degree of Nevin's familiarity with and fondness for the German Mediating philosophy and theology and with the dialogue between Hodge and Nevin about Schleiermacher.

78. See Gerrish, *Tradition and the Modern World*, 58–59, n. 200. See also Gerrish, "John Calvin and the Reformed Doctrine of the Lord's Supper," 85–98.

In the last few chapters, the focus shifts from the Reformers to the interlocutors' own theological commitments, with Nevin critiquing Hodge's "modern Puritanism," and Hodge indicting Nevin for a wide range of heretical tendencies.

Chapter 9: The Modern Theory Debated

We come now to material that for the most part will not appear as reworked material in "The Doctrine of the Reformed on the Lord's Supper." Nevin makes it clear in that text that he wants to focus on the historical argument and evidence. The debate however is inseparable from the theories upon which the men operated. So in chapter 9, Nevin declares an end to the historical part of the debate and takes up the criticism of "modern Puritan theology," which he had offered initially in *The Mystical Presence*, and of which Hodge has now shown himself to also be guilty. Here we meet also Hodge's counter-accusation, that Nevin is guilty of modern German theology, with all its errors. His periodical, the *Biblical Repertory and Princeton Review*, had been most critical of recent German science and theology, little of which had met with Princeton's approval. German idealist philosophy, along with its theory of historical development, were considered chief offenders. Our biographies of the two men above showed how deeply rooted was Princeton's antipathy toward modern German science.

In introducing the chapter, Nevin immediately flies in the face of Princeton dogma by asserting that while the faith of the church remains the same, dogmatic truths are modified over time in the understanding of the church. For Princeton, as the faith is never changing, so should theological dogma be. Theology's job is to render as precisely as possible the "truth once delivered to the saints," the Bible, and change accordingly is only the result of misunderstanding and error. For Nevin, such an approach almost guarantees that the historical evidence will be distorted in favor of current dogmatic preferences, as he believes it has in this case.

Hodge's critique, however, lodges a similar charge against Nevin—Nevin's system hangs on his theory of organic law, which is essentially Schleiermacher's. If it goes, so does his theory. Nevin is quite indignant at such a charge, denying any particular dependence on or fidelity to Schleiermacher, and Hodge is certainly exceedingly harsh in his prognostication. The doctrine contained in *The Mystical Presence* was close to Calvin's and holds a place of honor within the confessions of the Reformed bodies, although often misunderstood by those who declare their allegiance. Although the principle of organic law has not fared as well, nor perhaps the philosophy of Hegel and the theology of Schleiermacher, this does not automatically negate Nevin's work, and indeed there might still be something of value to learn from the insights of the German Mediating approach.[79] Likewise, though neither the faculty psychology of Princeton

---

79. Indeed, the understanding of history as a dynamic, living force is to be commended and has found its way into contemporary historical theory, and recently we have even seen a renewed interest in the historical philosophy of Hegel. To some extent this resurgence was sparked by Hans Küng's *Menschwerdung Gottes*, which was a sensation when it appeared in English in 1987 under the title *The Incarnation of God*. The author speaks frequently of the ongoing and recently renewed interest in Hegel's idea of history. See also the work of Karl Rahner; Charles Taylor, *Hegel*; Angelica Nuzzo, *Memory,*

nor the idealist psychology advanced by Rauch remain recognizable, the material of their early insights continue to inform our contemporary discussions of soteriology.

Chapter 10: Departures from Chalcedonian Orthodoxy

In the previous section, the worst charge that Hodge leveled at Nevin's theory was the accusation that it was essentially Schleiermachean (although Hodge also implied that this meant a kind of pantheism, by suggesting that Nevin's Christology would unite us with Christ in such a way that we would share in his divinity). In chapter 10, Hodge goes further, enumerating the various heresies that Nevin's German Mediating theology has involved him in, including the charge of Eutychianism. Nevin responds to the charge with a charge of his own: that Hodge in his christological dualism is moving dangerously close to Nestorius.

Hodge also offers a direct attack on Nevin's archetypal theology (which Nevin had learned from Ernesti, although Hodge believes he got it from Schleiermacher). Hodge says that in depicting Christ as the ideal man, he leaves open the possibility that in the end, although ideal, Christ is still a man or else that all who are in him are gods. This leads either to a Socinian humanizing of Christ or a pantheist deifying of man. The dual threat is obvious. One is either thrown into rationalism or into mysticism—which is precisely the unanswered question of the work of Schleiermacher: Was he a rationalist or a mystic?

To this challenge, Nevin answers that to be the ideal or perfect man is necessarily to be more than a mere man; it is to be at the same time the Son of God. He relies here on Karl Ullmann's corrective to Hegel, which we encountered in the preliminary essay to *The Mystical Presence*. This makes any thought of pantheism mistaken. Christ alone is the ideal and universal center to which all men must be drawn to share in the true ideal of humanity. In contrast, Hodge's view cannot recognize the way in which Christ's supernatural life has entered inwardly and organically into our human nature; it cannot explain how humanity is literally transformed into God-bearing people, rather than being merely inspired. The WORD, says Nevin, did not become inspirational, it became FLESH! Hodge, on the other hand, considers that the result of Nevin's position here is to undermine the function of the Holy Spirit, robbing him of his role in communicating Christ to the believer. He reiterates his insistence that there is among the early Reformed no such teaching of a theanthropic life being passed on to believers in Christ; the bond is made by the indwelling of the Holy Spirit in each individual believer.

Chapter 11: Departures from Protestant Orthodoxy

Hodge now focuses on the ways in which Nevin's theology departs from core Protestant and Reformed commitments, chief among them the atonement. Nevin, says Hodge, has effectively replaced a Reformed understanding of the atonement with the system of Schleiermacher, which intimates that salvation comes from achieving

---

History, Justice in Hegel; Catherine Malabou, *The Future of Hegel.*

"God-consciousness" through our relationship with Christ. In such a theory, there *is no* doctrine of the atonement—no propitiation, no satisfaction, and no verdict of divine justice!

In response, Nevin will cover this checklist of necessary theological terms, but he does depart from traditional Reformed language. Nevin is clearly applying nineteenth-century solutions to questions of sixteenth-century theology that he considered unresolved, especially as these questions impacted Christology. Nevin had been pleased with Calvin's sacramental doctrine, but the ideas of predestination and the decrees had long troubled him. To this, contemporary scholars will have to ask whether, in moving beyond Hodge's doctrine of the atonement, Nevin was also moving beyond the very tradition he was calling the Reformed back to. As Gerrish mused, "What becomes of the appeal to tradition if the tradition is divided against itself?"[80]

Hodge worried as much, clearly highlighting Nevin's novelty in his theory of the second Adam. Above all, Hodge is concerned not so much that Nevin departed from the words of sixteenth-century sacramental language as from the "spirit" of Reformation teaching. Nevin has replaced the evangelical spirit of the old Reformed with a "churchy" interpretation that is more catholic than Protestant. Of course, Nevin replies, that explains the low view of Hodge on the sacraments. He has replaced the role of the church with that of the Holy Spirit in subjective liaison with the believer. The church is nothing more than the assembly of those chosen by the Spirit, a conclusion that Nevin finds unacceptably poor and abstract.

Chapter 12: Final Criticisms

The debate draws to a close with Hodge's attack on Nevin's philosophical and theological "rationalism." This, Hodge says, is not meant personally—it is simply the nature of the speculative psychology[81] to which Nevin has committed himself, which Princeton has long opposed. If it avoids rationalism, it falls into pantheism, Hodge dolefully concludes. Nevin replies that the system of Princeton is a dead formalism. History is dissected and shorn of its dynamic, living quality. This leads to an abstract theory of the atonement that divorces the life of Christ from his people. To sound one last alarm bell, Hodge suggests that Nevin's theory is inadvertently Sabellian and thus anti-trinitarian. Nevin scoffs at this criticism, and takes the opportunity instead to clarify his relations to German theology, and to defend his reliance upon it, as a minister in the German Reformed Church.

Having addressed all of Hodge's criticisms, Nevin steals the last word, offering a valuable recapitulation of the two contrasting views, in which Hodge's system appears in unflattering colors as "outward," "mechanical," and "abstract." His concluding peroration evinces his confidence that the result of the interchange has been a decisive double vindication of the central claims of *The Mystical Presence*. On the one hand,

---

80. *Tradition and the Modern World*, 70.

81. Meaning here "philosophy of the mind." Hodge goes on to say that Ullmann recognizes its proximity to pantheism and mysticism. Rather, Ullmann believed it a corrective to pantheism and mysticism as might be detected in Schleiermacher.

Hodge's challenges to its historical claims have been refuted at every point, and the debate has indeed afforded the opportunity to pile on even more and stronger historical evidence than Nevin had offered in *The Mystical Presence*. On the other hand, Nevin's theological concerns about the unsacramental, unchurchly nature of contemporary Reformed Protestantism, he declares, have been proved sadly true in Hodge's article. Indeed, this is no small matter they have contended about, he concludes; nothing less is at stake than what it means to believe "in the holy catholic Church," as stated in the Apostles' Creed. With this dramatic pronouncement, Nevin declares his work done.

Conclusion

The debate was won by Nevin, but by reason of his mastery of the texts, as is often the case in debates of this kind. The question of who was right is more complex. Nevin gave the lion's share of influence to Calvin when it came to the authoritative teaching of the Reformed of the sixteenth century on the Lord's Supper; a viable claim, but perhaps overstated. Hodge, resisting the idea that doctrines evolve, undoubtedly erred in trying to grant equal authority to the early Helvetic material as, for example, the Heidelberg Catechism. As Gerrish points out, Ebrard confirmed Nevin's thesis by showing that "after the Wittenberg Concord of 1536, there emerged a third sacramental theology in Protestantism, distinct alike from crass Lutheranism and crass Zwinglianism . . . [and that it] formed an important bond of unity between the Lutheran and the Reformed branches of evangelical Protestantism." For historical idealists such as Schaff and Nevin, this emergence suggested a synthesis that incorporated "the inward life" of each communion. In this, however, Nevin perhaps saw more in this "inward life" than may have been warranted, as if the life existed without inconsistencies. Hodge was right to contest Nevin's attempt to see uniformity in the confessions. But with the exception of the Swiss, history does suggests that the bulk of the Reformers were as conservative as Calvin or more so, and the balance tipped toward Lutheran concerns over Zwinglian liberalism.

The consensus that Nevin identified included Bucer and Melanchthon, and would be an enormous influence on the German Reformed, especially those Germans from the Palatinate. Ursinus greatly appreciated Calvin—but Melanchthon as much as Calvin. And the Dutch Reformed became convinced by Calvin and revered the Heidelberg Catechism. The Huguenots too bear the unmistakable stamp of Calvin's influence and that of his associate Beza.

Nevertheless, Hodge was right to identify a swing back in the other direction among many Reformed of the next century. Confessions like Westminster are not of quite the same spirit as Heidelberg, the Gallican, or the Belgic, and certainly not of the Augsburg Confession. Perhaps Hodge would have been better served to state his preference for seventeenth-century sacramental theology and leave it at that. Still, given the insights of recent scholarship, it is important to resist too neat a conclusion regarding a single sacramental mind-set among the Reformed of the sixteenth century. A study of sixteenth-century liturgies has shown that many sources were contributing to the sacramental practice of worshippers as well as their theological convictions.[82] These practices and convictions must be read between the lines of the great confessions.

In any case, however, as Brian Gerrish points out, only to be more recently echoed by George Hunsinger, Calvin and the Reformed confessions cannot be taken seriously if we ignore their strong insistence that the sacraments are *not* "mere reminders"; that communion with Christ is *not* simply about beliefs in Christ; that the ecclesial body of Christ is *not* just an "association of like-minded individuals." In spite of the Reformed's difficulty in expressing what that "something more" is that they experience in the Holy Supper, says Gerrish, if they are to succeed in ecumenical theology, they will need to "throw their weight on Calvin's side of the Reformed boat."[83]

---

82. Nevin and Hodge both appear unaware of the importance of John a Lasco, and they may have underestimated the authority of Bucer and Peter Martyr as well.

83. Gerrish, *Grace and Gratitude*, 190. See also Hunsinger, *Eucharist and Ecumenism*.

1

Nevin Introduces the Debate[1]

MR. EDITOR:

Many of your readers, no doubt, would be pleased to see at least some parts of this article, transferred from the *Princeton Repertory* to the *Weekly Messenger*.[2] In these circumstances, may I be permitted to request that you will publish, in successive numbers, the whole? The article is indeed of some length; but the subject of which it treats is one of great interest, and the source from which it proceeds is such as to entitle it to more than common respect. Dr. Hodge stands before us as the central theological organ, in some sort, of the entire Old School Presbyterian Church[3] in this country; and the article itself is characterized throughout, by a corresponding consciousness of authority and power. The weight of his single name is with multitudes sufficient to outweigh any amount of favorable judgment on the other side. Such a man as Krummacher,[4] in this case, or any other evangelical *German* divine, can hardly be

1. ["Dr. Hodge on the Mystical Presence," *Weekly Messenger of the German Reformed Church*, New Series, vol. 13, no. 37, Wednesday, May 24, 1848. Published by the Board of the Synod of the German Reformed Church: Chambersburg, PA.—ed.]

2. ["Princeton Repertory" refers to the *Biblical Repertory and Princeton Review*, which began its life in 1825 as the *Biblical Repertory: A Collection of Tracts in Biblical Literature* by Charles Hodge. It was printed by D. A. Borrenstein and remained under the control of Hodge virtually until his death. The *Weekly Messenger of the German Reformed Church* was the English language newsletter of that denomination. The *Weekly Messenger* was published by the Board of Missions, but as it became a weekly, it was in the editorial hands of Benjamin S. Schneck—ed.]

3. [The "Old School Presbyterian Church" refers to a split that occurred among Presbyterians causing some to ultimately leave the denomination and form a separate synod. The division, which occurred in 1837, came for a variety of reasons with New Measures revivalism and a more fundamental approach to Scripture being two major issues. "Old Schoolers" remained traditional in their theological and ecclesiastical outlook. However, while Nevin, Hodge, and the Princeton professors identified with the Old School position, they often found the Old School leaders extreme and uncompromising. Both Nevin and Hodge worked to ease tensions and were utterly opposed to a split. For a comprehensive treatment of the rise of New School Presbyterianism see George Marsden, *The Evangelical Mind and the New School Presbyterian Experience.*—ed.]

4. [F. W. Krummacher was at that time a celebrated Pietist preacher in Prussia and a leading advocate of the German Reformed in America. Ultimately he would go on record as stating that the Mercersburg position was in keeping with contemporary orthodox German theology. Here Nevin compares the relative importance of Krummacher in German to that of Hodge in America. Yet in spite of Krummacher's

seen or felt; all would seem to be settled by the single voice of the *Princeton Repertory*. Such a voice deserves to be respectfully heard. The article besides is written with ability and force. Dr. Hodge is not Dr. Kurtz,[5] as this latter gentleman is proud to confess. He has some knowledge of the subject, and approaches it in a true and manly way.

It is expected on all hands, I believe, that I should *try* at least to make some defense, against this assault. The expectation too is reasonable. I have no right to be silent. Has Dr. Hodge convicted me of error, in the main positions of my book? I am bound, in the case of so momentous an interest, to let the fact be known. If not, it is due to all parties that I should show why I cannot yield to his argument. The only question has been, in my mind, with regard to the way of coming out. The *Repertory* would not of course admit a reply in its own columns; that in any case is against its rule. The *Messenger* does not come at all before the same reading public; and is beside, as a paper, for general popular use, not exactly the proper ground for a full formal reply. As however it seems desirable now to present the article of Dr. Hodge, the subject necessarily requires some sort of notice from my side in return. This it will be best to furnish, I think, in the form of notes or observations on the text of Dr. Hodge itself. Such informal and direct reply is likely to be of more account in the *Messenger*, than a long counter article following in a separate way.

I remain yours, J.W. N. *Mercersburg, May 15th, 1848*

REVIEW OF THE MYSTICAL PRESENCE [BY CHARLES HODGE]

We have had Dr. Nevin's work on the *Mystical Presence* on our table since its publication, some two years ago, but have never really read it, until within a fortnight. We do not suppose other people are quite as bad, in this respect, as ourselves. Our experience, however, has been that it requires the stimulus of a special necessity to carry us through such a book. Being called upon to investigate the question, What was the real doctrine of the Reformed church on the Lord's Supper? we naturally turned to Dr. Nevin's work, and we gratefully acknowledge the assistance derived from it. We differ from him, indeed, essentially, as to the whole subject, not only as to the historical question, but as to what is the true doctrine. We are, however, on that account only the more disposed to give him credit for the diligence with which he has collected materials (though almost entirely on one side) for the proper decision of the question. So much has of late been said by Dr. Nevin of the apostasy of the Reformed church; his uniform tone is so disparaging, if not contemptuous, when speaking of all the branches of that church,

favorable review of the *Mystical Presence*, he could not equal the influence of a negative review by Hodge in the United States. Krummacher's remarks were recorded by Schaff in his article in the *Weekly Messenger* of the German Reformed Church, August 11, 1847. Schaff quotes Krummacher that the work was "historically and exegetically impregnable throughout." See Nichols, *The Mercersburg Theology*, 245; Nichols, *Romanticism*, 88.—ed.]

5. [Benjamin Kurtz (1795–1865), retired Lutheran minister and avid revivalist, was the editor of the *Lutheran Observer*, which had previously published a series of articles in defense of the methods of the noted revivalist Charles G. Finney (1792–1875). See Nichols, *Romanticism*, 58. Kurtz and the *Observer* allied with other anti-Mercersburg leaders and periodicals.—ed.]

except his own; the charge of Puritanism and Rationalism is so constantly flowing from his pen, that he has reason, we think, to be surprised that all this has been so long endured in silence. We, however, do not propose on this occasion to travel out of the record, or do more than endeavor to answer the question, What is the true doctrine of the Reformed church on the Lord's Supper? Having done this however, we shall give our reasons for thinking that Dr. Nevin is tenfold further from the doctrines of our common fathers, than those whom he commiserates and condemns.

It is confessedly a very difficult matter to obtain clear views of what was the real doctrine of the Reformed church on the Lord's Supper during the sixteenth century. This difficulty arises from various sources. The subject itself is mysterious. The Lord's Supper is by all Christians regarded as exhibiting, and, in the case of believers, confirming their union with the Lord Jesus Christ. Whatever obscurity rests on that union, must in a measure rest on this sacrament. That union, however, is declared to be a great mystery. It has always, on that account, been called the mystical union. We are, therefore, demanding too much when we require all obscurity to be banished from this subject. If the union between Christ and his people were merely moral, arising from agreement and sympathy, there would be no mystery about it; and the Lord's Supper, as the symbol of that union, would be a perfectly intelligible ordinance. But the scriptures teach that our union with Christ is far more than this. It is a vital union, we are partakers of his life, for it is not we that live, but Christ that liveth in us. It is said to be analogous to our union with Adam, to the union between the head and members of the same body, and between the vine and its branches. There are some points in reference to this subject, with regard to which almost all Christians have agreed. They agree that this union includes a federal[6] or representative relation, arising from a divine constitution; and on the part of Christ, a participation in our nature. He that sanctified and they who are sanctified are all of one. On this account he calls them brethren. Inasmuch as the children are partakers of flesh and blood, he also himself likewise took part of the same (Heb. ii. 11–14). It is in virtue of his assumption of our nature that he stands to us in the intimate relation here spoken of. It is agreed, further,

---

6. [Hodge comes at union with Christ from this federal perspective. Union is contractual, in the sense that one voluntarily accepts the claims of Christ made upon the life of the believer. While Nevin allows for a forensic aspect to the atonement, he rejects, as stated by William B. Evans, an "extrinsic legal or federal union with Christ," and he recovers Calvin's doctrine of union with Christ. That is to say, Nevin recognizes that while our sin and God's justice demand a just verdict of guilt before God, our redemption and pardon do not result from God's arbitrary decree nor from any extrinsic declaration of forgiveness by God, but by receiving forgiveness and righteousness through our unity with Christ. The full development of the Reformed doctrine of imputation including Nevin's theory is well explained in Evans, *Imputation and Impartation*, 18. Hodge later wrote, "We are in Him by faith. There is indeed a federal union between Christ and his people, founded on the covenant of redemption between the Father and the Son in the counsels of eternity. . . . But it was also, as we learn from the Scriptures, included in the stipulations of that covenant, that his people, so far as adults are concerned, should not receive the saving benefits of that covenant until they were united to Him by a voluntary act of faith. . . . To be in Christ, and to believe in Christ, are, therefore, in the Scriptures convertible, and, therefore, the same effects are attributed to faith as are attributed to union with Christ" (*Systematic Theology*, III:104). Nevin would never conclude that union with Christ and faith in Christ are effectively the same thing, since for Nevin this ignores the whole question of physical incorporation into the actual body of Christ.—ed.]

that this union include on our part a participation of the spirit of Christ. It is the indwelling of the Holy Spirit, who is the Spirit of Christ, and dwells without measure in him as our head, who dwells also in his people, so that they become one body in Christ Jesus. They are one in relation to one another, and one in relation to him. As the human body is one by being animated and pervaded by one soul, so Christ and his people are one in virtue of the indwelling of one and the same Spirit, the Holy Ghost. It is further agreed that this union relates to the bodies as well as the souls of believers. Know you not, says the apostle, that your bodies are the members of Christ; know ye not that your body is the temple of the Holy Ghost, who dwelleth in you? The Westminster Catechism,[7] therefore, says of believers after death, that their bodies being still united to Christ, do rest in their graves until the resurrection. This union was always represented as a real union, not merely imaginary nor simply moral, nor arising from the mere reception of the benefits which Christ procured. We receive Christ himself, and are in Christ, united to him by the indwelling of his Spirit and by a living faith. So far all the Reformed at least agreed.

Do the scriptures teach, besides all this, that we are partakers of the human nature, of the real flesh and blood of Christ? This question Romanists and Lutherans[8] answer in the affirmative. They teach the actual reception and manducation of the real body of Christ. This the whole Reformed church denied, in England, Belgium, & Germany, as well as in Switzerland. But as Christ speaks of eating his flesh and drinking his blood, the question is in what way this is to be understood? All the Reformed answered, that by receiving the body and blood of Christ, is meant receiving their virtue or efficacy. Some of them said that it was their virtue as broken and shed, i.e., their sacrificial virtue; others said, it was a mysterious, supernatural efficacy flowing from the glorified body of Christ in heaven; and that this last idea, therefore, is to be taken into the account, in determining the nature of the union between Christ and his people. Apart, therefore, from the mysteriousness of the subject, the diversity of views among the Reformed themselves, is one reason of the difficulty determining the real doctrine of the church, on this subject. In some of the confessions we have the one, and in some the other of these modes of representation, brought to view.

Another source of difficulty is found in the fact that almost all the Reformed confessions were framed for the express purpose of compromise. One great object

7. [There are two catechisms, one the "longer" the other the "shorter." Compiled by the Westminster Assembly in 1647, they were the work of the synod appointed by the Long Parliament to bring about reform in the Church of England in a Presbyterian and Calvinistic direction. Hodge quotes here from Shorter Catechism Q. 38.—ed.]

8. [Roman Catholics adopted "transubstantiation," the belief that the whole substance of the elements of the Eucharist, the bread and wine, convert to the whole substance of the body and blood of Christ, while the "accidents," i.e., the appearances and outward properties of the bread and wine, do not change. Today, the view as stated in the *Catechism of the Catholic Church*, 1994, has hardly changed, "It is by the conversion of the bread and wine into Christ's body and blood that Christ becomes present in this sacrament" (p. 346). Lutherans historically attested to a doctrine called "consubstantiation" following the lead of Martin Luther. It holds that the substances of the bread and wine and the substances of the body and blood of Christ co-mingle (the latter being "in, with, and through" the former). Thus, when Lutherans eat the sacrament they ingest both bread and wine, and the body and blood of Christ.—ed.]

of Calvin's life, was to prevent the schism between the two branches of the Protestant church. He and the other authors of these symbols, therefore, were constantly endeavoring to frame a statement of this doctrine, which all parties, Lutheran, Zwinglian, and Calvinistic, could adopt. Union was at that time a matter of last importance,[9] not only on religious and ecclesiastical grounds, but for reasons connected with their political well-being and safety. The question about the Lord's Supper, was the only one which kept the parties separate. Here Luther was inflexible and most unreasonably violent. The Lutherans were at this time far more numerous and powerful than the Reformed. To conciliate Luther was, therefore, a constant object of desire and effort. Conference after conference was held for this purpose. The Reformed on all these occasions, and in all their confessions, went as far as possible to meet the views of the Lutherans. It is not wonderful therefore that their language, should at times, be hard to reconcile with what was in fact the real doctrine of the Reformed Church. We find Bucer[10] signing a formula which satisfied Luther, and Beza[11] signing another, which satisfied the Romish commissioners, at Poissy.[12] It is fair to infer from these historical circumstances, that while the Reformed held a doctrine which admitted of expression in the language adopted, it might be much more simply and intelligibly expressed in other terms. And we find in fact, that as soon as this pressure from without was removed, all ambiguity as to the Reformed doctrine as to the Lord's Supper ceased. No one pretends to misunderstand the language of Turretin and Pictet,[13] the contemporaries or immediate successors of Beza. This suggests a third source of difficulty on this subject, the ambiguity of the terms employed in these confessions. The words, presence, real, true, flesh, blood, substance, &c., are all employed, in many cases, out of their ordinary sense. We are said to receive the true body and blood but nothing material; the substance but not the essence; the natural body but only by faith. It is not easy to unravel these

---

9. [Today we would say "first importance."—ed.]

10. [Martin Bucer (1491–1551), in 1523 openly preached Lutheranism, but moved toward the Reformed theology of the Eucharist. He became a key leader of the Reformed in Switzerland and South Germany after the death of Zwingli. Bucer has been underrated in his contribution to the Palatinate reformation. This has been rectified to a great extent by Deborah Rahn Clemens in her doctoral dissertation, "Foundations of German Reformed Worship in the Sixteenth Century Palatinate" (1995). See also Wright, *Bucer*; Greschat, *Martin Bucer*.—ed.]

11. [Theodore Beza (1519–1606), a student of Calvin and head of the Geneva Academy from 1559. When Calvin died, he inherited Calvin's mantle as leader of the Genevan church and mentor of its disciples in France, the Netherlands, and England. He was responsible for crystallizing Calvinist doctrines such as predestination and Presbyterianism in the forms that would define Calvinist orthodoxy for centuries to come. See Raitt, *Eucharistic Theology*; Maruyama, *Ecclesiology of Theodore Beza*.—ed.]

12. [The Colloquy of Poissy, organized in September 1561 by the French regent, Catherine de' Medici, invited Reformed divines including Beza and a delegation of Roman Catholic bishops to seek to resolve religious differences in the realm. The Colloquy was inconclusive, with the matter of the Eucharist proving the ultimate sticking point. See Nugent, *Ecumenism in the Age of Reformation: The Colloquy of Poissy*.—ed.]

13. [Francis Turretin (1623–87), Swiss-Italian reformer, dogmatician and systematizer of Calvin's theology into what became known as "Calvinistic orthodoxy." His *Institutes of Elenctic Theology* were the text used by Hodge at Princeton. Benedict Pictet (1655–1724), Turretin's nephew and a Genevan preacher. He was the author of Christian Theology.—ed.]

conflicting statements and to determine what they really mean. Besides all this it is hard to tell where to look for the authoritative exhibition of the Reformed doctrine. Shall we look to the private writings of the Reformers, or to the public confessions? If to the latter, shall we rely on those of Switzerland or on those of the Palatinate, France or Belgium? These, though they have a general coincidence, do not entirely agree. Some favor one interpretation, and some another. Dr. Nevin chooses to make Calvin the great authority, and pronounces the confessions of the Swiss churches "chaotic and contradictory." The most satisfactory method of proceeding, as we conceive, will be to quote in the first instance, those authorities which represent the Swiss views; secondly, those which present the views of Calvin; and thirdly, those symbols in which both parties concurred. Having done this, we propose to analyze these statements and endeavor to determine their meaning.

CRITICISM [BY JOHN W. NEVIN]

The confession with which Dr. Hodge commences is not adapted certainly to inspire any very high confidence in his review. First, he feels no inward interest, it seems, in the subject; it is for him a heavy question altogether, this sacramental controversy, into which he is carried only by the "stimulus of a special necessity." He is indeed set apart to the science of theology as his proper vocation; but this subject has for him evidently little or no connection with theological science. He has no sympathy with the deep Christological inquiries of the fourth and fifth centuries; no power to enter into the great sacramental controversy of the sixteenth century, save as a matter of barren historical curiosity. His whole theology in this tract, as I shall show hereafter, betrays plainly the false posture of his mind, as we have it thus incidentally confessed, in regard to the region he is here called to explore. It is a theology that has to do almost exclusively with one side of Christianity only, at the cost of what belongs to it with equal right on another side; and which, for this very reason, is ever prone to run out into a system of mechanical abstractions,[14] with the loss of all hearty interest in the concrete realities of the old catholic creed. With all becoming respect however for Dr. Hodge (for he is a man whom I do greatly respect), I must protest solemnly against his competency to sit in judgment on my book, while under the power of *such* a mind. The sacramental question falls back at once upon the Christological question; which again lies at the foundation of the whole idea of the Church, and forms the *only* basis of an earnest and truly scientific theology in any direction. To take no inward interest in this, is just to be disqualified in full for every such investigation, as that which Dr. Hodge has here undertaken for the benefit of the Church.

And then, in the second place, how little trouble it has cost him to set the whole matter in its proper light! It is not to be supposed, of course, that his study of the

---

14. [This criticism is especially important for Nevin. In his view, Hodge's "modern Puritan system" views the world as "mechanism," where his theology understands the world as "organism." Hence, the contrasting systems are depicted by Mercersburg as "dead" on the one hand, and "living" on the other.—ed.]

subject has not been a good deal broader than the "fortnight" immediately preceding this review. It is evident enough however, that it has not been very special or full at any time; the subject had no living value for his mind; and he had besides all along a very decided judgment, as to how it *ought* to be settled, without going much into historical details. We find accordingly but little recourse to authorities, in the article, in the way of original examination.[15] Most of the quotations brought forward are simply borrowed from the *Mystical Presence* itself, with a sense put into them to suit the views of Dr. Hodge. This *ex cathedra* style of putting an end to so great and difficult a question, may find some apology possibly in the acknowledged learning of Dr. Hodge, and the strong vantage ground of his position in the Church; but of itself it is not suited to beget any very great confidence either in his argument or its results.

The "materials" collected in my book are said to be "almost entirely on one side." They will be found however to embrace *all* that can be counted primary and legitimate evidence, in the case; that is, such quotations from Calvin as cut off all room for doubt in regard to his theory, and extracts from all the symbols of the Reformed Church that are allowed to be of any force on the main question—unless indeed the *Consensus Tigurinus*[16] be supposed of material omission, which I am not prepared to allow. Turretin and Pictet are in no sense parallel authorities, with Calvin, Beza, Ursinus,[17] and the old Reformed Confessions. They belong to a later period.

I have not been particularly guilty, I think, of disparaging other branches of the Church *in favor of my own*. My views involve of course throughout the idea, that there has been a serious falling away, on the part of the Reformed Church generally (and with the Lutheran still more), from the sacramental faith of the sixteenth century; a change attributable in large measure to Puritanism, as a sort of second stage in the process of the great Protestant revolution. Why it should be unbecoming at all to speak of this plainly, in such light and under its own name, I am not able to see. In my book, I have a full array of evidence to show the fact of this falling away, and its true character. Dr. Hodge never notices this at all, but simply says I am much farther aside from the

15. [Of course, scholarship into the original sources themselves will become the only acceptable standard for judging the quality of historical research in the years that would follow. This had not previously been the case, however, particularly in American Protestantism, which in this respect particularly lagged behind German theological and historical science.—ed.]

16. [Much later (1877) Schaff published his *Creeds of Christendom* and did not include the *Consensus Tigurinus*, also called *The Consensus of Zurich*, 1549. Here he explained that the *Tigurinus* along with the *Genevan Catechism* and the *Geneva Consensus* were documents drawn up by Calvin, but much too long to include in his Creeds. Furthermore, the consensus documents "are not so much confessions of faith as elaborate theological and polemical essays on two doctrines—the one on the Lord's Supper, the other on Predestination . . . ." He concluded that "the Second Helvetic, the Gallican, the Belgic, the Scotch, and other Reformed Confessions . . . are sufficiently explicit and more authoritative." See Schaff, *Creeds of Christendom*, 3:232. Schaff wrote that Calvin stood between Luther and Zwingli, and felt an intense need to reconcile the parties. That was why he met with the groups as together they forged the Consensus Tigurinus. Until the later confessions appeared, the Zurich symbol was adopted by most of the Reformed with Basel being the last to agree (*Creeds*, 3:471–473).—ed.]

17. [Zacharias Ursinus (1534–84), trusted student of Melanchthon and chief author of the Heidelberg Catechism. He also published a commentary on the Catechism and a work on its defense. See Visser, *Zacharias Ursinus*.—ed.]

old faith than those whom I thus pity and condemn. It would have been more to the point to show, that I have not done *justice* to the Modern Puritan view.

With all I may have spoken in disparagement of Puritanism (as a theoretic *system*), it will be admitted, I think, that the *Princeton Repertory* is quite as free and sweeping in its judgments on all *German* theology.

It is well that Dr. Hodge admits, in the outset, a real *life-union* between Christ and believers, and allows it to be a "mystery." We shall find all this afterward, however, virtually excluded from his theological system. He admits too, that the *Lutheran* confession, one grand division of the original Protestant world, held that our union with Christ is such as to involve a participation in his human nature. Let this be borne always in mind. It will be easy to show, that the Calvinistic faith comprehended the *substance* of the very same mystery, only with a very material difference as to its mode, I have shown it already by incontrovertible evidence in the *Mystical Presence*, which Dr. Hodge has not condescended to notice, and might seem indeed not even to have read. But I will try to make the matter still more convincingly plain.

The way in which Dr. Hodge notices the "sources of difficulty" belonging to a right estimate of the sacramental question, as it stood in the early Reformed Church is curious and significantly characteristic. It puts one in the mind of the old *pragmatical* view of history (exemplified to some extent in Planck),[18] by which all is treated as a box of dry bones, that are to be put together with hooks and wires as to the skill of the operator may seem best. The idea of the past, as something which once had a real life of its own, that must needs be *reproduced*, in the spirit, from its own ground upwards, in order that it may be understood, is thrust aside in favor of the much more convenient imagination that it never had any right to be anything more than can be forcibly squeezed into modes of thought which prevail in our own time.[19] Dr. Hodge comes to the sixteenth century, in this case, with his whole mind conformed to a certain scheme in regard to the Church and the sacraments, which is assumed with full confidence, from the start, to be the only one that can at all bear examination. The rule, which he thus carries in himself, is made the measure for trying all that comes before him in the thinking of the reformers; what agrees with it is right and intelligible, what fails to do so must be resolved into some accidental obliquity or confusion belonging to the age. The old church view naturally clung still, in this age, to men's minds; there was a disposition towards conciliation and compromise on the side of the Reformed Church,

18. [Gottlieb Jakob Planck (1751–1833), historian of the Lutheran Church, professor at Göttingen whose chief work, *Geschichte der Entstehung der Verändeningen und der Bildung anseres protestantischen Lehrbegriffs von Anfang der Reformation bis zur Einführung de Konkordienformel* returned objectivity to the study of the Formula of Concord according to Schaff (*Creeds of Christendom*, 1:336). Nevin's depiction of Planck refers to a methodology still steeped in the rationalism of the late eighteenth century.—ed.]

19. [This sentence shows how firmly Nevin stood, methodologically, in the historical school of Hegel. It was August Neander who introduced Nevin into the philosophic system that had had such a great impact on Europe, including on the philosophy of Coleridge and the Oxford theologians, on the French with Victor Cousin (1792–1867) and of course all of Germany at the time. The organic concept of historical development was not discovered by Hegel alone, but he undoubtedly took it to its most advanced form in his idealist or speculative philosophy.—ed.]

&c. But what is all this more than saying, that the age stood in a different relation to the old catholic creed altogether, from that which is now common in the Protestant world, and to be understood at all must be taken in this respect as it *was*, and judged accordingly? Does it follow that our thinking is more worthy of trust, just because it is less bound by such catholic reminiscences and associations? That were at once to take for granted the whole question in dispute. What we want here, is not to be told what influences wrought, in the sixteenth century, to produce the semblance of high sacramental views; but so to force our way into the whole life to which such influences once belonged (leaving our own out of sight), that we may be able to understand it, and deal with it under its own living form.

When Dr. Hodge would have us believe that such men as Bucer, Calvin and Beza, *strained* the sense of their own creed to bring it into apparent correspondence with that of Luther, whilst it might have been "much more simply and intelligibly expressed in other terms," he betrays the hollowness of his own ground, by simply cutting a knot which he has no power to untie. There is full as much evidence, that they strained their language the other way, to accommodate the low tendencies of some in Switzerland. We have no right thus to resolve the divine earnestness of these great men, into diplomatic show and cunning. If ever there was a clear case, we have one when we say that they made *vital* account of the sacramental mystery, and used such language as they best could, to guard it from perversion, both on the right hand and on the left. Only let it be felt that they were in earnest here with their faith, and not simply playing a part (such as our modern consciousness is too often forced to play with the old symbols), and much of the ambiguity which is supposed to attach to their language will become sufficiently plain. The ambiguity comes from *our* position, in many cases, rather than from theirs. "We are said to receive the true body and blood, but nothing material; the substance, but not the essence; the natural body, but only by faith."

Conflicting statements, says Dr. Hodge, which cannot easily be unraveled. In the old Calvinistic system, however, studied within itself, and not Puritanized into modern proportions, all is clear enough. The contradiction grows out of the stand-point of Dr. Hodge, and is itself plain proof that he is not doing justice to the sixteenth century, but squeezing it into the shape of his own age. With the sacramental system of modern New England, for instance, in the mind of these old patrons of the Reformed faith, how is it conceivable at all that any such hyperbolic phrases should have come into such familiar use?

2

The Views of Zwingli and Calvin[1]

REVIEW, CONTINUED [HODGE]

First then, the Zuinglian View

Z UINGLE[2] SAYS:

> The Lord's Supper is nothing else than the food of the soul, and Christ instituted the ordinance as a memorial of himself. When a man commits himself to the sufferings and redemption of Christ, he is saved. Of this he has left us a certain visible sign of his flesh and blood, both which he has commanded us to eat and drink in remembrance of him.

This is said in a document, presented to the council of Zurich, in 1523. In his LXVII Articles published in 1523, he says, briefly on this subject, in art. 17, "Christ who offered himself once upon the cross is the eternally sufficient offering and sacrifice for the sins of all believers. Whence it follows that the mass is not a sacrifice, but the commemoration of the sacrifice made upon the cross, and, as it were, a seal of the

---

1. ["Dr. Hodge on the Mystical Presence, Article from the Repertory, Continued," *Weekly Messenger*, New Series, vol. 13, no. 38. Wednesday, May 31, 1848. Published by the Board of the Synod of the German Reformed Church: Chambersburg, PA—ed.]

2. [Hodge:] We use the name of Zuingle to characterize the form of doctrine which he actually taught, and which was adopted in the church of Zurich of which he was the pastor; not in the sense in which the term Zuinglian is popularly used, to designate what was really the Socinian or Remonstrant doctrine on the Sacraments. [The common spelling is Zwingli. What Hodge means by this is that he wants to differentiate between Zwinglianism and what ultimately became the view of Unitarians. Simply put, Zwinglianism denies the presence of Christ in the Lord's Supper. In contrast, Zwingli affirmed Christ's spiritual presence through the Holy Spirit. Ulrich Zwingli (1484–1531), educated at Bern, ordained a priest in 1506, ultimately a leader of the Swiss Reformation. His first Reformation tract appeared in April 1522. By 1524 Zwingli embraced the eucharistic "symbolism" he is famous for. He died on the field of battle. See Gabler, *Huldrych Zwingli, His Life and Work* and G. R. Potter, *Zwingli*.—ed.]

redemption effected by Christ."[3] In the *"Expositio Chr. Fidei,"*[4] written just before his death and published by Bullinger,[5] 1531, he says,

> The natural substantial body of Christ in which he suffered, and in which he is now seated in heaven, at the right hand of God, is not in the Lord's Supper eaten, corporeally, or as to its essence, but spiritually only.... Spiritually to eat the body of Christ, is nothing else than with the spirit and mind to rely on the goodness and mercy of God through Christ.... Sacramentally to eat his body, is, the sacrament being added, with the mind and spirit to feed upon him.[6]

And afterwards, "We assert therefore that the body of Christ is not eaten in the Supper in a gross carnal manner as the Papists pretend, but spiritually and sacramentally, with a devout, believing and homely mind, as St. Chrysostom says." In his *Epist. Ad princip. German.*[7] (Op. II. p. 546), he uses this language:

> When the bread and wine, consecrated by the very words of Christ are distributed to the brethren, is not the whole Christ, as it were sensibly (if words are required, I will say more that I am wont to do) presented to the senses? But how? Is the natural body handled and eaten? By no means; but offered to the mind to be contemplated, for the senses we have the sacrament of this thing.... We never have denied that Christ is sacramentally and *in mysterio* present in the Lord's Supper, as well on account of believing contemplation, as the whole symbolical service.

The confessions which most nearly conform to this view are the *Confessio Tetropolitana*, The First Basel, and The First Helvetic confession.[8] All these are apologetic. The last named protests against the representation that the Reformed regard the sacraments as mere badges of profession, asserting that they are also signs and means of grace. In art. 22, the Lord's Supper is called *coena mystica* ["the mystical supper"],

---

3. [These articles appear in Schaff, *Creeds of Christendom*, 3:197–207 in German and Latin. An English translation is given by Emil Buehrer in "Zwingli's Sixty-Seven Articles," 5–7.—ed.]

4. [This work can be found in James T. Dennison, ed., *Reformed Confessions of the 16th and 17th Centuries in English Translation: 1523–1552*, 3 vols. (Grand Rapids: Reformation Heritage Books, 2008–2012), 1:176–225.—ed.]

5. [Johann Heinrich Bullinger (1504–75), Swiss reformer and student of Zwingli. Bullinger replaced Zwingli as chief pastor of Zurich after the death of Zwingli. See Bromiley, *Zwingli and Bullinger*; Gordon and Campi, eds., *Architect of the Reformation.*—ed.]

6. [Hodge:] Niemeyer *Col. Conf.* p. 44, 47. [*Collectio, Confessionum in Ecclesiis Reformatis*, ed. H. A. Niemeyer (Leipzig: Klinkhardt, 1840). See Dennison, *Reformed Confessions*, 1:186–88.—ed.]

7. [Hodge is likely here using the *Huldrici Zuinglii Opera* edition edited by Melchior Schuler and Johannes Schulthess (Zurich: Friedrich Schulthess, 1829–42).—ed.]

8. [Tetrapolitan Confession, the oldest of the Reformed Confessions (1530). Written in great haste, it was prepared at the Diet of Augsburg by Bucer and is closely aligned to the Augsburg Confession. The First Basel Confession is of the Zwinglian family of confessions (1534). The first draft was done by Oecolampadius and finished by Myconius. It is a simple and moderate articulation of the evangelical faith. The First Helvetic Confession (also known as the Second Confession of Basel) was compiled in Basel in 1536 by Heinrich Bullinger, Myconius, Bucer, and others. While essentially Zwinglian in its sacramental theology, it does affirm the real spiritual presence of Christ in the Eucharist.—ed.]

in which Christ truly offers his body and blood, and hence himself to his people; not as though the body and blood of Christ were naturally united with the bread and wine, or locally included in them, or sensibly there present, but in so far as the bread and wine are symbols, through which we have communion in his body and blood, but of the spiritual or eternal life.[9]

The most concise and perspicuous statement of this form of the doctrine is to be found in "The Sincere Confession of the ministers of the church of Zurich," dated 1545.[10] Those ministers say:

> We teach that the great design and end of the Lord's Supper, that to which the whole service is directed, is the remembrance of the body of Christ devoted, and of his blood shed for the remission of our sins. This remembrance however cannot take place without true faith. And although the things, of which the service is a memorial, are not visible or present after a corporal manner, nevertheless believing apprehension and the assurance of faith renders them present in one sense, to the soul of the believer. He has truly eaten the bread of Christ . . . who believes on Christ, very God and very man, crucified for us, on whom to believe is to eat, and to eat, to believe. . . . Believers have in the Lord's Supper no other life-giving food than that which they receive elsewhere than in that ordinance. The believer therefore receives both, in and out of, the Lord's Supper in one and the same way, and by the same means of faith, one and the same food, Christ, except that in the Supper the reception is connected with the actions and signs appointed by Christ, and accompanied with a testifying, thanksgiving and binding service. . . . Christ's flesh has done its work on earth having been offered for our salvation; now it no longer benefits on earth and is no longer here.[11]

This is a remarkably clear and precise statement, and should be remembered; for we shall find Calvin and others whose language is often so different, avowing their concurrence with these ministers of Zurich, or at least uniting with them in the statement of this doctrine.

Views of Calvin and of the Confessions formed under his influence

Inst. IV. 17. 10:

> We conclude that our souls are fed by the flesh and blood of Christ, just as our corporal life is preserved by bread and wine, for the analogy of the signs would not hold, if our souls did not find their aliment in Christ, which, however, cannot be the case, unless Christ truly coalesce into one with us, and support us through the use of his flesh and blood. It may seem incredible indeed that the flesh of Christ should reach us from such an immense local distance, so as to become our food. But we must remember how far the secret power of the Holy Spirit transcends all our sense, and what folly it must be even to think of reducing his

---

9. [See Dennison, *Reformed Confessions*, 1:349 for a modern translation.—ed.]

10. [See Heinrich Bullinger, *Orthodoxa Tigurinae Ecclesiae ministrorum Confessio* (Zurich: Christoph Froschauer, 1545). Can be accessed at http://www.e-rara.ch/zuz/content/titleinfo/855784.—ed.]

11. [Hodge:] Guerike: *Symbolik*. S. 452. [Guerike, *Allgemeine christliche Symbolik* (Leipzig, 1839).—ed.]

immensity to our measure. Let faith embrace then what the understanding cannot grasp, namely, that the spirit unites things which are totally separated. Now this sacred communication of his flesh and blood, by which Christ transfuses his life into us, just as if he penetrated our bones and marrow, he testifies and seals in the holy Supper; not by the exhibition of a vain and empty sign, but by putting forth such an energy of his Spirit as fulfils what he promises. What is thus attested he offers to all who approach the spiritual banquet. It is however fruitfully received by believers only, who accept such a vast grace with inward gratitude and trust.[12]

In 1561 Calvin wrote, in answer to the Lutheran Hesshuss[13] and with a view to unite the two parties, his Tract *de vera participatione carnis et sanguinis Christi in sacra coena*.[14] In an appendix to that Tract, he says:

The same body then which the Son of God once offered in sacrifice to the Father, he daily offers to us in the Supper, that it may be our spiritual aliment. Only that must be held which was intimated as to the mode, that it is not necessary that the essence of the flesh should descend from heaven, in order that we may feed upon it; but that the power of the Spirit is sufficient to penetrate through all impediments and to surmount all local distance. At the same time we do not deny that the mode here is incomprehensible to human thought; for flesh naturally could neither be the life of the soul, nor exert its power upon us from heaven; and not without reason is the communication, which makes us flesh of his flesh, and bone of his bones, denominated by Paul a great mystery. In the sacred Supper we acknowledge it a miracle, transcending both nature and our own understanding, that Christ's life is made common to us with himself, and his flesh given us as aliment.

Again,

these things being disposed of, a doubt still appears with respect to the word *substance*; which is readily allayed, if we put away the gross imagination of a manducation of the flesh, as though it were like corporal food, that being put into the mouth, is received into the stomach. For if this absurdity be removed, there is no reason why we should deny that we are fed with Christ's flesh substantially, since we truly coalesce with him into one body by faith, and are thus made one with him. Whence it follows we are joined with him in substantial connection, just as substantial vigor flows down from the head into the members. The definition must then stand that we are made to partake of Christ's flesh substantially; not in the way of carnal mixture, or as if the flesh of Christ drawn down from heaven

12. [See John Calvin, *Institutes of the Christian Religion*, trans. Ford Lewis Battles, ed. John T. McNeill (Philadelphia: Westminster Press, 1971), 2:1370.—ed.]

13. [Tilemann Heshusius or, in German, Hesshusen (1527–88) who originally was a moderate with Melanchthon but grew into a vehement and contentious defender of local presence. He insisted on the oral manducation of Christ's literal body, but his divisive nature even forced him to depart from fellow hardliner Westphal over his carnal language in describing the "chewing" of Christ's body.—ed.]

14. [*Dilucida Explicatio Sanae Doctrinae de Vera Participatione Carnis et Sanguinis Christi, in Sacra Coena. Ad discutiendas Heshushii nebulas.* Translated by Henry Beveridge as "The True Partaking of the Flesh and Blood of Christ in the Holy Supper," in T. F. Torrance, ed., *Calvin's Tracts and Treatises*, 495–572.—ed.]

entered into us, or were swallowed by the mouth; but because the flesh of Christ, as to its power and efficacy, vivifies our souls, not otherwise than the body is nourished by the substance of the bread and wine.

We prefer giving these extreme passages as selected by Dr. Nevin, instead of others of a different character, which could easily be gathered from Calvin's works. Those of the latter class, will turn up in their appropriate places. We proceed to quote some of the confessions, which most manifestly bear the impress of Calvin's hand or spirit.

The Gallican Confession was adopted by the Protestants of France,[15] in 1559. In the 36th art. it is said:

Quamvis (Christus) nunc sit in coelis, ibidem etiam remansurus donec veniat mundum judicatures, credimus tamen, eum arcana et incomprehensibili Spiritus sui virtute nos nutire et vivificare sui corporis et sanguinis substantia per fidem apprehensa.[16] Dicimur autem hoc spiritualiter fiieri, non ut efficaciae et veritatis loco imaginationem aut cogitationem supponamus, sed potius, quoniam hoc mysterium nostrae cum Christo coalitionis tam sublime est, ut omnes nostros sensus totumque naturae ordinem superet, denique quoniam sit divinum ac coeleste, non nisi fide percipi at apprehendi potest.

Art. 37 Credimus, sicut antea dictum est, tam in coena quam in baptismo, Deum nobis reipsa, id est vere et efficaciter donare quicquid ibi sacramentaliter figurat, ac proindecum signis conjungimus veram possessionem ac fruitionem ejus rei, quae ita nobis offertur. Itaque affirmamus eos qui ad sacram mensam Domini puram fidem tanquam vas quoddam afferunt, vere recipere, quod ibi signa testificantur, nempe corpus et sanguinem Jesu Christi, non minus esse cibum ac potum animae, quam panis et vinum sunt corporis cibus.[17]

15. [This confession, also called The French Confession of Faith, prepared by Calvin with the help of his student De Chandieu, was actually adopted that year by the synod in Paris and later by the Synod of La Rochelle, in 1571. In addition it was delivered to Charles IX by Beza, and ultimately sanctioned by Henry IV. It first appeared in French. See Schaff, *Creeds of Christendom*, 3:356–82.—ed.]

16. [Hodge:] Why Dr. Nevin, in his translation of this passage, should refer *apprehensa* to *virtute*, instead of *substantia*, we cannot tell. [Nevin:] In so doing I simply followed my text as given in Niemeyer, *Col. Conf.* p. 338, which reads: *Arcana et incomprehensibili spiritus sui virtute per fidem apprensa, &c.* Common as such variations are in these old confessions, Dr. Hodge might easily have presumed that my translation was based on a text different in this way from the one he quotes. [Hodge likely used the Latin version of 1566 in the *Corpus et Syntagma Confess.* as listed in Schaff, *Creeds of Christendom*, 3:356.—ed.]

17. *Note by the Editor* [Samuel R. Fisher of the *Weekly Messenger*]—For the benefit of those of our readers who do not understand Latin, we have thought it proper to give as accurate a translation of the quotations in this language as possible. "Although Christ is now in heaven and will also remain there until he shall come again to judge the world, yet we believe, that he, through the secret and incomprehensible energy of his Spirit, nourishes and vivifies us with the substance of his body and blood apprehended by faith. We say, however, that this is done spiritually, not that we would substitute an imagination or thought in the place of efficacy and truth, but rather because this mystery of our coalition with Christ is so sublime, that it transcends all our senses and the whole order of nature; in fine, because it is divine and heavenly and cannot be perceived and apprehended, except by faith. We believe, as before said, that in the Supper as in baptism, God in fact, that is, truly and efficaciously, grants unto us all that is there sacramentally represented, and accordingly we join with the signs, the true possession and fruition of that which is thus offered to us. We therefore affirm that those who bring to the Lord's holy table pure faith, as if a certain vessel, truly receive what the signs there testify, namely, that the body and blood of

This is perhaps the proper place to state, though not in chronological order, that a meeting of the National Synod of France, in 1571, Beza being president, an application was made by certain deputies to have the clause in Art. 37 altered, which asserts that we are nourished with the "substance of Christ's body and blood." The Synod refused to make the alteration, and explained the expression by saying, they did not understand by it

> any confusion, commixture, or conjunction . . . but this only, that by his virtue, all that is in him that is needful for our salvation, is hereby most freely given and communicated to us. Nor do we consent with them who say we do communicate in his merits and gifts and spirit, without his being at all made ours; but with the apostle (Eph. V. 23), admiring this supernatural, and to our reason incomprehensible mystery, we do believe we are partakers of his body shed for us, so that we are flesh of his flesh, and bone of his bones, and that we receive him together with his gifts, by faith wrought in us by the incomprehensible virtue and efficacy of the Holy Spirit.[18]

This decision was considered by the ministers of Zurich as involving a condemnation of their doctrine, and they complained of it accordingly. The following year, 1572, therefore the Synod decided, that though they chose to retain the word *substance* in the sense explained, they did so "without prejudicing those foreign churches, which for reasons best known to themselves do not use the word substance." And instead of saying as they had done the year before, "that we must truly participate in the second Adam, *that we may derive life from him*;" they substitute for the last clause the words: "that by mystical and spiritual communication with him, we may derive that true eternal life." "And the Lord's Supper," they add, "is principally instituted for the communication of it; though the same Lord Jesus be offered to us both in his substance and gifts, in the ministry of the word and baptism, and received by faith."[19] In the articles adopted by the Synod of London, in 1552,[20] and sanctioned by the authority of Edward VI, the article on the Lord's Supper, gives in the first clause the scriptural language, "To those who receive it worthily and with faith, the bread which we break is the communion of the body of Christ," &c. The second clause rejects transubstantiation. The third denies the Lutheran doctrine, & asserts that as Christ is in heaven, *non*

Jesus Christ, are no less the meat and drink of the soul, than the bread and wine are the food of the body." [See Schaff, *Creeds of Christendom*, 3:380–81.—ed.]

18. [Hodge:] Quick's *Synodicon*, I. p. 92. [*Synodicon in Gallia reformata*, edited by John Quick. London, 1692.—ed.]

19. [Hodge:] Quick's *Synodicon*, I. p. 104.

20. [These articles, according to Schaff (*Creeds of Christendom*, 1:614), were begun with the accession to the throne of Edward VI, 1547. Having reformed English worship, Edward's church leaders set about to reform doctrine. The program started out as an attempt to articulate a creed with the help of German and Swiss reformers. This was abandoned for an all-English formula of public teaching, resulting in forty-two articles. The project was begun by Cranmer in 1549 and completed in 1552, with the approval of the Synod of London. The articles were published in 1553.—ed.]

debet quisquam fidelium carnis ejus et sanguinis realem et corporalem (ut loquantur) praesentiam in Eucharista vel creddere vel profiteri.[21]

In the *Thirty-nine Articles of the church of England*, adopted in 1562,[22] the article on the Lord's Supper corresponds in purport exactly in the first three clauses, with the article of Edward VI. Then follows these words: *Corpus Christi datur, accipitur, et manducatur in coena, tantum coeleste et spirituali ratione. Medium autem quo corpus Christi accipitur et manducatur in coena fides est.*[23] It is a remarkable fact that the Anglican confessions have decidedly a more Zuinglian tone than those of any other of the Reformed churches. This may in part be accounted for by the consideration that they were not irenical, drawn up to conciliate Lutherans.

In the *Scotch Con.* of 1560,[24] the language of Calvin is in great measure retained. The only sentence that need be quoted is the following:

> We confess that believers in the right use of the Lord's Supper thus eat the body and drink the blood of Jesus Christ, and we firmly believe that he dwells in them, and they in him, nay, that they thus become flesh of his flesh and bone of his bones. For as the eternal deity gives life and immortality to the flesh of Christ, so also his flesh and blood, when eaten and drunk by us, confer on us the same prerogatives.

In the *Belgic Conf.* adopted in 1563,[25] the following words occur, Art. 35.

> *Christus testificatur, nos, quam vere hoc sacramentum manibus nostris accipimus et tenemus, illudque ore comedimus et bibimus, (unde et postmodum vita nostra sustentatur) tam vere etiam nos fide (quae animae et manus et os est) in animis nostris recipere verum corpus et verum sanguinem Christi, unici servatoris nostri ad vitam nostram spiritualem. Nequaquam erraverimus dicentes, id quod comeditur esse proprium et naturale corpus Christi, idque quod bibitur proprium esse*

---

21. [WM Ed.:] "No believer ought either to believe or profess the real and corporeal presence (as they speak) of his flesh and blood in the Eucharist."

22. [Essentially the same as the Edwardian articles with the exception of some borrowings from the Augsburg Confession, a clause about Christ's descent into Hell, and the above quoted strong condemnation of Christ's bodily presence in the elements (Schaff, Creeds of Christendom, 1:614–15). For an excellent introduction to this text, see Oliver O'Donovan, *On the Thirty Nine Articles.*—ed.]

23. [WM Ed.:] "The body of Christ is given, received and eaten in the Lord's Supper only in a heavenly and spiritual manner. But the medium by which the body of Christ is received and eaten in the Supper is faith."

24. [The Scotch Confession appeared in Edinburgh in 1561 after the Parliament had met and directed John Knox and his company to prepare a confession of faith. This was following the death of the Queen Regent, and the expulsion of the French military. While the legal recognition of the Reformed Church of Scotland was years away, the spirit of the Reformation united the members of Parliament around covenantal faith. See Schaff, *Creeds of Christendom*, 3:437–79. The quotation here is found on page 469.—ed.]

25. [The Belgic Confession (1561) was originally composed by Guido de Brés and based on the Gallican Confession of 1559. It marked the acceptance of the Calvinistic theology for the Netherlands and sought to repudiate Anabaptist teaching. It was readopted by the Synod of Dort in 1619. Schaff, *Creeds of Christendom*, 3:383–436.—ed.]

sanguinem. At manducandi modus talis est, ut non fiat ore corporis, sed spiritu per fidem.[26]

It is not necessary to quote from other Confessions language of the same import with that already quoted. All the symbols above cited contain more or less distinctly the impress of Calvin's views, if we except perhaps those of the church of England, which as before remarked, are more of a Zuinglian cast. We come now to

Those symbols in which both Zuinglians and Calvinists agreed

Perhaps the most interesting and important of this class is the *Consensus Tigurinus*. Switzerland had long been greatly distracted by the controversy on the sacraments. After much persuasion on the part of his friends, Calvin was induced to go to Zurich and hold a conference with Bullinger in 1549. The result of that conference was the adoption of the articles previously drawn up by Calvin himself, and afterwards published with the title: "*Consensio mutua in re sacramentaria Ministrorum Tigurinae Ecclesiae, et D. Joannis Calvini Ministri Genevensis Ecclesie, jam nunc ab ipsis authoribus edita.*"[27] We have, therefore, in this document the well considered and solemnly announced agreement of the Zuinglian and Calvinistic portions of the Reformed church. The *Consensus* was soon made the object of vehement attack by the Lutherans. Four years after its date, Calvin felt himself called upon to publish an explanation and defense of it. In his letter, prefixed to that defense, and addressed to the ministers of Zurich and other Swiss churches, he says: The Lutherans now see that those whom they denounce as Sacramentarians agree, and then adds, *Nec vero si superstites hodie essent optimi et eximii Christi servi Zuinglius et Oecolampadius, verbulum in ea sententia mutarent.*[28] [29]

This *Consensus* embraces twenty-six articles, all relating to the sacraments, and especially to the Lord's Supper. In these articles there is not a word, which any of the

26. [WM Ed.:] "Christ testifies, that as truly as we receive and hold this sacrament with our hands, and eat and drink it with our mouth of the soul (by which also our life is sustained), so truly also do we by faith (which is both the hand and the mouth of the soul,) receive in our souls the true body and blood of Christ our only Savior, to the nourishment of our spiritual life. We by no means err, when we say that that which is eaten is the proper and natural body of Christ, and that which is drunk is his proper blood. The mode of manducation, however, is such that it is not done by the mouth of the body, but by the spirit through faith." [See Schaff, *Creeds of Christendom*, 3:429–30.—ed.]

27. ["Mutual consent on the matter of the sacrament of the ministers of the church of Zurich, and of John Calvin, minister of the church of Geneva, now edited by the authors themselves." For a modern translation of the *Consensus Tigurinus*, see "Mutual Consent of the Churches of Zurich and Geneva as to the Sacraments," in Torrance, ed. *Tracts and Treatises*, 2:200–20.—ed.]

28. [Hodge:] Compare with this the language of Dr. Nevin, who endeavors to represent the doctrine of Calvin and Zuingle on this subject to be as wide apart as the poles. He even says: "If Calvinism, the system of Geneva, necessarily runs here into Zuinglianism, we may, indeed, well despair of the whole interest. For most assuredly no church can stand, that is found to be constitutionally *unsacramental*." p. 74. [MTSS edition, p. 64.—ed.]

29. [Trans. "And even if the two excellent doctors, Zuinglius and Oecolampadius, who were known to be faithful servants of Jesus Christ, were still alive, they would not change one word in our doctrine." "Mutual Consent," 211.—ed.]

evangelical churches of the present day would desire to alter. We should like to print them all as the confession of our own faith on this whole subject. The first four are introductory. The fifth declares the necessity of our union with Christ, in order that we should partake of his life. The sixth declares that union to be spiritual, arising from the indwelling of the Spirit. The seventh sets forth the design of the sacraments. They are declared to be badges of profession and Christian communion, excitements to thanksgiving and to the exercise of faith, and to a holy life, and *syngraphae* ["promissory notes"—ed.] binding us thereto. Their principal end, however, is said to be that God therein may testify his grace to us, represent and seal it. For though they signify nothing not announced in the word, still it is a great thing, that they present, as it were, the living images before our eyes, and which affect our senses and serve to lead us to the thing signified, while they recall to mind the death of Christ and all his benefits, that our faith may be called into exercise; and besides this, what God had by his mouth declared, is here confirmed and sealed. The eighth declares that God inwardly works or communicates by his Spirit, the blessings signified by the sacraments. They are therefore, as stated in the ninth article, not naked signs, but as it is there expressed, "Though we distinguish, as is proper, between the sign and things signified, we do not disjoin the truth (or reality) from the signs; since all who by faith embrace the promises there presented, receive Christ with his spiritual gifts." In the tenth article, it is, therefore, said, we should look at the promise rather than the signs. The signs without Christ, are declared in the eleventh article, to be *inanes larvae* ["vain masks"—ed.]. The articles from the twelfth to the seventeenth, both included, relate to the efficacy of the sacraments. It is denied that they have any virtue in themselves, all their efficacy is referred to the attending power of God, which is exercised only in the elect, and therefore, it is added, the doctrine that the sacraments confer grace on all who do not oppose the obstacle of mortal sin, falls to the ground. In the eighteenth it is stated that the reason why the sacraments fail to benefit unbelievers is to be referred to their want of faith, and neither to the sacraments which always retain their integrity, nor to God. The nineteenth teaches that the blessings received in the sacraments are by believers received on other occasions. And moreover, as is said in the twentieth, the benefit received from the sacraments, is not to be restricted to the time of administration, but may follow long afterwards. Those baptized in infancy are often regenerated in youth or even old age. In the twenty-first art. all local presence of Christ in the Eucharist is denied. As a man he is in heaven, and is present only to the mind and faith. The twenty-second states that the words of institution, "This is my body," must be understood figuratively. In the twenty-third, it is taught that manducation of Christ's body implies no mixture or transfusion of substance,[30] but the derivation of life from his body and

---

30. [Hodge is within his right to demur on the clarity of Calvin's use of the term "substance." Gerrish called it "confusing." "At times he denies that the substance of Christ's body is given in the Supper, at other times he affirms it" (178–79). Certainly, some of this is due to the various meanings the term has. Likewise Calvin can mean substance in an "empirical way," rather than as St. Thomas had it in a "metaphysical way." But when Calvin says we become "one substance" with Christ—it is hard not to interpret it in a metaphysical way, although it is not the same use Thomas made of it. See Gerrish, *Grace and Gratitude*, 177–78.—ed.]

blood as a sacrifice. The last three articles are directed against transubstantiation, the Lutheran doctrine of local presence, and the adoration of the host.

The force of this document as an exhibition of the true doctrine of the Reformed Church on this whole subject is greatly impaired in this meager outline. We shall, however, have occasion to refer to its more explicit statements, in the progress of this investigation. The next witness to be cited is the *Heidelberg Catechism*. It was prepared at the command of Frederick III, elector of the Palatinate, by Caspar Olevian,[31] a disciple of Calvin, and Ursinus,[32] a friend of Melancthon,[33] and adopted by a general synod held at Heidelberg in 1563.[34] This catechism having symbolical authority, both in the German and Dutch Reformed Churches, is entitled to peculiar respect as a witness to the faith of the Reformed Church.

In answer to the 66th question the sacraments are declared to be "Sacred visible signs and seals, instituted by God, that through them he may more clearly present and seal the promise of the gospel, viz. that he, for the sake of the one offering of Christ accomplished on the cross, grants to us the forgiveness of sin and eternal life."[35]

In answer to the following question, it is stated that the design both of the word and sacraments is to direct our faith to the sacrifice of Christ on the cross as the only ground of our faith.

> Question 75. *How art thou reminded and assured, in the holy Supper, that thou art a partaker of the one offering of Christ on the cross, and of all his benefits?*

Ans. Thus, that Christ has commanded me to eat of this broken bread, and to drink of this cup and has promised first, that as surely as I see with my eyes the bread of the Lord broken for me, and the cup handed to me, so surely was his body broken

---

31. [Caspar Olevian (1536–87), Reformed theologian in Germany, very much under the influence of Calvin. While at Heidelberg (1560–76) he coauthored the Heidelberg Catechism. He was instrumental in introducing Reformed doctrine, polity, and discipline to the Palatinate. For Olevian and Ursinus see Bierman, Gunnoe, and Maag, *Introduction to the Heidelberg Catechism*.—ed.]

32. [Zacharias Ursinus (1534–84), trusted student of Melanchthon and chief author of the Heidelberg Catechism. He also published a commentary on the Catechism and a work on its defense. See Visser, *Zacharias Ursinus*.—ed.]

33. [Philipp Melanchthon (1497–1560), born Philipp Schwarzerd. He matriculated at Heidelberg and Tubingen and finally became professor of Greek at Wittenberg. Martin Luther had an enormous influence on him but as with so many others he fell out with Carlstadt. He was the force behind the Diet of Augsburg and the resulting confession was by and large his work. Melanchthon emerged as an irenic force in the bitter controversies of this time. He displayed a love of learning, which was common among the Reformers with whom a humanistic stripe was evident, and was not afraid to modify his views in the face of new insights and teaching. See Stupperich, *Melanchthon*; Maag, *Melanchthon in Europe*.—ed.]

34. [The Heidelberg Catechism came about in the midst of great anxiety, indeed, to the point that fights were breaking out in church chancels over communion practice. With Frederick III becoming Elector of the Palatinate in 1559, and with his lack of success at reconciling the various parties, he asked Ursinus and Olevianus to prepare an evangelical catechism at Heidelberg. See MTSS vol. 1, pp. 73–77, 302–4 for Nevin's full discussion of the background to the Catechism.—ed.]

35. [Hodge:] There is some slight variation as to the phraseology, between the German and Latin copies of this catechism. We unfortunately have not the authorized English version at hand, and therefore are obliged to translate, except where Dr. Nevin has given the English version, from the originals.

and offered for me on the cross and his blood shed for me. Second, that he himself as certainly feeds and nourishes my soul to eternal life with his crucified body, and shed blood, as I receive from the hand of the minister, and after a corporal manner partake of the bread and wine, which are given as the symbols of the body and blood of Christ.

Ques. 76. *What is it then to eat the crucified body and drink the shed blood of Christ?*

> Ans. It is not only to embrace with a believing heart all the sufferings and death of Christ, and thereby to obtain the pardon of sin and eternal life; but also, besides that, to become more and more united to his sacred body, by the Holy Ghost who dwells both in Christ and in us; so that we, though Christ is in heaven and we on earth, are notwithstanding, flesh of his flesh and bone of his bones; and that we live and are governed forever by one Spirit, as the members of the same body are by one soul.

In the answer to the 78th, it is said that as in baptism the water is not changed into the blood of Christ, nor is itself the ablution of sin, but the symbol and pledge of those things, so in the Lord's supper the bread is not the body of Christ, though from the nature of a sacrament and usage of scripture, it is so called.

In answer to Ques. 79th, it is said; the bread is called Christ's body, &c.,

> Not only thereby to teach us that as bread and wine support this temporal life, so his crucified body and shed blood are the true meat and drink whereby our souls are fed unto eternal life; but more especially, by these visible signs and pledges, to assure us, that we are as really partakers of his true body and blood (by the operation of the Holy Ghost), as we receive by the mouths of our bodies these holy signs in remembrance of him; and that all his sufferings and obedience are as certainly ours as if we had in our own persons suffered and made satisfaction for our sins to God.

In the following question, "What is the difference between the Lord's Supper, and the Popish mass?" the first clause of the answer is:

> The Supper of the Lord testifies to us that we have perfect remission of all our sins, on account of the one sacrifice of Christ which he himself made once for all upon the cross; and also that we, by the Holy Spirit, are united to Christ, who according to his human nature is only in heaven at the right hand of the Father, and is there to be adored by us.

There is nothing in this account of the Lord's Supper to which exception would even now be taken. There is something in the answer to the 75th question, which seems evidently intended to cover Calvin's peculiar opinion of a miraculous influence from the body of Christ in heaven, but it is also as evidently intended to cover Bullinger's view on that subject. It is language to which Zuingle and Oecolampadius,[36] as Calvin says on another occasion, would not object. This is the more remarkable

36. [John Oecolampadius (1482–1531), also Hussgen, was born in the Palatinate and became an important Reformer in Basel where he spent most of his career. He came under the sway of Luther before joining with the Reformed. He played an instrumental role in the Colloquy of Marburg (1529) where he defended the eucharistic views of Zwingli.—ed.]

when we consider the historical circumstances under which this catechism was drawn up, and its decidedly irenical objective. No part of Germany was more distracted by the sacramentarian controversy than the Palatinate. Nowhere was greater exertion made to conciliate the Lutherans by framing expressions which they could adopt. Yet this catechism, framed under these circumstances, teaches nothing to which the ministers of Zurich would be unwilling to subscribe.

The only other public symbol which it is necessary to cite, is the Second Helvetic Confession.[37] This on some accounts is the most authoritative of all the confessions of the Reformed Church. It was drawn up by Bullinger in 1562. In 1565, the Elector Frederick, above mentioned, alarmed by the furious contentions in his dominions, and annoyed by the misrepresentations of the Lutherans, wrote to Bullinger to send him a confession which could if possible unite the parties, or at least silence the clamours of the Lutherans, and which the Elector might present at the approaching diet of the empire to refute the calumnies directed against the Reformed. Bullinger sent this confession which he had prepared some years before. The Elector was perfectly well satisfied. To give it weight it was then sanctioned by the Helvetic churches, and soon became one of the most generally recognized standards of the Reformed in all parts of Europe. What it teaches on the Lord's Supper is entitled to be regarded as a fair exhibition of the real doctrine of the church. The fact that it was written by Bullinger, the successor of Zuingle at Zurich, the great opponent of what was considered peculiar in Calvin's views of this subject, would lead us to expect to find in it nothing but what the Zurich ministers could cordially adopt.

In the 19th ch., it is taught concerning the sacraments in general, 1. That they are mystic symbols, or holy rites, or sacred actions, including the word, sign, and things signified. 2. That there were sacraments under the old as well as under the new economy. 3. That God is their author, and still operates though them. 4. That Christ is the great object presented in them, the substance and matter of them, the lamb slain from the foundation of the world, the rock of which all our fathers drank, &c. 5. Therefore as far as the substance is concerned, the sacraments of the two dispensations are equal; they have the same author, the same significance and effect. 6. The old have been abolished, and baptism and the Lord's Supper introduced in their place. 7. Then follows an exposition of the constituent's parts of the sacrament. First, the word, by which the elements are constituted sacred signs. Water, bread and wine, are, in themselves, apart from divine appointment, no sacred symbols. It is the word of God added to them, consecrating or setting them apart, which gives them their sacramental character. Secondly, the signs, being thus consecrated, receive the names of the things signified. Water is called regeneration, the bread and wine, the body and blood of Christ, i.e. the symbols or sacraments of his body and blood. They are not changed in their own nature. They are called by the names of the things signified, because the two are sacramentally united, that is, united by mystical significance and divine appointment. 8. In the next paragraph the confession rejects, on the one hand, the Romish doctrine of

37. [The Latin text of this confession can be found in Schaff, *Creeds of Christendom*, 3:237–306. For a modern translation see Dennison, *Reformed Confessions*, 2:809–81.—ed.]

consecration; and, on the other, the opinion of those who either make the sacraments mere common signs, or entirely useless. 9. The benefits signified are not so included or bound to the sacraments, that all who receive the signs receive the things signified; nor does the efficacy depend on the administrator; nor their integrity, upon the receiver. As the word of God, continues his word, whether men believe or not, so it is with the sacraments.

The 21st chapter is devoted to the Lord's Supper. The following passages, which we prefer giving in the original, will suffice to exhibit the doctrine here taught:

> *Ut autem rectius et perspicacius intelligatur, quomodo caro et sanguis Christi sint cibus et potus fidelium, percipianturque a fidelibus ad vitam aeternam, paucula haec adjiciemus. Manducatio non est unius generis. Est enim manducatio corporalis, qua cibus in os percipitur ab homine, dentibus atteritur, et in ventrem deglutitur. . . .*

Nothing of this kind of course is admitted with regard to the Lord's Supper.

> *Est et spiritualis manducatio corporis Christi, non ea quidem, qua existimemus cibum ipsum mutari in spiritum, sed qua, manente in sua essentia et proprietate corpore et sanguine Domini, ea nobis communicantur spiritualiter, utique non corporali modo, sed spirituali, per spiritum sanctum, qui videlicet ea, quae per carnem et sanguinem Domini pro nobis in mortem tradita, parata sunt, ipsam inquam remissionem peccatorum, liberationem, et vitam aeternam, applicat et confert nobis, ita ut Christus in nobis vivat, et nos in ipso vivamus, efficitque ut ipsum, quo talis sit, cibus et potus spiritualis noster, id est, vita nostra, vera fide percipiamus. . . . Et sicut oportet cibum in nosmetipsos edendo recipere, ut operatur in nobis, suamque efficaciam exerat, cum extra nos positus, nihil nobis prosit; ita necesse est nos fide Christum recipere, ut noster fiat, vivatque in nobis, et nos in ipso. . . . Ex quibus omnibus claret nos, per spiritualem cibum, minime intelligere imaginarium, nescio quem, cibum, sed ipsum Domini corpus pro nobis traditum, quod tamen percipiatur a fidelibus, non corporaliter, sed spiritualiter per fidem. . . . Fit autem hic esus et potus spiritualis, etiam extra Domini coenam, et quoties, aut ubicunque homo in Christum crediderit. Quo fortassis illud Augustini pertinet: Quid paras dentem et ventrem? Crede, et manducasti.*
>
> *Praeter superiorem manducationem spiritualem, est et sacramentalis manducatio corporis Domini, qua fidelis non tantum spiritualiter et interne participat vero corpore et sanguine Domini, sed foris etiam accedendo ad mensam Domini, accipit visibile corporis et sanguinis Domini sacramentum.*[38]

38. [WM Ed.:] "But that it may be more correctly and perspicuously understood, in what manner the flesh and blood of Christ are the meat and drink of believers and are received by believers to eternal life, we add these few words. Manducation is not of one kind. For there is a corporal manducation by which food is received into the mouth by man, masticated with the teeth and passed into the stomach."

"There is also a spiritual manducation of the body of Christ, by which however we are not to suppose that the food itself is changed into spirit, but the body and blood of the Lord, preserving their own essence and peculiarity, are spiritually communicated to us, not in a corporeal, but in a spiritual manner, by the Holy Spirit, who thus applies to and confers upon us, those things which were prepared by the flesh and blood of the Lord delivered up for us in death, namely, remission of sins, freedom and eternal life, so that Christ may live in us and we may live in him; and causes that we receive him as our spiritual meat and drink, that is, as our life. . . . And as it must needs be that we receive food inwardly by eating, in order that it may operate in us and exert its efficacy, for whilst it is placed without us, it profits us

We have thus furnished, as it appears to us, adequate materials for a clear and decided judgment as to what was the real doctrine of the Reformed church as to the Lord's Supper. We propose now to review these materials and apply them to the decision of the various questions agitated on this subject.

GENERAL CRITICISM [NEVIN]

The authorities here presented, it will be seen, are to a great extent the same, as far as they go, which are to be found quoted in the *Mystical Presence*. Dr. Hodge has not gone into any original historical investigation of the subject, but has thought it sufficient to trust his general preconceptions in the case; simply applying them to the material here furnished to his hand, in such a way as to make it suit the object he had in view. The only new authority he brings forward which can be regarded as any account, is the familiar *Consensus Tigurinus*: which as it happens to sound most favorably to his cause, he insists on making the rule, or rather the Procrustean bed, by which to screw into proper shape the sense of all testimonies and symbols besides. This, however, is a most arbitrary requirement, to which no mind, at all at home in the theological literature of the sixteenth century, can be willing for a moment to submit. The *Consensus Tigurinus* has never been allowed to be at all of any such primary force, in the Reformed Church. Dr. Hodge talks of compromise and ambiguous phraseology, as entering into the sacramental statements of the age in other cases; but if there be room anywhere for such supposition, it is emphatically in the case of this *Consensus* of Zurich. It is acknowledged on all hands, that Calvin here condescended as far as he possibly could towards the Zuinglian extreme, for the purpose of assisting the Swiss Church, as it were, to come up to the higher ground on which he himself habitually stood. It has generally been considered indeed, that in some of his expressions he fell into actual contradiction with his own system, as previously taught and as he continued to hold it afterwards to the end of his life. At all events, it is a most violent assumption, on the part of Dr. Hodge, that his plain, unequivocal declarations on the subject of his own faith, a hundred times repeated throughout his works, are to be overruled by the authority of this one document, of most questionable sense, instead of allowing it to be interpreted rather by the hundred authorities that are explicit and clear.

But all this is spoken by concession. Even the "forlorn hope" of this *Consensus Tigurinus*, will be found to fail the cause it is brought up to support, when subjected to

---

nothing; so also it is necessary that we receive Christ by faith, that he may become ours, and may live in us and we in him. . . . From all which it is clear that, by spiritual food, we are to understand, not merely imaginary, I know not what kind of, food, but the body of the Lord itself delivered up for us, which, however, is received by believers, not corporally, but spiritually, by faith. . . . But this becomes spiritual meat and drink even without the Supper of the Lord, and as often or wherever a man shall believe in Christ. Whence perhaps that saying of Augustine, 'Why prepare teeth and stomach? Believe, and thou hast eaten.'

"Besides this higher spiritual manducation, there is also a sacramental manducation of the body of the Lord, by which the believer not only partakes spiritually and internally of the true body and blood of the Lord, but outwardly also, by approaching the table of the Lord, receives the visible sacrament of the body and blood of Christ." [See Dennison, *Reformed Confessions*, 2:866–67.—ed.]

true historical trial. Dr. Hodge approaches it in the spirit of his own time and position; as though it had been lately framed in Philadelphia or Boston; ignoring and forgetting, out and out, the sacramental views of the sixteenth century; and finds it tolerably easy, in this way, to put into it what he conceives to be a sound and satisfactory sense. "In these articles," he says, "there is not a word, which any of the evangelical churches of the present day would desire to alter. We should like to print them all as the confession of our own faith on this subject." I do not doubt, for a moment, the sincerity of Dr. Hodge, in this declaration. The articles could easily be signed by our modern churches generally, just as they can readily subscribe to the old *Apostles' Creed, taking all in their own sense.*

But could they do so, in the proper historical sense of the articles themselves? That is the only question of much account in the case. Happily, as regards the *Consensus Tigurinus*, we are not thrown simply on the general teaching of Calvin, to make out the sense in which it is to be taken. We have a full *exposition* of it, from his own hand, of which Dr. Hodge takes no notice. Could he subscribe to the sacramental doctrine of that? I shall show hereafter that he could not, unless prepared at the same time to adopt the tenth article of the Augsburg Confession.[39]

Dr. Hodge is pleased to say also, in view of the extracts given from our excellent Heidelberg Catechism: "There is nothing in this account of the Lord's Supper to which exception would even now be taken." He means of course again, however, provided all be construed in his own sense. In the *sense of Ursinus*, neither Dr. Hodge nor Dr. Kurtz (Lutheran though this last pretend to be), could endorse the Heidelberg Catechism at this point; just as little as either of them could sign, in good faith, the Augsburg Confession in Melancthon's sense. I have already furnished incontrovertible evidence of this from Ursinus himself, in my work the *Mystical Presence*. But I will offer evidence again still more overwhelmingly plain; so that no way-faring man, though a fool, need be left in any doubt hereafter, as to the true sacramental doctrine of this ancient and venerable symbol of the German Reformed Church.

Dr. Hodge shows little originality in the general *arrangement* of his witnesses, as in their selection. He intimates indeed that my use of the authorities has been one-sided, and such as to set them in a false light; and then we have them formally mustered under three divisions, for the purpose, as it might seem, of bringing order and light into their united testimony. This probably is regarded as the great strength of the article, by those who talk of its unanswerable ability.[40] But now, it is not true that in

---

39. [Nevin:] Art. 10 "Of the Supper of the Lord they teach that the Body and Blood of Christ are truly present, and are distributed to those who eat the Supper of the Lord; and they reject those that teach otherwise." [Augsburg Confession (1530), mainly the work of Melanchthon. Having received the support of Luther and Charles V, it became the standard Lutheran confession of faith. See Schaff, *Creeds of Christendom*, 3:3–73.—ed.]

40. [This attests to Hodge's enormous popularity. Nevin has already heard that Hodge's review is unassailable; that it puts the matter to rest by placing the topic in the spectrum of three divisions: 1) The Swiss Confessions, 2) The views of Calvin, and 3) Those places where the two agree. Here, at the last and in conclusion, Hodge would say that we have the definitive view—we have the doctrine of the Reformed on the Lord's Supper.—ed.]

the *Mystical Presence*, the authorities are adduced without our attempt at least to set them in their proper historical relations. A careful distinction is made throughout in the book between the confessions preceding and those following Calvin, as full notice is taken also of their respective relations both to Lutheranism on the one side and Zuinglianism on the other. In *my* survey however, the Zuinglianizing element is made to give way gradually altogether to the Calvinistic, which appears at last accordingly as the acknowledged ruling life of all the leading Reformed Confessions. This order of things is exhibited, not in the way of willful assumption, but on the ground of clear historical deduction. It suits not however, of course, the theory of Dr. Hodge; and so, without troubling himself at all to interrogate the actual course of history on the subject, he simply orders his classification in such a way, as to make his Zuinglian authorities at once co-ordinate in full with the Calvinistic, as though both ran parallel in time throughout, and at last settled into a sort of joint result, substantially agreeing with the Zuinglian doctrine, as this stood in the beginning! Never was there a more perfectly unhistorical mode of proceeding, in such a case.

It is pretty evident besides, that in his whole estimate of the subject, Dr. Hodge has been ruled unduly by the authority of Guerike,[41] as he is led to speak of several Reformed confessions in his *Symbolic*. Guerike, it is well known, is an ultra Lutheran, who in his zeal against the Reformed Church aims always to sink its sacramental orthodoxy to the lowest point. This is the fashion of the Old Lutheran school throughout; they will have it still, as they insisted on having it in his own day *against himself*, that Calvin's doctrine of the spiritual real presence differs not at all from the idea of a presence "in mere contemplation," as held, they say, by Zuingli. So Guerike of course forces this preconception on all the Calvinistic symbols; and Dr. Hodge (finding it acceptable to his different stand-point on the opposite side), quietly acquiesces in it as right and good. But not withstanding all this, it is a sheer theological prejudgment on both sides, that cannot stand the test of historical investigation, for a single moment.

This is not the place, of course, to take up the sense of these authorities. Let us see first the *use*, to which they are turned by Dr. Hodge, in the subsequent part of his article. The readers of the *Messenger*, in the mean time, we may trust, will be careful to preserve them for future reference and comparison.

Only one caution here, in the way of self-defense. Let all who take an interest in the subject, be sure that they keep before them always the true point in question. It is easy to feel, that in all this parade of authorities as given by Dr. Hodge, some advantage is taken (undesignedly I suppose on his part), of the strong tendency there is in the popular mind, particularly at the present time, to confound and mix things here which are in themselves entirely distinct. Quotations that go against *local* presence, a *material* flesh and blood, &c., or that make all to turn on *faith*, to be by the *Spirit*, through the

---

41. [Later, in his *Systematic Theology*, Hodge identifies Guerike as the German theologian who makes as a main point of disagreement with the Lutherans, the Reformed position that the Reformed reject any "inherent power" in the Lord's Supper, believing that the Holy Spirit works from outside the elements themselves, "*virtus Spiritus Sancti extrinsecus accidens*" (Guerike, *Allgemeine christliche Symbolik* [Leipzig, 1839], p. 378).—ed.]

virtue of Christ's body *spiritually* received, &c., are easily accepted, with such notions as most persons bring along with them to the inquiry, as full and satisfactory at once in regard to the point in hand; as though in some way, against all my protestations to the contrary, I had made the Calvinistic doctrine to involve a real presence in the flesh! I have most carefully described the doctrine, in the first part of the *Mystical Presence*, as excluding every conception of a local or material communication with Christ. Calvin admitted no real presence in the flesh, or as holding at all in the sphere of sense. But he *did* hold and teach, that simultaneously with the outward transaction of the sacrament, the *mystery* of a real communication with the very substance of the Savior's human life has place also for the soul of every true believer, by the power of the Holy Spirit, accomplishing thus for his whole person *all* that was supposed to be reached, in a different mode, by the doctrine of Luther himself. This Calvin believed, and this same view reigns in all the old Reformed symbols after his time. So much I affirm; and so much, if I understand it properly, this article of Dr. Hodge is intended to deny.

3

Christ's Real Presence in the Lord's Supper[1]

REVIEW, CONTINUED [HODGE]

In what sense is Christ present in the Lord's Supper?

THE AUTHORITIES ABOVE CITED, and the private writings of the Reformed theologians, are abundant in teaching that Christ is present in the Lord's Supper. They represent it as a calumny, when Lutherans asserted that the Reformed regarded the bread and wine as representing the body and blood of Christ in no other sense than a statue represents Hercules or Mercury. Zuingle says, we have never denied that the body of Christ is sacramentally and mystically present in the Lord's Supper. They admitted not only that he is present as God and by his Spirit, but in an important sense as to his body and blood. The whole controversy relates to this latter point, viz, to the mode in which the body and blood of Christ are present in the Lord's Supper. In deciding this point, the Reformed theologians are very accurate in determining the different senses in which a thing may be said to be present. The word *presence*,[2] they say, is a relative term, and cannot be understood without reference to the object said to be present, and the subject to which it is present. For presence is nothing but the application of an object to the faculty suited to the perception of it. Hence, there is a two-fold presence, viz., of things sensible and of things spiritual. The former are present, as the word imports, when they are *prae sensibus* ["prior to the senses"], so as to be perceived by the senses; the latter, when they are presented to the intelligence so as

---

1. ["Dr. Hodge on the Mystical Presence, Article from the Repertory, Continued, No. 3," *Weekly Messenger*, New Series, vol. 13, no. 39. Wednesday, June 7, 1848. Published by the Board of the Synod of the German Reformed Church: Chambersburg, PA.—ed.]

2. [Latin *praesentia*; the scholastics distinguished several modes or ways of being present including 1) locally or bodily in which finite things are physically present or present in body and can be circumscribed; 2) spiritually or virtually, in which the presence is immaterial and does not occupy space, but instead is manifest in the power it exhibits. It might apply to angels, souls, and the body of Christ; 3) Illocal or definitive presence, which refers to a finite spiritual being such as a soul; and 4) repletive presence, in which a spiritual being fills a place in such a way that it cannot be defined or contained by it. God alone has repletive presence. For a fuller treatment of this subject see, Muller, *Dictionary of Latin and Greek Theological Terms.*—ed.].

to be apprehended and enjoyed. Again, presence even as to sensible objects is not to be confounded with nearness. It stands opposed not to distance, but to absence. The sun is as near to us when absent at night, as when present by day. A thing therefore may be present as to efficacy and virtue, which is at a great distance locally. In which of these senses are the body and blood of Christ present in the Lord's Supper? All the Reformed, in answer to this question, say that it is not in the sense of local nearness. The bread is neither transmuted into the body of Christ, as Romanists say, nor is his body locally present in, with and under the bread, according to the Lutheran doctrine. The presence is to the mind, the object is not presented to the senses, but apprehended by faith. It is a presence of virtue and efficacy, not of propinquity. All these statements, both negative and positive, are found in the authorities referred to in the preceding pages. The [First] Helv. Conf. chap. 21, says:

> The body of Christ is in heaven at the right hand of God. . . . Yet the Lord is not absent from his church when celebrating his Supper. The sun is absent from us in heaven, nevertheless it is efficaciously present with us; how much more is Christ the Sun of righteousness, though absent as to the body, present with us, not corporeally indeed, but spiritually, by his vivifying influence.

Calvin, in the *Consensus Tigurinus*, art. xxi. says: "Every imagination of local presence is to be entirely removed. For while the signs are here on earth seen by the eyes and handled by the hands, Christ, so far as he is a man, is nowhere else than in heaven; and is to be sought only by the mind and by faith. It is therefore an irrational and impious superstition to include him in the earthly elements." In the 10th art. it is taught that he is present in the promise, not in the signs.

Ursinus, the principal author of the Heidelberg Catechism, in his exposition of that formulary, says:

> These two, the sign and the thing signified, are united together in this sacrament, not by any copulation, or corporal and local existence of one in the other, much less by transubstantiation, or changing the one into the other; but by signifying, sealing and exhibiting the one by the other. That is, by a sacramental union, whose bond is the promise added to the bread, requiring the faith of the receivers. Whence it is clear, that these things in their lawful use, are always jointly exhibited and received, but not without faith of the promise, viewing and apprehending the thing promised, now present in the sacrament; yet not present or included in the sign as in a vessel containing it; but present in the promise, which is the better part, the life and soul of the sacrament. For they want judgment who affirm that Christ's body cannot be present in the sacrament, except it be in or under the bread; as if forsooth, the bread alone, without the promise, were either the sacrament, or the principal part of the sacrament.[3]

---

3. [Hodge:] Quoted by Dr. Nevin, p. 91 [of *The Mystical Presence* (see p. 80 of the MTSS edition). Nevin is quoting from Ursinus's *Commentary* on the Catechism, edited and published in Latin by his student David Pareus, and translated into English by D. Henry Parrie (Oxford: Joseph Barnes, 1587). This passage is from p. 434 of the 1645 edition. For a modern translation, see G. W. Williard, trans., *Commentary on the Heidelberg Catechism.*—ed.].

There is, therefore, a presence of Christ's body in the Lord's Supper; not local, but spiritual; not for the senses but for the mind and to faith; not of nearness but of efficacy. This presence (as Zuingle said, "if they want words,") the Reformed were willing to call *real*; if by real was understood not essential or corporal, but true and efficacious, as opposed to imaginary or ineffective. So far as this point is concerned there is no doubt as to the doctrine of the Reformed church.

CRITICISM [NEVIN]

Here we may see at once the need of the *caution*, which I have already given in my own defense. Evidence is arrayed to show, that the old Reformed doctrine excluded the idea of a *local* presence of Christ's body and blood in the Lord's Supper, as though that point had in some way been called in question. Certainly, Calvin taught no local presence, no comprehension of Christ's body in the elements, no presence of any sort in the sphere of sense; and no such doctrine is to be found in any of the Reformed symbols. All this is fully granted and affirmed, over and over again, in the *Mystical Presence*. But then, let it be well observed, that Dr. Hodge is utterly at fault, when he seems to take it for granted that the only alternative to a local presence, must be a presence in "the intelligence" or simple influence from abroad. This is a fallacy which the popular mind is ever ready to run into, and it is only by taking advantage of it that the representation here before us comes to have any plausible show of force whatever. Calvin never meant to oppose a simply intellectual presence to a gross sensible presence; either of these was for him a presence in the sphere of mere nature or flesh. What he insisted upon was a *spiritual* presence as something different from both; a presence *en pneumati*, not under any natural mode of existence, but in a way peculiar to a higher order of life that transcends altogether the conditions and limitations of our present mortal state. All belongs, not to the world of nature nor to the world of logic, but to the world of faith, and is strictly a *mystery*, which we are bound to acknowledge and receive in this character, and in this character alone. Zuingle indeed speaks of mere "contemplation" in the case, as Dr. Hodge would appear also to resolve all into an act of "intellectual apprehension;" but such was by no means the view of Calvin and the later Reformed symbols. Their *sacramental* presence always signified a mystical real presence, not in the flesh, but *in the Spirit*, not in space, but in true substantiality and power. This is amply shown by the quotations given in my work, and will be farther confirmed hereafter.

REVIEW, CONTINUED [HODGE]

What is meant by feeding on the body and blood of Christ?

This question does not relate to the thing received, but simply to the mode of receiving. What is intended by sacramental manducation? In reference to this point, all the Reformed agreed as to the following particulars: 1. This eating was not with the mouth, either after the manner of ordinary food, which the Lutherans themselves denied, or in any other manner. The mouth was not, in this case, the organ of reception. 2. It is only by the soul that the body and blood of Christ are received. 3. It is by faith, which is declared to be the hand and the mouth of the soul. 4. It is by or through the power of the Holy Ghost. As to all these points there is a perfect agreement among the symbols of the Reformed church. *Con. Tig*, art. 23, "That Christ feeds our souls with his body and blood, here set forth, by the power of the Holy Ghost, is not to be understood as involving any mixture or transfusion of substance, but that we derive life from his body once offered as a sacrifice, and from his blood shed as an expiation."[4] Belgic Con. art. 35. God, it is said, sent Christ, as the true bread from heaven, "which nourishes and sustains the spiritual life of believers, if it be eaten; that is, if it be applied and received by the Spirit through faith." *Ursinus*:

> There is then in the Lord's Supper a double meat and drink, one external, visible and terrene, namely bread and wine; and another internal. There is also a double eating and receiving; an external and signifying, which is the corporal receiving of the bread and wine, that is, that which is performed by the hands, mouth and sense of the body; and an internal, invisible, and signified, which is the fruition of Christ's death, and a spiritual engrafting into Christ's body; that is, which is not performed by the hands and mouth, but by the spirit and faith.[5]

As to the question whether there is any difference between eating and believing, the authorities differ. The Zurich confession and the Helv. quoted above distinctly say there is not. The former says: "Eating is believing, and believing is eating." The latter says: "This eating takes place as often and whenever a man believes in Christ." So the Belgic confession, just quoted. Calvin, however, makes a distinction between the two; eating, he says, is not faith, but the effect of faith. "There are some," he says,

> who define in a word, that to eat the flesh of Christ and to drink his blood, is no other than to believe on Christ himself. But I conceive that in that remarkable discourse, in which Christ recommends us to feed upon his body, he intended to teach us something more striking and sublime; namely, that we are quickened by a real participation of him, which he designates by the terms *eating* and *drinking*, that no person might suppose the life which we receive from him to consist in simple knowledge. . . . At the same time, we confess there is no eating but by faith, and it is impossible to imagine any other; but the difference between me and those whose opinion I now oppose, is this . . . they consider eating to be faith itself, but I apprehend it to be rather a consequence of faith.[6]

We do not see the force of this distinction. It all depends upon the latitude given to the idea of faith. If you restrict it to knowledge and assent, there is room for the distinction between eating and believing. But if faith includes the real appropriation of Christ, it includes all Calvin seems to mean by both terms, eating and believing. This question is of no historical importance. It created no diversity of opinion in the church.

4. ["Mutual Consent," in Torrance, ed., *Tracts and Treatises*, 2:219.—ed.]

5. [Pareus, ed., *Summe of the Christian Religion*, 470.—ed.]

6. [See McNeill, ed., *Institutes*, 2:1365.—ed.]

The question, whether eating the flesh of Christ, and drinking his blood, is confined to the Lord's Supper; in other words, whether there is any special benefit or communion with Christ to be had there, and which cannot elsewhere be obtained, the Romanists and Lutherans answer in the affirmative; the Reformed unanimously in the negative. They make indeed a distinction between spiritual and sacramental manducation. What is elsewhere received by faith, without the signs and significant actions, is in the sacraments received in connection with them. This is clearly taught in the confession of Zurich, 1545, quoted above; also in the second Helv. Confession as has already been shown. That confession vindicates this doctrine from the charge of rendering the sacrament useless. For, as it says, though we receive Christ once, we need to receive him continuously and to have our faith strengthened from day to day. Calvin teaches the same doctrine in the *Con. Tig.* Art. 19, "The verity which is figured in the sacraments, believers receive *extra eorum usum* ["outside their use"—ed.]. Thus in baptism, Paul's sins were washed away, which had already been blotted out. Baptism was to Cornelius the laver of regeneration, though he had before received the Spirit. And so in the Lord's Supper, Christ communicates himself to us, though he had already imparted himself to us and dwells within us." The office of the sacraments he teaches is to confirm and increase our faith. In his defense of this *Consensus*, he expresses surprise that a doctrine so plainly proved by experience and scripture, should be called into question (Niemeyer's Col. p. 212). In the decree of the French National Synod of 1572,[7] already quoted, it is said, "The same Lord Jesus, both as to his substance and gifts, is offered to us in baptism and the ministry of the word, and received by believers."[8]

We find the same doctrine in the Book of Common Prayer of the Church of England. In the office for the communion of the sick, the minister is directed to instruct a parishioner who is prevented receiving the sacrament, "that if he do truly repent him of his sins, and steadfastly believe that Jesus Christ hath suffered death for him on the cross, and shed his blood for his redemption, earnestly remembering the benefits he hath thereby, and giving him hearty thanks therefore, he doth eat and drink the body and blood of our Savior Christ profitably to his soul's health, though he do not receive the sacrament with his mouth." On this point there was no diversity of opinion in any part of the Reformed church. There was no communion of Christ, no participation of his body and blood, not offered to believers and received by them, elsewhere than at the Lord's table and by other means. This is exalting the grace of God without depreciating the value of the sacraments.

---

7. [The Eighth National Synod held at Nimes, May 6, 1572. The manual for Church discipline among the French Reformed, the *Discipline Ecclésiastique*, was finalized here. See Sunshine, *Reforming French Protestantism.*—ed.]

8. [Quick, *Synodicon*, 10.—ed.]

CRITICISM [NEVIN]

Here again I must refer to my "caution." Dr. Hodge might seem to his readers, in what he says of the mode of sacramental manducation as taught by the Reformed Church to be urging something not admitted in the *Mystical Presence*. Every one, however, who has read the book knows that this is not the case. Take a single quotation:

> The Reformed Church taught that the participation of Christ's flesh and blood in the Lord's Supper is *spiritual* only, and in no sense corporal. The idea of a local presence, in the case, was utterly rejected. The elements cannot be said to comprehend or include the body of the Savior, in any sense. It is not *there*, but remains constantly in heaven, according to the scriptures. It is not handled by the minister, and taken into the mouth of the communicant. The manducation of it is not oral, but only by faith. It is present in fruition accordingly to believers only in the exercise of faith; the impenitent and unbelieving receive only naked symbols, bread and wine, without any spiritual advantage to their own souls. *Mystical Presence*, p. 60.[9]

Dr. Hodge admits here however, that Calvin made a distinction between believing and spiritual eating; the force of which, he candidly tells us, he is unable to see.[10] The question, he adds, is of no historical importance, as "it created no diversity of opinion in the Church." But he has no right to dispose of it in this summary way. There is then this much involved in it, that it sunders Dr. Hodge completely, with his "mind presence" substituted for a mere "sense presence," from the position of Calvin and the Calvinistic confessions. It depends on this question, whether the force of the sacrament is to be regarded as at all objective, or as only and altogether subjective. Dr. Hodge, in conformity, with what may be considered the reigning Puritan view at this time, reduces all to the mere action of faith, as the mind of the subject brought simply into a certain relation to the general truth of the gospel; and it is not strange therefore, that he should not understand Calvin, when he talks of "something more striking and sublime, namely, that we are quickened by a real participation of Christ, which he designates by the terms *eating* and *drinking*, that no person might suppose the life which we receive from him to consist in simple knowledge."[11] So precisely Dr. Dick,[12]

9. [MTSS edition, 49.—ed.]

10. [It is clear that Calvin did not make "eating the same as believing." Eating the flesh and blood of Christ is not therefore believing. Moreover, insofar as the flesh and blood are signs pointing to the cross and the benefits there achieved, communion with Christ cannot be achieved without a continuous partaking of that offering. Hence, the Supper is the way by which believers can enjoy the Lord "all the time." See Gerrish, *Grace and Gratitude*, 130–33.—ed.]

11. [Calvin, *Institutes*, ed. McNeill, 2:1365.—ed.]

12. [John Dick (1764–1833), ordained in the Secession Church of Aberdeen in 1786. He served a church just outside of Edinburgh. No doubt barred from theological study in the Presbyterian seminaries, Dick received his Doctor of Divinity degree from the "college" of Princeton in 1815. In 1819 the professorship of Systematic Divinity came open at the Seminary of the Secession Church in Glasgow where he taught until his death. His *Lectures on Theology*, II Vols., were published in Edinburgh beginning in 1834. Their importance has been overlooked. Dick's *Lectures* are known to have been a textbook at Princeton as well as Mercersburg Seminary. Hodge's similarity in method to Dick's is abundantly clear. The recent reprint (2010) includes a "Memoir" written by Dick's son and it captures this beautifully.

standing on the same ground with Dr. Hodge, takes Calvin to task as uttering unintelligible nonsense, when he speaks of "some inexplicable communion in this ordinance with the human nature of Christ." (See *Myst. Pres.* p. 114.)[13] All this, however, only shows the general nature of the chasm, which has come to hold here between the old Calvinistic and the Modern Puritan theory of the Lord's Supper, as I have shown at large in the second chapter of the *Mystical Presence*. Right or wrong, Calvin held and taught, all his life, that we have more in the Lord's Supper than a mere occasion for the exrcise of our faith; that it carries in itself, by the Holy Ghost, an objective mystical force, by which directly we are made to participate in the true mediatorial life of the blessed Redeemer, as the element of immortality as well as righteousness. And if this created, as we are told, "no diversity of opinion in the Church," it was simply because the same view entered prevailingly into its creed as a whole. Whatever indistinctness there may seem to be on the point, in any of the earlier confessions, it gave way before the clearer consciousness that was introduced by the instrumentality of Calvin; which is to be found plainly enough expressed accordingly in the leading confessions after this time. They teach us, with one voice we may say, in the language of our own Heidelberg Catechism, that by these visible signs and pledges, "*we are as really partakers of his true body and blood,* BY THE OPERATION OF THE HOLY GHOST, *as we receive by the mouths of our bodies these holy signs in remembrance of him.*"[14] They assert an objective, and not simply a subjective force, in the holy mystery.

They do not indeed confine our participation of Christ's life to the Lord's Supper. On the contrary, they assume the fact of a mystical life union as necessarily at hand in the previous relation of the believer to Christ, to make room for the special mystery of the sacramental manducation. But certainly they do not make the sacramental manducation, to be the same thing simply with the ordinary exercises of Christian penitence and faith. They reject of course the idea of a magical introduction of Christ's life into the body of the worshipper apart from his central consciousness, through which alone our nature can be entered in a spiritual way; differing in this respect from the Romanists and Lutherans; but they question not the presence here of a *special* and *extraordinary mystery*. This I have shown in the way of contrasts between the Calvinistic and Puritan systems, in the second chapter of the *Mystical Presence*.[15]

"He was distinguished by the strictness with which he adhered to the great Protestant rule of making the Bible, in its plain meaning, the source of his religious creed, and the basis of his theological system. His distrust of reason, as a guide in religion, was deeply sincere, and never wavered; and so was his confidence in revelation; both were the result of inquiry: and the perfect reasonableness of his faith was in nothing more evident than the limits which he set to it; for he had taken pains to ascertain the bounds of revelation, and within these he was as teachable as a child; to everything beyond them, where we are left to our own resources, no one could apply the test of reason with more uncompromising boldness" (xiv). See *Lectures on Theology by the Late Rev. John Dick*. See also, J. R. McIntosh, *Dictionary of Scottish History and Theology,* edited by Nigel Cameron.—ed.]

13. [*Lectures on Theology by the Late Rev. John Dick. D. D.*, Lec. XCII; quoted in MTSS edition p. 101.—ed.]

14. [Question 69.—ed.]

15. [See MTSS edition, pp. 104–6.—ed.]

REVIEW, CONTINUED [HODGE]

What is meant by the body and blood of Christ as received in the sacrament?

The language employed in answer to this question is very various. It is said, we received Christ and his benefits, his flesh and blood, his true body, his natural body, his substance, the substance of his flesh and blood. All these forms of expression occur. Calvin says we receive the substance of Christ. The Gallican Confession says, "We are fed with the substance of his body and blood." The Belgic Confession, that we receive "his natural body." The question is, what does this mean? There is one thing in which all parties agreed, viz., that our union with Christ was a real union, that we receive him and not his benefits merely; that he dwells in his people by his Spirit, whose presence is the presence of Christ. Though all meant this, this is not all that is intended by the expressions above cited. What is meant by saying we receive his flesh and blood, or the substance of them? The negative answer to this question given by the Reformers uniformly is, they do not mean that we partake of the material particles of Christ's body, nor do they express any mixture or transfusion of substance. The affirmative statement is, in general terms, just as uniform, that these expressions indicate the virtue, efficacy, life-giving power of his body. But there are two ways in which this was understood. Some intended by it, not the virtue of Christ's body and blood as flesh and blood, but as a body broken and of blood shed, that is, their sacrificial atoning efficacy. Others, however, insisted that besides this there was a vivifying efficacy imparted to the body of Christ by its union with the divine nature, and that by the power of the Holy Ghost, the believer in the Lord's Supper and elsewhere, received into his soul and by faith this mysterious and supernatural influence. This was clearly Calvin's idea, though he often contented himself with the expression of the former of these views. His doctrine is fully expressed in the following passages.

> We acknowledge, without any circumlocution that the flesh of Christ, is life-giving, not only because once in it our salvation was obtained; but because now, we being united to him in sacred union, it breathes life into us. Or, to use fewer words, because being by the power of the Spirit engrafted into the body of Christ, we have common life with him; for from the hidden fountain of divinity life is, in a wonderful way, infused into the flesh of Christ, and thence flows out to us.[16]

Again: "Christ is absent from us as to the body, by his Spirit, however, dwelling in us, he so lifts us to himself in heaven, that he transfuses the life-giving vigor of his flesh into us, as we grow by the vital heat of the sun."[17] From these and many similar passages, it is plain, Calvin meant by receiving the substance of Christ's body, receiving its virtue or vigor, not merely as a sacrifice, but also the power inherent in it from its union with the divine nature, and flowing from it as heat from the sun.

The other explanation of this matter is that by receiving the substance of Christ's body or by receiving his flesh and blood was intended receiving their life-giving

16. [Hodge quotes from Calvin's *Consensionis Capitum Expositio*, in Niemeyer 214. See "Exposition of the Heads of Agreement," in Torrance, ed., *Tracts and Treatises*, 2:238.—ed.]

17. [See ibid. 240.—ed.]

efficacy as a sacrifice once offered on the cross for us. This view is clearly expressed in the Zurich Confession of 1545. "To eat the bread of Christ is to believe on him as crucified. . . . His flesh once benefitted us on earth, now it benefits here no longer, and is no longer here." The same view is expressed by Calvin himself in the *Con. Tig.* 1549. In the 19th article we are said to eat the flesh of Christ, "because we derive our life from that flesh once offered in sacrifice for us, and from his blood shed as an expiation." With equal clearness the same idea is presented in the Heidelberg Catechism, 1560. In question 79, it is his crucified body and shed blood which are declared to be the food of the soul. The same thing is still more plainly asserted in the Helv. Confession 1566, c. 21. In the first paragraph, it is said, "Christ as delivered unto death for us and as a Savior is the sum of this sacrament." In the third paragraph this eating is explained as the application, by the Spirit, of the benefits of Christ's death. And lower down, the food of the soul is declared to be *caro Christi tradita pro nobis, et sanguis ejus effuses pro nobis.*[18] Indeed as this confession was written by Bullinger, minister of Zurich, the great opponent of Calvin's peculiar view, it could not be expected to teach any other doctrine. In what is called the Anglican Confession, drawn up by Bishop Jewell[19] 1562, the same view is presented. It is there said: "We maintain that Christ exhibits himself truly present . . . that in the Supper we feed upon him by faith and in the spirit (*fide et spiritu*) and that we have eternal life from his cross and blood."[20] To draw life from the cross is here the same as to draw it from his blood, and of course must refer to the sacrificial efficacy of his death.

The question now arises which of the two views above stated is entitled to be regarded as the real doctrine of the Reformed? The whole church united in saying believers receive the body and blood of Christ. They agreed in explaining this to mean that they received the virtue, efficacy or vigor of his body and blood. But some understood, thereby, the virtue of his body as broken and of his blood as shed, that is, their sacrificial efficacy. Others said that besides this, there was a mysterious virtue in the body of Christ due to its union with the divine nature, which virtue was by the Holy Spirit conveyed to the believer. Which of these views is truly symbolical?[21] The fairest answer to this question probably is, neither to the exclusion of the other. Those who held to the one, expressed their fellowship with those who held the other. Calvin and

---

18. [Trans. ". . . even so the flesh of Christ delivered for us, and his blood shed for us." Dennison, *Reformed Confessions*, 2: 867. It is hard to see how this quote makes Hodge's point (except indirectly in the sacrificial allusion), although the whole paragraph surrounding it is a warning against thinking in terms of corporeal consumption, so it fits with Hodge's argument.—ed.]

19. [John Jewel (1522–71) was a disciple of Peter Martyr Vermigli during the Edwardian phase of the English Reformation (1547–53), and returned from exile under Mary to become Bishop of Salisbury (1560) and a leading theologian in Elizabeth's church. He is known chiefly for his famous defense of the Church of England, *Apologia Ecclesiae Anglicanae* (to which Hodge here alludes), and for mentoring the young Richard Hooker. See J. E. Booty, *John Jewel.*—ed.]

20. [Hodge is quoting from John Jewel's *Apology of the Church of England*, II.15. The 1888 edition, edited by Henry Morley (London: Cassell, 1888), may be found at http://anglicanhistory.org/jewel/apology/.—ed.]

21. [That is, "confessional."—ed.]

Bullinger united in the *Consensus Tigurinus* from which the later view is excluded. Both views are expressed in the public confessions. Some have one, some the other.

But if a decision must be made between them, the higher authority is certainly due to the doctrine of sacrificial efficacy first mentioned. 1. It has high symbolical authority in its favor. Its being clearly expressed in the *Con. Tig.*, the common platform of the church, on this whole subject, and in the Second Helv. Con., the most authoritative of all the symbols of the Reformed church, and even the Heidelberg Catechism, outweighs the private authority of Calvin or the dubious expression of the Gallican, Belgic, and some minor Confessions. 2. What is perhaps of more real consequence, the sacrificial view, is the only one that harmonizes with the other doctrines of the church. The other is an uncongenial foreign element derived partly from the influence of previous modes of thought, partly from the dominant influence of the Lutherans and the desire of getting as near to them as possible, and partly, no doubt, from a too literal interpretation of certain passages of scripture, especially John vi. 54–58, and Eph. v. 30.[22]

It is difficult to reconcile the idea that a life-giving influence emanates from the glorified body of Christ, with the universally received doctrine of the Reformed Church, that we receive Christ as fully through the ministry of the word as in the Lord's Supper. However strongly some of the Reformed asserted that we partake of the true or natural body of Christ, and are fed by the substance of his flesh and blood, they all maintained that this was done whenever faith in him was exercised. Not to urge this point however. All the Reformed taught, Calvin perhaps more earnestly than others, that our union with Christ since the incarnation is the same in nature as that enjoyed by the saints under the old dispensation. This is perfectly intelligible if the virtue of his flesh and blood, which we receive in the Lord's Supper, is its virtue as a sacrifice, because he was the Lamb slain from the foundation of the world. His sacrifice was as effectual for the salvation of Abraham as of Paul, and could be appropriated as fully by the faith of the one as by that of the other. But if the virtue in question is a mysterious power due to the hypostatical union, flowing from Christ's body in heaven, it must be a benefit peculiar to believers living since the incarnation. It is impossible that those living before the advent could partake of Christ's body, in this sense, because it did not then exist; it had not as yet been assumed into union with the divine nature. We find therefore that Romanists and nominal Protestants, make the greatest distinction as to the relation of the ancient saints to God and that of believers since the advent, between

22. [The Dutch theologian Gerrit P. Hartvelt, in a later study (*Verum Corpus: Een studie over een central hoofdstuk uit de avondmaalsleer van Calvijn.* Delft: W.D. Meinema, 1960) shared Hodge's fear that this was a dangerous alien invasion into Reformed theology, in which the ordinary lean of Reformed theology toward Antiochene categories is replaced by an appeal to Alexandrian Christology. Still, Hartvelt's Calvin is essentially Nevin's. Gerrish, while largely endorsing Nevin's reading, suggests that this mysterious "vital power" needs to be set alongside Calvin's many other metaphors of communion with Christ, including the way that we ascend to Christ and he descends to us, as well as Hodge's preferred metaphor of the Spirit as the conduit through which Christ's body exercises a "powerful force or influence on believers." Calvin also uses the metaphor of the sun's influence, for which reason he is sometimes accused of being a "energist" (receiving the power of Christ who is himself above in heaven). See Gerrish, *Grace and Gratitude*, 177–78.—ed.]

the sacraments of the one dispensation and those of the other. All this is consistent and necessary on their theory of the incarnation, of the church and of the sacraments, but it is all in the plainest contradiction to the doctrine of the Reformed Church.[23] Here then is an element which does not accord with the other documents of that church; and this incongruity is one good reason for not regarding it as a genuine portion of its faith.

Another good reason for this conclusion is, that the doctrine almost immediately died out of the church. It had no root in the system and could not live. We hear nothing from the immediate successors of Calvin and Beza, of this mysterious, or as it was sometimes called, miraculous influence of Christ's heavenly body. Turretin, Beza's contemporary, expressly discards it. So does Pictet, who followed Turretin, and so do the Reformed theologians as a body.[24] As a single indication of this fact we refer to Craig's catechism, written under an order of the General Assembly of the church of Scotland, of 1590, and sanctioned by that body in 1592.[25] It will be remembered that the Scotch confession of 1560, before quoted, follows the very language of Calvin on

23. [Hodge:] "If any one doubts this assertion, let him read Calvin's *Institutes* B. iv. c. 14 § 20–25. This subject however will come up in another place." [Hodge has in mind a rather large section from the *Institutes* where Calvin goes a long way in showing how the Old Testament "sacraments" such as circumcision, were no less effective than the New Testament sacraments of baptism and the Lord's Supper. Likewise, the Old Testament sacraments imparted Christ, and that was why they were effective. Calvin wrote in the section referred to by Hodge (*Institutes*, ed. McNeill, 2:1296–1301): "But we utterly reject that Scholastic dogma (to touch on it also in passing) which notes such a great difference between the sacraments of the old and new law, as if the former only foreshadowed God's grace, but the latter give it as a present reality. Indeed, the apostle speaks just as clearly concerning the former as the latter when he teaches that the fathers ate the same spiritual food as we, and explains that food as Christ [1 Cor. 10:3]" (1299). However, if Hodge means to suggest that Calvin saw *no* difference between the sacramental dispensations, his case weakens. Calvin concluded his chapter 14 writing, "Yet in this respect also we admit some difference. For both attest that God's fatherly kindness and the graces of the Holy Spirit are offered us in Christ, but ours is clearer and brighter. In both Christ is shown forth, but in ours more richly and fully, . . . when Christ was revealed sacraments were instituted, fewer in number, more majestic in signification, more excellent in power" (1303). So, then, Hodge is essentially correct when he says, "All the Reformed taught, Calvin perhaps more earnestly than most others, that our union with Christ since the incarnation is the same in nature as that enjoyed by the saints under the old dispensation." Of course, the key word is "nature." It may be the same union in nature, but Calvin is clear to state that it is not entirely the same. See the first volume in this series for a thorough presentation in "Doctrine of the Reformed Church on the Lord's Supper," the chapter "Historical Trial" (244–314) and especially the section *Ad Discutiendas Nebulas.—*ed.]

24. [Hodge:] We had transcribed various authorities as to this point, but are obliged to exclude them for the want of space. We refer the reader only to Turretin's statement of the question as between the Reformed and Lutherans, where he will see this whole matter ventilated with that masterly discrimination for which Turretin is unrivalled. *Theol. Elenct.* III. p. 567. [See Francis Turretin, *Institutes of Elenctic Theology*, 3 vols., ed. James T. Dennison, trans. George M. Giger.—ed.]

25. [John Craig (1512?–1600), educated at St. Andrews and after a time abroad returned to Scotland in 1560. The following year he was ordained minister at Holyrood. As a colleague of John Knox his influence was significant and he participated in the drawing up of various forms, confessions, and articles. The catechism was used specifically as a form for examination prior to Holy Communion. It may be found online at http://www.swrb.com/newslett/actualNLs/communca.htm (taken from Dunlop, ed., *Collection of Confessions of Faith, Catechisms, Directories, Books of Discipline, Etc.*, vol. 2.—ed.]

this particular point. In Craig's catechism however, we have the following exhibition of the subject.

> *Quest. [70]* What signifieth the action of the Supper? Ans. That our souls are fed spiritually by the body and blood of Jesus Christ. John vi. 54. *Ques. 71* When is this done? Ans. When we feel the efficacy of his death in our conscience by the spirit of faith. John vi. 33. . . . *Ques. 75* Is Christ's body in the elements? A. No, but it is in heaven. Acts i. 11. *Ques 76.* Why then is the element called his body? A. Because it is a sure seal of his body given to our souls.

In the "Confession of Faith used in the English congregation in Geneva," the very first in date of the symbols of the Scotch church, it is said: "So the Supper declareth that God, a provident Father, doth not only feed our bodies, but also nourishes our souls with the graces and benefits of Jesus Christ, which the scriptures calleth eating of this flesh and drinking of his blood."

It is of course admitted that a particular doctrine's dying out of the faith of a church, is, of itself, no sufficient evidence that it was not a genuine part of its original belief. This is too obvious to need remark. There is, however, a great difference between a doctrine's being lost by a process of decay and by the process of growth. It is very possible that a particular opinion may be engrafted into a system, without having any logical or vital union with it, and is the more certain to be rejected, the more vigorous the growth and healthful the life of that system. The fundamental principles of Protestantism are the exclusive normal authority of scripture, and justification by faith alone. If that system lives and grows it must throw off everything incompatible with those principles. It is the fact of this peculiar view of a mysterious influence of the glorified body of Christ, having ceased to live, taken in connection with its obvious incompatibility with other articles of the Reformed faith, that we urge as a collateral argument against its being a genuine position of that system of doctrine. According to the most authoritative standards of the Reformed church, we receive the body and blood of Christ, as a sacrifice, just as Abraham and David received them, who ate of the same spiritual meat and drank from the same spiritual drink. The church is one, its life is one, its food is one, from Adam to the last of the redeemed.

CRITICISM [NEVIN]

Of course, the case excludes every thought of corporeal contact, transfusion of material substance, &c. All is spiritual and mystical, by the power of the Holy Ghost and faith, a fact not belonging to nature but transcending it *in the Spirit*. I have never represented the doctrine of Calvin in any other light. The true question is, however, What did the Reformed Church of the sixteenth century mean by "feeding on the substance, virtue or efficacy of Christ's body and blood" in the Spirit, that is, in the transcendent mystery of the sacramental transaction. Dr. Hodge is evidently embarrassed with this whole phraseology. It goes far beyond his system, & is taken plainly to be a sort of extravagant accommodation on the part of the age to the superstition of former times. Our common Puritan style of thinking, is in no danger certainly of falling into such strange expressions. He is forced to admit in the first place generally, that to receive Christ's flesh and blood in the sacrament means, in the old symbol, *more* than the common indwelling of the Spirit in our hearts. This is a very great admission, however, which goes far to notify the whole aspect in which he has been trying to present the subject before. Then there is a *special* mystery here after all, in the sense of the old Church; and it is not quite so clear, that no objective supernatural force was supposed to be comprehended in the ordinance, but only an outward help to good thoughts and pious feelings. But Dr. Hodge is compelled to go still farther with his admission. Calvin at least, he tells us, *did* hold that a vivific efficacy extends from Christ's body to his people. But this is the very point on which may be said to hinge, so far as this great reformer is concerned, the whole controversy of Dr. Hodge with my book. I have asserted and proved, that he held and taught the mystery of a real participation in the substance of Christ's mediatorial human life, in the Lord's Supper. This the article of Dr. Hodge makes a *show* at least of denying, and is generally taken as doing so in fact. But here, the whole point is surrendered. Calvin plainly taught, says Dr. Hodge, that to partake of Christ's body, is not merely to have part in his atonement, but in the very virtue or energy besides of his human life. The admission is fatal, in the end, to the whole cause which Dr. Hodge is endeavoring to uphold.

It may be said indeed, that the "virtue, efficacy and life-giving power" of Christ's body are not to be considered as the same thing with the proper life of his body itself. Dr. Hodge probably has some such idea as this in his mind. He thinks of the vivific power here noticed, as a sort of mysterious *influence* simply supposed to emanate from Christ's corporeal presence in heaven, like the power that flows from the sun; and it is no wonder that he finds it in such view hard to understand or adopt. For what sense in truth can anyone attach to the notion of vivific influence, going forth in this way from the body of Christ, as something in no farther connection with our life? But it was no such meaning as this, the words virtue, efficacy, substance, vital energy, &c., of Christ's body, were employed to express in the sixteenth century. The idea intended was the presence of Christ's veritable living nature itself. This was not regarded as standing in the case in anything that could be apprehended by sense, every thought of matter must be excluded, the existence of Christ *en pneumati*, in the Spirit, was of a higher order, all activity and power, and not capable of being measured or approached at all in an outward fleshly way. Now to express the presence of such a life, the inmost substance of it, the very thing itself and not simply an attribute belonging to it, what terms *could* Calvin have used, over against the crass conceptions of Romanists and Lutherans, other than such as those just quoted, which we find him to have used always in fact? It is vast wrong then to his memory, as well as to the Reformed faith generally in his age, to endeavor to drag them down to any lower sense. I have furnished abundant evidence already, in the *Mystical Presence*, and hope to furnish more in the progress of this present discussion, that Calvin intended to express by the vivific virtue of Christ's body, *all* that Luther was laboring for by his oral manducation, and indeed, as he always believed and said himself, a great deal more.[26]

Against this view however, Dr. Hodge arrays another, which he represents as more generally prevalent in the Reformed Church, more consonant with its true genius, and of such force as finally to dispel the Calvinistic peculiarity from the general creed. Here we are brought to the very gist of the whole historical question; the true relation namely of the *sacrifice* of Christ and his *life*, as concerned, according to the faith of the original Reformed Church, in the Christian salvation generally and in the mystery of the Lord's Supper in particular. Dr. Hodge is right, in saying that the Reformed doctrine of the Eucharist shows two phases, in the sixteenth century, as taking its complexion sometimes from the idea of the atoning efficacy of Christ's death, and at other times from the vivific power of his life. But he is wrong, when he conceives of these two views as bearing at best only an outward and temporary alliance in the same system, and sinks the last into character of merely accidental importance as compared with the first. The Reformed doctrine starts in Switzerland under the first aspect, but completes itself finally, through Calvin, under the second; not in such a way as to drop the old view, but so as to bring it to its full significance, by joining it to its proper basis in the other. *This union of the two views forms the true sacramental creed of the Reformed Church, as it appears in all the later confessions.* It is the misery of our modern divinity, on the other hand, that it has so widely fallen away again from this divine synthesis, sundering the atonement of Christ from its necessary ground in his life, and then arraying the one against the other as though they were opposite and rival powers! For what less than this is it, when we hear such a man as Dr. Hodge gravely asserting, that the doctrine of a life-giving power mysteriously flowing from Christ's person, as taught by Calvin, is incompatible with the Protestant doctrine of justification by faith, and on this account could not hold its place, as a foreign element, in the faith of the Reformed Church! Alas for the memory of Luther, that *he* should not have understood better the sense of his own great article of a standing or falling Christianity.

This whole subject is of vast importance, and it will be necessary now to pause a little with Dr. Hodge's article, for the purpose of placing the question here brought into view, so far as the case may allow, in its true historical light.

26. [Calvin saw himself as an ally or "disciple" of Luther, and his greater allegiance was to Wittenberg over Zurich. Moreover he favored the Augsburg Confession over most others with the exception of the French Confession (1559) of which he was the principal author. It was Calvin's view that the Swiss did not so much reject Luther's core sacramental teaching—as they did not fully "grasp it." See Gerrish, *Grace and Gratitude*, 138–40.—ed.]

4

Nevin on the Ancient Reformed Creeds[1]

HISTORICAL EXCURSUS [NEVIN]

Dr. Hodge, as we have seen, brings up his witnesses from the sixteenth century in a promiscuous body, and questions them in a heap, without the least care to determine, in the first place, their true *historical* standing and weight. In the *Mystical Presence*, I have endeavored at least to do some justice to the actual relations of the age, by tracing the progress of the Reformed doctrine, from its somewhat confused incipient form in Switzerland, onward through the architectonic agency of Calvin, to the complete character in which it appears in the later confessions. But this does not suit the purpose of Dr. Hodge; and so, in virtue simply of his own good pleasure in the case, he turns all into "a rude and undigested mass," which he then proceeds to work into use in the most free and independent way. "It is hard to tell," we hear him saying,

> . . . where to look for the authoritative exhibition of the Reformed doctrine. Shall we look to the private writings of the Reformers, or to the public confessions? If to the latter, shall we rely on those of Switzerland, or on those of the Palatinate, France or Belgium? These, though they have a general co-incidence, do not entirely agree. Some favor one interpretation, and some another. Dr. Nevin chooses to make Calvin the great authority, and pronounces the confessions of the Swiss Churches chaotic and confused.

And so Dr. Hodge, to mend the matter, thinks it best to give up the idea of *all* historical order, and apply to the case a purely mechanical classification (after the fashion of botany), exhibiting, in the first place, "those authorities, which represent the Swiss views, secondly those which present the views of Calvin, and thirdly those symbols in which both parties concurred." A very convenient equalization of witnesses truly, but historically hollow and worthless throughout.

---

1. ["Dr. Hodge on the Mystical Presence, Article from the Repertory, Continued, No. 4," *Weekly Messenger*, New Series, vol. 13, no. 40. Wednesday, June 14, 1848. Published by the Board of the Synod of the German Reformed Church: Chambersburg, PA.—ed.]

The case, however, even in this form, refused to come immediately straight. Calvin at least talks strangely of our being fed with the virtue of Christ's body; and some of the confessions are implicated, but too plainly, in the same mystical theory. Even Dr. Hodge himself is forced to see and confess the fact. This view then must be violently set aside, as having no right to appear in the Reformed creed. Happily *another* view is at hand, in the same creed, which is supposed to make this exclusion perfectly regular and easy. In the earlier confessions especially, all stress is laid on the *sacrificial* force of Christ's death, as the great object to be appropriated by faith in the Lord's Supper. Thus we have two conceptions of sacramental communion, in the old Reformed creed, one referring to the atonement, the other to the life also of Christ's body. These, Dr. Hodge thinks, cannot well stand in the same system; and so the question comes up, which must be required to give way to the other, in our estimate of the original Reformed doctrine of the Lord's Supper. The proper answer to this, would seem to lie in an appeal to history. But Dr. Hodge chooses to settle the point, in a different way. He knows how it *ought* to be settled, on the inward merits of the case itself, and he proclaims it settled accordingly. "The higher authority," he tells us, "is certainly due to the doctrine of sacrificial efficacy." Buy why? The answer is ready. Because, 1. "It has high symbolical authority in its favor;" 2. "It is the only one that harmonizes (Dr. Hodge being judge) with the other doctrines of the Church. The other is an uncongenial foreign element derived partly from the influence of previous modes of thought, partly from the dominant influence of the Lutherans, and the desire of getting as near to them as possible, &c." How pragmatic! 3. "The doctrine almost immediately died out in the Church. It had no root in the system, and could not live." In such most unhistorical style is it, that Dr. Hodge contrives, to his own satisfaction, to *speculate* out of the way the Calvinistic idea of a real life—communication with Christ in the holy sacrament, as though it never belonged in fact to the ancient Reformed creed; from which notwithstanding it continues to stare upon us upbraidingly, I had almost said like the ghost of Banquo,[2] to the present day.

But there is a history in this business, which we may not thus make or unmake at our theological pleasure. I have tried before to expound it, to some extent, in the *Mystical Presence*; an analysis, which Dr. Hodge has not pretended to examine or refute, but simply nullifies by convenient silence. Providentially, I am now assisted by a new ally, on this field, in whose favor I feel more at liberty to bespeak attention and respect. I refer to the second volume of Ebrard's great work, *Das Dogma vom heiligen Abendmahl*, which is devoted especially to the history of the sacramental controversy, as it was agitated in the age of the Reformation. Favorable notice is taken of the *first* volume of the work in the *Mystical Presence*, and a regret expressed that the second had not then appeared; as it might have much facilitated my own investigations, as

---

2. [A character in Shakespeare's 1606 play *Macbeth*. Banquo was made a ghost by the murderous hand of a jealous and suspicious Macbeth, and in a famous scene, disrupts a banquet by appearing (only to Macbeth) and staring accusatorily at him. Interpreters debate whether the ghost was simply a figment of Macbeth's fevered and increasingly deranged imagination; it may be that Nevin intends to hint that Hodge's treatment too proceeds from such an unstable imagination.—ed.]

directed towards the same ground. It is on the whole well, however, that this was not the case. Exhibiting as it does now the results of a wholly separate inquiry, it is of so much the more force to confirm and complete the investigation contained in my book. I need not say that it has been highly gratifying to me, to find myself so ably backed and supported from such a quarter. Professor Ebrard (formerly of Zurich, now of Erlangen) is indeed a *German*, which may be considered by some a serious drawback on his authority; but he is, at the same time, a zealous *Reformed* theologian, and his *scholarship* is acknowledged on all hands to be of the very highest order. He has made it his business moreover to *study* the subject here in hand, in the most full and patient use of *all* the original sources of knowledge, not to see how things *should* have been, but to learn of history how they were in fact. The result is the present volume of 800 octavo pages, reproducing the sacramental life of the sixteenth century, as we have it exhibited in no work besides; and tracing in particular the rise and progress of the Reformed doctrine, as distinguished from the high Lutheran, in such a way as to leave almost nothing to be desired, in relation to the whole subject. The work, thus complete, corroborates and sustains, with unanswerable evidence, every material historical position presented in the *Mystical Presence*, and just as clearly, of course, convicts Dr. Hodge of error and mistake.

In any true historical study of the case, it must appear at once that we have no right to mix and confound authorities, in the style pursued by Dr. Hodge. The earlier Swiss confessions can never be allowed to stand parallel with the later Reformed symbols (much less to take precedence of them) without such violence to history as may be said to kill it altogether. It is arbitrary, in the extreme, to exalt the *Consensus Tigurinus* to the rank of a supreme law for the whole creed of the Church. No less arbitrary is it, to question the right of Calvin to be regarded as the great organ, by which the creed came to its full and final expression. All history has but one voice here.[3] Beyond every sort of rational doubt, Calvin *does* form the medium of clear transition, from the older Helvetic faith to a higher power, as we may call it, of the same faith as presented in the later confessions; *all* of which express here his theory, with most remarkable agreement, and can be rightly interpreted in no other sense. The only proper classification of the confessions, is into those before Calvin and those that follow; and the only proper relation between the two classes, is that which subordinates the first entirely to the second, as the acknowledged consummation at last of the whole confessional process. The earlier symbols lost their authority in fact, with the appearance of the later, Gallic, Scotic, Belgic, Second Helvetic Confessions, and the Heidelberg Catechism.

According to this division, it is true that the older Swiss doctrine of the Lord's Supper lays weight mainly (though not exclusively), on the sacrificial interest in Christ, whilst it is in the later confessions mainly that we find urged also the idea of a

---

3. [Nevin clearly overstates his case somewhat here, displaying what had been a common error committed by post-Enlightenment historical science, with its deterministic confidence and resulting reductionistic character. Rahn-Clemens in her dissertation (citing Thompson as well) demonstrates the greater complexity involved in attributing influence, authorship, and authority to a confession. Still, this does not excuse Hodge's error. See Bard Thompson, "Melanchthon and the German Reformed Church," 162–85. See also Rahn-Clemens, "Foundations of German Reformed Worship."—ed.]

participation in his life. The second view might seem in this way to have supplanted the first, rather than to have been expelled by it as a foreign element from the system. The truth is, however, the two views stand in no such hostile and mutually exclusive relation to each other, as is imagined by Dr. Hodge. That they should seem to do so in *his* theology, only shows that this itself is something different from the old Reformed creed. With Calvin, the idea of a life-union with Christ stood not at all in the way of the sacrificial interest which it had been the great object of Zuingli and the first Swiss divines generally to assert. On the contrary, that interest for him could not be properly supported in any other view; and it was his zeal for all that is precious in the doctrine of the atonement, which along with his zeal for all that is precious in the believer's union with Christ, engaged him to insist on this last so constantly as the indispensable basis of the first. The merit of Christ was not, in his view, as it seems to be to the view of Dr. Hodge, a mere thought in God's mind to be set over to the credit of sinners in an outward way; it was something real and concrete, which as such could never be sundered from the life to which it belonged; on which account this life itself must be made to reach over to all who are to have the benefit of it, as the necessary and only bearer of such high grace. Christ *first, & then* his merit; the life of the Son of Man made ours, in order to a true and full interest in the wealth of this life; such was the steady, unvarying order of Calvin's creed, a hundred times repeated, from the commencement of his ministry to its close. And in this form, it passed into all the later Reformed Confessions; not with the sacrifice certainly of the old Zuinglian way of looking at the subject; but so, at the same time, as to carry this forward to its full sense, by coupling it with the idea of the mystical union, completing thus the whole doctrine in the proper combination of its two different sides.

Zuingli and Luther

Both of these great men were led to take their position in regard to the Lord's Supper, in an independent way, and without any reference on either side to the other. The view of Zuingli was called out primarily, in opposition to the Roman doctrine of the mass, and had regard to the general act of the Church in the sacramental solemnity, rather than to its power inwardly for the individual worshipper. Is the Lord's Supper in itself a true sacrifice for sin, repeating perpetually the propitiatory act of Christ's death? To this question Zuingli answered, against the Romanists: No; it is simply a memorial or *sign* of the one Christian sacrifice originally made on Calvary. In such reference, of course, the answer was correct. The Eucharist does not repeat, but only commemorates, Christ's death. Zuingli was right too in referring the ordinance, as he did, to the idea of the atonement, as the great object to be apprehended in order to our salvation. The words: This is my body *broken*, and my blood *shed*, do look undoubtedly, in their direct sense, to Christ on the cross. We are saved by the merit of his death, made ours by faith. But the question still remains: *How* come we to have such part in Christ's death?

Luther, by his whole nature and inward history, had his mind turned more to the question: What is the significance and value of the Lord's Supper for the subjective life of the particular communicant? Hence his tendency was, from the start, to lay emphasis on the idea of a communion in it with Christ's *life*, rather than with his death. He made large account also, of course, of the sacrificial side of Christianity. But this we appropriate through the ordinary actings of faith in his view, as something purely objective, in opposition to all personal activity in the way of merit, as taught by Rome. In proportion however, as objective and subjective were thus held asunder, faith coming to no real union with the life of its object, in the reception of Christ's righteousness, it became the more necessary with him to provide for this union (*felt* to be indispensible to all true salvation) in a different way; and hence he was led to resolve it into another order of grace altogether, secured through the mystery of the holy sacraments. The Lord's Supper especially became for him the medium of a direct communication with what might be considered the outward person of Christ; and he was led to refer it accordingly, not to his death so much as to his life, and so of course to this only under its present glorified character. With such inward frame, he fell into collision first with the wretched rationalism of Carlstadt;[4] a man, with whom, to their credit be it spoken, the Swiss divines never made common cause. Against his shallow destructional spirit, Luther stood forward, as against the whole tribe of the Anabaptists also, in an earnestly and severely conservative tone. The idea of a real life-union with Christ in the Lord's Supper, as it had been held by the holy Catholic Church from the beginning, he made to be just as necessary to Christianity as the idea of justification by faith without works. In all this however, laudable as his zeal was in its own nature, he was naturally brought to overlook too much, the other side of the sacramental transaction, its reference namely to the atonement. The idea of Christ's death here was thrust aside, to make room for the idea of his glorified life.

Thus differently conditioned by their different rise and growth, the Zuinglian and Lutheran views came at last, a. 1526, to a direct and open conflict. This went forward actively afterwards, with much more dignity on the side of Zuingli than on that of Luther, till the parties were brought finally to a personal meeting, a. 1529, in the memorable conference in Marburg.

This whole controversy was very important, as opening the way for a deeper apprehension of the sacramental question in a following period. It is easy to see, however, that in itself it did not bring this question to its true ground. Both Luther and Zuingli were to a certain extent right in their different positions; while, on the other hand,

4. [Carlstadt named for his birthplace, his real name being Andreas Bodenstein (1480–1541). German Reformer who in coming to Protestantism came under the influence of Luther. However, his extreme views led to a falling out with Luther who denounced him as the new "Judas." He was a notorious iconoclast, who angered many by his removing many of the venerated images from churches. He rejected the Mass, denied the bodily presence of Christ in the Eucharist, and insisted on shouting the liturgy in German. In spite of Luther's feeling that Carlstadt was too radical and pushing too aggressively for reform, Schaff paints a somewhat different picture, saying criticism of Carlstadt was overstated, that he often moved with diplomatic constraint and was willing to show reserve when civil authorities chastised him (Schaff-Herzog, 414).—ed.]

both became wrong again, by refusing to see and acknowledge the truth that lay on the contrary side. Luther had good reason to insist on the idea of a real life-union with Christ in the sacrament; but he had no right to deny, at the same time, the direct reference it bears to the sacrificial value of his death. Here palpably Zuingli showed himself more sound than his opponent, by intonating as he did the commemorative relation of the ordinance to the broken body and shed blood of the Redeemer, and insisting on the metaphorical sense in the words of institution. But he had no right on the other side, to press this view, at the cost of the mystical union. To such extreme antagonism however, the controversy, as in all similar cases, naturally tended throughout; and we find both parties accordingly, at the Marburg conference, as also more or less before, firmly planted on their opposite portions of truth, in the way of abrupt contradiction, as though one must be necessarily all right and the other all wrong.

How far Zuingli may have had a correct apprehension of the life-union of believers with Christ, is not clear. Dr. Ebrard, who shows himself throughout his great admirer and zealous apologist, puts him in this respect on a higher ground than I have assigned to him in the *Mystical Presence*. His idea is that Zuingli all along regarded an inward union with Christ's life, as the necessary foundation of all the grace that is brought nigh to us in the Lord's Supper, and that it was only his fear of losing the other interests that led him, in the pressure of controversy, to thrust it more and more out of sight. How precisely this may have been, I will not pretend to say; Ebrard brings forward some strong passages, it must be confessed, from his earlier writings, in support of what he supposes; and it would be a great satisfaction certainly to have the point fully established, in favor of a man whose memory has so many claims on our affectionate respect. There is much, however, in the case to create perplexity and doubt, and it is not easy to forget the unfavorable judgment given him by Calvin. But so much in any view we owe to his great name, not to estimate his position from relations that come into view only after his death, but to take him as he stood, in the first stadium of the sacramental controversy, and entangled in the false *Gegensatz* ["opposition"], or issue which it carried in his controversy with Luther. As we have no right to burden a father of the third century with Christological consequences that hang on new issues created in the fourth, so also it is unbecoming to saddle Zuingli with sacramental consequences, that come fairly and fully into view, only under a wholly new phase of the controversy in the days of Calvin and Joachim Westphal.[5] The Calvinistic issue was never clearly presented either to him or Luther. Had it been exhibited in full form at the conference at Marburg, it is by no means improbable that it would have brought both these patriarchs of the Reformation to join hands on the same ground; unless indeed the pride of *committal*, strong as we all know ever in partially sanctified minds, might have stood in the way. But this could not well be, in the process of the controversy itself. That first abrupt antagonism was itself needed, to make room for

---

5. [Joachim Westphal (1510–74) was a fiery Lutheran minister adamantly opposed to the Swiss position, who remained an opponent of the later Calvinistic view arguing that there was no appreciable difference. A recent work that gives particular attention to the debates between Westphal, Heshusius, and Calvin on the Eucharist is Chung-Kim, *Inventing Authority.*—ed.]

the deep ironical view that followed. Still it is consoling to know, that neither Zuingli nor Luther ever distinctly negativated the sacramental doctrine of Calvin; for it was not properly at hand to them, for any such purpose. Zuingli, in this view, is no proper representative of the low rationalistic theory of the Lord's Supper, which is now so prevalent unhappily in our *evangelical* churches. It may indeed, well be doubted, as I have said in the *Mystical Presence*, "whether he could have been deliberately satisfied at all with the poor, bald conception, which is too often made to pass under the authority of his name at the present time."[6] My own full persuasion is that most of this modern thinking, as illustrated for instance in such a man as Dr. Kurtz, finds its true historical type, not in the genial faith of Zuingli, but in the far less respectable spiritualism of Andrew Bodenstein Carlstadt.

Luther and the Wittenberg Concord

The Marburg conference seemed, in one view, to be a failure. Luther and Zuingli parted, as they met, without agreement, each to appearance more firmly fixed than before in his own mind. In another view, however, the occasion was of vast importance. It made the parties better acquainted with each other than they had been previously. It brought the old controversy to its utmost tension; and in doing so opened the way for a salutary remission and pause, in which room was found for a new and better view of the whole question to take root extensively in the mind of the Church. It is remarkable, that both Oecolampadius and Melancthon, from this time seem, to have modified considerably their previous theories, approaching each other on what was felt to be deeper ground. Evidently indeed, in different directions, both in Germany and Switzerland, a tendency was at work towards a conception of the sacrament, which promised finally to reconcile and unite the interests so long divided in this unhappy conflict. Even Luther himself showed signs of being at least wearied with the strife, and in the end carried his concessions in favor of union much farther, than could have been expected of him at an earlier day.

The divines of Strasburg, with the excellent Bucer at their head, were particularly active in seeking such a reconciliation. Placed by geographical position *between* Saxony and Switzerland, and in intimate friendly communication with both, they were led to assume also, almost from the start, a sort of middle ground in the sacramental controversy, on which it became their great interest and endeavor subsequently to effect a junction of the Lutheran and Zuinglian views. Unfortunately, however, they had no clear insight into the nature of the real point of difference between these views, and the true sense of their own position as including in fact a real advance of the whole question to new and higher ground. So instead of addressing themselves to the business of an *inward* settlement of the difficulty, as they should have done, by proper exposition and criticism, we find them throughout laboring rather for a merely external reconciliation, in which the difficulty was to be simply hushed, or treated as though

---

6. [This quote appears in the *Mystical Presence* (p. 53, note 33 of the MTSS edition) in a long footnote about Zwingli.—ed.]

it did not exist.[7] Bucer tried to persuade himself that both sides in reality meant the same things, and then toiled heroically to bring them to the same opinion. The effort of course could not be successful; but it formed not withstanding a vastly important act in the progress of the great theological drama to which it belonged.

In the year 1530, the *Augsburg Confession* was formed. On the subject of the Lord's Supper, it affirmed, in the tenth article, that "the true body and blood of Christ are actually present, taken and received, under the form of bread and wine," (that is, under *both* forms, and not simply the form of bread as taught by the Romanists) in the sacred ordinance. It did not assert a local inclusion of the body and blood in the elements; avoided thus in truth Luther's conceit of an *oral* manducation; while, at the same time, it proclaimed, with proper antithesis to Zuingli's tendency to resolve all into a simply monumental character, the fact of an actually present fruition of the Savior's mediatorial life.

Southern Germany at the same time, under the guidance particularly of Bucer, presented a separate confession (the so called *Tetrapolitan*), in which Christ is said to give in the sacramental mystery his true body and blood, "to be truly eaten and drunk as the food and drink of souls, by which they may be nourished into everlasting life." This at once raises the mystery distinctly into the sphere of the spirit, and corresponds fully with the view of Calvin. It expressed, however, only the sense of the Augsburg confession itself, as it stood at least in Melancthon's mind; and we find the "four cities"[8] accordingly admitted, on this basis, to the general Lutheran confederation.

Zuingli's life was brought to an untimely end, soon after, a. 1531, on the bloody field of Cappel. Luther was so affected with the intelligence, as he tells us himself, that his sleep was turned into a night of weeping and tears. Alas that he had not wept sooner, when challenged by the streaming eyes of Zuingli at their only meeting in Marburg![9]

Now followed, through a series of years, the well meant, but badly conducted, negotiations of Bucer, to effect a general concord. These we have not room here, of course, to follow in detail. First, it was necessary to satisfy Luther, that the Tetrapolitan confession itself involved no essential variation from that of Augsburg. Next we have Bucer, on his first campaign, a. 1533, in Zurich, trying to persuade the Helvetic divines, that they might easily come to a similar pacification. They were too honest, however, to fall in with his imagination that the difference could be thus reduced to nothing; and charged him with being unfair either to them or Luther, in pretending to agree with both. After proper preliminary preparations, we find him, a. 1535, again on the field; negotiating

7. [Rahn-Clemens will show that Bucer was well supported by the likes of Melanchthon, Vermigli, Zanchi, and others all laboring in the cause of unity, and that it might be somewhat simplistic to broadly paint the early affair as fixated on mere externals ("Foundations of German Reformed Worship").—ed.]

8. [Strasbourg, Memmingen, Lindau, and Constance—hence the name "Tetrapolitan."—ed.]

9. [Thompson and Bricker wrote: "This is heavily romanticized. Luther had no love for Zwingli in any respect, and considered his death a matter of divine judgment. See Roland H. Bainton, *Here I Stand*, 322" (p. 419).—ed.]

now with Melancthon and Luther; coming to the result finally of the "Declaration of Cassel," in which the bread and wine were said to be *exhibitive* signs involving, by *sacramental* union, the simultaneous presence of Christ's flesh and blood. Then came the third and last campaign, a. 1536, resulting in the celebrated Concord of Wittenberg. The object was first to unite the Helvetic Church in the Cassel declaration. Switzerland, at this time, was not itself of one mind. Nearest to Strasburg stood Basel, whose First Confession, as drawn up by Oecolampadius, contained in truth the very view of Bucer. Zurich was more disposed to adhere to the Zuinglian conception, though favorably inclined also to the project of union. Bern for a time clung most stiffly of all to Zuingli's particular stand point, under the influence especially of Megander:[10] a zealot on the Swiss side, who may be taken as a fair counterpart to Westphal subsequently on the Lutheran side. A strong counter influence, however, gained ground here also, more and more. Finally, Bucer and Capito[11] were empowered to represent the general Helvetic church, and to negotiate on its behalf articles of agreement with Luther and the Saxon divines, on the basis substantially of the First Helvetic Confession published a short time before. This negotiation led to the Wittenberg Concord; a contradictory formula, which first denies the local inclusion of the body of Christ in the bread, and then asserts that it is truly received with it by unbelievers as well as believers.

To *such* a concord, of course, Switzerland could not consent; and all pains were taken to let the fact be known. A delegation waited on Bucer from Basel, to protest. Eight days he labored to satisfy them; but in vain. Grynaeus[12] told him plainly, that he wrested the sense of Luther in trying to bring it into harmony with that of the Helvetic church. Then came new public transactions in Switzerland; in which Bucer labored still in vain to reconcile the Swiss to his construction of the Wittenberg Concord. At last, it was determined to write to Luther himself on the subject, and get his sense as it were directly from his own mouth. Honest Helvetians! How little evidence we see in all these transactions of a disposition to "conciliate Luther," at the cost of truth and sincerity, or to bend and strain their own true creed, as much as possible, "to meet the views of the Lutherans," or to frame confessions "for the express purpose of compromise;" according to the general charge preferred by Dr. Hodge, against the whole Reformed Church of this period. Clearly their great care was to avoid every sort of misunderstanding, as well to shun even the most remote implication in what they conceived to

10. [Kasper Grossmann (Megander), 1495–1545. Megander was devoted to a Zwinglian perspective. He became a fierce opponent of Bucer, such that in spite of the Wittenberg Concord and the resulting revised catechism, Megander refused to accept the alterations and returned to Zurich to continue his resistance to the efforts of Bucer.—ed.]

11. [Wolfgang Capito (1478–1541), Protestant Reformer whose given name was Kopfel; he was a close associate of Bucer at Strasbourg. Educated at Freiberg, he came under the influence of Erasmus, which led him to an admiration of Luther. His temperament was such that he practiced a tolerant approach in applying the principles of the Reformation. See Kitchen, *Wolfgang Capito*.—ed.]

12. [Simon Gryner (Grynaeus), 1493–1541. A schoolmate of Melanchthon, he was a significant contributor to the First Helvetic Confession and urged acceptance of the Wittenberg Concord. He was the only representative of the Swiss at Worms. After visiting Melanchthon in Wittenberg, he became professor of Greek in Heidelberg (1524). He favored Zwingli's view of the Eucharist and corresponded with Oecolampadius.—ed.]

be the great error of Luther's doctrine, the idea namely of anything like a local presence or oral manducation in the mystery of the holy supper.

In the letter to Luther now mentioned, the Swiss divines laid before him a copy of Bucer's exposition of the Concord, and declared that if *this* were its true sense, they were ready to accept its articles. Then, to cut off all possible mistake, they state their general creed, and their view of the Lord's Supper in particular. In this sacrament, they say, "the main thing is God's gift, namely the body and blood of Christ, yea the *body which has been delivered to death for us, and the blood which has been shed on the cross to wash away our sins.*"—"We deny not that the body and blood of Christ are eaten and enjoyed, in the Supper, as the food of souls and unto eternal life. But this have we with our predecessors denied, and deny it still to *this* day, that the body of Christ is eaten in itself corporeally or as flesh, or that he is everywhere present with his body in a corporeal and natural way."

This letter was carried to Luther by Bucer himself. His answer came nine months afterwards; respectful and friendly; and, strangely enough, acquiescing in their explanation and position.

Thus the old controversy came to at least a sort of outward pacification, which continued in force subsequently for fifteen years. During this calm, time and opportunity were allowed for the quiet development of what may be denominated the Melancthonian and Calvinistic theory, in opposition to crass Lutheranism on the one side and crass Zuinglianism on the other. The way was already open, in different directions, for this auspicious advance. There was indeed a portion of the Swiss Church, represented by such men as Megander, which was disposed to cling to the separate standpoint of Zuingli, even when it was becoming clear that it needed to be made complete, by admitting the presence of Christ's *life* in the sacrament, though not in Luther's sense; but the other deeper view, as held by men like Oecolampadius, Myconius,[13] Grynaeus, and we will add Bullinger also, and as we have it exhibited in the First and Second Confessions of Basel (See *Myst. Pres.* p. 65–67)[14] was gradually unfolding itself, at the same time, more or less clearly also, on all sides, in the general consciousness. The Helvetic Church is exhibited to us under an aspect of confusion (not without some contradiction), in the process of an inward transition towards the true Reformed creed as subsequently spoken with clear full voice, not of course with

---

13. [Oswald Myconius (1488–1552), formerly Geisshäusler, a humanist Swiss Reformer who studied at Basel before going to Zurich. He was forced from Lucerne because of his Protestant convictions, returning to Zurich to become an important collaborator with Zwingli. He succeeded Oecolampadius in Basel and remained there until the end of his life. Myconius was both revered and scorned for his attempts at reconciliation with the Lutherans.—ed]

14. [See MTSS edition, pp. 55–57. Nevin is referring to the developing idea of the communication of Christ's actual life: "But the mystical supper is that in which the Lord offers His body and His blood, that is, His own self truly to His own, for this purpose, that he might live more and more in them and they in Him," "The First Helvetic Confession" (also known as the Second Confession of Basel), in Dennison, *Reformed Confessions*, 1:349.—ed.]

the abandonment of Zuingli's doctrine as absolutely false, but so as to save its true force rather in a higher conception and definition.[15]

This is *not* the period then to which we are to look primarily, for finally definitive testimony in regard to the sacramental doctrine of the Reformed Church in the sixteenth century. To make it the measure of interpretation for the period immediately following, is to do violence to all history. The Church gained a new stadium, by the ministry of Calvin. He did not indeed create or originate its faith; but he was beyond all controversy, the organ or medium, by which it came at last to its full expression.

"To learn the true character of the Eucharistic doctrine of the Reformed Church in the sixteenth century," I repeat from the *Mystical Presence,*

> we must have recourse to the time when the doctrine had become properly defined and settled in the Church itself. The representations of this period are not to be ruled and interpreted by statements drawn from an earlier day, but on the contrary, these earlier statements, springing as they do from a comparatively rudimental state of Protestant theology, must be of right interpreted and ruled by the form in which the doctrine is made to appear afterwards, when the same theology had become more complete. This later form of the doctrine moreover, as developed and enforced especially by Calvin, is the same which is found to carry in the symbolical books of the Church generally, and in this view again must be regarded of course as of paramount and exclusive authority in the present inquiry.—pp.64–65.[16]

"Dr. Nevin *chooses* to make Calvin the great authority," says Dr. Hodge—as though all hung here on arbitrary hypothesis. He might as well speak of my choosing, to make General Washington the father of his country, in the American Revolution. It is history here that speaks, and we are bound to regard her voice.

With this preparation we pass on now to the doctrines of the mystical or spiritual real presence, as held and taught by the great reformer of Geneva.

---

15 [Nevin intends to stress that the older confession was not abandoned willy-nilly, but was, as the German theologians of the day said, sublimated into the new emerging doctrine, while maintaining continuity with the older view. Nevin's historicist suggestion that the confession itself was evolving and growing into maturity was something Hodge could not abide.—ed.]

16. [MTSS edition, p. 54.—ed.]

5

Sacramental Doctrine of Calvin[1]

M R. EDITOR:
The following article is long; but it seemed desirable to condense the whole
question, as regards Calvin separately, into a single view. I applied to one of our religious reviews (*not* the *Repertory*) for permission to publish an article, in its columns
simply on the *historical* question.[2] But it was politely refused, for fear of giving offence
and provoking controversy. Our evangelical press, in part at least, seems strangely dis-
inclined to let the voice of history come, in this sense, to any fair hearing.

J. W. N.

HISTORICAL EXCURSUS, CONTINUED [NEVIN]

We have glanced rapidly over the *first* section of the sacramental history of the sixteenth century, extending from the birth of the Reformation to the formation of the
Wittenberg Concord, in the year 1536. The whole controversy, through this period,
turned on the antithesis or issue first joined between Zuingli and Luther. The first,
in opposing the mass, had been led to press the simply monumental side of the holy
mystery; the second, by his inward and outward relations, had his mind more turned
towards its mystical, directly life-giving value for the individual worshipper. Zuingli
insisted on the *sacrifice* of Christ as the great object of appropriation in the ordinance;
Luther on the presence of his glorified *life*. Both had a right on their side, so far as
their main positions were concerned; but each fell into wrong again, in refusing to
recognize and admit the truth maintained by the other. To save his conception, Luther
required a sort of *outward* entrance of Christ's life into ours; it must be by the mouth,
and independently even of faith. This Zuingli, with good reason, rejected. Such participation seemed to him carnal and useless. What we need in Christ is his sacrifice

---

1. ["Dr. Hodge on the *Mystical Presence*, Article from the Repertory, Continued, No. 5," *Weekly Messenger*, New Series, vol. 13, no. 41. Wednesday, June 21, 1848. Published by the Board of the Synod of the German Reformed Church: Chambersburg, PA.—ed.]

2. [Again, this is what will appear in the *Mercersburg Review* as "The Doctrine of the Reformed Church on the Lord's Supper" (1850), and was published along with the *Mystical Presence* as volume 1 of this series.—ed.]

already made for sin; this we reach by faith; which is the only organ of communication with him in the Lord's Supper, as well as in all other acts of worship. The words of institution he made accordingly to be figurative; and in this he was right; they do refer certainly to the power of his death immediately, and not to the idea of his glorified life. Luther's exegesis here was always pedantic and violent in the extreme. But was it necessary for the two views absolutely to exclude each other?

The controversy, in this first form, in due time spent its force. We find it lulled to rest finally in the Wittenberg Concord. Zuingli had gone to his reward. Luther never came to a clear sense of the precise defect of his own system; but evidently he had some misgivings in relation to it, which prevented him from taking any firm stand against the new tendency, that was silently at work on all sides, during the latter part of his life. When he met with Calvin's view of the subject, he remarked that if the controversy had been managed in *this* style, it might long since have been adjusted without trouble. Then a year after the date of the Concord, a. 1546, he fell asleep in Jesus.

Oecolampadius and Melancthon

Meanwhile, as already intimated, a *new* view of the sacramental presence was quietly striking its roots into the consciousness of the Protestant world, and mounting upwards to mature strength. This was not confined to any one section of the Church, but comes before us rather as the spontaneous product of its general life, starting forth at various points from the fermenting process which had gone before. We find it widely active in the German Church, under the banner of the Augsburg Confession. Its main representative here was Melancthon himself, the author of the confession; and one striking evidence of it, is exhibited to us in the alteration introduced into the tenth article of this symbol, by his own hand. The alteration simply expressed the sense of the article, as understood by himself, in its first form; and that he was not singular at all in such view, appears from the fact that the alteration was at once very generally accepted as fully right and valid. And yet the article, so defined, makes no account of a local presence or oral communication whatever. It simply affirms the *fact* of a real participation in Christ's mediatorial life, without determining the *mode*. It soon appeared, that a large part of the Lutheran Church rested in this Melancthonian view as the only proper sense of the Augsburg Confession. In the Helvetic Church, as we have seen, there was a parallel movement, that served to bring in gradually a very material modification of the Zuinglian doctrine. The significance of the Eucharist as a memorial of Christ's sacrifice was still insisted on as at first; but attention was now turned besides, more than in the beginning; to the idea of a real participation in his life, as the necessary condition and support of the other interest. The question came into view: Admitting our communion with Christ here to be, not by the mouth but only by faith, not in the flesh but only by the Spirit, does it not still involve in this way an actual appropriation of the life or substance of his person, as the bearer of his merit and righteousness? How Zuingli might have replied to this question, sundered entirely from the old Lutheran antithesis, is not clear; it was not properly the issue on which he was called to pronounce. We know, however, how it was answered by Oecolampadius, in the latter part of his life. We know too, that his view, as expressed for instance in the First Confession of Basel, became always more and more predominant as the true sense of the original Helvetic faith.

"We firmly believe," it is said in this Confession,

> that Christ himself is the food of believing souls unto eternal life; and that our souls, by true faith upon Christ crucified, are made to eat and drink the flesh and blood of Christ; so that we, members of his body as our only head, live in him as he also lives in us; whereby we shall at the last day, by him and in him, rise to everlasting joy and blessedness.[3]

As in the Lutheran Church we meet afterwards an interest, led by such men as Westphal and Hesshuss, which violently refused to quit the old Lutheran standpoint, even after it had become plain that it could be made complete only by being advanced to the ground occupied by Melancthon; so in the Swiss Church also a like one-sided tenacity of the past discovered itself, in men like Megander, against the corresponding advance of which we now speak. This gave rise to a good deal of confusion and contradiction. Megandrian Zuinglianism and Flaccian Lutheranism[4] are the opposite sides of the old antithesis, refusing to follow now the stream of history towards a true union of these divided interests in a higher view. That higher view, as it comes out at last in its full proportions, may be denominated Melanchthonian Calvinism.

Calvin did not create this system, and then convert the Swiss Church to it as a new theory. Nothing can well be more unhistorical, than to conceive of the Helvetic divines, with Bullinger at their head, as standing, down to the time of the *Consensus Tigurinus* for instance, in the same relation precisely to the sacramental question, in which they stood at Zuingli's death. The question in fact was no longer the same, and as a general thing they were no longer on the same ground. Zuinglian still, so far as the old issue went, they felt very widely the necessity of so extending their system as to include in it the substance also of what had been contended for by Luther. In these circumstances it was, that Calvin, admirably formed for such service by the whole constitution of his mind, became the distinguished organ in God's hands for unfolding into clear and full statement the sense which the Church was struggling to reach; all with so happy a success, that Zuinglianism was brought in a very short time to surmount itself completely in the true position of the Reformed Church, as we have it embodied subsequently in all the symbolical books of that age.[5]

3. [See Dennison, *Reformed Confessions*, 1:291.—ed.]

4. [Matthias Flacius (1520–75) was a Lutheran theologian who joined Luther and Melanchthon in Wittenberg and became a professor of Hebrew. He came to reject the milder teachings of Augsburg and the consensus building done by Melanchthon, asserting himself as a strict dogmatist, which resulted in his ejection from Wittenberg by Melanchthon.—ed.]

5. [Perhaps it is not so clear as Nevin would like it. Gerrish records Calvin's subtle changes of position in the editions of the *Institutes*. "He seemed to stumble between the rival opinions of Luther and Zwingli rather than harmonize them, wavering on both the Real Presence and sacramental causality." But neither Nevin nor Hodge should be blamed, as the sixteenth-century confusion over Calvin's position is mirrored as much today as then. And as the question of causality frustrated Calvin's contemporaries, it

"This view," says Professor Ebrard,

> was not brought in, as modern polemics may represent, in the way of temporary
> compliance towards the Lutherans, as though the Reformed Church had to thank
> the Lutheran for such a morsel of truth as she came thus to possess; but we find
> it, long before Bucer's negotiations, independently uttered by Oecolampadius in
> the *Confessio Mylhusiana*,[6] and Calvin independently also brought it with him
> from France.

Calvinistic Theory

Calvin published the first edition of his *Institutes*, a. 1535, in the twenty-sixth year of
his age, and before he had come into connection with either the Lutheran or Helvetic
system of thinking. Here we find very distinctly stated, the sacramental doctrine which
he continued to hold to the end of his life. With Zuingli, he rejects every idea of a *local*
presence, and places Christ's body circumscriptively at the right hand of God;[7] but will
not allow this to stand in the way at all of a real communication of his mediatorial life
to our persons. With Luther, he asserts an actual presence of Christ's life in the sacrament; but he will not admit the thought of any corporeal ubiquity for this purpose.
The mystery transcends all the conditions of common natural experience; falls not
within the sphere of sense; holds out of space and above it; and is not therefore to be
apprehended or explained by the natural understanding. It is effected, superlocally, by
the spirit. Christ's flesh and blood are at hand, not in the bread and wine as such, but
in the transaction; not materially or by mechanical contact in space, but *dynamically*,
in the way of living substance and power; not for the outward man primarily and
separately, as Luther contended, but for the *soul* (by no means to be confounded here
with mere understanding or mind), as the central life of the whole person, so as to flow
out from this to the *body* also as the true pabulum of immortality. The circumscription
of Christ's person, says Calvin, soaring in this thought above both Luther and Zuingli,
is not to impose any restriction on his activity;

> that he should not put forth his energy wherever he may please, in heaven or on
> earth; or exhibit himself as present in power and virtue; or be always at hand to

---

frustrates his interpreters today. Had he had his way, he would have turned the debate away from the
question of how is it we swallow Christ's body, to the infinitely more important question of "why is there
a Lord's Supper at all?" See Gerrish, *Grace and Gratitude*, 10, 13.—ed.]

6. [Or First Confession of Basel (*Confessio Fidei Basileensis prior*), of which the first draft was prepared by Oecolampadius, then edited by Oswald Myconius the following year (1532) and finally published in 1534 with a preface by Adelberg Meyer. By 1537 it was adopted by the city of Mühlhausen,
hence the name *Confessio Mühlhusana* (or *Mylhusiana*). It is moderate in temperament and asserts that
Jesus Christ is the food of the soul that leads to everlasting life. For a modern translation see Dennison,
Reformed Confessions, 1:286–96.—ed.]

7. [Calvin accepted Zwingli's view that the Lord's ascension is crucial in understanding what hap-
pened in the Supper. If Jesus is in heaven he cannot be "enclosed" on earth in the bread. This made a
literal consumption impossible. Thus the bread and wine are analogous and the eating is spiritual. See
Gerrish, *Grace and Gratitude*, 9.—ed.]

his people; live in them, sustain, confirm, quicken and preserve them, as fully as though he were at hand in the body.[8]

It is easy of course, to turn all this into the common place thought, that Christ, by his Spirit or in virtue of his divinity, sways a universal empire in the Church from which his proper human life is excluded; but no one at all familiar with Calvin, can suppose *him* to be chargeable with any such frigid sense in the use of such strong language. He means to assert a real presence of Christ's full mediatorial being, only under a superlocal order of existence. Those who choose to do so, may pronounce this unintelligible mysticism;[9] our business here is not to defend it, but only to represent it as a historical fact. And yet, why should it be deemed so incredible for Him, who is raised in our nature over all material limitations (in the *full* sense of the eighth psalm, the whole world under his feet), to reveal the force of his entire being wherever he may please? Have we not analogies enough even in our present natural sphere, to show that the separation in space is no bar whatever to the most intimate and complete *dynamic* union? Is not the root of the tree *in* its branches, and the head of the body *in* its members, far more really than they could possibly be by any mechanical juxtaposition or conjunction? See *Myst. Presence*, p. 172, 173.[10] To the profound and comprehensive mind of the great Christian philosopher, Leibnitz,[11] this idea carried no absurdity or insuperable difficulty whatever. The true reconciliation of the two confessions, Reformed and Lutheran, he finds just in this; "that the substance of the body consists in its *primitive power*, active and passive, and that the immediate application of this power forms the *presence* of such substance, *even without dimensions*."[12] It is a

8 [Nevin:] *Hoc regnum nec ullis locorum spatiis limitatum, nec ullis dimensionibus circumscriptum, quin Christus virtutem suam, ubicunque placuerit, in coelo et in terra exerat, quinse praesentem potentia ac virtute exhibeat, quin suis semper adsit, in iis vivat, eos sustineat, confirmet, vegetet, conservet,* non secus acsi corpora adesset. *Instit. ed. prim.* p. 246; as quoted by Henry. ["This Kingdom is neither bounded by location in space nor circumscribed by any limits. Thus Christ is not prevented from exerting his power wherever he pleases, in heaven and on earth. He shows his presence in power and strength, *is always* among his own people, . . . and *lives* in them, sustaining them, strengthening, quickening, keeping them unharmed, *as if he were present in the body*." Calvin, *Institutes*, ed. McNeill, 2:1381. The allusion to Henry is to Paul Henry, *Das Leben Johann Calvins*, 3 vols. (Hamburg: Perthes, 1835–44). An English translation by Henry Stebbing was published, *The Life and Times of John Calvin, the Great Reformer* (London: Whittaker, 1849).—ed.]

9. ["The suspicion has never quite been laid to rest that even when Calvin's language appears to affirm a real presence and the efficacy of the sacred signs, he could not honestly have meant it." Gerrish, *Grace and Gratitude*, 9. —ed.]

10. [MTSS edition, pp. 153–54.—ed.]

11. [Gottfried Wilhelm Leibniz (1646–1716), German philosopher, scientist, mathematician, historian, and diplomat. He is perhaps best known today for his philosophical monism. He viewed God's creation as a harmonious whole, which was undoubtedly a feature that attracted Nevin to his philosophy. His book on theodicy, *Essais de Théodicée sur la bonté de Dieu, la liberté de l'homme et l'origine du mal* (Amsterdam, 1710), while unsystematic, was a compilation of his views over many years. While both transubstantiation and consubstantiation harmonize with his theory of substance, Nevin believed it was Calvin's theory that best suited Leibniz's views. Both Nevin and Ebrard were attracted to the philosophy of Leibniz.—ed.]

12. [Nevin:] *Pensees de Leibnitz*, Paris 1803, p. 106, as quoted by Ebrard [*Das Dogma*, II:413—ed.]: *que la substance du corps consiste dans la puissance primitive, active et passive, et que c'est dans l'application*

most low view of the body, in any case, to make it consist of given quantum matter in space; its fundamental character is found only in the psychic force which comes to its revelation in this form. So Calvin saw and felt; and in such view it is, that he rejects the crass notion of Luther; not to sunder the body of Christ from the mystery of the holy Eucharist, but only make the one more sure of its presence in its true vital energy and virtue.

Soon after, a. 1536, we find Calvin settled in Geneva. A very important ecclesiastical convention, the so called *September Synod*, was held the following year, a. 1537, at Bern. On this occasion, the three Geneva divines, Farel,[13] Calvin and Viret,[14] presented their memorable "confession of faith in regard to the Eucharist" (quoted, *Myst. Pres.* p. 124).[15] It well deserves here our special attention. "The spiritual life which Christ bestows upon us," it is here affirmed, "consists not merely in this, that he vivifies us *by his Spirit*, but that by the power of his Spirit also he makes us to partake of his *life-giving flesh* (*carnis suae vivificae*) by which participation we are fed unto everlasting life."[16]

This is the Calvinistic *mystical union*, as it enters into the general Christian life. It holds only through the soul, as the proper center of the new man, and is wrought by the Spirit in conjunction with the activity of faith; but it is notwithstanding a real making over of Christ's human life dynamically to his people, in such a way that this is carried out into their bodies also as the principle of the resurrection and the pabulum of immortality. How far this goes beyond the notion of the mystical union as held by Dr. Hodge, I need not say. Calvin shows here a clear sense of the central unity of our life, as embracing corporeity and spirituality at last in the form of a single fact; and it

---

immediate de cette puissance que consiste la presence de la substance, meme sans dimensions. Gerrish wrote in *Grace and Gratitude* that Leibniz took an interest in Protestant/Catholic relations and felt that Calvin "was moving toward a fresh conception of the substance of Christ's body precisely as its force or power, so that the substance is present, albeit in a non dimensional way, wherever its power is applied. This conception, Leibnitz believed, held out the best prospect for harmony between the two Protestant confessions." This, says Gerrish, was brought out by the German theologian Ebrard, but Gerrish said he could not find the source of the quote which Ebrard cited as "Leibniz, *Pensees sur la religion et la morale*, 2d ed. (Paris: Nyon, 1803), 106." This is as Nevin has it. Yet Gerrish says in his footnote that he had seen a later edition of the *Pensees* where he found the quote (2 vols. Brussels: Societe Nationale pour las Propagation des Bons Livres, 1838, page 322 of volume 1.) The *Pensees* described the selection as an extract from a letter to Fabricius. Gerrish writes that Ebrard, drawing from the conclusion of Leibniz, believed that Calvin was able to merge the Lutheran idea of real union with the body of Christ and the Zwinglian idea of the material circumscription of Christ's body (Ebrard, 2:413; Gerrish, 180).—ed.]

13. [Guillaume Farel (1489–1565), influential Reformer of Switzerland; he became interested in Protestant thinking in Paris and was banished under the suspicion he was a follower of Luther. While in Basel he criticized Erasmus and again was forced to leave. In 1535 he and Pierre Viret successfully established Geneva in the Reformed faith. The very next year he convinced Calvin, as he journeyed through Geneva, to join him in the struggle. From that time on the fates of the two were intertwined. See Bruening, *Calvinism's First Battleground*.—ed.]

14. [Pierre (Peter) Viret (1511–71), a Swissman who studied in Paris, came under Farel's influence in 1531, was ordained by Farel, and in 1533 became his assistant in Geneva. Later he became a major leader of the French Reformed Church. See Berthoud, *Pierre Viret*.—ed.]

15. [MTSS edition, p. 110, note 23.—ed.]

16. [See "Confession of Faith concerning the Eucharist," in Reid, ed., *Calvin: Theological Treatises*, 168.—ed.]

is only the stubborn dualism which too generally characterizes our modern thinking, that makes it so hard for many to get at his sense. Our union with Christ is not outward or mechanical; it rests in no local descent of contact; but it is in the fullest sense vital, and involves an actual organic reproduction or birth in us of his very life. So the confession goes on: "When therefore we speak of the communion which believers have with Christ, we mean that they *communicated with his flesh and blood not less than with his Spirit,* so as to possess thus the *whole Christ.*" This is said to be clearly the sense of the Scriptures, & it is added: "Nor is it a small or common thing the apostle teaches, when he asserts that we are *flesh of Christ's flesh and bone of his bones,* but he so designates the admirable *mystery* of our communion with his *body,* which no one may adequately describe in words."[17]

All this, it is next said, requires no *local* presence; "for the efficacy of his Spirit is not so limited by any bounds, but that he can *truly copulate and gather into one,* things that are locally disjoined. We acknowledge accordingly that his Spirit is the bond of our participation in him"—not so however, let it be well noticed, as if the Spirit simply flowed here from Christ to us in an outward way, leaving *his* proper life behind, in the way represented by Dr. Hodge—"but so, that he *feeds us truly with the substance of the Lord's flesh and blood* unto *immortality* and vivifies us by *their* participation."[18] Then comes the relation of the general mystery to the Eucharist: "This communion of his flesh and blood, Christ *offers and presents* in his holy supper, under the symbols of bread and wine, to all who rightly attend upon it in its proper character."[19] Here is the

17. [See ibid., 168.—ed.]

18. [See ibid., 168.—ed.]

19. [Nevin:] *Vitam spiritualem quam nobis Christus largitur, non in eo duntaxat sitam esse confitemur, quod spiritu suo nos vivificat, sed quod spiritus eitiam sui virtute carnis suae vivificae nos lacit participes, qua participatione in vitam aeternam pascamur. Itaque cum de communione, quam cum Christo, fideles habent, loquimur, non minus carni et sanguini ejus communicare ipsos intelligemus, quam spiritui, ut ita totum Christum possideant. Siquidem cum asserte testetur scriptura, carnem Christi vere nobis esse cibum, et sanguine ejus vere potum, ipsis vero nos educari opotere constat, si vitam in Christo quaerimus. Jam nec exiguum quiddam aut vulgare docet apostolus, cum nos carnem de Christi carne et ossa de ossibus ejus esse asserit, sed eximium nostrae cum ipsius corpore communionis mysterium ita designat, quod nullus verbis satis pro dignitate exlicare queat. Ceterum istis nihil repugnant, quod Dominus noster in coelum sublatus, localem corporis sui praesentiam nobis abstulit, quae hic minime exigitur. Nam utcunque nos in hac mortalitate perigrinantes in eodem loco cum ipso non includimur aut continemur, nullis tamen finibus limitata est ejus spiritus efficacia, quin vere copulare et in unum colligere possit, quae locorum spatiis sunt disjuncta. Ergo spiritum ejus vinculum esse nostrae cum ipso participationis agnoscimus, sed ita, ut nos ille carnis et sanguinis Domini substantia vera ad immortalitatem pascat, et eorum participatione vivificet. Hanc autem carnis et sanguinis sui communionem Christus sub panis et vini symbolis in sacrosancta sua coena offert et exhibet omnibus, qui eam rite celebrant juxta legitimum ejus institutum.* Henry, *Leben Calv. I. Beilage 5.* [See Henry, *Das Leben,* vol. 1, appendix 5. Trans. "We confess that the spiritual life which Christ bestows upon us does not rest on the fact that he vivifies us with his Spirit, but that his Spirit makes us participants in the virtue of his vivifying body, by which participation we are fed on eternal life. Hence when we speak of the communion which we have with Christ, we understand the faithful to communicate not less in his body and blood than in his Spirit, so that thus they possess the whole Christ. Now Scripture manifestly declares the body of Christ to be verily food for us and his blood verily drink. It thereby affirms that we ought to be truly nourished by them, if we seek life in Christ. It is no small or common thing that the apostle teaches, when he asserts that we are flesh of Christ's flesh and bone of his bone. Rather he points out the great mystery of our communion with his body, whose sublimity no one

objective force of the sacrament, recognized in full. It is a real *act,* on the side of Christ. Along with the outward service, proceeds an inward divine mystery, *actus in actu,*[20] of which the outward is to be regarded as the symbol and pledge. Christ "offers and presents," in a real way, the very thing (viz., the living and vivific virtue of his flesh and blood) which the elements of bread and wine externally represent.

This confession is exceedingly important. It was presented to a synod of the Helvetic Church, fully alive on all sides to the bearing and force of its several positions, and by no means disposed to fall blindly over into Luther's arms. A strong Megandrian interest prevailed in Bern, and just at this time no small amount of prejudice was roused by the negotiations connected with the Wittenberg Concord. Bucer and Capito found it necessary to attend the synod, in their own defense. The subject led to large discussion and debate. Such, however, was the prevailing tendency, that in the end the scale turned, even here in Bern, in favor of Bucer's view. Megander felt himself defeated. He had formed a Catechism, in which the Lord's Supper was declared to be a mere *memorial* of Christ's death; this the Synod ordered to be changed; and another section was substituted for this part of it accordingly, not long after, composed by Bucer. "The epidemic of Bucerism," it was said complainingly by Megander and his friends, "spread daily more and more." The Genevan divines stood openly of course on the same ground. Bucer and Capito subscribed their Eucharistic confession, and it became, in fact, an official act of union, "between the Strasburgers and the Swiss."

Calvin at Strasburg

Soon after, we find Calvin fairly in the bosom of the Lutheran Church itself. His banishment from Geneva, a. 1538, led him subsequently to Strasburg, where he was settled as minister and theological teacher for a period of between two and three years. Here of course he signed the Augsburg Confession.[21] It is not clear, whether in its altered or unaltered form; but this is a point of no consequence whatever, as the first only

---

is able to explain adequately in words. For the rest it is no contradiction with this that our Lord is exalted in heaven, and so has withdrawn the local presence of his body from us, which is not here required. For though we as pilgrims in mortality are neither included nor contained in the same space with him, yet the efficacy of his Spirit is limited by no bounds, but is able really to unite and bring together into one things that are disjoined in local space. Hence we acknowledge that his Spirit is the bond of our participation in him, but in such manner that he really feeds us with the substance of the body and blood of the Lord to everlasting life, and vivifies us by participation in them. This communion of his own body and blood Christ offers in his blessed Supper under the symbols of bread and wine, presenting them to all who rightly celebrate it according to his own proper institution." "Confession of Faith concerning the Eucharist," in Reid, ed., *Calvin: Theological Treatises* (Philadelphia: Westminster Press, 1954), 168.—ed.]

How any scholar can pretend to question Calvin's faith in a real life communication for believers in Christ's humanity in the face of such a passage, it is not easy to comprehend.

20. [Literally translated as, "The act within the act," in other words, "the divine act of the Holy Spirit which takes place within the liturgical act of the Eucharist." See Gerrish, *The Old Protestantism and the New,* 322.—ed.]

21. [Nevin:] *Nec vero Augustanam confessionem repudio, qui pridem volens ac lubens subsripsi, sicut eam autor ipse interpretatus est.* Letter to Schaling, a. 1557. [Trans. "Truly I, who previously subscribed willing and glad, do not reject the Augsburg Confession, just as the author himself explained it." Epistola 2607, *Corpus Reformatorum, Calvini Opera,* IX, 430.—ed.]

expressed the sense which was attached to the second by Melancthon himself. Calvin thus had no difficulty with either. He stood on common ground with Melancthon, Bucer, and a wide section of the Lutheran Church besides, and considered himself of the same confession without the least force put on his previous convictions. The case required no explanation, and cost no sort of trouble. And yet, as we have seen, the tenth article of the Augsburg Confession explicitly affirms, that the body and blood of Christ are truly presented, in the Lord's Supper, along with the bread and wine. Did Calvin play the hypocrite here? Or was he the clever church politician simply, paying outward court to Lutheran prejudice and power? It needs some courage, to say or think anything so bold as that.

More than this. During his settlement at Strasburg, Calvin is found entering, without the smallest embarrassment, into ecclesiastical relations and transactions of a wholly Lutheran character, as one fully naturalized and at home in his new church sphere. In 1539, he attended the Frankfort convention; in 1540, the conferences at Hagenau and Worms; 1541, the transactions at Regensburg, as a delegate from the Strasburg church, and was looked upon as altogether Lutheran, no less than Bucer himself. At Frankfort, he met first with Melancthon, and had full communication with him on the subject of the Lord's Supper. "He assured me," says Calvin, "that he had no other view than the one my words expressed." The two great men entered into a bond of the most intimate friendship, which lasted through life; with the full understanding that on the mystery of the real presence they thought alike.

So little however did Calvin find it necessary to conceal or modify his sacramental doctrine in Strasburg, in favor of Luther's theory, that we find him here writing and publishing on the whole subject exactly as before. The second edition of his *Institutes* was issued from this place. Here also he published his *Catechism*, in its last complete form; also his admirable tract *de Coena*, the great object of which was precisely to carry the whole question above the old Zuinglian and Lutheran antithesis, to the higher form in which this had come to an end in his own mind. Not the shadow of a wish do we see to *strain* the doctrine as he held it, either toward one side or the other.

The Catechism repeats in full the view presented at the September Synod in Bern. Quotations here would carry us too far. (See specimen, *Myst. Pres.* p. 70, 71.)[22] The Christian life is represented as holding always in the form of a mystical union with Christ, accomplished by the Spirit through the soul or central principle of our twofold life, but extending from this into the whole man; in the Lord's Supper, this communication, always only partial in our present state, is *confirmed* and *increased*; the bread and wine are symbols, of no power aside from the action of the Spirit, but along with them is offered really and truly the life-giving virtue of Christ's flesh and blood; they are not merely *significative*, but also *exhibitive*. Signs; whence the catechumen is made to say: "I do not doubt, but that as the words and signs testify, so he makes us *partakers also of his substance*, that we may *coalesce* with him into one life." By substance is meant of course, not matter in any sense, but the virtue & active energy in which pre-eminently,

22. [MTSS edition, pp. 60–61.—ed.]

Calvin supposes Christ's glorified body to consist. All again as a mystery, transcending the categories of space and sense; "by the miracle and hidden power of his Spirit, for whom it is not difficult to bind together things which are otherwise locally far apart."[23] We must look then not to the bread and wine as such, but to Christ in heaven; not however in the flat sense of reaching him only by our subjective thought and feeling; and still less in the dream of anything like real local ascent of the soul to his presence, such as some have charged Calvin with teaching, to make his theory absurd; but in such a way as to expect from him superlocally, and not from the local signs in any material mode, the objective grace of the holy sacrament, a true participation namely, by the mirific[24] power of the Holy Ghost, in the very substance of Christ's life. Such is the clear sense of Calvin's Catechism.

The tract *On the Supper* (*de Coena*) is only a more extended and minute exposition of the same doctrine (See Calv. OP. T. IX. pp. 1–9).[25] He blames both Luther and Zuingli, for pushing their separate views to an extreme. The elements are signs; but they are sure pledges also of the accompanying presence of the things they represent. Christ hangs out here no *false colors*.[26]

> We have a very fair parallel, in an analogous case. When the Lord was pleased to manifest his Spirit at Christ's baptism, he represented it under the figure of a dove. John the Baptist, narrating the event, says that he was the Holy Ghost descending. If we look at it closely, we will perceive that he *saw* nothing but the dove; for the essence of the Holy Spirit is invisible. As he knew however that the vision was no vain show, but the most sure sign of the presence of the Holy Spirit, he hesitates not to say that he saw it, as having been represented in such way as the case allowed. So in the communion which we have in Christ's flesh and blood, we must say, the mystery is spiritual, such as cannot be seen with the eyes nor comprehended by human understanding. It is shown to us accordingly by figures and signs that fall under the cognizance of sense, as is required by the imbecility of our nature; in such way however, that it is *not naked and simple figure*, but joined also *with its own truth and substance*. The bread thus is of right termed Body; since it not only represents this, but actually offers it to our use.[27]

Could any statement well be more explicit and clear? Calvin employs the same striking parallel elsewhere also, to illustrate his view of the mystical or sacramental presence.

---

23. [Calvin, "The Catechism of the Church of Geneva (1545)," in Reid, *Calvin: Theological Treatises*, 137.—ed.]

24. [I.e., performing miraculous acts.—ed.]

25. [The reference here is most likely to vol. 8 (not, in fact, IX) of the *Ioannis Calvini noviodunensis Opera omnia: In novem tomos digesta*, which contains his *Tractatus Theologici Omnes* (Amsterdam: John Jacob Schipper, 1667). The tract, entitled, "A Short Treatise on the Lord's Supper," can be found in Reid, *Calvin: Theological Treatises*, 142–66.—ed.]

26. [In Calvin's view, Zwingli's shortcoming was in "reducing" the sacraments to signs that "*attest*" our faith, instead of signs that "*strengthen*" our faith. However, Calvin appreciated Zwingli's position in its secondary role in which the sacraments are "a confession of faith." Gerrish, *Grace and Gratitude*, 186.—ed.]

27. [Ibid., 147—ed.]

"Calvin rendered an incalculable service here to the Church," says his biographer Henry,

> in directing the attention of one wide section of it to the force and power of the Lord's Supper, which some in Switzerland were disposed to turn into a mere commemoration. Millions of Christians in the Reformed Church owe it to him, that they have enjoyed the supper in its right sense, so as to partake in it of the true, spiritual, glorified Christ. His deep view moreover has almost everywhere become prevalent now in the Evangelical Church.[28]

This last remark is made of Germany of course, and not of our evangelical American churches. It is somewhat queer, that the same number of the *Princeton Repertory* which sinks the Reformed doctrine of the Eucharist so low, in its review of the *Mystical Presence*, has an article highly commendatory of *Calvin's Life* by Henry.[29]

The Consensus Tigurinus

Such was Calvin in Strasburg. In 1541, he was restored again to Geneva. Switzerland, in the mean time, continued to rise more and more to the proper ground, in regard to the sacraments. Bern had come to stand in great part with Strasburg; Basel leaned strongly the same way; only the small territory centering in Zurich refused to obey the onward movement, and seemed disposed to stick in Megandrian Zuinglianism, as the absolute truth. Calvin undertook now to bring up this interest to the proper line, and to unite thus the whole Helvetic Church in the same sacramental doctrine. In the face of such design indeed, an unfavorable reaction was created, towards the close of Luther's life, bearing strongly in the opposite direction. Still Calvin persevered mildly in his good endeavor. The case required, first of all, that he should come to a right understanding with Bullinger, the worthy and influential *antistes* or superintendent of Zurich. Bullinger held him in considerable suspicion, not knowing fully his sacramental views. This was allayed to some extent by proper correspondence. Finally, Bullinger invited him to a personal interview, on the subject, in Zurich. Calvin declared that no letter was ever more welcome to him than this; and two days after he was on his way to the place, in company with his friend Farel. The conference lasted several days, and resulted in the articles of the famous *Consensus Tigurinus*, which became now, a. 1549, the basis of agreement for the Swiss Church in general.

These articles go as far as the case could possibly allow towards the Helvetic side, in the old controversy; exclude distinctly Luther's local presence and oral communication; and lay marked stress on the sacrificial interest, as contended for by Zwingli [*sic*]. But it is not true that they involved, as ultra Lutherans have pretended, an abandonment of the ground previously occupied by Calvin himself in Strasburg and Geneva.

---

28. [Henry, *Das Leben.*—ed.]

29. [Nevin:] In this article the sacramental controversy of the 16th century is spoken of, as a foul excrescence simply on the Reformation; and Luther is said to have disgraced himself by his unexampled "revilings lavished on Zuingli and *Calvin*." The *Repertory* quietly assumes moreover that the Old Calvinistic faith here was just its own; which however, as we see from Henry himself, was by no means the case.

On the contrary, they show the triumph of Calvinism over what was still defective in the old Swiss view. Zuinglianism here completes itself publicly, by associating with its primary position distinctly the enunciation of the sacramental *life* mystery, as the necessary basis of all interest in the *sacrifice* to which the transaction refers. It is Bullinger that rises above his old position, as Farel had done before, in free obedience to the superior mind of Calvin; not Calvin that descends, as Dr. Hodge would seem to imagine, to common Megandrian ground.[30] Every such supposition as this last is unhistorical in the extreme. It turns Calvin into either a fool or a knave. No one however can suppose him a fool; it was not possible for such a man to make so great a transition, and not be aware of the change, if it actually occurred. It comes to this then, that he played a false game either at Strasburg or Zurich. The case is of too grave a character entirely, to be resolved into holy policy and skill. To say that Calvin played a part here, in such a style, is just to pronounce him an unworthy hypocrite throughout. All can see where he stood before, and where he continued to stand afterwards. Even Dr. Hodge himself is forced to admit, that he attributed a mystical efficacy of some sort to Christ's body, which *he* cannot allow or comprehend. And yet he will have it, that this *Consensus Tigurinus* is down to a full level, with the sacramental faith of our modern American churches generally! If it be so, Calvin was a crafty Jesuit indeed.

The seventh article is quoted by Dr. Hodge in such a way as to obscure (undesignedly of course) its true sense. Among other ends of the sacraments, it is there said,

> this one is the *principle*, that by them God may *attest, represent,* and *seal* to us his grace. For although they signify nothing different from what is announced in the word itself, it is still a *great thing,* that they are set before our eyes as if *living images,* that may the better affect our senses by conducting as it were to the thing; while they bring to mind the death of Christ and all his benefits, that faith may be the more exercised, and *besides this confirm and ratify, as with seals,* what God by his mouth declared.[31]

Dr. Hodge refers the idea of *sealing,* no doubt, to the general grace of God as proclaimed in the gospel. But it lies in the whole doctrine of Calvin as elsewhere declared, and also in the phraseology of the age, that it should be taken in the sense of an authentication of what is at hand mystically in the sacramental transaction itself. The elements have not merely a doctrinal, but also a *pignoral*[32] force (like the dove in the Baptist's vision), attesting the presence of Christ's life at the time, not locally but superlocally by the Spirit, for the fruition of all believing communicants. This accordingly is expressly asserted in the next article. "What the sacraments *figure* to our eyes and other senses, the Spirit truly works *within,* namely, that we first enjoy *Christ*

30. [Calvin was able to convince Bullinger of his adjusted position—that while the physical feasting on the body and blood of Christ occurs in the sacrament, an inward spiritual eating occurs at the same time. The adjustment represented a "weaker" but acceptable formula to the Swiss. "Where Calvin and Bullinger never agreed was over Calvin's belief that God performs the inward *through* the outward." Gerrish, *Grace and Gratitude,* 166–67.—ed.]

31. ["Mutual Consent," in Torrance, ed., *Tracts and Treatises,* 2:214.—ed.]

32. [I.e., having to do with a pledge.—ed.]

as the fountain of all blessings, and then are reconciled to God by the benefit of his death, &c." All of course depends on the invisible side of the transaction: the elements are "inanes larvae" ["worthless masks"—ed.] separately considered[33] (and the Baptist's dove was no better); but still the sacraments are *organs*, by which God works "efficaciously" where it seems good. Most plainly the *Consensus Tigurinus* understands by *signs, seals, fruition of Christ*, &c, something far more deep and real than the simply mental process into which all is resolved apparently by Dr. Hodge.

Let us hear however Calvin's own testimony on this point, as given officially in his *Exposition* attached to the articles of the Consensus by his own hand (*Op. T.* ix. pp. 653–659). Speaking of the concern of the Lutheran theologians for the idea of real divine *contents* in the sacramental mystery as distinguished from naked signs, he says:

> When they hear us confess on our side, that the sacraments are *neither empty figures, nor outward badges simply of piety*; but *seals of the promises of God efficaciously (efficaciter)*, works in his elect; and that the signs thus, although *distinct* from the things signified, are still not *disjoined* from them and *separate*; that they are given to ratify and confirm what God has promised by his word, and especially to *seal the mysterious communication we have with Christ*: surely there is no cause left, for thrusting us into the rank of enemies. When, as I have said, their cry is on all sides that they wish only this doctrine to stand good, namely, that God employs the sacraments as helps for promoting and increasing faith, that the promises of eternal salvation are *engraven on them* so as to be offered by them to our consciences, and that they are *not* empty signs, since God joins with them the *efficacy* of his Spirit; all these points granted, what is there to hinder now their cheerfully giving us their hand? And not to turn to secondary private authorities, *our readers will find in this* Consensus *all that is contained in the so called Augsburg Confession, as published at Regensburg*, provided only it is not strained, through fear of the cross, to please the papists. The words are: *In the holy supper, with the bread and wine are truly given Christ's body and blood.* Far be it from us, either to rob the Eucharistic symbol of its *truth*, or to deprive pious minds of such vast benefit. We say accordingly, lest our senses should be mocked with bread and wine, that *to their outward figure is joined this true effect*, that believers *there* receive the body and blood of Christ.[34]

So Calvin.[35]

---

33. [Nevin:] *Sed externae eorum representationi*, it is said in the *Exposition, conjunctam esse Spiritus efficacia*, ne inanes sint picturae. [Trans. "But that the efficacy of the Spirit is conjoined with their outward representation, *lest they should be empty pictures*." "Exposition of the Heads of Agreement," in Torrance, ed., *Tracts and Treatises*, 2:227.—ed.]

34. [See ibid. 224–25.—ed.]

35. [Nevin:] "By the terms of this agreement, it was now plain that the Swiss in the main matter were one with the Lutherans. For until this time there might be a doubt, whether they admitted in the Supper a true substance of Christ's body and blood, but now doubt was no longer possible. A true presence and a real participation of Christ's body was settled. The difference regarded only the manner in which Christ is present, the Lutheran view binding the Lord's body or its substance by miracle to the sign, the Calvinistic making the believer rise to Christ to be united with him; this rising however was only metaphorical, as Christ is spiritually present." *Das Leben von Calvin's*, Paul Henry, abridged edition, p. 278 [vol. 2, p. 472 of full edition cited above—ed.].

Is it not strange now to hear Dr. Hodge say: "In these articles there is not a word, which any of the evangelical churches of the present day would desire to alter? We should like to print them all as the confession of our own faith on this subject." Perfectly honest of course; but spoken from the standpoint of a very different consciousness, from that which reigned in the Reformed Church of the sixteenth century.[36]

Calvin and Westphal

Next comes the *second* great sacramental war, to which this *Consensus Tigurinus* served in part as an outward occasion; although its true cause lay much deeper, in the bosom of the Lutheran Church itself. The issue here was widely different from the old antithesis between Luther and Zuingli. Both parties move, to a great extent, under the common banner of the Augsburg Confession. The controversy lay between ultra Lutheranism, and the widely extended doctrine of Melancthon and Calvin; resulting finally in the formal rupture of the general Church into the distinction of Lutheran and Reformed. I have given some account of it in the *Mystical Presence*, and still more fully in my *History of the Heidelberg Catechism*.[37]

Westphal came out with a public assault on the Swiss churches, a. 1553. The next year a second pamphlet followed from the same violent pen. Calvin replied, with an exposition and defense of the *Consensus Tigurinus*. Westphal wrote again, a. 1555.

---

36. [Nevin:] The use which Dr. Hodge tries to make of the *Consensus Tigurinus*, shows how little trouble he has taken to go to the bottom of the whole historical question; for it is not to be supposed, for a moment, that such a man would willfully conceal or misrepresent what he knew, in favor of a cherished preconception. He affects throughout to pass off the articles of this document, in the sense of the current modern view, as expressed for instance in Craig's catechism. [John Craig d. 1600—colleague of John Knox and author of two catechisms, the larger printed by Henrie Charteris in 1581, saying that the sacraments compare to the word. The word is given to the ear and the sacraments to the eye.—ed.] This too in the face of the full "*Capitum Expositio*" of 1554, and the following "Second Defense" against Westphal, in which Calvin, over and over again, protests indignantly that every such construction did him violent wrong; & at the same time re-asseverates, again and again, the very mystery which the *Consensus* is thus supposed by Dr. Hodge to exclude. "The sacraments," says the Exposition, "are helps and media, by which we are either inserted into the body of Christ, or being so inserted coalesce with it more and more, till he unites us with himself in full (*solide*) in the heavenly life." We must "coalesce into Christ's body," to have part in his grace; he "diffuses his life into us, only as he is our head, from which the whole body," by joints and hands, grows. Christ truly acts what the signs show; it is no "theatrical pomp;" nothing is signified "which is not given." The pledge is accomplished with the very thing it brings to view. It is no perception simply in the way of "thought or memory;" the "*flesh* of Christ is truly vivific;" life, "from the fountain of the Godhead is wondrously poured into Christ's flesh" (as a general reservoir for our fallen nature), "from whence it flows into us," by the space transcending power of the Holy Ghost, "so that we have with him one and the same life." No crass carnal mixture is to be imagined here, of course, "We grant the mystery too sublime for our apprehension." He "transfunds [i.e., "transfuses"—ed.] into us the life giving energy of this flesh." [These quotations can all be found in "Exposition," 226, 238, 240. Fuller versions of the quotations, in Latin and translation, can be found in MTSS vol. 1, pp. 269–70.—ed.] Such is the style of the Exposition. How *could* Dr. Hodge leave it out of sight so completely, in his attempt to *modernize* the *Consensus Tigurinus*?

37. [John Williamson Nevin, *The History and Genius of the Heidelberg Catechism* (Chambersburg, PA: Publication Office of the German Reformed Church, 1847); slated to appear in vol. 9 of the present series.—ed.]

Calvin's *Second Defense* appeared in 1556.[38] The controversy thickened now on all sides. Calvin added, in 1557, his "*Last Admonition* to Joachim Westphal."[39]

In these publications, we have in full again the very same sacramental doctrine he had taught before in Strasburg. It will be observed too, that all has regard to the *Consensus Tigurinus* in the way of vindication and commentary; and the case is made still more interesting from the fact, that the very same use seems to have been made of this document by Westphal, only with a different view, that is now made of it by Dr. Hodge. Throughout indeed, there is a very remarkable correspondence between the treatment of Calvin by the ultra Lutheran school, and that to which he is now generally subjected from the opposite extreme. In both directions, it has been insisted that he played an adroit game, stretched his own convictions to please the Lutherans, paltered in double sense, and ambiguous terms, involved himself in contradictions, and took refuge in unintelligible distinctions. Westphal calls him an *eel*, which no one could hold by the tail. Dr. Hodge is more respectful, but it comes much to the same thing at last. Now it so happens, that the charges of both (for they are directly or by implication the same) are met in the publications here before us by Calvin himself, and very summarily disposed of as "calumnies." I am sorry that my limits do not allow me to notice these in detail. One of the best replies to the article of Dr. Hodge, so far as Calvin is concerned, would be simply a republication in full of his Second defense "*adversus Joachimi Wesphali calumnias.*"

Against the imputation of dishonest policy and intrigue, he always protests that he sought not to please men but God. And surely he *should* be considered one of the very last men who was likely to be swayed, on a great question like this, by any such sinister references and aims. His whole character and history combine to prove the contrary.[40]

But he rejects a local, material, natural presence, exclaims Westphal, and in this way upsets the sacramental mystery.—Calvin admits the first, but denies the second. The mystery holds in a higher sphere.

Westphal.—He makes the elements mere *signs*.[41]

38. ["Against the Slanders of Joachim Westphal." A modern edition of this text is "Second Defense of the Pious and Orthodox Faith concerning the Sacraments in Answer to the Calumnies of Joachim Westphal," in Torrance, ed., *Tracts and Treatises*, 2:245–344.—ed.]

39. ["The Last Admonition to Joachim Westphal." See Torrance, ed., *Tracts and Treatises*, 2:345–494.—ed.]

40. [Nevin:] *Hoc quidem mihi jure vindico, nunquam me ambigua loquendi forma, capitose aliud prae me tulisse, quam sentirem*—11. *Def.* [Nevin quotes throughout from the Amsterdam edition, *Tractatus Theologici Omnes.* Trans. "What I justly claim for myself is, that I never by employing an ambiguous mode of expression captiously brought forward any thing different from my real sentiment." "Second Defense," 253.—ed.]

41. [This ingenious section recapitulates the literary debate between Calvin and Westphal in the form of a continuous dialogue. Although most of it is condensed paraphrase, rather than direct quotation, Nevin sticks fairly close to the original texts, and includes copious footnotes throughout this section to provide the original Latin on particularly important points. A somewhat different version of the same can be found in MTSS vol. 1, pp. 272–80.—ed.]

Calvin.—Signs certainly; but by no means naked signs. Christ uses here no false colors. The verities represented accompany the signs. The last vouch the presence of the first.[42]

Westphal.—All is resolved thus into the exercises of the worshipper. The verities are present only in thought and contemplation, as embraced in the action of faith.

Calvin.—I mean not so. The verities are at hand objectively, the inward grace in the outward transaction. Faith is only the condition, not the cause of our mystical participation of Christ in the Supper. God forbid, that I should think of turning the process into a mere mental exercise of any kind.[43]

Westphal.—You make all spiritual; the agency of the Holy Ghost simply exciting faith, love, and other graces.

Calvin.—Spiritual the process is, as distinguished from your crass conception of an oral manducation. The mystery centers in the soul, and is wrought by the vivific power of the Holy Ghost, under a mode of existence that transcends all natural experience and conception. But it is not a mere influence. The Spirit actually binds Christ and his people into one life; not as a river joins two cities a hundred miles apart, by flowing through both; but as the actual medium (*"modus habitationis Christi in nobis"*) of his indwelling presence.[44]

---

42. [Nevin:] *Testamur passim in scriptis nostris longe differre ab inanibus figuris quae Dominus nobis reliquit gratiae suae testimonia et sigilla. Diserte hoc* Consensus *praedicat. Dominum qui verax est, intus praestare suo Spiritu quod oculis figurant Sacramenta; nec quam distinguimus inter signa et re signatas disjungere a signis veritatem.—Adv. Westph. Op. T. IX* p. 666. [Trans. "We uniformly testify in our writings, that the sacraments which the Lord has left us as seals and testimonies of his grace, differ widely from empty figures. Our *Agreement* distinctly declares, that the Lord, who is true, *performs* inwardly by his Spirit that which the sacraments figure to the eye, and that when we distinguish between the signs and the things signified, we do not disjoin the reality from the signs." "Second Defense," 274.—ed.]

43. [Nevin:] *Ubique resonant scripta mea, differre manducationem a fide, quia sit fidei effectus. Non a triduo ita loqui in coepi, nos credendo manducare Christum quia vere participes ejus facti in ejus corpus coalescimus, ut nobis communis sit cum eo vita. Iam anni compluresfluxerunt, ex quibus non destiti hoc subinde repetera. Quam turpa igitur Westphalo fuit, quum disserte verba mea sonent, manducare aliud esse quam credere quod ego fortiter nego, quasi ame profectum impudenter obtrudere lectoribus?* p. 669. [Trans. "My writings everywhere proclaim, that eating differs from faith, inasmuch as it is an effect of faith, I did not begin only three days ago, to say that we eat Christ by believing, because being made truly partakers of him, we grow up into one body, and have a common life with him. Years have now elapsed since I began, and have never ceased to repeat this. How base then was it in Westphal, while my words distinctly declare that eating is *something else* than believing, impudently to obtrude, what I strenuously deny, upon his readers, as if it had been actually uttered by me?" "Second Defense," 283.—ed.]

44. [Nevin:] *Haec nostra definitio est, spiritualiter a nobis manducari Christi carnem, quia non aliter animas vivificat, quam pane vegetatur corpus; tantum a nobis excluditur substantiae transfusio. Westphalo non aliter caro vivifica est, quam si ejus substantia voretur.—Neque enim simpliciter Spiritu suo Christum in nobis habitare trado, sed ita nos ad se attollere, ut vivificum carnis suae vigorem in nos transfundat.* p. 669. [Trans. "Our exposition is, that the flesh of Christ is spiritually eaten by us, because he vivifies our souls in the very manner in which our bodies are invigorated by food: only we exclude a transfusion of substance. According to Westphal, the flesh of Christ is not vivifying unless its substance is devoured. Our crime then is, that we do not open our arms to the embrace of such a monster." "Second Defense," 283.—ed.]

Westphal.—You refer then, of course only to his *divine* nature.

Calvin.—Not at all. The communication extends to his humanity also, his real flesh and blood.[45]

Westphal.—You must mean a merely imaginary body.

Calvin.—I mean the same that hung upon the cross, and is now glorified in heaven.[46]

Westphal.—But how can this be at such vast distance?

Calvin.—As I have said already, it is a mystery in the sphere of the Spirit. Dynamically and organically things may be joined into one that are wide apart in space.[47]

Westphal.—But you confess this to be only for the soul or mind of the communicant; not for his body.

Calvin.—Not for the body indeed in a direct and outward way, as your theory requires; but just as little either for the mind separately considered. Soul and mind are not the same thing. I mean by the soul, the central principle of our whole life, which in the end reaches out to the body also no less than the spirit. In this way, Christ is the true food, by which our whole nature is nourished unto immortality.[48]

Westphal.—Still you will not allow, that we partake of his *substance*.

---

45. [Nevin:] *Ita Christum corpore absentem doceo nihilominus non tantum divina sua virtute quae ubique diffusa est, nobis adesse, sed etiam facere ut nobis vivifica sit sua caro.* p. 669. [Trans. "Thus I teach that Christ, though absent in body is nevertheless not only present with us by his divine energy, which is everywhere diffused, but also makes his flesh give life to us." "Second Defense," 285.—ed.]

46. [Nevin:] *Dico igitur illo corpore, quod in cruce pependit, non minus in spiritualem vitam animas ipsas vegetari, quam pane terreno corpora nostra aluntur.* p. 668. [Trans. "I say, then, that by the body which hung on the cross our souls are invigorated with spiritual life, just as our bodies are nourished by earthly bread." "Second Defense," 280.—ed.]

47. [Nevin:] *Mihi certa est ac expedita defensio, ut detur Christi corpus, minime tamen requiri prae-sentiam: quia jam ante exposui, quod ex locorum distantia obstaculum ingeritur, immensa Spiritus virtute superari. Dari corpus utrinque fatemur, praesentiam quae inde minime consequitur, perperam inferri dico.* p. 671. [Trans. "My sure and simple defence is, that to the giving of the body, its presence is not at all requisite: for as I have already explained, the obstacle arising from distance of space is surmounted by the boundless energy of the Spirit. We both acknowledge that the body is given; but I hold that a bodily presence is thence erroneously inferred." "Second Defense," 291.—ed.]

48. [Nevin:] *Carnem ergo Christi, sine ullis ambagibus, fatemur esse vivificam; non tantum quia semel in ea nobis salus parta est, sed quia nunc dum sacra mutate cum Christo coalescimus, eadem illa caro vitam in nos spirat, vel ut brevius dicam, quia arcana Spiritus virtute in Christi corpus insiti, communem habemus cum ipso vitam. Nam ex abscondita Deitatis fonte in Christi carnem mirabiliter infusa est vita, ut inde ad nos flueret.* p. 657. [Trans. "We acknowledge, then, without any equivocation, that the flesh of Christ gives life, not only because we once obtained salvation by it, but because now, while we are made one with Christ by a sacred union, the same flesh breathes life into us, or, to express it more briefly, because ingrafted into the body of Christ by the secret agency of the Spirit, we have life in common with him. For from the hidden fountain of the Godhead life was miraculously infused into the body of Christ, that it might flow from thence to us." "Exposition," 238.—ed.]

Calvin.—Not of the outward material of his nature certainly in any way; but still of its actual substantial life; the vivific virtue of his true flesh and blood.[49]

Westphal.—Aye, there it is; a mere virtue or influence, emanating from him through the Spirit. You mean at last simply the efficacy and value of his death, applied to us of God, and appropriated by faith.

Calvin.—Not so at all. Christ *first*, and only *then* his merits and his benefits. By "virtue" or "efficacy," in this case, I understand always the essential vital reality of Christ's body. This in its glorified state is all "life and spirit;" a body of course still; but not such as belongs to our present moral condition. It is capable thus of reaching over, with organic reproductive force, by the Spirit and *in* the Spirit, into the person of his people; just as the root can live itself into the branches, or the head assert its presence in all the members which it animates in like manner.[50]

Westphal.—Ah; you are skulking behind unintelligible phrases. This is only to conceal your real meaning.

Calvin.—I own here the imbecility of my poor intellect; but before God I use no prevarication. The apostle himself pronounces the whole a "great mystery." My faith bows before it, with childlike homage.[51]

Such I conceive to be a fair statement of Calvin's doctrine, as it may be extracted from this controversy with Westphal, as well as from his writings in general. Even the difficulty of the Old Testament saints is urged against him by Westphal, as a sort of *argumentum ad hominem*, in the same way that Dr. Hodge now brings forward to show that he held no such doctrine. How he dispenses of it, we will see hereafter.

His last tract on the Supper was published against Hesshuss, a. 1561, near the close of his life.[52] It reiterates strongly the same doctrine. Dr. Hodge pronounces the

49. [Nevin:] *De voce substantiae si quis litem moveat, Christum asserimus a carnis suae substantia vitam in animas nostras spirare; imo propriam in nos vitam diffundere, modo nequa substantiae transfusio fingatur.* p. 660. [Trans. "Should any one raise a dispute as to the word substance, we assert that Christ, from the substance of his flesh, breathes life into our souls; nay, infuses his own life into us, provided always that no transfusion of substance be imagined." "Second Defense," 248.—ed.]

50. [Nevin:] *Carnem Christi nobis edendam proponi signis sincere et luculente tradit, ego unus sum ex numero: modum tantum definio, quod Spiritus sui virtute Christus locorum distantiam superet, ad vitam nobis e sua carne inspirandam.* p. 670. [Trans. "If any sincerely and distinctly teach that the flesh of Christ is set before us to be eaten by us, I too, am of the number: I only explain the manner, viz., that Christ overcomes the distance of space by employing the agency of his Spirit to inspire life into us from his flesh." "Second Defense," 287.—ed.]

51. [Nevin:] *De modo si quis me interroget, fateri non pudebit, sublimius esse arcanum, quam ut vel meo ingenio comprehendi vel enarrari verbis queat; atque, ut, apertius dicam, experior magis, quam intelligam. Inst.* IV. 17. 32. [Trans. "If anyone should ask me how this takes place, I shall not be ashamed to confess that it is a secret too lofty for either my mind to comprehend or my words to declare. And, to speak more plainly, I rather experience than understand it." *Institutes*, ed. McNeill, 2:1403. —ed.]

52. [Nevin:] His whole sacramental doctrine is brought out, under its most round & complete form, in the *third edition* of the *Institutes*, a. 1559. It is strange that any one should read this, and make any question about Calvin's faith in the mystical presence of Christ's flesh and blood in the Eucharistic transaction. By calling himself the bread of life, our Lord teaches, he says, "not only that we are saved by believing in his death and resurrection, but also that by the true communication of himself, *his life*

69

extracts from this tract in the *Mystical Presence* "extreme passages," and says it would be easy to gather others of a different character from Calvin's work. But why then has he not done so? The representation is a mistake (honest of course) on the part of Dr. Hodge. The passages are not extreme. They are amply sustained by other quotations in the *Mystical Presence*, and they are in full keeping only with all that Calvin has written on this subject. On this, as on all other questions, he is beyond all writers of the age true to himself, without change or contradiction, from the beginning of his theological career to its close. Nor is it at all difficult to know what his theory was, as distinguished from the Lutheran and Modern Puritan. All we need is to drop our stubborn preconceptions, and consent to hear him speak from his own standpoint instead of ours; then all becomes uncommonly clear. The *how* of the mystery remains; but the *what* affirmed of it is just as plain, as the doctrine of the trinity in the writings of Athanasius.

The case is too plain for contradiction. Calvin at least *did* hold and teach the real presence of Christ's body, not locally but dynamically, in the Lord's Supper.[53] All his writings prove it. It is shown by the violent suppositions it is found necessary to resort to, in order to get clear of it. He signed the Augsburg Confession, and made common cause openly with the Melancthonian part of the Lutheran Church. He always declared himself one with Luther as to the *mystery*, and only at variance with him in regard to its mode. The best informed theological scholars have always admitted this to be the case. So, for instance, the profoundly clear sighted Schleiermacher.[54] So to quote one for many, that prince of thinkers, Leibniz. "I have gone over the *Institutes* of Calvin," says this great man,

> as well as all his other writings in which he treats of the Eucharist, and have made from them many such extracts, as prove that this author has seriously, constantly, strongly, inculcated the *real* and *substantial* participation of the body of our Lord; and when he denies the real presence, he is to be understood undoubtedly as speaking only of a *dimensional* presence.[55]

For the Weekly Messenger.

---

is made to pass over into us and become ours, just as bread taken as food, conveys vigor to the body" [*Institutes*, ed. McNeill, 2:1365.—ed.]. This life is lodged in his *flesh* into which it wells from the divinity as a perennial fountain, for our use. All through the "*arcana Spiritus sancti operatio*" ["the secret work of the Holy Spirit"—ed.], which it is presumptuous for us to think of understanding. In the Lord's Supper, the mystery of this communication is not only represented, but sealed and certified as a present fact.

53. [In Hodge's *Systematic Theology* he ultimately grants Nevin his argument, saying, "While Calvin denied the real presence of the body and blood of Christ in the Eucharist, in the sense in which that presence was asserted by Romanists and Lutherans, yet he affirmed that they were dynamically present" (3:628).—ed.]

54. [Friedrich Daniel Ernst Schleiermacher (1768–1834), highly influential German theologian and preacher. Studied at Halle and later became a member of the Romantic Movement. Afterward, he moved away from the Romantic agenda and developed a unique theology in the idealist tradition. He is famously known as the one who taught that religion was based on feeling and intuition. His *Religion: Speeches to Its Cultured Despisers* (1799) was enormously influential, so much so that many consider Schleiermacher, with this work and the rest of his brilliant writings, to have altered the course of Christian theology in the nineteenth century.—ed.]

55. [Nevin:] Quoted by Ebrard [from Leibniz's *Pensees*. See note 12.—ed.].

6

Sacramental Doctrine of the Reformed Confessions[1]

WE HAVE NOW ASCERTAINED and settled fully, by clear historical evidence, the Calvinistic theory of the Lord's Supper, as held and taught by Calvin himself. The case is not one that leaves room at all for any rational controversy or doubt. The doctrine of Calvin on the Eucharist is just as plain as his doctrines on the decrees. To talk of ambiguity and contradiction here in *his* creed, may suit the convenience of such as are too indolent to examine for themselves, or too heady to allow even history itself to have a voice different from their own. But it is all idle and contrary to fact. Calvin wrote much on this subject, in his *Institutes*, in his Commentary, in his Catechism, in particular controversial tracts; it is not only here and there his peculiar system comes into view, but it may be said to be interwoven with his entire theological life from its commencement to its close; it is not only in a general way that it thus challenges our attention, but every point belonging to it is handled again and again, in most minute and careful detail. And yet the same unvarying representation is exhibited throughout. The same definitions and distinctions, the same forms of expression, the same images and illustrations, everywhere come in our way. In meeting the false constructions put upon his doctrine by Westphal, the same that are now forced upon it by the *Princeton Repertory*, he appeals to his uniform statements to the contrary, as a hundred times repeated, again and again reiterated, of long public notoriety, &c.; and at times loses all patience with the pertinacious determination shown to burden him with the very views, which he had taken the greatest pains to repudiate. Altogether his faith in the *mystery* of the holy sacrament, as an actual exhibition of the body of Christ for the use of believers, is just as clear as the fact of his residence in Strasburg or Geneva.

And this Calvinistic doctrine, in all its essential features—not as something opposed to the primitive Helvetic faith, but as the necessary and proper completion of its tendency and sense—passed over now, with the close of Calvin's life, into *all* the great

1. ["Dr. Hodge on the *Mystical Presence*, Article from the Repertory, Continued, No. 6," *Weekly Messenger*, New Series, vol. 13, no. 42. Wednesday, June 28, 1848. Published by the Board of the Synod of the German Reformed Church: Chambersburg, PA.—ed.]

national symbols of the Reformed Church. These are the Gallic, Old Scotch, Belgic, and Second Helvetic Confessions, together with the Heidelberg Catechism.

We may here see, without much trouble, how utterly unhistorical is the form, in which Dr. Hodge has seen fit to present his array of authorities, for the settlement of the general question in hand. The earlier Swiss testimonies are treated precisely as if they were uttered from the latter half of the sixteenth century; not the least regard is had to the broad difference there was between the *first* sacramental war and the *second*; the Zuinglian and Calvinistic positions are taken as fixed quantities, to be reckoned with as in an algebraic problem; Bullinger and the Helvetic divines, it is taken for granted, never moved an inch from the point occupied by them in the beginning; and so when we find them at last on common ground with Calvin, as in the *Consensus Tigurinus* it must be viewed as an outward confederation, involving in fact the triumph of the old form of thinking over the new, as the permanently accredited creed of the Reformed Church. So we have Zuinglian confessions, Calvinistic confessions, and Zuinglo-Calvinistic confessions, all as it might seem of contemporaneous and co-ordinate rank; without the least care or pains taken, to show what clear and sure result could the question ever be brought, by any such chaotic process of inquiry.

Dr. Hodge has no right to parade his first class of authorities (purely Zuinglian as he calls them) as a sort of parallel offset to the second. They belong wholly to a different period. As it is, they go far, in part at least, as we have already seen, to assert the very same doctrine which is more distinctly uttered at a later period. In any view, they form part of the *growing* life of the Helvetic Church, and not of its mature and settled manhood. This comes into view in the period of Calvin, with the corresponding maturity of the Reformed Church as a whole. Calvinism is the Zuinglian faith, carried out to its true and healthful symmetry and strength; in opposition to Megandrianism, which sought then, and still seeks, to stunt its growth, by keeping it pedantically to the single position in which it first started. We may not make the older confessions then the measure by which to try the later, but are bound rather to look of the full sense of the first in these last; as we find that they were superseded by them in truth, after Calvin's time. Dr. Hodge's *third* class, in which he pretends to find a sort of outward compromise between Calvinism and Zuinglianism (this last taken in *his* Megandrian sense), is very much the creature of his own imagination. The Heidelberg Catechism, as we shall see presently, is decidedly Calvinistic; the *Consensus Tigurinus* was considered to be so also by Calvin himself; and the Second Helvetic Confession must be interpreted in the same way. We have in fact, after the time of Calvin, but one class of authoritative symbols, and these are all Zuinglo-Calvinistic indeed; not however in the way of external amalgamation; but in such sort, that the old Zuinglian position, as asserted against Luther, is completed by development into the view of Calvin. The recognized standards of the Reformed Church, in this complete stage, are the five great symbols which have now been named. All older confessions, Calvin's Catechism and the *Consensus Tigurinus* among them, lost their force and importance with the appearance of these more perfect systems. They alone are the true ultimate rule, for determining the faith of the Reformed Church in the sixteenth century.

The Four Confessions

The Gallic, Scotch, Belgic, and Second Helvetic Confessions all made their appearance between the years 1559 and 1563. See *Mystical Presence*, p. 79–83.[2] No one at all familiar with the distinctive points of Calvin's sacramental theory, and the phraseology employed to represent them in his writings, can fail at once to recognize it in each of these publications. The same stress is not laid in each case indeed on the same points; one aspect is made more prominent here, and another there; but in all of them the doctrine is so fully characterized as to preclude every construction, by which it might be sought to explain it away. The language is rational with a Calvinistic interpretation, but becomes extravagant and absurd, the moment we try to take it in any less sublime and mysterious sense.

In every case, of course, the Reformed positions are firmly taken against the Roman and high Lutheran theories. No local presence, no oral manducation, no inclusion of Christ in the elements, no participation for unbelievers; all by the *Holy Ghost* and through the organ of *faith*, and for the *soul* primarily of the pious communicant. The elements, aside from the attendant grace of God, are powerless and vain. Christ's body remains locally in heaven. We feed upon it, not in any natural or outward way, but sacramentally and mystically only. As to all these points, there is no room for question or doubt. The Reformed Confessions, as with one voice, make common cause here throughout with Zuingli.

So also undoubtedly they assert, with unequivocal emphasis, the Zuinglian idea of the *sacrificial* interest exhibited in the ordinance, as a "commemoration" of the atoning virtue of Christ's broken body and shed blood. It is emphatically the *death* of Christ, as a past fact, which is here shown forth, by lively signs, to the faith of his people, to be appropriated by them in its efficacy and value to take away sin.

But now it is a most rash and precipitate conclusion, to infer from all this at once, as Dr. Hodge and many others seem inclined to do, that the doctrine of the Reformed Confessions ends with the positions here named, in such a way as to shut out the mystical side of the sacramental transaction, as we have already been made familiar with it in the writings of Calvin.

To deny a local presence, is not to make the presence itself a mere figment. The alternative to sense and flesh, is not necessarily naked thought and contemplation. To lay stress on the covenant in Christ's blood, is not to exclude the idea of a true fellowship with his life as its necessary basis. The *mystery* of the Lord's Supper is not overthrown, by being simply lifted from the sphere of nature into the sphere of Spirit.

If we feed not on Christ with the mouth, just as little can we be said to do so with the understanding or mind. Neither *dente* ["with the teeth"] nor *mente* ["with the mind"], not "in *ventrem*" ["into the stomach"] and yet just as little "in *mentem*" ["into the mind"] was the current Reformed distinction in regard to the subject in the period of which we now speak.[3] Our common modern view resolves all into a mental

2. [MTSS edition, pp. 69–72.—ed.]

3. [Nevin quotes his *Mystical Presence*; MTSS edition, p. 82.—ed.]

process, upsetting thus in full the old mystery of a real communication with Christ's true divine-human life. The process is made to be purely subjective, involving at most certain gracious influences of God's Spirit, and corresponding moral exercises in the worshipper's soul, parallel precisely with the use that may be made of any other means of spiritual edification. But this is *not* the doctrine of the old Reformed symbols. They hold fast to the "mystery," and make high account of it as lying at the bottom of the whole sacramental transaction.

Thus, while faith is required as the necessary condition of our union with Christ, it is not allowed to be its cause. The main force of the sacrament is found in the objective action of the Holy Ghost.

This again is no general influence merely, but a real making good of what the signs represent. The elements are only bread and wine, visible symbols of Christ's flesh and blood; but they are not void signs; the verities they signify go with them, in another sphere, by the Spirit.

True, Christ's body is in heaven, and not in the bread, but still its vivific power, that in which its true substance consists, is by the mysterious action of the Holy Ghost actually joined to our souls in the sacramental transaction; so that we are fed by it in a dynamic, though not of course in an outward fleshy way.

This participation is accordingly through the soul, as a spiritual process, and not in any sense by the mouth; but the soul in this case is not the mind, as one side simply of our general life; it is the center of our being as a whole (which is not dualistic but monadic or single), and determines in the end both form and contents for the entire man. Thus centrally to feed upon Christ's substantial life; is to be nourished in truth by his flesh and blood, in our whole persons, unto everlasting life.

Let any one, I say, honestly examine the sacramental doctrine of the *Gallic, Scotic, Belgic,* and *Second Helvetic* Confessions, with a full sense of the Calvinistic definitions in his mind, as they prevailed in that age, and he will find all these positions clearly embraced in it, beyond the shadow of doubt.

"Through the secret and incomprehensible energy of his Spirit, he nourishes and vivifies us by the substance of his body and blood."—"This mystery of our coalition with Christ is so sublime, that it transcends all our senses, and so also the whole course of nature" (*Gallic Confession*).[4]—"In the Lord's Supper, rightly used, Christ is so united to us as to be the very nutriment and food of our souls." Believers, by the operation of the Holy Ghost overcoming the barriers of space, "eat the body and drink the blood of Jesus Christ, so as to become thus flesh of his flesh and bone of his bones; for as the eternal divinity has imparted life and immortality to the flesh of Jesus Christ, so likewise his flesh and blood, when eaten and drunk by us, confer upon us the same prerogatives" (*Scotch Confession*).[5]—The sacraments are means or organs, "through which God himself works in us through the power of the Holy Spirit." Christ "per-

4. [Article 36. The full context from which these excerpts are taken can be found in MTSS vol. 1, p. 293. See also Dennison, *Reformed Confessions*, 2:152–53.—ed.]

5. [Article 21. See MTSS vol. 1, p. 294 for full quote. See also Dennison, *Reformed Confessions*, 2:201–2.—ed.]

forms in us really all that he represents to us in these sacred signs; although the mode is such as to surpass the apprehension of our mind, and cannot be understood by any, inasmuch as the operation of the Holy Spirit is hidden and incomprehensible" (*Belgic Confession*).[6]—"Believers receive what is given by the minister of the Lord, and eat the Lord's bread and drink the Lord's cup; inwardly, however, at the same time, by the work of Christ though the Holy Spirit, they partake also of the Lord's flesh and blood, and are by the same fed unto everlasting life" (*Second Helvetic Confession*).[7]

This last confession was drawn up by Bullinger, a. 1562, and afterwards acquired general authority in the Swiss Church. Dr. Hodge assumes that it must occupy low ground, because it came from Zurich; and then, on the strength of its widely extended authority, sinks the whole Calvinistic doctrine, in its true final sense, down to the same level. But this is to make no difference between the Zurich of 1530 and the Zurich of 1562. It is begging the whole question, to make the sacramental doctrine of Bullinger and the Helvetic divines at this time, parallel with that of Craig's catechism and this article in the *Biblical Repertory*. We have seen already how wide of the mark every such supposition is, in the case of the *Consensus Tigurinus*. And we may easily see it also, in the case of this Second Helvetic Confession. It speaks plainly enough for itself; and the fact of its favorable reception in the Palatinate, a. 1565, where we *know* most certainly that the Calvinistic doctrine stood in full force, should of itself be enough to rescue it from all suspicion of any such Megandrian character, as we find apparently forced upon it by Dr. Hodge.

The language of the "Belgic Confession," the symbol of the Reformed Dutch Church, is admirably strong and distinct. For the "soul," as the seat of the Christian life, so liable to be confounded with the notion of mere *mind*, we have here the idea of the "new man" (embracing our total nature, soul and body), the product of our second nativity "in the union of Christ's body." Christ is the pabulum of this new man; faith is "the hand or mouth" for its reception; the Eucharistic symbols are divine certifications of its being actually at hand; what is represented, is made good by Christ himself, in the mysterious transaction; the mode of the mystery is such as transcends all understanding; it falls within the invisible abyss of God's power; "what is eaten, however, is the very natural body of Christ (*ipsissimum* Christi corpus *naturale*), and what is drunk his true blood." Alas, that it should be so hard for us, at the present time, to climb even in thought to the plain literal sense of so sublime and magnificent a creed!

The Heidelberg Catechism

For an account of the formation of this most ecumenical, and in some respects most complete of all the Reformed symbols, the reader is referred to the *Mystical Presence*, p. 83–90,[8] and more extensively still to my small work entitled *The History and Genius*

---

6. [Article 35. See MTSS vol. 1, pp. 294–95 for full quote. See also Dennison, *Reformed Confessions*, 2:445–47.—ed.]

7. [Article 21. See MTSS vol. 1, p. 295 for full quote. See also Dennison, *Reformed Confessions*, 2:865–69.—ed.]

8. [MTSS edition, pp. 73–82. See also pp. 299–304.—ed.]

of the Heidelberg Catechism. Dr. Hodge notices it as a sort of irenical compromise "between the Zuinglians and Calvinists," and thinks there is nothing in its sacramental doctrine "to which exception would even now be taken," meaning of course from the Megandrian standpoint represented in his review. Mosheim,[9] I believe, has a remark of the same sort about the Catechism, and it is from him mainly perhaps that we find it repeated frequently by others. I have never been able however to find the least evidence of any such compromise, in the actual history of its production. On the contrary, all the circumstances of this show every such supposition to be unnatural in the extreme. The controversy which gave rise to it, was not the old question at all that lay between Zuingli and Luther; but the new issue created in the bosom of the Lutheran Church, between the doctrine of mystical presence in the Spirit, as held by Melancthon and his school, and the crass conception of a corporeal presence in the bread, as contended for by the part which finally produced the Form of Concord. The first view was the same that Calvin held in the Reformed Church, the Zuinglo-Calvinistic as it might be termed, matured from the old Zuinglian stock into becoming consistency and perfection. As for Megandrian Zuinglianism, we hear not a word of its influence in the Palatinate. The truth is, the Reformed Church here springs properly from the spirit of Melancthon; as it is his spirit also which, through his favorite disciple Ursinus, more than that of any other of the older Reformers, pervades every page, we may say, of the Heidelberg Catechism.

I am glad to find my general judgment of the constitution and character of this admirable symbol, as given particularly in the second of the two works to which I have just referred, strongly supported by Professor Ebrard. "We need not offer a panegyric," he says,

> on the merits of the Catechism; it speaks its own praise. Its wonderful union of doctrinal precision and inward earnestness, easy comprehensibility and pregnant depth, leave it without a parallel in its way. It is at once a system of divinity and a book of practical edification; every child can understand it on the first reading, while yet the catechist finds in it the richest material for profound elucidation.

Its sacramental doctrine is plainly such as it might be expected to contain, in the circumstances to which it was formed. The distinction of Lutheran and Reformed was not yet at hand in the German Church; no ecclesiastical revolution was thought of, in the ground now taken by the Palatinate; it was regarded only as a declaration in favor of Melancthonian Lutheranism against the crass conceptions of such men as Westphal, Timann,[10] and Hesshuss; the banner of the Augsburg Confession was

9. [Johann Lorenz Mosheim (1694–1755), educated at Kiel he became professor of theology at Helmstedt and Göttingen. He was a noted ecclesiastical historian whose reputation was based on his novel objective approach, making him a candidate for the first modern historian. Nevin, however, believes Mosheim's view of the Catechism is distorted by his Lutheran point of view.—ed.]

10. [Johann Timann (1500–57), was a Lutheran hard-liner intractable in his holding to Luther's theory of the Eucharist. He published a tract in which he claimed that all church leaders agree with Luther on his doctrine of the Eucharist. He then insisted that the ministers of Bremen sign the tract. When several of the pastors refused, it set off a great controversy.—ed.]

allowed to float quietly over the national church as before. Discussion and disputation, under the most public form, attended the movement; all turning on the question simply of mode, and not of fact, as respected the sacramental mystery. The mystery itself was allowed on all hands. At the imperial diet at Naumburg, a. 1561, the elector Frederick III. renewed his signature, with the other German princes, to the Augsburg Confession; the Catechism was published under his auspices in 1563; and yet three years after, a. 1566, we hear him again, at another diet, appealing to this very subscription in proof of his orthodoxy, and publicly ratifying it as still valid for his hand and heart. So little sense had either he or his theologians of any essential variation in the new symbol, from what they conceived to be the true meaning of the Augsburg creed. The Catechism accordingly just expresses the sense of this creed, as it was held by Melancthon and the Melancthonian party in the Lutheran Church; the sense in which it had been signed by Calvin at Strasburg; the true Calvinistic doctrine itself, as we find it authoritatively established in all the later Reformed confessions.

Throughout here, we have the two great aspects of the ordinance carefully distinguished, and yet just as carefully held together. All looks to the sacrifice once offered on Calvary, the covenant of pardon and peace established in Christ's bloody *death*; but all is made immediately to turn again on the power of a real union with his present *life*, now glorified in heaven, as the only stream by which it is possible for such vast grace to be conveyed into our souls.

Thus in the 75th question, we are told that the transaction involves a divine certification from Christ of the atonement as already made, "*and further,* THAT HE FEEDS AND NOURISHES MY SOUL TO EVERLASTING LIFE BY HIS CRUCIFIED BODY AND SHED BLOOD, *as assuredly* as I receive from the hands of the minister, and taste with my mouth, the bread and cup of the Lord, as certain signs of the body and blood of Christ."[11] Here we have a full distinction between the signs and the things signified; as *broken* and *poured out*, the symbols attest the death of Christ for our sins; as *eaten* and *drunk*, they certify also our communion in his life as a present fact.

What is it then to eat and drink thus Christ's body and blood? Is it to partake simply of the fruits of his death by imputation? No, we are told in the answer to the following question, but in order to this something still more inward and deep. It is *not only* to embrace the benefit of Christ's suffering and death;

> but also *besides that* TO BECOME MORE AND MORE UNITED TO HIS SACRED BODY, BY THE HOLY GHOST, who dwells both in Christ and in us; so that we, though Christ is in heaven and we on earth, are notwithstanding "*flesh of his flesh and bone of his bone;*" and that we live, and are governed forever by one spirit, as members of the same body are by one spirit.

Could any statement well be more plain, for an unsophisticated mind, in the least degree familiar with the theological terminology of the sixteenth century? Here are all the Calvinistic or Melancthonian points, in clear and precise enunciation; the memorial

---

11. [See MTSS vol. 1, pp. 304–5, for full quotations of this and the following. See also Dennison, *Reformed Confessions*, 2:786.—ed.]

of the atonement; our present fruition[12] of Christ's life, as the ground of all interest in his death; the local barrier surmounted by the Holy Ghost; and so a real participation, dynamically, in the very substance or vivific vigor of his glorified person.

Question 77 affirms this to be the true and proper sense of the words of institution.

In the next question, it is declared that the bread and wine remain unchanged.

Then all is summed up in the 79th question. "Why then doth Christ call the bread his body, and the cup his blood, or the new covenant in his blood in Christ?" *Ans.* "Christ speaks thus not without great reason, namely, *not only* thereby to *teach us*"—in the way of symbolic show—"that as bread and wine support this temporal life, so his crucified body and shed blood are the true meat and drink whereby our souls are fed to eternal life; but *more especially* by these visible signs and pledges to *assure us*"—in the way of divine certification "that we are *really* partakers of his *true body and blood* (BY THE OPERATION OF THE HOLY GHOST), as we receive by the mouths of our bodies these holy signs in remembrance of him; and that all his sufferings and obedience are as certainly ours, as if we had *in our own persons* suffered and made satisfaction for our sins to God."

Is it not strange that any question should be made, with regard to the sense of language so plain and full? How could it be more strongly asserted than it is here said in fact, that in the holy Eucharist by the act of Christ objectively through his wonder-working Spirit, and not simply by our act, we are made to participate, not orally and outwardly, but mystically, dynamically and substantially, through the inmost soul-center of our being, in the divine life that wells up perpetually through the fountain of his humanity, as Calvin has it, for the use of our dreary and dying nature?

Ursinus

If there could be any doubt with regard to the true sense of the Catechism, it ought to vanish from the most incredulous mind before the testimony of its author. This may be found to some extent, in the *Mystical Presence*, p. 90–94.[13]

The Catechism called forth violent opposition, particularly from the theologians at Wurttemberg. It became necessary thus for Ursinus and his colleagues at Heidelberg, to stand forward in its vindication and defense. In this way, its sacramental doctrine especially was brought under full and long discussion; so that we are not left to conjecture at all in what relations it actually stood to the theology of that time. On what ground is it then that we find the theologians of the Palatinate taking their stand in this controversy? The case is historically clear as the light of day. They contended not at all for Megandrian Zuinglianism, as held for instance by Dr. Hodge, but only for Melancthonian Calvinism, as the form in which the old Zuinglian faith had come to be complete. The issue was in no sense that between Zuingli and Luther, but the new question wholly on the *mode* of the sacramental mystery, as it lay now between the oralists and spiritualists, as they might be called, in the bosom of the Lutheran

---

12. [In the older sense of "enjoyment."—ed.]

13. [MTSS edition, pp. 80–82.—ed.]

Church itself. Heidelberg affirmed the fact of a real participation in Christ's human life as firmly and strongly as Wurttemberg; the only difference was, in answering the question: *How* is the mystery brought to pass?

I have quoted some passages in the *Mystical Presence*, from the *Commentary of Ursinus on the Catechism* as published by David Pareus, that show unanswerably what doctrine here it was designed to teach. Passing by all this however at present, I beg leave to fix attention on the following extracts from the "*Gruendlicher Bericht,*" or True Doctrine of the Sacraments,[14] drawn up by his pen, and published in the name of the whole Heidelberg faculty, in the way of solemn apology and defense of their faith; a most interesting and valuable testimony truly, for which I am indebted to Professor Ebrard, not having the original work unfortunately within reach.[15]

In the *second part,* which treats of the Holy Supper, it is said:

> That we might live eternally by Christ, it was not enough for him to become a sacrifice for us, but he must also *incorporate us with himself,* that we may become by him again a habitation of God, John 15. Hence he makes us partakers *not only of his merit,* but also *of himself,* that is, of his *person, substance,* and *essence (substanz und Wesens),* and *thus* also of his power and operation, or of his condition, property and glory.—Himself he gives over to us, by *dwelling in us truly with his Spirit,* and by so joining and uniting us, through this Spirit which dwells both in him and us, *with his true essential body,* that we hang to him as limbs to the head or branches to the vine, and *have life out of him.* For Christ is our head and vine, according to his divinity, he abides in us essentially along with the eternal Father and the Holy Ghost, John 14:23; but according to his humanity, he is not *within* our body. For as the head in the natural body is not in the arm or foot, nor the arm in the head, and as the stock of the vine is not within the branches nor the branches within the stock, but all members so hang and grow to the head, and all branches to the vine, by their veins, hands and joints, that they draw thence their life, whether far off or near as regards *place*; so also the body of Christ is not in ours, as our body also is not in his, but the Holy Ghost, which dwells in him and in us, is the living eternal, *incomprehensible bond* between him and us, by which our MORTAL FLESH IS INCORPORATED AND KNIT TO THE LIVING FLESH OF CHRIST A THOUSAND TIMES MORE CLOSELY, FIRMLY AND STRONGLY, *than all the members of our body are joined by their veins and fleshly bands to our head,* and we are made members of Christ, *of his*

14. [The full title of this text is *Gründlicher Bericht Vom Heiligen Abendmal unsers Herrn Jesu Christi, aus einhelliger Lehre der H. Schrifft, der alten Rechtglaubigen Christlichen Kirchen und auch der Augspurgischen Confession* (Complete Commentary on the Holy Communion of Our Lord Jesus Christ, according to the Authoritative Teaching of the Holy Scriptures, of the Ancient Orthodox Christian Church and Also the Augsburg Confession). It was published at Neustadt in 1590 and again in 1604; both editions may be found at the Post-Reformation Digital Library (prdl.org).—ed.]

15. [Nevin:] I wish some friend of our Seminary would take it into his head to procure a full copy of the works of Ursinus, for its library. They ought to be there certainly, if nowhere else to be found in the country. It would be a handsome and valuable present, which could not fail to do honor to any name with which it might be associated; and if the means of the donor should allow him to add to it a full apparatus of the old theological literature of the Palatinate, it would redound to his praise still more. Ursinus is not as much known as he deserves to be. Few names in the sixteenth century have a stronger title to respect and veneration.

flesh and of his bone, it matters not whether the body of Christ be *as to situation and place* near at hand or far off.

What could be more fully in point, for the whole question with which we are here concerned? Who will dare to turn the bold phraseology of the 76th and 79th questions of the Catechism into a mere flourish of speech, in view of so clear a statement under the hand of Ursinus himself? The clear sighted man, no less than Calvin himself, knew full well what he meant to assert, by resolving the sacramental mystery into the POWER OF THE HOLY GHOST, as transcending all local limitations. What at last is any merely mechanical union, as compared with the organic, plastic force that binds together dynamically here the subjects of a common life? "It is a great misunderstanding or perversion," we are told again,

> that some so take and give the word *spiritual*, as though it did not signify what actually occurs, but were only a thought or imagination. For as *corporeal*, in this question, expresses what is perceived and one with the senses and members of the body, so also *that is spiritual which takes place by the operation of the Holy Ghost*. Hence, the body of Christ also, although it is no spirit, but true human, natural, visible and palpable flesh and blood, is notwithstanding a *spiritual* gift and bestowment, since the participation of it is spiritual, that is, comes to us by the Holy Ghost.

Weighty interpretations, says Ebrard, of a most weighty idea!

The ninth and last part of this "*Gruendlicher Bericht*" is devoted to the object of showing that the sacramental doctrine of the Heidelberg Catechism is in full harmony with the true and proper sense of the tenth article of the Augsburg Confession.

Dr. Hodge finds this Catechism nearly as digestible as the *Consensus Tigurinus*!

The Declaration of Thorn

To the five proper confessions now noticed may be joined with good reason the celebrated DECLARATION presented, by the Reformed theologians, to the General Synod held at *Thorn* in the year 1645.[16] It is not indeed a confession in the strict view; but we have in it a most weighty and solemn exposition of the creed of the Reformed Church, as exhibited in previous confessions, certifying to us in the most authentic form the sense in which it was understood at this time. The object of the Synod was irenical; but when this failed, there was no disposition shown on the side of the Reformed Church, to retreat at all from the ground on which she had here professed

16. [The Colloquy of Thorn, AD 1645, was convened in the violence of the Thirty Years' War, making success very unlikely. It was an attempt to heal the discord by the Catholic king of Poland, Wladislaus IV, by bringing together the Protestant and Catholic parties in the Lutheran town of Thorn, in West Prussia. The parties were asked to present their positions, but the Protestant statements were routinely rejected by the Catholic representatives, and unfortunately disputes among the Reformed and Lutherans strengthened the position of the Roman Catholics. The resulting rancor may have done more harm than good. However, the Declaration of Thorn, which was the statement of the Reformed at the Colloquy, was one of the most carefully crafted confessions of the Reformed and the only one of the statements from Thorn that had practical benefit. It was later adopted by the three Brandenburg Confessions. In regard to the sacramental controversy, it stated agreement with the altered Augsburg Confession.—ed.]

to stand. On the contrary, this *Declaration of Thorn* was at once erected into permanent symbolical authority in Poland, and also in Prussia and Brandenburg; along with the *Helvetic Confession*, let it be well observed, in the first country, and in connection with the Heidelberg Catechism in the last. For the *German* Reformed Church thus, in particular, it must be taken as of absolutely conclusive force, in regard to the whole subject which we have now under consideration. Let us attend then to its sacramental doctrine. The chapter on the "Supper" consists of 14 articles.

I. As Baptism is the sacrament of our spiritual *regeneration* in Christ, so the Holy Supper is declared to be the sacrament of our spiritual *nutrition* in the same, through the communication of his body and blood once offered for sin.

II. It consists thus of two sides or parts, terrene and celestial, which are so joined as to be both exhibited to us "in the *most true, real* and *present* way;" the first outwardly to the senses, the last, "under a *spiritual, mystical* and *celestial mode*," inscrutable to reason and sense, and accessible only to *faith*; by which we apprehend both the promise and the *thing promised*, namely "Christ crucified with all his benefits."[17]

III.

> Hence the terrene things, bread and wine, are properly styled Christ's body and blood, as being so, not indeed substantially or corporeally, but *sacramentally* and *mystically*, through and on account of the *sacramental union*; which does not consist in mere signification or obsignation, but also in this *joint* and *simultaneous exhibition* and *communication* of the terrene and celestial things, under their different modes.

—No flesh and blood *in the elements*, as Luther would have it; but still the true vivific power of Christ's life, made over to us *in the transaction*.

IV.–V. In what sense the early fathers speak of the elements as changed into Christ's body and blood, and of the whole ordinance of a Eucharistic sacrifice.

VI.–IX. A rejection in full of *transubstantiation* and every sort of *local inclusion* or *co-existence*, or *corporeal* or *oral* communication in any way whatever, together with the *mass* and worship of the *host*.

X. Still the signs are not nude and vain, but

> *simultaneously* exhibit what they represent and seal, as most certain media and *efficacious instruments*, by which the body and blood of Christ, and so Christ himself with all his benefits, are *exhibited* and *offered* to all communicants, as to believers they are actually *given* and *conferred* so as to be by them *received* for saving and life-giving food to the soul.

---

17. [Unfortunately, Nevin provides no indication of his source edition for these citations, and we have been unable to locate an English edition of this obscure *Declaration*. It is most likely he translated either from the Reformed *Declaratio Thoruniensis*, Latin, in Niemeyer (669–89) or *Die Bekenntniss-Shriften Der Evangelisch-Reformirten Kirche* in the German, edited by Böckel (865–84).—ed.] An English translation of the Declaration is slated to appear in volume 4 of Dennison, ed., *Reformed Confessions*, forthcoming 2013.

—Objective in full.

XI.

> Nor do we by any means deny the *true presence* of Christ's body and blood in the Supper, but only the local and corporal mode of presence, and a substantial union with the *elements*; the presence itself *with us*, we sacredly believe, and this *not* as imaginary, but as *most true, most real,* and *most efficacious,* namely, that very *mystical union* of Christ with us, which *he himself,* as he promises by word and by symbol offers, by his Spirit also *effects,* and which we *through faith accept* and by love feel agreeably to that ancient saying: The motion is felt, the mode unknown, the presence believed.

—How objective action, and subjective condition again are here held asunder!

XII.

> Whence it is clear, that not merely the *virtue, efficacy, operation* or *benefits* of Christ, are presented and communicated to us, but especially the *substance itself of Christ's body and blood,* that self-same victim which was given for the life of the world and slain upon the cross, that by believing communion with the victim and union with Christ himself, we might in *consequence* partake also of the merits and benefits procured by his sacrifice, and abide in him even as he does in us.

XIII.

> And this, *not only as to the soul,* but also *as to our body.* For although, as by the bodily mouth we receive the terrene part, so it is by faith as the proper *organ* of the heart, (*cordis*) that we receive the celestial part; according to that old line, "*ventrem, quod terimus, mentem, quod credimus, intrat*";[18] still by the mediation of this faith, *not merely our souls,* but also our *bodies themselves,* are inserted and united into Christ's *body* BY HIS SPIRIT, unto the hope of the *resurrection* and everlasting life, that we may be flesh of his flesh and bone of his bone, and so one mystical body with himself, which the apostle with good reason has styled a great mystery.

—What a repudiation here of the abstract spiritualism, which *now* pretends so widely to palm itself upon the world as the true sense of the old Reformed faith! The soul or heart, acted upon by the Holy Ghost in this GREAT MYSTERY, is not the understanding simply as a separate existence, but the ground principle and inmost living center of our whole nature, out from which in a real way the organic force of Christ's life is reproductively carried into both mind and body, transmuting them, as Hooker expresses it, from sin to righteousness, from death and corruption to immortality and life. "*Christi caro,*" in the beautiful language of Calvin, "*instar fontis est divitis et inexhausti, quae vitam a divinitate seipsam scaturientem ad nos transfundit.*"[19] Let those

18. [Trans. "What we chew goes into the stomach; what we believe, into the mind."]

19. [Trans. "The flesh of Christ is like a rich and inexhaustible fountain that pours into us the life springing forth from the Godhead into itself." *Institutes,* ed. McNeill, 2:1369. Nevin has found a key image in the thinking of Calvin. Gerrish wrote, Calvin recognized that in Scripture the attributes of God are not so much described as depicted. "The pivotal description of God as source or fountain of good

who choose set aside this "old wine" for the more spirituous produce, as they may take it, of our modern divinity; there are not a few still we may trust, whose hearts will say: *The old is better.*

XIV. The last article insists on the use of the cup for the laity, as well as the bread.

What a luminous commentary is this declaration of Thorn, in particular, on the sacramental doctrine of the GERMAN *Reformed Church, and the sense of the* HEIDELBERG CATECHISM, as its primary symbolical book. Must we betake ourselves to Princeton or modern New England, to be told what *we* are bound to believe here, in order that we may be orthodox in our own communion, with this full plain exposition of the old Prussian Church in our hands? Against such humiliation and wrong, who that has the least particle of German blood in his veins (which I have *not*), must not stand ready earnestly and solemnly to protest!

General Result

We have now completed our historical review, and are prepared to return once more to the article of Dr. Hodge. Those who have had patience to accompany me in this excursus, will find themselves, I trust, better fitted than before, to come to some proper estimate of the points here brought into discussion. Much of the argumentation of Dr. Hodge will of itself fall at once to the ground, as being directed against positions that nobody calls in question; much will be found to turn on the fallacy of taking the words of one age in the wholly different sense of another; and *all* will be shorn of its title to respect, by the perfectly unhistorical hypothesis, which is made to underlie its use of authorities from beginning to end. At the same time the defective character of Dr. Hodge's own theological position, as contrasted with the old faith of the Calvinistic or Reformed Church, is brought into view, in such a way as must serve materially to shake its credit, with such as are competent to judge in the case. He sunders the *sacrifice* of Christ from his *life*, in the Christian mystery, and entangles himself thus in consequences, which I at least, with all my respect and esteem for him, should be very sorry to accept at his hands. In the old Reformed doctrine, as we have now seen, sacrifice and life are made to go together, the first borne and carried always in the bosom of the second.

---

reappears . . . countless times elsewhere in Calvin's writings, and it clearly determines his entire conception of what genuine religion is." See *Grace and Gratitude* (25–26).—ed.]

7

What It Means to Receive the Body and Blood of Christ[1]

[NEVIN]

ONE GREAT OBJECT OF the historical inquiry through which we have now passed, it will be borne in mind, has been to show that the *sacrificial* and *vivifical* sides of the holy Eucharist, its force as a memorial of the atonement made by Christ's sorrowful *death* and its force as a seal or pledge of present participation in Christ's triumphal *life*, by no means exclude each other, as Dr. Hodge supposes, in the proper constitution of the Reformed doctrine, but on the contrary go necessarily together to make this inwardly perfect and complete. Dr. Hodge is disposed to lay all stress on the sacrificial interest, as it was originally insisted upon by Zuingli and the old Helvetic Church; while he does not hesitate to say of the other that "it is an uncongenial foreign element" derived from abroad, "which does not accord with the other doctrines of the Church," and is not to be regarded therefore "as a genuine portion of its faith." This, as we shall soon see, forms a most weighty point in the whole controversy here in hand, and furnishes we may say the key to all that is distinctive in the theology of Dr. Hodge, as contrasted with that of Calvin and the Reformed symbols. We have nothing to do now of course with the theological question itself, as such, which is here brought into view. There are few indeed more important, or more deserving at this time of the serious attention of all sections of the Protestant Church. On it turns to a great extent the claims of sacramental, churchly, catholic piety, as set over against the pretensions of that merely individual spiritualism, which now affects so widely to be the whole truth of Christianity, footing itself before God on its own naked frames and states, and making a boast of its rupture with all church antiquity. It is the question at last in fact, whether religion be a thing of mere thought and feeling, or the power in truth of a new real creation in the world, embracing an objective and substantial life of its own. But it is only the *historical* side of the subject, that we are concerned with here; and this we have now been enabled happily to place in its proper light. What Dr. Hodge is

---

1. ["Dr. Hodge on the *Mystical Presence*, Article from the *Repertory*, Continued, No. 7," *Weekly Messenger*, New Series, vol. 13, no. 43. Wednesday, July 5, 1848. Published by the Board of the Synod of the German Reformed Church: Chambersburg, PA.—ed.]

thus bent on sundering, the old sacramental doctrine of the Reformed Church joined together; and the union is in such a form as to show, that it was not simply accidental and mechanical, the outward juxtaposition only of heterogeneous elements, as we are told by Dr. Hodge; it stands before us as the product of a real concrete growth; it is at once inward and organic.

In the early Church, all stress was laid at first on the resurrection and ascension of Christ, in such a way as to leave out of sight greatly the mystery of his birth. In due course of time however, the Christian consciousness fell back on the full sense of this last, as the necessary ground and support of its own contents in the other view. The ecclesiastical year, representing the glorious cycle of redemption, started with the festivals of Easter and Pentecost, only to complete itself afterwards in the festival, first of Epiphany, and then of Christmas. Not as though the miraculous conception had not belonged to the original creed; we know that it did; but the higher nativity so filled the eye of the Church, as for a time to eclipse in some sort the fundamental significance of that primary birth in the flesh, in which was involved the glory of all that followed.[2] So in the case before us, as we have seen, the Reformed Church of the sixteenth century was led at first, by the circumstances in which it was placed at the time, to intone with special emphasis the relation of the Lord's Supper to the sacrifice of Christ as a *past* transaction; but only in such a way as to fall back distinctly afterwards upon its relation to the *present* power of his everlasting life, as the necessary basis of the other grace. So we have it fully developed in Calvin. *He* saw no opposition (as even Dr. Hodge himself admits) between the two conceptions here brought into view. On the contrary, it was precisely to save the first, as originally insisted upon by Zuingli, that he felt it necessary to insist with like zeal upon the second. "Truly I see not," he tells us, "how anyone can trust that he has redemption and righteousness by the *cross* of Christ, and life by his *death*, if he have not in the first place a true communion with *Christ* himself; for these benefits could never reach us if Christ did not first make himself ours." *Inst.* IV.17.11. And to be ours in this way, it was not enough with Calvin that he should be mentally apprehended; it must come to a real participation in his flesh and blood, that is, in his veritable mediatorial life, as now exalted to glory in heaven. To have part in the sacrifice, we must have part in him who was sacrificed and slain, in whose being alone is still borne and carried all its atoning value.

Such moreover is the doctrine of the whole Church, clearly uttered in the Gallic, Scotic, Belgic, and Helvetic Confessions, and the Catechism of the Palatinate. Dr. Hodge is entirely mistaken, when he speaks of the authority of these symbols, as being divided between the two conceptions now in view, and pretends accordingly to *outweigh* with the clear testimony of the *Consensus Tigurinus*, the Helvetic Confession, and strange to add the Heidelberg Catechism, what he is pleased to designate as "the

---

2. [Nevin:] See this whole point well represented by Dorner in the first part of his Christology. [See Isaak August Dorner, *Entwicklungsgeschichte der Lehre von der Person Christi von den ältesten Zeiten bis auf die neuesten* (Stuttgart: Berlin, 1845–53). In English see *History of the Development of the Doctrine of the Person of Christ*, trans. by William Lindsay Alexander (Edinburgh: T & T Clark, 1884). Nevin may have had access to the form in which the work first appeared as two essays in *Tübinger Zeitschrift*, no. 4, 1835, and no. 1, 1836.—ed.]

private authority of Calvin" and the "dubious expression" of some of the other confessions. The case carries no such doubtful aspect whatever. It is just as clear as language could well make it, that all the symbols just named, connect our interest in the commemorated sacrifice of Christ, always with our interest in his abiding glorified life, as jointly comprehended in the same sacramental mystery. Such, we are assured by Calvin himself in the most explicit and solemn terms, is the doctrine of the *Consensus Tigurinus*. It is the Helvetic Confession which says that believers, along with the outward signs outwardly received, at the same time, "BY THE OPERATION OF CHRIST THROUGH THE HOLY GHOST, partake also of *the Lord's flesh and blood*, and are fed by them unto eternal life." And then what shall we say of the Heidelberg Catechism, with the loud witness of Ursinus and his colleagues still ringing in our ears? Five times over, to say the very least, in the 75th, 76th, 77th, 79th, and 80th questions, we have the idea of a life communion with Christ, in the holy Supper, solemnly proclaimed, as lying at the ground of our communion with his death. If it had been designed to anticipate and confound the very representation here made by Dr. Hodge, it could hardly have been worded more effectively for such purpose than we find it to be in fact. And yet it utters only the universal, and well understood doctrine, of the whole Reformed Church at the time. While the mass teaches a daily repetition of Christ's sacrifice for sin, and the actual presence of his body under the form of bread and wine as a fit object of worship (Quest. 80), the Lord's Supper as distinguished from it, we are here told, "testifies to us, that we have a full pardon of all our sin *by the only sacrifice* of Jesus Christ," as a fact once for all accomplished on the cross; and along with this, "that we BY THE HOLY GHOST *are engrafted into Christ*, who according to his human nature is now not on earth, but in heaven." No new sacrifice and no bodily presence, as the Romanists are accustomed to pretend; but still no disjunction of sacrifice and life, as contended for by Dr. Hodge; a view, on the contrary, lying between both these extremes; the virtue or efficacy namely of the old sacrifice, always new and fresh by coming to us through the medium of the body in which it was once accomplished, made nigh to us for this purpose, not in a material way, but still really and truly, under a higher mode of existence, by the *mystic action of the Holy Ghost*. Such was the doctrine of the Reformed Church.

So much then is plain. In divorcing the sacrifice of Christ from his life, Dr. Hodge is no true representative of the sacramental faith of the Reformed Church, as this stood in the sixteenth century. This of course does not at once settle the question, whether in doing so he is to be regarded as theologically right or wrong. He tells us how the doctrine *ought* to have stood at any rate, in order to be solid and firm; and he has a full right, of course, to dissent at this point, if he may see proper, from the authority of Calvin and the old confessions; they are not to be considered by any means infallible. But in such case, the fact of this dissent should be openly acknowledged. It may be true too, that the doctrine soon cleared itself of the feature (Calvin's private whim!) which Dr. Hodge imagines should never have belonged to it; something of the same sort is admitted and affirmed in the *Mystical Presence*; only with this difference, that what is there regarded as an unhappy falling away from its original and proper life, is here attributed by Dr. Hodge to the action of its "healthy growth." All this however, touches not, in any way, the merits of the historical question, as such; and it is with this alone that we are here occupied, at the present time. Whatever may be thought of the subject in a purely theological view, it is at least of very considerable interest to see and know, that the old Reformed doctrine of the holy Eucharist, as we have it clearly represented in the writings of Calvin, the Gallic, Scotic, Belgic and Helvetic Confessions, and the Heidelberg Catechism, differs on the point now before us, we may say *toto coelo*, from the view exhibited to us by Dr. Hodge. What they join together in the sacramental mystery, Christ's sacrifice and life, he insists on tearing asunder.

Having in this way come to some clear apprehension of the question of history, as it lies between the sixteenth century and Dr. Hodge, in regard to the main point, the nature and design namely of the holy Eucharist as held by the early Reformed Church, it will not be difficult to dispose of what is said subsequently of its proper efficacy and value. On the subject of our union with Christ, in the first place, we have the following statement.

REVIEW FROM THE REPERTORY, CONTINUED [HODGE]

What is the effect of receiving the body and blood of Christ?

This question is nearly allied to the preceding. In general terms it is answered by saying, that union with Christ, and the consequent reception of his benefits, is the effect of the believing reception of the Lord's Supper. In the Basel confession, it is said, "So that we, as members of his body, and as our true head, live in him and he in us." The Geneva catechism says the effect is "That we coalesce with him in the same life." The Scotch Confession says, "We surely believe that he abides in them (believers) and they in him, so that they become flesh of his flesh and bone of his bones." The Heidelberg catechism has much the same words, adding, "and ever live and are governed by one Spirit, as the members of our body by one soul." The Second Helv. Confession says, the effect of the Lord's Supper is, such an application of the purchase of Christ's death, by the Holy Spirit, "that he lives in us and we in him." So the Aug. Confession and others.

In explaining the nature of this union between Christ and his people, the Reformed standards reject entirely, as we have already seen, everything like corporeal contact, or the mixture or transfusion of substance. The proof of this point has already been sufficiently presented. We add only the language of Calvin. He says in opposition to the Lutherans: "if they insist that the substance of Christ's flesh is mingled with the soul of man, in how many absurdities do they involve themselves?"[3] See also his *Inst.* IV.17.32.[4] In this negative statement, as to the nature of this union, all the Reformed

---

3. [Hodge:] See his defense of the *Consensus Tigurinus*. [See "Exposition of the Heads of Agreement," in Torrance, ed., *Tracts and Treatises*, 2:239.—ed.]

4. [See *Institutes*, ed. McNeill, 2:1403–5. Hodge is probably referring to this passage, "Meanwhile, I frankly confess that I reject their teaching of the mixture, or transfusion, of Christ's flesh with our soul. For it is enough for us that, from the substance of his flesh Christ breathes life into our souls—indeed, pours forth his very life into us—even though Christ's flesh itself does not enter into us" (1404).—ed.]

agreed. They agreed also in the affirmative statement that we receive Christ himself and not merely his benefits. The union with Christ is real, and not an imaginary or merely moral one. This is often expressed by saying we receive the substance of Christ, i.e. as they explain it, Christ himself, or the Holy Spirit, by whom he dwells in his people.[5] Their common mode of representation is that contained in the *Con. Tig.*, *Haec spiritualis est communicatio quam habemus cum filio Dei, dum Spiritu suo in nobis habitans faciat credentes omnes, omnium, quae in se resident, bonorum compotes.*[6] The mode in which this subject is represented in scripture and in the Reformed standards, is, that when the Holy Spirit comes to one of God's chosen with saving power, the soul is regenerated; the first exercise of its new life is faith; Christ is thereby received; the union with him is thus consummated; and on this follows the imputation of righteousness and all saving benefits.[7]

The only question is whether besides this union effected by the Holy Spirit, there is on our part any participation of Christ's human nature as such. This takes us back to the question already considered, relating to the mode of reception and the thing received, when it is said in scripture, that we eat the flesh and drink the blood of the Son of Man. As to these questions, it will be remembered the Reformed agreed as to the following points: 1. That this reception is by the soul. 2. Through faith, not through the mouth. 3. By the power of the Holy Ghost. 4. That this received Christ's body is not confined to the Lord's Supper, but takes place whenever faith in him is exercised. 5. That it was common to believers before and after the coming of the Son of God in the flesh. We have here a complete estoppel of the claim of the authority of the Reformed church in behalf of the doctrine that our union with Christ involves a participation of his human body, nature, or life. If it be asked, however, in what sense that church teaches that we are flesh of Christ's flesh, and bone of his bones? the answer is, in the same sense in which Paul says the same thing.[8] And his meaning is very plain. He tells

5. [Hodge:] All these forms of expressions, illustrated and interchanged as they are in the Confessions, occur also in the early Reformed theologians. Thus Turretin says: "The union between Christ and us is never in scripture spoken of as bodily, but spiritual and mystical, which can only be by the Spirit and faith." Tom. III. p. 576. "The bond of our union . . . is on the part of Christ the efficacious operation of his Spirit, on our part, faith, and thence love." p. 578. This union he adds, is called substantial and essential in reference to its verity. He asserts that we receive "the substance of Christ." "Because Christ is inseparable from his benefits. The believers under the Old Testament are correctly said to have been made partakers of Christ himself, and so of his body and blood, which were present to their faith; hence they are said to have drunk of that rock, which was Christ." p. 580. [Hodge cites here from Francis Turretin, *Institutes of Elenctic Theology*, vol. 3. Hodge likely used either the 1734 edition (Utrecht: Jacob Pools), or possibly the 1847 edition (Edinburgh: J. D. Lowe), published in four volumes.—ed.]

6. [Trans. "The spiritual communion which we have with the Son of God takes place when he, dwelling in us by his Spirit, makes all who believe capable of all the blessings which reside in him." "Mutual Consent," in Torrance, ed., *Tracts and Treatises*, 2:214.—ed.]

7. [Calvin's understanding of sanctification may not have been so methodical. Calvin did not think of receiving Christ in terms of a "crisis decision," but rather in terms of a "magnitude subject to variation." Not that justification is partial. It is not! But the ounce of faith required for justification can multiply into a fuller enjoyment of Christ. "It is with this fuller possession that the Eucharist has to do." See Gerrish, *Grace and Gratitude*, 134.—ed.]

8. [Eph 5:25–33.—ed.]

us that a husband should love his wife as his own body. He that loveth his wife loveth himself. His wife is himself, for the Scriptures say, they are one flesh. All this, he adds, is true of Christ and his people. He loves the church as himself. She is his bride; flesh of his flesh and bone of his bones. If the intimate relationship, the identification of feelings, affections and interests, between a man and his wife, if their spiritual union, justifies the assertion that they are one flesh, far more may the same thing be said of the spiritual relationship between Christ and his people, which is much more intimate, sublime and mysterious, arising as it does from the inhabitation of one and the same Spirit, and producing not only a union of feeling and affection, but of life. The same apostle tells us that believers are one body and members one of another, not in virtue of their common human nature, nor because they all partake of the humanity of Christ, but because they all have one Spirit. Such as we understand it is the doctrine of the Reformed church and of the Bible as of the mystical union.

CRITICISM [NEVIN]

Caution: It is admitted on all hands, and nowhere more fully than in the *Mystical Presence*, that Calvin and the Reformed standards "reject entirely everything like corporeal contact, or the mixture or transfusion of substance." Our union with Christ they make to be, by the Holy Spirit, not material and local, but mystical and dynamic. This is not the question at all between Dr. Hodge and my book. The question is simply, after all these admissions have been made: *What* does the union involve?

Is there, says Dr. Hodge, *besides this union effected by the Holy Spirit*, any participation on our part of Christ's human body or of his human nature as such? Here we see at once, to what his notion of mystery comes. "The union with Christ is real, and not an imaginary or merely moral one," we are told. This looks like a full concurrence with the old symbols; but in the very next breath, all is unsaid again by the form into which the conception of such vital conjunction is thrown. Christ dwells in his people by the Holy Spirit; and so it is violently inferred at once that all must resolve itself into a purely intellectual process, in which, by the mediating influence of the Holy Ghost, the mind of Christ is brought into communion with the mind of his people. Dr. Hodge seems to have no other conception but this, of an apprehension of Christ by faith, through the Spirit; this is for him the sense of a real life union with the Son of Man, and it is another question accordingly altogether, whether *besides this* we have any part in his human body or nature as such.

But surely this is to mock us with empty words as a substitute for veritable things. A real *life union*, which yet leaves the life of Christ wholly on the outside of ours, and for its actual presence gives us only a divine influence under an entirely different form? The Spirit that dwells in Christ, dwells also in his people now, as he dwelt of old in Abraham, Moses and David, and by this outward bond of a third party they are made to be mystically one, even as God is in Christ and Christ in God! Our union then with Moses, is just of the same order with the union that binds us to our blessed Redeemer. The same Spirit is the bond in both cases, precisely in the same way. The mystery is just as great in the first instance, as it is in the second. There is no "mystery" properly speaking in the whole business, more than such as may be supposed to lie in the general idea of divine influences exerted upon men by the Holy Ghost. It is something parallel only in the spiritual world, with the junction of two cities, some hundred miles apart, by the presence of a river that flows through them both.

What an idea too of Christ's *life*, to ask if it includes necessarily his human nature. This of itself shows how little real, after all, nay how perfectly imaginary, the believer's union with the person of the Savior is taken to be, in this scheme of Dr. Hodge. Is not the *humanity* of Christ then an essential part of his life? Can this possibly be sundered, as a real subsistence and not a mere figment of the brain, from its relation to his *body* as one perpetual side of its being and power? Is it not then a mere abuse of language, to talk of a mystical union with Christ, a true life junction with his LIFE, that is not admitted still to extend to the human side of his general being? To me every such view, so far as it may pretend to allow any such mystery whatever, is always of a decidedly Nestorian aspect.[9] It introduces a dualistic breach into the great "mystery of godliness" itself, as exhibited to us in Christ's person, and in this way tends to overthrow ultimately all sound theology. Nestorianism in fact, as I shall have occasion to show more fully hereafter, would seem to be the reigning defect in the whole system of Dr. Hodge.

But now this conception of our union with Christ, by which all is reduced to an abstract influence apart from his real life, is not more contradictory and solecistical in its own nature, than it is at full variance also with the original faith of the Reformed Church. On this point, I join issue with Dr. Hodge direct and firm. When he says: The whole Reformed Church in England, Belgium and Germany, as well as in Switzerland, denied that we are partakers of the human nature, the real flesh and blood of Christ (p. 239), the case requires, that he should be met with plump, though always of course respectful, contradiction. There is only one way of sustaining any such position; that is, to make the idea of Christ's body at once synonymous here with outward material flesh that can be apprehended only under a local form and in some physical way. *Then* indeed it becomes easy to show, that the Reformed Church admitted no such participation. But then too, the whole argument becomes a work of sheer supererogation, on which no learned man should be willing to waste an hour's discussion. Who doubts at all, that the Reformed Church has always rejected every sort of local, oral, material communication of Christ's body with the persons of his people? But to make this the question here at issue, would be to play the part of a cunning juggler simply, who so shifts things by sleight of hand that one is made to pass for another altogether different. Such fallacy, in the case before us, is especially easy. The popular mind can hardly be kept indeed, from running into it perpetually of its own accord. But I should be sorry to suspect any disposition at all to make capital out of it, on the side of Dr.

9. [Fifth-century heresy named for Nestorius, Patriarch of Constantinople (c. 386–c. 451). Nestorius was accused of undermining the personal unity of Christ by asserting the independent subsistence of the human nature that Jesus took from Mary. Nevin in turn was accused by Hodge of having Monophysite or Eutychian characteristics. In contrast to the doctrine that Christ had both a divine and human nature, Eutyches seems to have taught that Christ had but one nature that combined both the divine and the human.—ed.]

Hodge; and I must take it for granted therefore, that no such reserved quibble is intended to lie hid in his propositions. It is in such a view, that I pronounce it incorrect. The Reformed Church of the sixteenth century, did *not* deny that believers participate in the human life of Christ, but on the contrary steadily asserted this great mystery as an essential part of its creed.

Who that has followed me with any sort of attention in the historical survey, through which we have lately passed, can have any doubt with regard to this point? Calvin's doctrine is plain; and it is plain also that the same view was accepted by the Church at large, as a true exposition and statement of her proper faith. The five great symbols, Gallic, Scotic, Belgic, Helvetic, and Palatinate, all utter here the same voice. Most explicitly, they affirm the very thing which Dr. Hodge here charges the church with denying, that believers namely, in the Lord's Supper are fed with the flesh and blood, that is, with the true human nature of Jesus Christ, unto everlasting life. All by the POWER OF THE HOLY GHOST, it is true, through the organ of faith and not by the mouth; but only all the more surely and really, for this very reason. Not in the way of an influence merely exciting to acts of faith and love; but in the way of almighty objective causation, actually making over to our lives organically the living substance of Christ's life, as truly as the same thing has place between trunk and branches, head and members, in the natural world. A participation indeed by the *soul*, excluding thus of course all mechanical transplantation of material elements; not therefore, however, only for the mere understanding or mind; but for the soul as the inmost seat of our whole life in such a way as to reach forth from this again, with true reproductive force, to the entire "new man," in Christ Jesus, as the same is to be revealed hereafter in the full glory of the resurrection.

Or will it be pretended, that the "vivific *virtue*" of Christ's body, in the old Calvinistic doctrine, is to be taken in the sense of something *less* than its true and proper life? Dr. Hodge seems disposed to get clear of it in some such way; as it must prove fatal indeed, in any other view, to the whole cause he has undertaken to support. He admits that Calvin, and others also to some extent, attributed to the body of Christ, in consequence of its union with the divine nature, a peculiar virtue, a certain "mysterious and supernatural *influence*" as he calls it, that is made to extend from him in some way to the souls of his people; which, however, he himself chooses to treat very much as an unmeaning fancy, that could find no room subsequently in the settled doctrine of the Church. But this is to do vast violence to the whole subject. Calvin was not a man, to cling thus, all his life long, to a mere blind whim or crotchet; and to be so pedantically set upon it, as to insist on making it, at the same time, the very center of his whole sacramental doctrine; and it is a strange compliment surely to the age of the Reformation, to suppose that any such whim should have been passively received from him also into the old symbols, as sound only that included no corresponding sense. This idea of the "life-giving virtue of Christ's flesh," as made over to his people "by the operation of the Holy Ghost," is quite too striking and prominent in the old Reformed doctrine, & too fully interwoven with its whole structure, to be set aside in any such summary way. Dr. Hodge is bound at least, in all respect to Calvin's memory, to say what *was* thought of under a phraseology so very strange, if it be not allowed to refer to the true and proper life of Christ. Anyone who may choose to attempt this, with an honest and candid mind, must soon find himself shut up to the one only conclusion which the case admits. By the life-giving virtue or efficacy of Christ's body, Calvin means always the very substance of Christ's life itself under its divine *human* form. What other mode of speech could he employ to express this idea, as distinguished from the crass conception of Romanists and Lutherans on one side, and the figment of mere spiritualism, on the other? For him, the body of Christ, in that new order of existence to which it has been advanced by the resurrection, is no longer under law to nature as before; it has become all "spirit and life"; having its place indeed in heaven, but in such a way as to be capable of reaching forth at once, over all outward local limits, with its inmost substance and force, to the souls of his people (and *so* to their bodies also) in every part of the world. To express all this, he avoids carefully every word that might imply locality or matter, but insists, with only the more emphasis and stress on all that it is included in the true conception of life in its invisible dynamic character. The human nature of Christ is made thus to be the reservoir of a life which flows into it from the divine nature (and what else this than his own living constitution itself) for the use of the race; the vivific virtue which it thus comprehends, the true in-ward substance of his flesh and blood, is conveyed over to us by the OPERATION OF THE HOLY GHOST; and as the result of the whole process, we are so joined to him as to become flesh of his flesh and bone of his bone, and his life reaches into us precisely as the root lives *in* its branches and the head *in* its members, in the world of nature, only under a far more inward and vital form. Westphal charges me, he says, with deny-ing that Christ gives us his body, because I affirm that he transfunds into us the vivific vigor of his flesh while he himself remains in heaven; "when, however, I say that Christ descends to us by his VIRTUE, my meaning is *not* to substitute anything different, which may overthrow the donation of his body" (*Ego vero, quum dico, Christum ad nos sua* virtue *decendere, nego me substituere aliquid diversum, quod donationem corporis aboleat*).[10]

To one indeed who has become in some good degree familiar with the Protestant Church in the sixteenth century, during the *second* sacramental war, as distinguished from the first, there can be no room whatever for any question with regard to the point here brought into view. This war had no regard at all to any such doctrine or view, as Dr. Hodge would now fain place to the credit of the Old Reformed Church. His statement is such as to thrust the MYSTERY of the sacramental transaction, as a real communion with Christ's flesh and blood, entirely out of sight. But in regard to *that*, there was no controversy in the period to which we now refer. Both sides stood on the same ground, in affirming the fact of this mystery, as involving a living participation of the true & real human life of the blessed Redeemer. They differed only in regard to the mode in which this was supposed to take place. The high Lutheran party charged the opposite side indeed with virtually rejecting the mystery, by the view they took of

10. [Nevin quotes here from Calvin's "Second Defense." See Torrance, ed., *Tracts and Treatises*, 2:279.—ed.]

its mode; but the other party never admitted the justice of this charge. On the contrary they always protested loudly and solemnly, with Calvin at their head, against every such consequence burdened upon them, as false and unfair. It is precisely such "*calumnies*," for the most part, that are met and indignantly repelled, in the tracts against Westphal. However the matter may now appear to Dr. Hodge, it is very certain that Calvin, standing in the midst of this great struggle, always considered himself, and the Reformed Church too, as holding substantially the very same doctrine with Luther in regard to our union with Christ in the sacramental mystery, and as being divided from him only by a circumstantial question, which with all its importance touched not the substance of the mystery itself in any material way. So he always said; and so, being dead, he still continues to speak, in all his works; and it is hard to see certainly, why on *such* a question at least, he is not entitled to full as much credit as the *Princeton Repertory* and Dr. Hodge.

It is not correct of course then to say that our participation of Christ in the Eucharist amounts to nothing more, according to the old Reformed doctrine, than the common actings of our faith at other times. The mystical union is not confined indeed to the Supper; it holds in the general Christian life, and must be to some extent previously at hand to make room for the special grace of the holy sacrament. The order too of our new life must be regarded as in itself always the same; not for the soul in one case and then for the body separately in another, as Luther seemed at least to think; it would be active, in any case, only through the spiritual center of our being as a whole, in the exercise of our faith. But Dr. Hodge may depend upon it, this was not supposed to bring the mystery of the holy sacrament to a level simply with the ordinary exercises of this faith at other times; and though in one case the very same thing, and no more, had place *with* the use of signs, which more commonly in the other had place *without* them. To what must the "mystery" be reduced, on any such supposition as this? Dr. Hodge himself admits, that Calvin at least made the sacrament to be more than an occasion merely for the exercise of faith. Eating and believing with him are by no means the same thing; there is an efficacious force in the transaction itself, *by the power of the Holy Ghost*, to unite us more and more with the life of Christ's sacred body. In the most distinct terms, he attributes to it an objective, mystical power in this way, which is altogether its own, and not to be confounded with the actings of the ordinary Christian life. So also the old Reformed Confessions. Along with the signs for outward use, go always, they tell us, the substantial verities thus represented, for the use of the inward or new man, not in the way of mere thought or contemplation, but so as to be actually at hand by the Spirit as a divine pabulum unto everlasting life. "Christ performs in us really," says the Belgic Confession, "all that he represents to us in those sacred signs,"[11] though in a mystical, incomprehensible mode; "Believers receive what is given by the minister of the Lord, and eat the Lord's bread and drink of the Lord's cup; inwardly, however, *in the mean time* [*interim*, that is, with simultaneousness or concomitant force], by the *operation of Christ* through the Holy Spirit [not from any

---

11. [See Dennison, *Reformed Confessions*, 2:446.—ed.]

subjective working only of their own faith, but by the mystical act of Christ himself], they partake also of the Lord's flesh and blood, and are by them fed unto everlasting life." So speaks the Helvetic Confession,[12] Dr. Hodge's pet authority among the later symbols; how widely aside from his own view, need not be farther said or shown. The same confession distinguishes expressly between sacramental and spiritual manduca-tion; not in such a way as to make all turn on the presence or absence of an outward sign, as Guericke pretends, and after him Dr. Hodge; but by ascribing to the sacrament expressly the force of an *objective application* of Christ's body and blood. The case is parallel, according to Calvin, with the relation of natural life to the life-giving agencies by which it is upheld and supported. Life must be at hand, for instance, to admit a vitalizing action on the part of the sun; its rays falling on a dead carcass produce only corruption and decay; but the vitalizing action is not, for this reason, the ordinary process of life itself. So faith, or spiritual receptivity, must be at hand to admit the vivific stream that flows from Christ's body in the holy sacrament but faith is not this stream itself, nor the measure even of its salutary power; it is a divine reality, which flows in upon the animated subject objectively, by the operation of the Holy Ghost, actually to strengthen and increase the life which is at hand, just as food nourishes the outward body. So, very clearly and fully, Calvin utters himself, in opposition to the misrepresentations of Westphal.

Case of O.T. Saints

But, says Dr. Hodge, "all the Reformed taught, Calvin perhaps more earnestly than most others, that our union with Christ since the incarnation is the same in nature with that enjoyed by the saints under the old dispensation." A complete *estoppel*, we are triumphantly told, to all claim of authority here in behalf of the doctrine, that the mystical union "involves a participation of his human body, nature or life." So it may be possibly for such as are previously prepared to take their historical knowledge, in this great case, as well as their theology itself, on mere authority & trust. But it is well to look into the matter a little more closely. Dr. Hodge, as we have already found, is sometimes betrayed into a rather cavalier treatment of history, by his own overween-ing mastery of the whole subject under an *a priori* form. He means of course to be true and honest; but he has such a profound apprehension of what *ought* to have been, that he cannot bring himself into the right posture always (a troublesome business frequently at any rate), for seeing what *has* been in truth and in fact. Witness his use of the *Consensus Tigurinus*, his pell-mell classification of the authorities generally, his undervaluation of Calvin over *against* Bullinger, his deliberate attempt to purge the Reformed doctrine of its Calvinistic peculiarity as a "foreign element" that had never any business to be there, &c. *Possibly* this present "estoppel" may not be so complete after all.

In the first place, Dr. Hodge himself admits, that Calvin at least and a part of the Church besides, allowed our union with Christ to include the idea of vivifying efficacy,

---

12. [See Dennison, *Reformed Confessions*, 2:866.—ed.]

extended to us from his body. And yet the same Calvin, it is said, contended "more earnestly perhaps than others," that the union of the Old Testament saints with Christ was the same that is enjoyed by saints now. What becomes then of the estoppel, in his case? Is it any more easy to conceive of a vivific influence proceeding from Christ's body *before his incarnation*, than it is to admit as much of his veritable human life itself? Dr. Hodge feels that it is not, and so advances, with right hardy courage, to expel the whole conception from the sacramental doctrine of the Reformed Church, as an uncongenial intrusion. Hear what he says:

> All the Reformed taught, Calvin perhaps more earnestly than most others, that our union with Christ since the incarnation is the same in nature as that enjoyed by the saints under the old dispensation. This is perfectly intelligible if the virtue of his flesh and blood, which we receive in the Lord's Supper, is its virtue as a sacrifice, because he was the lamb slain from the foundation of the world. His sacrifice was as effectual for the salvation of Abraham as of Paul, and could be appropriated as fully by the one as by that of the other. But if the virtue in ques-tion is a mysterious power due to the hypostatical union, flowing from Christ's body in heaven, it must be a benefit peculiar to believers living since the incarna-tion. It is impossible that those living before the advent could partake of Christ's body, in this sense, because it did not then exist; it had not as yet been assumed into union with the divine nature. We find therefore that Romanists and nominal Protestants, make the greatest distinction as to the relation of the ancient saints to God and that of believers since the advent, between the sacraments of the one dispensation and those of the other. All this is consistent and necessary on their theory of the incarnation, of the Church and of the sacraments, but it is all the plainest contradiction to the doctrine of the Reformed Church. Here then is an element which does not accord with the doctrines of that church; and this in-congruity is one good reason for not regarding it as a genuine portion of its faith.

But now who does not see that in all this argument for the ejection of the "uncon-genial foreign element," as at variance with Calvin's view of the Old Testament saints, it is precisely the acknowledged peculiarity of Calvin himself that Dr. Hodge is thus seeking to confound and destroy? And what then, in all common sense, becomes of the unanswerable "estoppel?" If it had not power to stop Calvin himself, it is not easy to see surely why it should be of any more force, on the *historical* question, for anybody else. Let Calvin be charged with the theological contradiction, if it seem proper; that is all fair and open ground; but surely Dr. Hodge is asking too much, when he wishes to turn the contradiction, as he holds it, into an estoppel of the very *fact* itself on which the whole charge is made to rest. A specimen of Homeric dormitancy, of a truth![13]

But to make the case still worse, the very difficulty here urged against Calvin is one that he had fully before his own mind, and repeatedly notices, for the very purpose of *obviating the wrong use* now made of it by Dr. Hodge. For it so happens, that in this

---

13. [Although "dormitancy" does not appear in any standard dictionary, the sense is fairly clear— "sleepiness, nodding off," so that the phrase "Homeric dormitancy" alludes to the proverb, "even Homer nods" (attributed to the Latin poet Horace)—even the greatest writers have occasionally lapses of incon-sistency or carelessness. Of course, in this context, Nevin means to suggest that to attribute *such* a lapse to someone of Calvin's stature is simply implausible.—ed.]

point, as well as in most every other, Dr. Hodge has been anticipated by Westphal, and the ultra-Lutheran school of the sixteenth century; only from a different standpoint and with a different design.

In his commentary on 1 Cor. X. 14, Calvin insists that sacramental signs and realities were as much bound together under the Old Testament, as they are under the New. The saints then participated truly in the life of Christ, as they do now. But here, he says, rises this question; "Inasmuch as we now in the Supper eat the body of Christ and drink his blood, how could the Jews have partaken of the same spiritual meat and drink, when there was yet no flesh of Christ which they might eat?" To this follows a very direct answer:

> The flesh which as yet was not, served them notwithstanding for food. Nor is this a vain or sophistical subtlety; for their salvation hung on the benefit of Christ's death and resurrection, and so upon his flesh and blood; whence it was necessary for them to partake of Christ's flesh and blood, in order that they might communicate with the benefit of redemption. This participation (perception,) was the mysterious work of the Holy Ghost, who so wrought, that the flesh of Christ, *though not yet created*, became in them efficacious. They are to be understood however, as having eaten in their mode, which was *different from ours*; and this is what I have before said, that Christ is now exhibited to us more fully as regards measure of revelation. For in our time, the manducation is substantial, which it could not be then; that is, Christ feeds us with his own flesh, slain for us and appointed unto us for meat, and we draw thence life.[14]

A hard saying all this, some may be tempted to exclaim, and not to be listened to with patience even from the respect-compelling lips of Calvin. We have to do with it at present, however, only in the form of *history*. In the face of it, what becomes of Dr. Hodge's "estoppel?"

Westphal tried indeed to use it against Calvin, on the basis of this very passage itself. He would have it, that the manna and rock were *only* figures, and that Calvin then of course made the New Testament sacraments to be no better. "Let him settle it with Paul," Calvin replies, planting himself on the literal text in his own sense, not unlike Luther here, with his *Hoc est corpus meum,* at the Marburg conference; "why is he displeased with me, and not rather with the apostle, whose words are so plain?" But Christ had not yet put on flesh, Westphal argued. "If he had any candor," Calvin returns,

> he would notice the solution I have given of this knot in my commentary; where I say, that the mode of eating for the fathers was different from ours, inasmuch as the manducation is *substantial* which it would not be then; namely, as Christ feeds us with his flesh sacrificed for us, that we may draw life *from its substance*. As the lamb is said to have been slain from the foundation of the world, so it was necessary for the fathers under the law to seek spiritual nourishment; from the flesh and blood, which we now enjoy more richly, not only as regards a fuller measure of revelation, but because the flesh of Christ *once offered* in sacrifice is *daily* extended to us for fruition. When therefore Westphal infers, that we equal

14. [*Calvin's Commentaries*, 22 vols. (Grand Rapids, MI: Baker, 2003), 20:319.—ed.]

the figure to the truth, it only shows his too arrogant malice, when he knows well enough that I mention distinct grades. *II Def. adv. Westhp. Calumnias. Op. ix. p. 671.*[15]

"I everywhere profess," he says in another place,

> that the same Christ who was set forth under the law, is more richly and fully exhibited now to us; I add also, that with the flesh of Christ, which exerted its force before it was created in the fathers, we are now *substantially* fed; which is more than enough to expose the dishonesty of Westphal, who calumniates us as confounding those grades, which as is proper we carefully distinguish. *Adm. Ult. Op. ix. p. 697.*[16]

This is not the place to canvass the sense or value of this part of Calvin's doctrine, in itself considered. So much at least is clear historically; first, that he did *not*, after all, make the participation of the O.T. saints in Christ to be the same with ours, as is affirmed by Dr. Hodge and secondly, that his view of it, whatever it was, was held as not to detract in the least from the fullness of his faith, a hundred times repeated, that in the Lord's Supper it is our privilege to communicate, really and truly, with the very substance of Christ's human life.

But apart from the specific testimony now presented in bar of Dr. Hodge's sweeping "estoppel," must it not be counted a very bold pretension, in any view, to think of arguing out of the way the general sacramental history of the sixteenth century, in any such purely logical style? Dr. Hodge shows himself a second *Hegel*,[17] we may say, in making the idea mistress of the fact.[18] Suppose a full contradiction in the case before us, and no attempt made whatever to solve the knot; could this, by any possibility, nullify the full, clear evidence we have the general fact notwithstanding, to which our attention is now directed? It is no dubious or obscure point that is here involved; the Eucharistic faith of the Reformed Church in the sixteenth century, was not spoken in a corner; it was proclaimed upon the house tops, and is now written so plainly on the scroll of past time that he who runs may read. That Calvin especially held and taught always a real union on the part of believers with the human nature or life of Christ, is just as plain as it is that he taught the doctrine of election. If his view of Old Testament grace come into conflict with this, as Dr. Hodge supposes, be it so; it is not necessary to

---

15. ["Second Defense," 283, 284.—ed.]

16. ["Last Admonition," in Torrance, ed., *Tracts and Treatises*, 2:401.—ed.]

17 [Georg Wilhelm Friedrich Hegel (1770–1831), German idealist philosopher educated at Tübingen where he aligned with Schelling and together they began to work out the speculative method that would make them famous. Hegel led the way from Kant and Fichte in developing a philosophy/theology of *Geist*, in which Christianity is rendered a philosophic system of Absolute knowing. For quite some time Hegel's was the reigning philosophical system in Germany. His influence on the host of subsequent philosophers, including Rothe, Baur, Feuerbach, and Marx, illustrates his importance to the history of philosophy.—ed.]

18. [Nevin's observation is a common if misguided critique of Hegel in general—that his system subjects the facts of history to the control of predetermined philosophical concepts. On the specific matter of the case before us, i.e., Calvin, the OT saints, and bodily union with Christ, Nevin is accusing Hodge of similarly making the facts of history serve his theological system.—ed.]

count either him or the confession infallible. But let us not, for any such reason, close our ears against the voice of facts. Let us not muzzle history, by a wholesale presumption of mere logic. What is an *a priori* negative of this sort worth, when confronted with such an avalanche of positive historical affirmation as we have here, from the opposite side?

Marriage Relation

Dr. Hodge exposes fully the flatness of his whole system, in what he says on the apostle's parallel between the mystery of marriage and our union with Christ. We have not room here of course to take this up minutely; and it is not easy from the nature of the subject, under any circumstances, to do it full justice in the way of popular representation. But who, with any proper *inwardness* of spirit, is not made to feel the vast wrong it is here made to suffer, under the frigid exegesis of Dr. Hodge? It is not true that the marriage union, as it holds between husband and wife, stands simply in "an identification of feelings, affections and interests;" they are mysteriously, at the same time, made to be *one flesh*, one joint life, in conformity with the original symbolical order of woman's creation, in which Eve, as Hooker expresses it, appears as "a pure native extract" out of Adam's body. It is this *mystery*, as plain as language can say it, that forms the pivot of the entire parallel; and the whole representation implies that the comparison is not merely outward and accidental; but that the marriage relation is, in very truth, a mystical prophecy, in a lower sphere, of the transcendental mystery of our union with Christ, which must be regarded as holding accordingly, in its own higher sphere, under a form of real analogy and correspondence. We *are*, says the apostle, members of his body, of his flesh and of his bones. Dr. Hodge falls here to the same rationalistic level precisely, with Pelagius, Episcopius, and DeWette.[19] Paul assuredly never designed to utter, with such solemn pomp, so poor and flat a sense. How much more rich and deep, the exegetical judgment of Calvin. He lays hold of the MYSTERY in its broadest form; and refers all especially to the holy Eucharist, as the central act through which is consummated, continually more and more, the full life-communion of the Savior with his glorious Church. So all the best commentators, at the present time. "The passage," says Calvin,

> is classic on our mystical communion with Christ. It is not to be taken in this view as hyperbolical, but literal; and it not only signifies that Christ partakes of our nature, but is designed to say something more deep and emphatic. For the words of Moses, Gen. 2:24, are quoted. And what now is the sense? As Eve was

19. [Pelagius (c. 354–c. 420/440) famously opposed Augustine by arguing that God gave mankind the ability to choose the good, and consequently that mankind can take the first steps to salvation without the benefit of divine grace, teachings subsequently condemned as heresy. Nevin thus sees as "rationalism" any attempt to explain in purely human terms the transcendent mystery of divine activity. It is on this same basis that he condemns Simon Episcopius (1583–1643), a leading follower of the Dutch theologian Arminius and his teachings on the role of human will in salvation. With Wilhelm Martin Leberecht DeWette (1780–1849), Nevin brings the controversy to his own back door and Mercersburg's reaction to the rationalism that had won so many theologians over in Germany and the Continent. DeWette can be depicted as stripping Christianity of its metaphysical base.—ed.]

formed out of the substance of her husband Adam, so as to be true members of Christ, coalesce with him by communication of his substance into one body.

In conclusion he adds:

> They are preposterous, who allow here only what they can grasp with their own measure of wit. When they deny the presentation of Christ's flesh and blood to us in the holy Supper, *Define the mode,* they exclaim, *or you will not convince us.* But as for myself, I am confounded (*in stuporem abripior*) with the grandeur of the subject. Nor am I ashamed to confess with Paul, admiringly, my own ignorance. For how much better is that, than to dwarf with my own fleshly sense what the apostle proclaims a HIGH MYSTERY.[20]

---

20. [See *Calvin's Commentaries,* 21:325.—ed.]

8

The Sacramental Efficacy of the Lord's Supper[1]

[NEVIN]

IT MUST HAVE BECOME sufficiently plain by this time to all who have given dispassionate attention thus far to the present discussion, that the sacramental theory of Dr. Hodge is something quite different from the old Calvinistic doctrine of the Reformed symbols, and that any *appearance* of agreement in the case turns altogether on the sound of quoted testimony divorced from its true historical sense. It is fashionable, with the school here represented, to speak of Calvin as wanting in clearness and consistency on this subject; but his theory in truth flows like a pellucid stream, always within the same channel, from the commencement of his public life to its close. It is our modern divinity that has become confused and muddy, and hard to understand, on this entire question of holy Eucharist. It talks of sacramental grace, and yet turns it the next moment into a mere fancy; affirms a mystical union with Christ, and yet resolves it all into a divine influence; pretends to find something great in the ordinance as compared with Arminian or Socinian spiritualism, and yet empties it at last of all objective contents in precisely the same flat style. Throughout his whole article, as we have seen, Dr. Hodge plays between the objective and subjective schemes of sacramental grace, in such a way that while he appears at times to accept the language of the first, it is only to fall in reality into the common-place sense of the second. With Calvin and the old confessions, he rejects a local presence and oral communication, and lays stress on the spiritual character of the transaction; taking it quietly for granted, the while, that this is all which is needed to identify his position with theirs. To a presence in the *flesh*, he knows no other opposite, it might seem, than a presence *in the mind*. The old terminology then may be admitted, though not without some feeling of hyperbolic exaggeration; only however, of course, to be translated forthwith into modern conceptions, more consonant in supposition with reason and common sense. All runs out thus into vague indetermination. The correspondence with the old

---

1. ["Dr. Hodge on the *Mystical Presence*, Article from the *Repertory*, Continued, No. 8," *Weekly Messenger*, New Series, vol. 13, no. 34. Wednesday, July 12, 1848. Published by the Board of the Synod of the German Reformed Church: Chambersburg, PA.—ed.]

doctrine lies after all only in its negations, and not in what it positively affirms. The phraseology, *spiritual presence, perception of Christ's flesh and blood, virtue of his life, participation by faith, operation of the Holy Ghost*, &c., carries quite a different meaning in the system of Calvin from that which is allowed to it in the system of Dr. Hodge and yet by Dr. Hodge himself scarcely any regard is had to this difference whatever; he makes the whole over to his own credit and use, with the most cool matter-of-course air, as though it could come into nobody's head to dispute his legal right to it in such wholesale way.

We have this general character of the article strikingly illustrated, in the following passage, winding up its "ventilation" of the old Reformed doctrine, in answer to the question: *What efficacy belongs to the Lord's Supper as a sacrament?*

REVIEW FROM THE REPERTORY, CONTINUED [HODGE]

On this point the Reformed, in the first place, reject the Romish doctrine that the sacraments contain the grace they signify, and that they convey that grace, by the mere administration, to all who do not oppose an obstacle. Secondly, the Lutheran doctrine, which attributes to the sacraments an inherent supernatural power, due indeed not to the signs, but the word of God connected with them, but which is nevertheless always operative, provided there be faith in the receiver. Thirdly, the doctrine of the Socinians[2] and others, that the sacraments are mere badges of profession, or empty signs of Christ and his benefits. They are declared to be efficacious means of grace; but their efficacy, as such, is referred neither to any virtue in them nor in him that administers them, but solely to the attending operation or influence of the Holy Spirit, precisely as in the case of the word. It is the *virtus Spiritus Sancti extrinsecus accidens*,[3] to which all their supernatural or saving efficacy is referred. They have, indeed, the objective moral power of significant emblems and seals of divine appointment, just as the word has its inherent moral power; but their efficacy as means of grace, their power, in other words, to convey grace depends entirely, as in the case of the word, on the cooperation of the Holy Ghost. Hence the power is in no way tied to the sacraments. It may be exerted without them. It does not always attend them, nor is it confined to the time, place or service. The favorite illustration of the Lutheran doctrine is drawn from the history of the woman who touched the hem of our Savior's garment. As there was always supernatural virtue in him, which flowed out to all who applied to him in faith, so there is in the sacraments. The Reformed doctrine is illustrated by a reference to our

2. [The name "Socinianism" derives from Lelio Francesco Maria Sozini (1525–62) and Fausto Paolo Sozzini (1539–1604), nephew of Lelio. Early in his career Lelio Sozini considered the ideas of mysticism and of the Reformation and in 1548 he settled in Switzerland. But in spite of an acquaintance with Melanchthon and Calvin, he engaged Calvin in a debate over the Trinity, where his views were not rejected outright (he satisfied Bullinger), but clear evidence of his anti-trinitarian views began to emerge. His nephew Fausto began his controversial career with rejection of the essential divinity of Christ. Later he wrote in rejection of mankind's natural immortality. Ultimately he sought the favor of John Sigismund, the ruler of Klausenburg and a well-known anti-trinitarian. He spent the rest of his life promoting early Unitarian views. See Cory, *Faustus Socinus*.—ed.]

3. [Trans. "the strength of the Holy Spirit occurring externally."—ed.]

Savior's anointing the eyes of the blind man with clay. There was no virtue in the clay to make the man see, the effect was due to the attending power of Christ. The modern rationalists smile at all these distinctions and say it all amounts to the same thing. These three views however are radically different in themselves, and have produced radically different effects, where they have severally prevailed.

All the points, both negative and positive, included in the statement of the Reformed doctrine, above given, are clearly presented with perfect unanimity in their symbolical books. In the Gall. Conf., art. 34, it is said, "We acknowledge, that these external signs are such, that through them God operates by the power of his Holy Spirit."[4] Helv. Conf. ii. [Second Helvetic Confession] c. 19: "We do not sanction the doctrine that grace and the things signified or included in them, that those who"[5] receive the signs receive also the blessings they represent. When this fails, the fault is indeed in the receiver, just as in the case of the word, God in both offers his grace. His word does not cease to be true and divine, nor do the sacraments lose their integrity, because men do not receive them in faith and to their salvation (see ch. 21, at the end).[6] The *Consensus Tigurinus* teaches, as we have already seen, that the sacraments have no virtue in themselves, as means of grace; *Si quid boni nobis per sacramenta confertur, id non fit propria eorum virtute . . . Deus enim solus est, qui Spiritu suo agit* (art. 12).[7] In the following articles it is taught that they benefit only believers, that grace is not tied to them, that believers receive elsewhere the same grace, and the blessing often follows long after the administration. The Scotch Conf. ch. 21, teaches that the whole benefit flows "from faith apprehending Christ, who alone renders the sacraments efficacious."[8] In the Geneva Cat. the question is asked: "Do you believe that the power and efficacy of the sacrament, instead of being included in the element, flow entirely from the Spirit of God?" *Ans.* "So I believe, that is, should it please the Lord to exercise his power through his own instruments to the end to which he has appointed them."[9] It is not worthwhile to multiply quotations, for as to this point, there was no diversity of opinion. We would only refer the reader to Calvin's *Inst.* IV. 14, a passage, which though directed against the Romanists, has a much wider scope. He there declares it to be purely diabolical error to teach men to expect justification from the sacraments, instead of from faith; and insists principally on two things, first, that nothing is conferred through the sacraments beyond what is offered in the word;[10] and, secondly,

4. [See Dennison, *Reformed Confessions*, 2:152.—ed.]

5. [See Dennison, *Reformed Confessions*, 2:863.—ed.]

6. [For the whole of chapter 21, see Dennison, *Reformed Confessions*, 2:865–69.—ed.]

7. [Trans. "If any good thing is bestowed upon us through the sacraments, it is not because of any inherent virtue. . . . For it is God alone who works by his Spirit." Dennison, *Reformed Confessions*, 1:541–42.—ed.]

8. [See Dennison, *Reformed Confessions*, 2:202.—ed.]

9. [See Dennison, *Reformed Confessions*, 1:510–11.—ed.]

10. [Gerrish argued that neither Hodge nor Nevin "did justice to Calvin's persuasion that by faith in the proclaimed word Christ becomes 'flesh of our flesh,' " which is to say neither really appreciated the way in which the word in Calvin took on sacramental significance. But likewise, the sacrament took on the character of proclamation! Calvin's innovation was to have word assume the role previously

that they are not necessary to salvation, the blessings may be had without them. He confirms his own doctrine by the saying of Augustine: *Invisibilem sanctificationem sine visibili signo esse posse, et visibile rursum signum sine vera sanctificatione.*[11]

Such then, as we understand it, is the true doctrine of the Reformed Church on the Lord's Supper. By the Reformed church, we mean the Protestant churches of Switzerland, the Palatinate, France, Belgium, England, Scotland and elsewhere. According to the public standards of these churches: The Lord's Supper is a holy ordinance instituted by Christ, as a memorial of his death, wherein, under the symbols of bread and wine, his body as broken for us and his blood as shed for the remission of sins, are signified, and by the power of the Holy Ghost, sealed and applied to believers; whereby their union with Christ and their mutual fellowship are set forth and confirmed, their faith strengthened, and their souls nourished unto eternal life.

CRITICISM [NEVIN]

This *is* ventilation truly, such as may be said to blow the entire sacramental mystery into chaff! We have Calvinistic terms and distinctions, backed with a few plausible quotations; but underneath the whole is made to lurk a poor modern sense, that Calvin himself would have repudiated with sacred indignation.

Certainly the efficacy of the Lord's Supper is referred, by the old Reformed Church, not to any magical virtue supposed to be included in the elements as such, but to the attending power of the Holy Ghost. But why should so plain a truism as this be paraded by Dr. Hodge, as touching at all the subject in debate? Is there a word to contradict it, in the *Mystical Presence*? We all know surely, how earnestly Calvin labored to turn men's minds off from all superstitious trust in the sacramental elements as mere objects of sense, and to fasten them on the interior side of the transactions, as holding in the mirific action of the Holy Ghost. But it is a huge *non sequitur*, to draw from all this the consequence which is here hurried upon us by Dr. Hodge, that the sacraments namely include in themselves no grace, and stand related to the ends they are made to serve only as accidental outward occasions. This, we confidently maintain, is *not* the sense of the old Reformed doctrine. It is not necessary surely to re-quote authorities here, in support of this position. If historical evidence can be made to prove anything,

---

held by the sacraments in medieval theology. His point of departure was the theology of Augustine, who recognized that the words uttered over the sacrament were not some magical formula. Rather the authentic word is the word operating in the sacrament, which becomes effective because it is believed. "The difference between the word and sacrament is simply that the sacraments picture what the word declares: namely Christ." Thus, for Calvin, there was no antagonism between the pedagogical and sacramental operations of the word. But what is not to be misunderstood is that Calvin was not elevating the word at the expense of the sacraments. His unique elevation of the significance of the word in his theology effectively cast the word in what had been traditional eucharistic language. So it was not so much the elevation of the word above that of the sacraments, so common in nineteenth-century Protestant America, as it was the elevation of the word to *equal* status with the sacraments. See Gerrish, *Grace and Gratitude*, 76, 82–86, 107.—ed.]

11. [Trans. "There can be invisible sanctification without a visible sign and, on the other hand, a visible sign without true sanctification." Calvin, *Institutes*, IV.14.14, ed. McNeill, 2:1290.—ed.]

it has been amply shown already that the old doctrine included always the idea of an objective mystical force, in the sacramental transaction itself; the very thing which Dr. Hodge in the passage before us ventures to deny. His representation then, however honestly intended on his own part, must be regarded as grossly injurious to the subject which he has in hand. It is nothing less in fact than a violent distortion, by which this is wrested out of its true and proper proportions into another shape altogether.

In denying that the outward elements possess any saving efficacy in their own separate nature, Calvin and the Reformed symbols did not mean to deny such efficacy to the sacraments in their full sense; for this, we have had full opportunity to see, was supposed to include this very conception as a necessary part of their constitution. Occasionally indeed the mere outward side of the service is denominated the sacrament, which then of course is represented as having no power in itself for sacramental ends; it is only the accompanying grace of Christ's Spirit, which can make it to be of any account. But in any full view of the case, these two things are regarded as going together in the constitution of the sacrament itself. Here it is, that Dr. Hodge is wholly at fault. His idea plainly is, that the relation of inward and outward is to be counted just as loose and free in the sacraments, as in the case of any other occasions that may be turned into means of grace by the concurring influence of God's Spirit; and this view he endeavors also to impose on the old Reformed Church. But who that has listened at all to Calvin or Ursinus, or attended in any measure to the clear sense of the old symbols, can fail to see how greatly they are wronged by every imagination of this sort. A sacrament, they tell us perpetually, consists of two sides, one outward and the other invisible and inward, which must be always taken together to complete the presence of the mystery. The holy Eucharist consists thus of a terrene part, objects and acts that fall within the sphere of sense; and a celestial part, other objects and acts, parallel with the first, which have place only in the sphere of the spirit. The outward things are in this view signs only and pictures of realities belonging to a higher order of existence; the inward things are these invisible realities themselves. And how now are these two sides of the ordinance bound together? Just as the cataract of Niagara, Dr. Hodge would tell us, may be employed by God's Spirit, if he see proper, to fill us with admiring and adoring thoughts of the mystery of Jehovah himself. A mere powerless sign in itself, the Holy Ghost can yet make use of as an occasion for exciting and supporting a spirit of devotion. Need we say however, that it was under no such loose and general relation as this, that the outward and inward were made to go together in the old Reformed doctrine of the Lord's Supper? They were considered always as constituent sides both, and one not a whit more so than the other, of the same sacramental transaction. The bond uniting them, according to the doctrine, is not physical or mechanical in any way; implies no local contact or inclusion, as the Romanist and Lutherans might seem to teach; falls not at all within the range of experience under any other form. To express this peculiar character, it is denominated a *sacramental* union; by which however is never meant that it is simply nominal or national, but only that it is extraordinary and peculiar to this case. It is regarded in fact as most intimate and necessary. Though not joined together in the same way, inward and outward meet here simultaneously in one fact, as really as soul and body are united in the constitution of our common life. The sacrament is not the elements used in its celebration, nor the outward service only in which this consists, but a divine TRANSACTION, comprehending in itself, along with such visible and earthly forms, the invisible power of the very verities themselves that are thus symbolically represented.

All this is strongly and clearly expressed, in the following statement, extracted from a confession presented at the *Colloquy of Worms*,[12] a. 1557, by Beza and other ministers in the name of the Gallic churches.

> We confess that in the Supper of the Lord not only the benefits of Christ, but the very substance itself of the Son of Man; that is, the same true flesh which the Word assumed into perpetual personal union, in which he was born and suffered, rose again and ascended to heaven, and that true blood which he shed for us; are not only signified, or set forth symbolically, typically or in figure, like the memory of something absent, but are truly and really represented, exhibited, and offered for use; in connection with symbols that are by no means naked, but which, so far as God who promises and offers is concerned, always have the thing itself truly and certainly joined with them, whether proposed to believers or unbelievers.
>
> As regards the mode now in which the thing itself, that is, the true body and true blood of the Lord, is connected with the symbols, we say that it is symbolical or sacramental. We call a sacramental mode not such as is figurative merely, but such as truly and certainly represents, under the form of visible things, what God along with symbols exhibits and offers, namely, what we mentioned before, the true body and blood of Christ; which may show that we retain and defend the presence of the very body and blood of Christ in the Supper. So that if we have any controversy with truly pious and learned brethren, it is not concerning the thing itself, but only concerning the mode of the presence which is known to God alone, and by us believed.[13]

This testimony is strong, but it goes not at all beyond the general sense of the Reformed Church as elsewhere expressed. "The papists confound sign and thing," says Calvin, "profane men, such as Schwenckfeld[14] and others, rend them asunder; let *us* keep the

---

12. [Although the Augsburg Religious Peace (1555) brought religious freedom to the churches of the Augsburg Confession, a true unity was still longed for by many. With the death of Luther a leader had not emerged that could provide the leadership desired by the princes, and even Melanchthon was under attack in his own party. Despairing that a counsel would succeed, Ferdinand ordered a conference to be held at Worms, August 24, 1557. The presidency went to Bishop Julius von Pflug, and the Protestant leaders included Melanchthon, Brenz, and Schnepf, among others. The conference actually began on September 11 and divisions once again dogged the Protestants, so much so that repeated interruptions led to suspensions in the proceedings. Beza, Farel, and other colleagues decided to attend the colloquy on behalf of the Protestants imprisoned in Paris by Henry II. The Germans had requested a confession of faith and Beza produced one entirely in agreement with the Augsburg Confession except the article on the Eucharist. It did, however, hold out hope that there might be a future agreement. In the end the colloquy fell apart and little in the way of union was achieved.—ed.]

13. ["*Confessio fidei doctrinaeque de Coena Domini exhibita illustrissimo Principi Virtembergensi, authoribus Th. Beza et Guilhelmo Farello*," May 14, 1557. See Johann Wilhelm Baum, *Theodor Beza, nach handschriftlichen Quellen dargestellt* (Leipzig: Weidmannsche Buchhandlung, 1843), I.405–9.—ed.]

14. [Caspar Schwenckfeld (1490–1561), Silesian theologian of the Reformation who initially came

middle; that is, let us hold the *conjunction* established by the Lord, but with proper *distinction*, so as not to transfer rashly to one what belongs to the other."[15]

So, as we have seen, he makes the dove at the baptism of Jesus parallel with the outward side of the Lord's Supper, in its relation to the invisible reality it represented. Here was no accidental connection only; the dove indeed as such, was not the Holy Ghost; but the presence of the one was bound to that of the other really and truly, as inward and outward sides simply of one and the same mysterious fact. And thus it is, that inward and outward go together also, not by identification or physical conjunction of any sort, but sacramentally and mystically, in the holy Eucharist. "It is to me beyond all controversy," we hear Calvin saying, "that the reality is here joined with the sign, or in other words, that so far as spiritual virtue is concerned, we do as truly partake of Christ's body as we eat the bread." The Confessions utter distinctly the same language.

> We join with the signs the true possession and fruition of what is thus offered to us. *Gal. Conf.*[16]

> We do utterly condemn the vanity of such as affirm, that the sacraments are nothing else but mere naked signs. *Scotch Conf.*[17]

> They were visible signs and seals of an invisible thing, *by means whereof* God worketh in us by the power of the Holy Ghost. Therefore the signs are not in vain or insignificant, so as to deceive us; for Jesus Christ is the true object presented by them, without whom they would be of no moment.—Now as it is certain and beyond all doubt, that Jesus Christ has not enjoined to us the use of his sacraments in vain, so he works in us all what he represents to us by these holy signs, though the manner surpasses our understanding. *Belgic or Reformed Dutch Conf.*[18]

> He that partakes of the sacrament outwardly with true faith, partakes not of the sign only, but enjoys also, as already said, the thing itself which this represents. [Second] *Helv. Conf.*[19]

> —He feeds and nourishes my soul to everlasting life, with his crucified body and shed blood, as assuredly as I receive from the hands of the minister, and taste with my mouth, the bread and cup of the Lord, as certain signs of the body and blood of Christ. *Heid. Cat.*[20]

Will anyone pretend to escape from all this, by saying it is only the general spiritual grace of the gospel, as it may be enjoyed at any time, which is supposed to be

---

under the influence of Luther. Soon he criticized major Reformation doctrines including justification by faith and Luther's doctrine of the Lord's Supper. His teachings were radical enough to receive violent criticism from both Roman Catholics and Protestants. See Erb, *Schwenckfeld in His Reformation Setting*; McLaughlin, *Caspar Schwenckfeld.*—ed.]

15. [Calvin, Commentary on 1 Cor 10:3 (*Commentaries*, 22:317)—ed.]

16. [See Dennison, *Reformed Confessions*, 2:153.—ed.]

17. [See Dennison, *Reformed Confessions*, 2:201.—ed.]

18. [See Dennison, *Reformed Confessions*, 2:444, 446.—ed.]

19. [See Dennison, *Reformed Confessions*, 2:868.—ed.]

20. [See Dennison, *Reformed Confessions*, 2:786.—ed.]

signified and pledged by the outward side of the sacrament, in this bold phraseology? To do so, can only betray great ignorance, or most stubborn prejudice, or rather no small combination of both. Is it necessary to quote again the strong language of Ursinus, on the point? Or must we still, pile proof upon proof from Calvin? The inward reality represented by the outward signs in the Lord's Supper is always taken by the old Reformed Church as at hand *simultaneously with the signs themselves;* and as entering thus, not indeed into the elements as such, but *into the transaction,* as a necessary part of its proper constitution. This precisely is what is meant, when it is declared so frequently, and with so much emphasis, that the signs here are not vain or nude. This they *would* be, it is supposed always, if they were not mystically attended with the very substance of the divine verities or things which they represent. And it is not necessary now surely to spend farther time, in showing that this inward reality in the case of the Lord's Supper was held to be nothing less than what was called for by the sacramental signs themselves; not the thought or memory merely of a sacrifice long since past, but the very power of the life in which all the value of this sacrifice stands, the true substance of Christ's flesh and blood.

How *could* Dr. Hodge, in the face of so much clear historical evidence to the contrary, be so carried away with the mere *sound* of a few quotations, as to affirm of the Reformed doctrine of the Lord's Supper, that it *did not bind any objective reality or force to the ordinance answerable to the sense of its signs!* His quotations after all came only to this, that the outward side of the sacrament has no power to confer grace of itself, and that the inward side of it, depending of course on the operation of the Holy Ghost, can avail to the benefit of the worshipper only under the condition of faith. But they are of no force whatever to show, that the two sides were not regarded as entering alike into the constitution of the sacrament itself, or that its full objective force in this view was considered as ceasing where no organ was at hand for its reception. Their objective power was never held to be that of signs simply, or mere occasional piety, but the actual presence of the thing signified, in real sacramental union with the signs, as inward and outward sides in the same mystical transaction. Of course, Calvin considered it a diabolical error to look to the sacraments for justification, without faith. But can this show, against his own testimony, page upon page, to the contrary, that he ascribed no force to the sacraments in their own constitution, which *with faith* is as truly efficacious as the action of the sun on natural life? The unfortunate *Consensus Tigurinus* is again pressed into service. But this instrument expressly styles the sacraments "*organs by which God efficaciously works*" in his people; while it is pointedly interpreted by Calvin himself, as teaching that the outward side of them is always attended with the actual presence of what they represent. That Westphal should represent the contrary, is treated as foul slander.

> Everywhere in our writings we testify, that the evidences and seals of his grace left us by our Lord, differ widely from empty figures. Expressly is this asserted in the *Consensus*, that the Lord, who is true, by his Spirit inwardly brings to hand what the sacraments figure to the eyes; and that when we distinguish between the signs and the things signified, we do not sunder from the signs their truth.

This topic is still more clearly and fully handled in our exposition. The sum is, however, that Christ is truly offered to us by the sacraments, in order that being partakers of him we may enjoy all his benefits, and that he finally may live in us and we in him.—According to us, the bread so signifies the body, that it invites us truly, efficaciously and in reality, to the communication of Christ. For we say that the truth which the promise contains, is *there at hand*, and that the *effect is annexed* to the eternal symbol. The trope by no means evacuates the sign, but shows rather how it is *not* void. Op. T. ix. p. 666, 667.[21]

The first part of Dr. Hodge's review closes with the following paragraph, which is worthy certainly of the general historical inquiry, whose results it is made to embrace in the way of summary recapitulation.

Christ is really present to his people, in this ordinance, not bodily, but by his Spirit; not in the sense of local nearness, but of efficacious operation. They receive him, not with the mouth, but by faith; they receive his flesh, not as flesh, not as material particles, nor its human life, but his body as broken and his blood as shed. The union thus signified and effected, between him and them is not a corporeal union, nor a mixture of substances, but spiritual and mystical, arising from the indwelling of the Spirit. The efficacy of this sacrament, *as a means of grace*, is not in the signs, nor in the service, nor in the minister, nor in the word, but solely in the attending influence of the Holy Ghost. This we believe to be a fair statement of the doctrine of the Reformed Church.

This is characteristic truly. The article affects to expound the Reformed doctrine historically, *in opposition* to the view taken of it in the *Mystical Presence*; and here we have a flourish of results and conclusions, that are intended plainly to be passed off on the unwary reader, as fully sustaining this magisterial pretension. And yet strange to say, with the exception of a single proposition, there is nothing here which is not fully admitted and endorsed by the *Mystical Presence* itself. This anyone may see with very little trouble, who has interest enough in the subject to examine the book with his own eyes. But what then? Are the two views taken of the old sacramental doctrine, found to mean in this way at least the same thing? By no means. It is only to a certain point after all, and for the most part under what may be called its negative aspect, that the proper Calvinistic doctrine, as presented in the *Mystical Presence*, is here covered by the statement of Dr. Hodge. The points of difference lie beyond. All that is required to reveal them, is that the statement should be pushed somewhat farther forward in the way of positive affirmation. It would then appear, that Dr. Hodge is in no harmony with the old doctrine whatever, and that when he uses to a certain extent the same words and phrases, it is only to give currency to an altogether different sense. This may easily be illustrated, by simply adding to his statement now quoted, such clauses as are needed to complete it in the true Calvinistic sense. These will be seen at once, to diverge in full from the sense of Dr. Hodge. To make this immediately palpable, the added clause will be given in small capitals.

21. ["Second Defense," in Torrance, ed., 274–75.—ed.]

Christ is really present to his people, in this ordinance, not bodily, but by his Spirit, AS THE MEDIUM OF A HIGHER MODE OF EXISTENCE; not in the sense of local nearness, but of efficacious operation, NULLIFYING MIRIFICALLY THE BAR OF DISTANCE, AND BRINGING THE VERY SUBSTANCE OF HIS BODY INTO UNION WITH THEIR LIFE. They receive him, not with the mouth, but by faith, AS THE ORDINARY ORGAN BY WHICH ONLY THE SOUL IS QUALIFIED TO ADMIT THE DIVINE ACTION NOW NOTICED; they receive his flesh, not as flesh, not as material particles, BUT DYNAMICALLY IN THE INWARD POWER OF ITS LIFE (SO THAT THE CLAUSE "nor its human life" IS NOT CORRECT); his body as broken and his blood as shed, THE VALUE OF THAT SACRIFICE CARRIED IN THE VIVIFIC VIRTUE OF THE SAME BODY NOW GLORIOUSLY EXALTED IN HEAVEN. The union thus signified and effected between him and them, is not a corporeal union, nor a mixture of substances, IN THE ROMAN OR LUTHERAN SENSE, but spiritual and mystical; NOT MERELY MENTAL, BUT INCLUDING THE REAL PRESENCE OF CHRIST'S WHOLE LIFE UNDER AN OBJECTIVE CHARACTER, AND REACHING ON OUR SIDE ALSO THROUGH THE SOUL INTO THE BODY; arising from the indwelling of the Spirit, NOT AS THE PROXY ONLY OF AN ABSENT CHRIST, BUT AS THE SUPERNATURAL BOND OF A TRUE LIFE CONNECTION, BY WHICH HIS VERY FLESH IS JOINED TO OURS, MORE INTIMATELY FAR THAN THE TRUNK TO ITS BRANCHES, OR THE HEAD TO ITS MEMBERS, IN THE NATURAL WORLD. The efficacy of this sacrament, *as a means of grace*, is not in the signs, SEPARATELY TAKEN, nor in the service, OUTWARDLY CONSIDERED, nor in the word, but solely in the attending influence of the Holy Ghost, AS THE NECESSARY COMPLEMENT OR INWARD SIDE OF THE DIVINE MYSTERY ITSELF OF WHOSE PRESENCE THE OUTWARD SIGNS ARE THE SURE GUARANTY AND PLEDGE, AND WHOSE MIRIFIC ACTION CAN NEVER FAIL TO TAKE EFFECT OBJECTIVELY WHERE THE SUBJECT IS IN A STATE TO ADMIT IT BY FAITH. This we believe, SO FILLED OUT WITH POSITIVE CONTENTS, to be a fair statement of the doctrine of the Reformed Church.

Serious Contrasts

Dr. Hodge then has unwittingly wronged and misrepresented the old Reformed Church, throughout his entire article. Nor is this of course the whole result, to which we are thus brought by the present discussion. It is equally plain, that his own doctrine of the holy sacraments involves a material departure from the creed of this Church, as it stood in the age of the Reformation. In the *Mystical Presence*, the charge of such a falling away is urged against what is there styled the Modern Puritan system generally, and a pretty full array of evidence is exhibited at the same time in support of the accusation. There is nothing disrespectful certainly to Puritanism, in all this. It is a simple question of history (of great theological interest also indeed) which we should desire, on all sides, to see properly and truly resolved. Dr. Hodge however makes no attempt to meet it, but holds it sufficient apparently to give the world his own *word*, that "Dr. Nevin is tenfold further from the doctrines of our common fathers, than those whom he commiserates and condemns." This was as much perhaps as could well be expected, in the circumstances. For it now appears, that Dr. Hodge himself is fully committed to this very scheme, and strongly bent besides on forcing it into the rights of the old

Reformed doctrine. This, I confess, is more than I expected. Whatever exception might be taken to the form given to the subject in my book, I never anticipated on the side of Princeton so plump a denial of all objective force & all mystical relation to Christ's true human life, in the holy sacrament, as we have presented to us in this article of Dr. Hodge. This of course is a proper occasion for sorrow and regret; but it serves, at the same time, powerfully to sustain and enforce all that is said in the *Mystical Presence*, on the subject now named. No one can compare attentively the modern system, as here brought into view, with the old doctrine of Calvin and the Reformed Confessions, and not be struck at once with the difference as very broad and serious. Dr. Hodge may be said indeed, in a certain sense, so to have forced the points of distinction into view, that it is hardly possible they should not be seen now and acknowledged on all sides. We have his own confession even that the old doctrine included, at least to some extent, an element, that was afterwards lost; only he thinks this loss involved an actual gain. We shall see however, that it comes in the end to the whole result of what others have been led to deplore, as the falling away of modern Puritanism from the sacramental faith of the sixteenth century.

According to the old Reformed doctrine, a real inward *sacramental grace*, dependent of course on the Holy Ghost but still bound to the ordinance, was supposed to accompany the outwards signs, as a celestial side joined to the earthly side of one and the same transition. But this Dr. Hodge denies, allowing no other connection between the visible and invisible here, than in any other case where an outward object or event may be employed by God's Spirit as an occasion for calling forth pious thoughts and feelings. The idea of a *sacramental* or *mystical* copulation of the outward and inward, terrene and heavenly, once so familiar in the Reformed Church, would seem to have no place in his mind whatever.

According to the old doctrine, the Lord's Supper includes in itself thus an objective force or power, in other words, the true presence mystically of the unseen verities it represents. This again Dr. Hodge denies. All resolves itself with him into the subjective states and frames of the worshipper. He talks indeed of a "moral objective power" belonging to the sacraments as significant emblems and seals; but by this he means simply that they bear a relation in this way to truth in its general form; and not at all that they have any specific virtue in themselves for the ends they propose to reach.

According to the old doctrine, the ordinance involves for believers a mystical participation of the flesh and blood of Christ; that is, as clearly explained, of his veritable human life now glorified in heaven. But this also Dr. Hodge very plumply refuses to admit; and goes so far as to say, in the face of all history, that such a conception never entered into the faith of the Reformed Church! It is not merely of a crass outward communication he thus speaks, but of all real conjunction with the substance of Christ's life, however spiritual, in a truly organic way.

According to the old doctrine, we have in the sacramental transaction always, the presence of a profound, incomprehensible MYSTERY. Calvin shows just as much sense of this as Luther. By the whole Reformed Church of the sixteenth century, it is constantly granted. To make any question of it was held to be profane. Only its *mode* was in debate; as here raised from the sphere of the flesh into the sphere of the spirit; not to rarefy it at all into an ideal or imaginary form, but on the contrary to make it only the more firmly real, *as a mystery*, in its original and proper sense. The action of the Holy Ghost in the case was not only by any means taken to be his influence simply on the worshipper's mind, but is spoken of always as a mysterious supernatural power, by which in a real objective way the very substance of Christ's life, notwithstanding all local obstruction, is made mirifically to reach over into the persons of his people, so as to knit them more and more to his own blessed body as flesh of his flesh and bone of his bones. But now, as we have seen, Dr. Hodge does not believe a word of any such sense of confounding doctrine. He may call the sacrament a mystery, in obedience to old church custom; but most assuredly, not at all in the old church signification of this high word. The action of the Holy Ghost on the human mind, in any case, may be counted incomprehensible and mysterious; and so far, it is easy to admit something above sense also in the transaction of the holy Eucharist. But the same thing can be done just as easily in the case of any outward spectacle, the cataract of the Niagara for instance or a moving picture, that may serve, by the agency of God's Spirit, to connect us in lively thought with the realities of the invisible world. It is hard to see any greater mystery than this in the Lord's Supper, as viewed by Dr. Hodge. It is very common indeed to hear the people warned, on sacramental occasions, not to think of anything more than such monumental force in the institution, lest they should be guilty of popish superstition; and so far as this article goes, Dr. Hodge would seem to have precisely the same view.

To cut off all room for mistake, he has himself brought clearly into light the radical divergency between the old doctrine and his own, by a statement which is found at once to cover all the points of difference now noticed. Two views of the meaning of the Lord's Supper, he admits, struggled for authority in the old Reformed Church, at least for a time; one referring it to Christ's *death* as something past, and the other referring it also to his *life* as something present. But the latter, he thinks, was a foreign element (one of Calvin's crotchets) that had no right ever to belong to the doctrine; contradicting as it did Calvin's own constant testimony in regard to the Old Testament saints, and refusing besides to coalesce harmoniously with the doctrine of justification by faith, as the same is held by Dr. Hodge. So it "died out of the Church" as it deserved to do, relic as it was of a by-gone age. We hear nothing of it even in Craig's Catechism. It was fairly and fully ejected from the system in which it once appeared, in the way of wholesome historical *development* and growth.

Most significant and momentous concession! This is precisely what I have endeavored to show in the *Mystical Presence*, and now again in this present discussion. Here of a truth is the grand issue, involved in the whole historical controversy, plainly settled against Modern Puritanism by the testimony of Dr. Hodge himself. What he calls a "process of growth" is nothing more nor less than what I have chosen to regard as a "process of decay." The general fact is granted. Its radical nature moreover is rightly described. The only question is in regard to its theological value and force. This however has nothing to do with the historical aspect of the subject. Here is an acknowledged departure from the sacramental doctrine of the sixteenth century, as regards one whole side of its meaning; for we have shown by abundant evidence, that this part of the doctrine was not peculiar at all to Calvin, nor of accidental character, but runs through the Reformed symbols, as an organic portion of its life; so that it is the general sacramental creed in this way which has been forsaken, and not simply some partial form of it, as insinuated by Dr. Hodge. The old doctrine made the Eucharist the bond of union with Christ's life, as well as the memorial of his death. Dr. Hodge rejects the first conception in full, and reduced all to the second. The sacrament is for him a monumental ordinance simply, through which faith, as a mental act lays hold of the atonement once made on Calvary; the idea of a real communication with the very living nature itself in which only the atonement is of perennial force, he holds to be "in the plainest contradiction to the doctrine of the Reformed Church." How then should he allow sacramental grace, objective virtue, participation of Christ's human life, or the presence of a true divine MYSTERY under any proper view whatever, in the transaction of the holy Eucharist?

Theological Consequences

And now as the difference thus brought into view is very clear, all who look at it must feel also that it is very important. It extends necessarily, in the end, to the whole theory of the Christian salvation.

This is not the place of course, to show in detail the theological consequences that are necessarily involved in the sacramental system of Dr. Hodge. They come into view more or less, throughout his whole article, and condition at almost every point his unfavorable judgment of the *Mystical Presence*. How could it be otherwise, in a case where the great endeavor has been to join in full union, according to the old Reformed doctrine, what Dr. Hodge so earnestly insists on putting asunder?

The original life of the Reformed Church includes two sides. It is not simply protestant, but in the true sense catholic also, as still bound by the old idea of an objective churchly Christianity. The great problem of Protestantism was to bind these different tendencies together, in permanent organic union. Evidently at the same time, it stood strongly exposed, by its very constitution, to the danger of sacrificing the second in favor of the first, just as Rome had fallen before into precisely the opposite extreme. To such a rupture in fact, the movement in due time widely came. The change exhibited in the doctrine of the holy Eucharist, is only an index of what has occurred under a more general form. THE SACRIFICE OF CHRIST HAS BEEN DIVORCED FROM HIS LIFE. This Dr. Hodge counts to be clear gain; the catholic element in the old doctrine was in his view a sort of foreign substance, which was soon expelled out of it by its own healthy action. There are those however who differ from this judgment, and see in the fact here mentioned a disease of Protestantism rather than a sign of health. In the view of such, of course, the great desideratum in the case, is to bring up once more to its proper position in the Christian scheme the interest which has been left behind. This requires no hostile attitude towards the opposite side; but goes on the assumption only that it can never be complete, except as organically and inwardly joined to the catholic life from which it has been so unfortunately divorced. It is believed that the *synthesis* aimed at by the original Reformed Church, and so widely abandoned since, is in itself still the true conception of Christianity, and that this never can accomplish its full mission under any different form. Religion must be at once objective and subjective, churchly and experimental, in one word Catholic as well as Puritan. This calls precisely for the restitution of the old idea of Christ's *life*, to the place originally assigned to it in the Protestant creed. What God had joined together, the sacrifice of Christ namely and his life, justification by faith and sacramental grace, let no man put asunder.

To sever the atonement from its true and proper living ground, in the case of the Lord's Supper, is virtually to do the same thing in the case of the Christian system as a whole. In this way, Christianity resolves itself into a doctrine, a thing to be apprehended only in the way of thought, rather than into the power of concrete fact. It is made to find its principle, or fontal force, not in the historical person of Jesus Christ, but in an outward decree or purpose of God. The mystery of the incarnation is viewed as a divine device simply, by which instrumentally this abstract purpose is carried into effect. The atonement thus is a mere thought in God's mind, to be set over to the account of men in an outward way, and to be by them embraced through faith in this form & in this form only. The incarnation then involves no new order of existence for the world, in its own constitution. In this respect, the Old Testament and the New form one and the same dispensation. Thus we are entangled in the conception of an Ebionitic,[22] or at best simply Nestorian Christ, in whose constitution the human and divine come after all to no abiding organic union, more than they may be supposed to have reached before.[23] Of course, in this way, the old catholic idea of the Church is completely lost. The sacraments sink into monumental or moral signs. The sublime realities of the ancient creed, are made to give room to a scheme of spiritualistic abstraction and we are shut up altogether to the power of an arid, angularly orthodox theology, in which the heart finds it difficult at any point to come to a full understanding with the brain.

Can anyone fail to recognize in this brief description, the general character of the theological system presented to us in the article of Dr. Hodge? It is not strange certainly that such a system should be led to make war on the *Mystical Presence*; and it is easy besides to understand and appreciate several points of assault, involved in the general attack. All grow out of the cardinal difference, which Dr. Hodge himself brings into view. Let him do justice to the old synthesis of the Reformed Church, and allow the LIFE of Christ its proper rights in the Christian system, as the bearer of SACRIFICE, and his other difficulties with the *Mystical Presence* may be adjusted with comparatively little trouble.

22. [From the Hebrew meaning "poor men," the sect was a Palestinian and Syrian form of Christianity observed by Jews who believed Jesus to have been a prophet who followed Jewish law. Nevin is focusing on their rejection of Christ's divinity, which was the mark that came to identify them outside the Christian mainstream and led to their brand of heresy.—ed.]

23. [See Nevin, *Antichrist: Or the Spirit of Sect and Schism*, where this theme is more fully developed (to be reprinted in vol. 5 of the present series).—ed.]

Relation to Catholicism and Lutheranism

There are two wholesale indications of the false theological position of Dr. Hodge, in regard to the general question here brought into view, which well deserve in conclusion our most serious attention. He makes no account whatever of the old *Catholic* doctrine of the sacraments; and the authority of the *Lutheran* Church in the case is treated with the most profound general contempt.

Our great argument with him against the Calvinistic conception of a life communication with Christ in the Lord's Supper, is that the same idea had held a central place in the Church as it stood previously; just as though, *every* departure from this must needs be a true advance in the Protestant direction. But was there no truth then in the ancient Church at all? And especially are we bound to believe that an idea so central to all its life, so interwoven with its very constitution from the beginning, as we know this of the Eucharistic MYSTERY to have been, was notwithstanding all along a grand *lie*, which as "uncongenial foreign element" the true life of Protestantism required it to expel? God forbid. The Rationalist and Unitarian, so far as this argument goes, have just as much to plead in favor also of *their* improvements. To fall away from the faith of the universal ancient Church is not as a matter of course to fall into the arms of truth. On the contrary, it is enough to create misgiving in any serious mind, only to know that the system of Dr. Hodge, in diverging as it does confessedly from the old Calvinistic doctrine of sacramental grace, involves at the same time a full falling away from the sacramental faith of the Holy Catholic Church, as it stood in all ages before. The proper MYSTERY of the Lord's Supper, this system renounces and denies. But to do so is practically to charge with folly and superstition, in its central interest, the worship of the Church from the beginning. A powerful presumption certainly *against* the position of Dr. Hodge, and not at all in its favor.

And then again, is no respect due on this great subject to the posture of the Lutheran Church, the other grand division of the Protestant interest itself? Not according to Dr. Hodge. The truth with regard to the sacraments lay from the start wholly on the side of the Reformed Church; and here not in its tendency *towards* the Lutheran doctrine, as shown in Calvin and the old confession, but rather in its tendency the other way, and the possibility it included of losing the idea of sacramental grace altogether; a possibility happily *actualized*, as Dr. Hodge tells it, at a later day. Of course, the entire sacramental position of the Lutheran Church, must be set down for gross superstition. Lutheranism may be allowed some respect on other grounds; for it is still convenient to glorify Luther himself as the great coryphaeus[24] of the Reformation; but this always in spite of the huge drawback now noticed, which every fool in divinity is supposed to be capable, at the same time, of estimating at its true worth. But, what we may well ask, is Lutheranism, as a distinct confession, when thus sundered from the substance of its old sacramental doctrine? Every such distinction is nugatory altogether. To treat with contempt the Lutheran idea of the sacraments, is necessarily at

---

24. [This term, originating from Greek drama, referred to the leader of the chorus. It likewise refers to the leader of any company, party, or movement.—ed.]

the same time to treat with contempt the entire theology and Church life of this wide spread venerable Protestant communion; as Lutheranism itself divorced from this idea, becomes necessarily all the world over, for every discerning eye, a parody upon its own name. Dr. Hodge, in fact, thus turns the Lutheran Church into a theological nullity. Occasionally the true state of his mind in regard to it, finds utterance in the way of open vilification; but in addition to this, his article is an insult to all genuine Lutheran feeling, from beginning to end.[25] The question of which it treats, historically intertwined as it is with the inmost life of Lutheran theology, is just disposed of as though such a theology had never been known. Dr. Hodge could hardly say more plainly in words than he here says by his silence: The Lutheran Church never had any sense in regard to this whole subject; WE are the people, and with us all the theological wisdom must live or die; if they wish to be right in any way, let them cast their old symbols to the *moles* and bats, and come and learn submissively at *our* feet. And yet, for one who looks at it rightly, what an enormous pretension is involved in all this? Can any sane man, with full understanding of the case, deliberately and seriously believe, that the old Lutheran issue in regard to the sacraments, convulsing the age of the Reformation as it did, was really after all of no meaning or value whatever? It is not possible, I firmly believe, to cherish a rational and intelligent respect for the Reformation itself with any such view. If we have faith in the Reformation as God's work, and not the wild sport of Satan, we must feel that the truth contained in it was divided between the two confessions; and that in the case now before us, the true problem for the Protestant Church as a whole is the union of the Lutheran and Reformed sacramental theories in an inward and organic way, and not their full everlasting diremption, as aimed at in this article of Dr. Hodge.

Such want of respect for Lutheran theology, in such a case, is a most fair ground for distrust. I am no Lutheran; but I owe too much to the rich fund of life and thought that is treasured up in the history of this Church, not to utter here a bold and open protest against the general wrong it is made to suffer at the hands of our Puritan thinking. Whether we lay it to heart or not, the genius of Lutheranism can never be sundered from the cause of the Reformation, without confusion to the whole interest. No union of the two confessions can ever be legitimate and true, that may fail to take up into itself, in large measure, the original characteristic life of this communion. That Lutheranism itself should seem so widely disposed, in this country, to renounce and nullify itself in favor of the opposite tendency (satisfied to keep only its ancient *name*), should be regarded as a calamity for the interests of American Protestantism generally.

25. [Nevin:] Who must not have admired the spaniel-like humility of the Lutheran *Observer*, in licking the foot to which it stands indebted for such disgrace, greeting with wild bark of joy the spittle flung into its own face! "O ANDREW BODENSTEIN CARLSTADT." [Nevin had a long-standing feud with the *Lutheran Observer*'s Benjamin Kurtz (1795–1865), retired Lutheran minister and avid revivalist. He was a founder of the General Synod and of Gettysburg Theological Seminary. Prior to the debate, the *Observer* openly rejected the idea of communion with the humanity of Christ and attributed the view to pure superstition. Furthermore, Kurtz described Nevin's view as "Con-corporation" and "semi-Romanism in relation to the Eucharist." Kurtz concluded that he was pleased that the Lutheran Church in America had since abandoned the antiquated views of the past. See the *Mystical Presence* (93–94).—ed.]

We may rest assured, no church life can be permanently sound, no theology can be firmly solid, in which the deep, vast significance of the Lutheran Church is treated as though it carried not in it the weight of a feather. This alone I consider a fatal defect in this whole article of Dr. Hodge. It goes on the supposition, that the proper truth and sense of the Reformed Church, lie away off on the side of its life which is farthest removed from the life of the Lutheran Church; and that they are to be asserted successfully only ignoring and annihilating, as much as possible, all right that has ever been claimed in this opposite quarter. But I can have no confidence whatever in any such process. The truth of the Reformed confession is to be sought, on the side *towards Lutheranism,* and under the sense of old Catholic ideas that are so deeply lodged in its constitution, *not by falling away from it completely* in the style too common at the present time. I have no mind, especially on this great sacramental question, to sit at the feet of any man, who shows himself whether it be through want of knowledge or lack of inward sympathy, insensible to the mighty merits of Lutheran theology both ancient and modern. For such a defect, in a case of this sort, no amount of credit and authority in any other view can be taken as a sufficient compensation. Not to have seen and *felt* the force of the Lutheran antithesis, in this question of the Lord's Supper, is just to be morally disabled at once for all sound judgment or voice in regard to its merits.

9

The Modern Theory Debated[1]

[NEVIN]

WE COME NOW TO the second part of this Princeton article, in which the theory of the "*Mystical Presence*" is briefly considered and condemned.

It is very necessary to hold fully apart the two different objects, which are joined together in that work. In the first place, it aims to furnish a simple historical exhibition of the old doctrine, in contrast with the form in which the subject is viewed for the most part at the present time. In the second place, it is an attempt to rescue the old doctrine from certain difficulties which have been felt to attend it, by giving it a shape suitable to the demands of modern theological science. This, it was supposed, might be done without the least wrong to the substance of the doctrine itself; since it is well known that all Christian truths are necessarily more or less modified for the understanding of the Church, though not changed in matter for its faith, as they are carried forward from age to age in the great life process of history. Still of course the two general objects now stated are in themselves entirely distinct. If the scientific exposition attempted in the *Mystical Presence*, should be found altogether unsatisfactory, the exhibition it gives of the actual faith of the original Reformed Church would not on this account fall to the ground. It must carry with it still its full force as a true statement of history, unless set aside by direct evidence depriving it of this character. The theological and historical questions here we are bound to keep carefully asunder.

Let it be borne in mind then, that we are now, for the present, done with the historical question, so far as this article of Dr. Hodge is concerned. If he can show my theory, as he calls it, to be unphilosophical and false, it is all very well. In such case, let the theory be given to the winds. I have brought it forward in good faith as a contribution to the cause of theological science, and out of true zeal for what I conceive to be the central mystery of Christianity. If however it be of no value for this object, let it perish as it deserves. I have no wish or care certainly that it should be otherwise. But

---

1. ["Dr. Hodge on the *Mystical Presence*, Article from the *Repertory*, Continued, No. 9," *Weekly Messenger*, New Series, vol. 13, no. 45. Wednesday July 19, 1848. Published by the Board of the Synod of the German Reformed Church: Chambersburg, PA.—ed.]

let us beware well, that we be not blinded in this way to the claims of other interest. Let us not dream, as Dr. Hodge would seem at times to do, that the old sacramental doctrine itself must stand or fall with any particular theory that may be employed, in this way, to commend it to the understanding. The *historical* fact still stands before us in all its force; the old doctrine recognized in the Lord's Supper a divine *mystery*, involving on the part of true believers a real participation of Christ's flesh and blood, or in other words of his veritable glorified human life. The question only comes back upon us, then: What shall we do with it at the present time? If one theory be found insufficient to relieve it from acknowledged difficulties, shall we try to assist ourselves by another; or shall we rest in the old statement simply without thought; or shall we give up the whole substance of the doctrine as the superstition of a by-gone age, and quietly transfer its terminology as we best can to a different system altogether?

Dr. Hodge, as we have seen, in common with the reigning Puritan tendency of the age, has recourse to this last expedient. To get clear of the difficulties which he finds in the old Calvinistic doctrine, he simply renounces and rejects the doctrine in full. One whole side of it, that namely by which it asserted the mystical presence of Christ's life in the Eucharist, he proclaims openly as an "uncongenial foreign element," that could never be assimilated properly to the general Reformed creed; and the great design and drift of his article is accordingly to bring it into discredit. If there be any force at all in historical evidence, it is clear for anyone who will take the least pains to inquire, that the sacramental doctrine of Dr. Hodge involves, in this way, an essential falling away from the doctrine of Calvin and the old Calvinistic symbols. It sunders professedly what they constantly make a prime point of joining together, the sacrifice of Christ and his life; it nullifies the whole inward side of the transaction, which they always exhibit as sacramentally bound to the outward; it empties it of all objective force, on which they continually insist; it admits no mystical communion with Christ's flesh and blood, which they most solemnly assert; it discards altogether the idea of any such mystery in the case as was held by the whole ancient church, which they count it ever a sacred duty to maintain. Dr. Hodge, while he undertakes to make out *my* theory wrong in regard to the old Reformed doctrine, brings in no other theory by which to save its proper substance, but with the most cool indifference gives it up in full to its enemies. While I should be very sorry to identify him with such bad company in any other respect, it cannot be disguised that the view he takes of the Lord's Supper is materially the same with that of the original Arminians,[2] and amounts to what would

2. [Jacob Arminius (1560–1609), Dutch theologian. Studied theology at Leyden. Later as preacher in Amsterdam (fifteen years) his theological views began to change. His views on election and reprobation in his exposition of Romans raised objections from the strict Calvinist party and when his public lectures on predestination became known it divided the university. The Calvinists wanted the matter settled by the synod, but instead the courts were used as were frequent deliberations up until the death of Arminius. Some of the Calvinists of that time thought that Arminius was diminishing the role of grace and allowing a role of mankind in procuring his own salvation. However, Arminius in his own right was more cautious than that. He could not agree with "double predestination" as he believed it made God the author of sin. Instead he taught a conditional predestination and placed more emphasis on personal faith, for which the charge of Pelagianism was leveled and has never been removed. Confusion over Arminius's sacramental position, along with its role in subsequent Remonstrant and Wesleyan theology,

have been regarded by Calvin, Beza and Ursinus, as a complete abandonment of the true symbolical ground of the Reformed Church.

This of course needs to be kept in mind. We found occasion for some distrust of this review, at the start, in Dr. Hodge's confessed want of all earnest inward interest in the sacramental question; and then again in his acknowledgment of having given it only a very cursory and general attention, of which we have had besides abundant evidence in our examination thus far of the review itself. But now we have another plea, in bar of its title to confidence and respect. The review rests throughout on a theory of Christianity, which departs materially from that of the Reformed Church in the sixteenth century. It rejects in form the distinctive substance of the old Calvinistic doctrine of the sacraments, and substitutes for it another of quite different constitution. Now it is not at once impracticable, we know, for a critic, in no sympathy himself with a particular standpoint, to pronounce judgment correctly on variations from it, under some different form, on the part of another. But the case would seem to require at least, that the critic so exercising his judgment should be properly sensible of his own position, and prepared also to acknowledge it without reserve. Dr. Hodge however refuses to see and admit in his general theory any such falling away from the old Reformed faith, as is necessarily implied by the view taken of it in the *Mystical Presence*. In these circumstances, all must see that he is not exactly qualified to measure the orthodoxy of the book, as related to the Calvinistic creed. The theory and argument of the *Mystical Presence* proceed throughout on the assumption, that the old Reformed doctrine of the sacraments is in substance sound and sacred; the work is for such as stand *within* the mystery of this doctrine, by their faith, rather than for such as stand *without*. Let Dr. Hodge rise first himself to the true Calvinistic platform in regard to the holy sacraments, and he will have more right to speak of "a radical rejection of the doctrine and theology of the Reformed Church," in the case of the others.

To make the case still worse, it will be found that the points on which Dr. Hodge takes the *Mystical Presence* to task, resolve themselves to a great extent, as already intimated, into the very article at last, in regard to which he makes a merit openly of

---

is equally persistent such that disagreement with Calvin was exaggerated. Arminius wrote, "We lay down the form in the relation and the most strict union, which exist between the signs and the thing signified, and the reference of both to those believers who communicate, and by which they are made by analogy and similitude something united. From this conjunction of relation, arises a two-fold use of signs in this sacrament of the Lord's Supper—the first, that these signs are representative—the second, that, while representing, they seal Christ to us with his benefits. VI. The end is two-fold: The first is, that our faith should be more and more strengthened towards the promise of grace which has been given by God, and concerning the truth and certainty of our being engrafted into Christ. The second is, (1.) that believers may, by the remembrance of the death of Christ, testify their gratitude and obligation to God; (2.) that they may cultivate charity among themselves; and (3.) that by this mark they may be distinguished from unbelievers." (*The Private Disputations of James Arminius*, "Disputation 54: On the Lord's Supper," in James Nichols, trans., *The Works of James Arminius*, Vol. 2. Public Domain: http://www.ccel.org/ccel/arminius/works2.iii.lxiv.html. Nevin's harsh indictment of Arminius may require closer scrutiny, for while it is certain the drift toward the more rationalistic theory was under way and may be said to exist in the thought of Arminius, a strict reading of the above fails to pin the charge so clearly on the author. See also Muller, *God, Creation and Providence in the Theology of Jacob Arminius*; Olson, *Arminian Theology*.—ed.]

having swerved entirely from the line of Calvin's faith. He affects indeed to consider this variation a mere circumstance on his own side; while at the very same time he represents the old view, most inconsistently, as carrying in itself an element of *fatal* self-contradiction, from which it could be saved only in this way. What is of such fatal force under the second aspect however, may not be so turned at once into a mere trifling accident under the first. If Calvin's idea of the *life* of Christ, as the necessary present bearer of the value of his sacrifice, involved such deep contrariety as Dr. Hodge supposes to the other parts of the Reformed system, it needs no great sagacity surely to perceive that very deep and far reaching consequences *must* be involved also in its abandonment. These come into view here, in part at least, in this article of Dr. Hodge, and constitute as now said the main burden of its quarrel with the *Mystical Presence*. Dr. Hodge sunders the Christian atonement throughout from its ever-living basis in the Redeemer's person; turns it into an abstraction, a mere thing of thought and doctrine; and in this way subverts the sacramental side of religion, almost entirely at a single stroke. The great object of the *Mystical Presence*, on the contrary, is to re-assert the old Protestant synthesis, and to bring thus the whole theory of our salvation to its true concrete ground in the *perennial* presence of Christ's LIFE.

REVIEW FROM THE REPERTORY, CONTINUED [HODGE]

Dr. Nevin's Theory[3]

Having already exceeded the readable limits of a review, we cannot pretend to do more in our notice of Dr. Nevin's book, than as briefly as possible state his doctrine and assign our reasons for considering it a radical rejection of the doctrine and theology of the Reformed church. It is no easy thing to give a just and clear exhibition of a theory confessedly mystical, and which involves some of the most abstruse points both of anthropology and theology. We have nothing to do however with anything beyond this book. We do not assume to know how these things lie in Dr. Nevin's mind;[4] how

---

3. [Hodge:] In calling the theory in question by Dr. Nevin's name, we do not mean to charge him with having originated it. This he does not claim, and we do not assert. It is, as we understand it, the theory of Schleiermacher, so far as Dr. Nevin goes.

4. [This is a bit disingenuous on the part of Hodge. As pointed out in the introduction to our edition of the *Mystical Presence* (36), Hodge read the *Weekly Messenger* and was "keenly aware of the various controversies surrounding the emerging Mercersburg theology . . . something very contentious was stirring at the early period. In the year that Nevin's series on the Catechism appeared in the *Messenger*, the *Repertory* published in its section 'Quarterly List of New Books and Pamphlets,' Hodge's review of Nevin's 'Eulogy on the Life and Character of the Late Rev. Dr. Frederick Rauch' (Chambersburg, PA, 1841, 23). After a paragraph in praise of the piety of the 'learned' Dr. Rauch and after lamenting how he will be missed, the reviewer writes that he wished he 'could pass in silence one feature of this discourse, which we notice, we confess, with more pain than surprise' (*BRPR* vol. 13, 1841, 464). Clearly Hodge was already aware of and concerned by the direction Nevin was going in. He continues, 'There is a tone of apology for some of the worst systems of German philosophy, a designating of destructive errors by the respectful appellation of "foreign forms of thought," which we think unworthy of the steadfastness and fidelity of a teacher of Christian doctrine. We know very well that nothing we could say on this subject would have the least effect upon the author of this Eulogy.' . . . Hodge held out the one hope that Nevin, having the 'anchor' of an American education, might be saved from the 'cataract' and 'hell of waters he

he reduces them to unity, or reconciles them with other doctrines of the Bible. Our concern is only with that part of the system which has here cropped out. How the strati [*sic*] lie underneath, we cannot tell. Dr. Nevin, in the full consciousness of the true nature of his own system, says the difficulties under which Calvin's theory of the Lord's Supper, labors, are "all connected with psychology, applied either to the person of Christ or the persons of his people," p. 156.[5] The difference then lies in the region of psychology. That science has assumed a new form. It has made great progress since the Reformation. "Its determinations," he says, "have a right to be respected in any inquiry which has this subject for its object. No such inquiry can deserve to be called scientific, if it fails to take them into view," p. 162.[6] There may be truth in that remark. It is, however, none the less significant as indicating the nature of the system here taught. It is a peculiar psychology applied to the illustration and determination of Christian doctrine.[7] It is founded on certain views of "organic law," of personality, and of generic and individual life. If these scientific determinations are incorrect, the doctrine of this book is gone. It has no existence apart from those determinations, or

---

seems to be drawing perilously near.' Hodge concluded sardonically that he hadn't the courage to follow Nevin into what Hodge regards as blatant heresy. Can there be any doubt that prior to even the earlier Mercersburg period in which Nevin composes his series on the Catechism (well before the arrival of Schaff), Princeton held his ideas in deep suspicion, even though Hodge still saw him as an ally on some fronts (such as new measures revivalism)." Moreover, with regard to Nevin's understanding of Calvin's sacramental theology, Nevin had already revealed in his series on the Heidelberg Catechism, printed in the *Weekly Messenger*, that Calvin taught the Real Presence of Christ in the sacrament.—ed.]

5. [See MTSS edition, 138—ed.]

6. [Ibid., 144—ed.]

7. [Nevin:] Does Dr. Hodge mean to object here to the use of *psychology* in the determination of Christian doctrine; or does he mean only, that no psychology is to be trusted which is *new*? There is a certain class, we know, who make a merit of denouncing all philosophy of whatever kind in the sphere of religion; they want nothing but the plain sense of the bible, out of which to build their scheme of theology; assuming, with supreme self complacency, that *they* bring with themselves no refracting medium of previous thought through which to admit the rays of its inspiration. But Dr. Hodge surely has too much sense to fall in with any such miserable slang. *He* knows that there can be no theology, however poor, without a corresponding philosophy; and that those who decry all theory in this form as inimical to religion, are always in fact bound hand and foot, beyond most others, in some wretched scheme of their own, that cannot bear a moment's intelligent examination. So there can be no theory in the Christian salvation, which does not involve a particular psychology. Dr. Hodge has his *psychology* too, and is very manifestly ruled by it throughout his entire theological system. There is room at the same time, in the nature of the case, for the science of psychology, like any other doctrine must necessarily undergo, *for the understanding*, a corresponding modification. Or does Dr. Hodge really think, that it should continue unaltered through all phases of intellectual science? We *know* at all events, that it has not done so in fact. Dogmas have their history in the past life of the Church, just as clearly exhibited as that of outward usages and rites. The great matter in the case is, that under all varying aspects of *science*, the inward substance of the Christian *faith* be carried forward and upheld still, at each point, in its original freshness and power.—*J. W. N.* [This footnote, among other things, allows us to see that what they called psychology, we would call the philosophy of the mind, or perhaps even better, hermeneutics. We would think of such English writers as Locke, Hume, and Reid and such German writers as Kant, Fichte, and Hegel. Of course, all of these writers wrote about more than the philosophy of the mind, but a significant portion of their work was directed precisely at that subject. Nevin had himself reviewed his colleague at the seminary, Frederick Rauch's *Psychology*, which was precisely a philosophy of the mind, or *spirit* as the Germans preferred.—ed.]

at least independent of them. Our first object is to state, as clearly as we can, what the theory is.

There is an organic law or life which gives unity wherever it exists, and to all the individuals through which it manifests itself. The identity of the human body resides not in the matter of which it is composed, but in its organic law. The same is true of any animal or plant. The same law may comprehend or reveal itself in many individuals, and continually propagate and extend itself. Hence there is a generic as well as an individual life. An acorn developed into an oak, in one view is a single existence; but it includes a life which may produce a thousand oaks. The life of the forest is still the life of the original acorn, as truly one, inwardly and organically, as in any single oak. Thus in the case of Adam; as to his individual life, he was *a* man, as to his generic life, he was the whole race. The life of all men is at last one and the same.[8] Adam lives in his posterity as truly as he ever lived in his own person. They participate in his whole nature, soul and body, and are truly bone of his bone and flesh of his flesh. Not a particle of his body indeed has come down to us, the identity resolves itself into an invisible law. But this is an identity far more real than mere sameness of particles.[9] So also in the case of Christ. He was not only *a* man, but *the* man. He had not only an individual but generic life. The Word in becoming flesh, did not receive into personal union with himself the nature of an individual man, but he took upon himself our common nature. The divinity was joined in personal union with humanity.[10] But wherever there is personality there is unity. A person has but one life. Adam had not one life of the soul and another of the body. There is no such dualism in our nature. Soul and body are but one life, the self same organic law. The soul to be complete to develop itself as a soul, must externalize itself, and this externalization is the body.[11] It is all one process, the action

8. [See ibid., 142–44 for Nevin's development of these points.—ed.]

9. [See ibid., 145–47 for Nevin's development of these points.—ed.]

10. [See ibid., 147–49 for Nevin's development of these points.—ed.]

11. [Hodge:] To be sure, the separate existence of the soul after death, and absence from the body is an ugly fact. But we know so little of the intermediate state, it would be a pity to give up a theory, for so obscure a fact. [Nevin:] This caricature is unworthy of Dr. Hodge, and is no better than a miserable slur, when all is done, as regards the point it affects to settle in such summary style. In the *Mystical Presence*, p. 171, 172, the difficulty here noticed is fully brought into view, as holding however not against a particular psychological theory, but against the form in which the subject is present in the bible itself. The bible, it is there said, proceeds throughout on the assumption, that the life of the *body* is necessary to complete the life of the *soul*, and that the immortality of one is the immortality also of the other. The temporary separate existence of the soul, in the view of the bible, is only its transition over into the full development by which the unity of our life is to become complete finally in the resurrection of the body. Does Dr. Hodge believe, we may seriously ask, that soul and body in man are *not* one life, but two different lives joined together in such a way as to admit their separation again in the intermediate state? This is implied certainly by his language. No wonder he should quarrel with modern psychology. And yet the *Princeton Repertory* some time ago endorsed the work of the late President Rauch on this subject, as substantially safe and sound (free in particular from all *Hegelian* leaven, without the slightest caveat in regard to the point here noticed; which notwithstanding comes forward in that work (p. 169–174, 1st edition) under the most broad and prominent representation). Soul and body, we are told here, are one life in their origin, "a twofold expression of the same energy," the inward and outward sides simply of the one indivisible fact which is presented to us in the idea of our proper human personality. There may be difficulties in this view; but Dr. Hodge ought to know certainly that still greater difficulties press on the

of one and the same living organic principle.[12] The same is true as regards Christ. If he is one person, he has one life. He has not one life of the body, another of the soul and another of his divinity. It is one undivided life. We cannot partake of the one without partaking of the others. We cannot be united to him as to his body, without also being united also with his soul and divinity. His life is one and undivided, and is also a true human life. This is communicated to his people. The humanity of Adam is raised to a higher character by its union with the divine nature, but remains, in all respects, a true human life.[13]

The application of these psychological principles to the whole scheme of Christian doctrine is obvious and controlling. In the first place, the fall of Adam was the fall of the race. Not simply because he represented the race, but because the race was comprehended in his person. Sin in him was sin in humanity and became an insurmountable law in the progress of its development. It was an organic ruin; the ruin of our nature; not simply because all men are sinners, but as making all men sinners. Men do not make their nature, their nature makes them. The human race is not a sand heap; it is the power of a single life. Adam's sin is therefore our sin. It is imputed to us, indeed, but only because it is ours. We are born with his nature, and for this reason only are born also into his guilt. "A fallen *life* in the first place, and on the ground of this only, imputed guilt and condemnation" (p. 164, 191, &c. &c.)[14]

In the second place, in order to our salvation it was requisite that the work of restoration should not so much be wrought for us as in us. Our nature, humanity, must be healed, the power of sin incorporated in that nature must be destroyed. For this purpose the Logos, the divine Word, took our humanity into personal union with himself. It was our *fallen* humanity he assumed. Hence the necessity of suffering. He triumphed over evil. His passion was the passion of humanity. This was the atonement. The principle of health came to its last struggle with the principle of disease, and gained the victory. Our nature was thus restored and elevated, and it is by our receiving this renovated nature that we are saved. Christ's merits are inseparable from his nature; they cannot be imputed to us, except so far as they are immanent in us. As in the case of Adam, we have his nature, and therefore his sin; so we have the nature of Christ and therefore his righteousness.

---

dualistic view, into whatever shape it may be cast; and as a man of science he should not think to throw all these into the rear, by simply sticking his head for the moment, like the ostrich, into a heap of sand. He ought to know too, that his dualistic psychology is of *heathen* origin, and not at all the product of the bible.—J. W. N. [Indeed, Rauch's *Psychology* was favorably received by Princeton—and the section to which Nevin refers is emphatic. Rauch redefines "body" removing from it the merely material. "The true and genuine body must be that which retains and preserves its *organical* identity in all these changes which remains the same in the never-ceasing stream of matter. But what is this organical identity? The life or power which connects the gases, earths, metals, and salt, into one whole, which penetrating them, keeps them together, or dismisses some and attracts others. No sooner does this penetrating power retire, than the body becomes a corpse, and the elements fall asunder. The power is the true body; it is invisible, but connecting the elements according to an eternal and divine law, it becomes manifest by its productions" (p. 182–83, 4th edition) of Rauch's *Psychology*.—ed.]

12. [See MTSS vol. 1, 152–54 for Nevin's development of these points.—ed.]

13. [See ibid., 149–52 for Nevin's development of these points.—ed.]

14. [Ibid., 167n31.—ed.]

The nature we receive from Christ is a theanthropic nature. For, as before remarked, being one person, his life is one. "His divine nature is at the same time *human*, in the fullest sense" (p. 174).[15] All that is included in him as a person, divinity, soul and body, are embraced in his life. It is not the life of the Logos separately taken but the life of the Word made flesh, the divinity joined in personal union with our humanity; which is thus exalted to an imperishable divine life. It is a divine human life. In the person of Christ, thus constituted, the true ideal of humanity is brought to view. Christ is the archetypal, ideal man. The incarnation is the proper completion of humanity. "Our nature reaches after a true and real union with the nature of God, as the necessary complement and consummation of its own life. The *idea* which it embodies can never be fully actualized under any other form" (p. 201).[16]

In the third place, Divine human nature as it exists in the person of Christ, passes over into the church. He is the source and organic principle of a new life introduced into the center of humanity itself. A new starting point is found in Christ. Our nature as it existed in Adam unfolded itself organically, in his posterity; in like manner, as it exists in Christ, united with the divine nature, it passes over to his people, constituting the church. This process is not mechanical but organic. It takes place in the way of history, growth, regular living development.[17] By uniting our nature with the divine, he became the root of a new life for the race.

> The word became flesh; not a single man only, as one among many; but flesh as humanity in its universal conception. How else could he be the principle of a general life, the origin of a new order of existence for the human world as such? (p. 210).[18]

> The supernatural as thus made permanent and historical in the church, must, in the nature of the case, correspond with the form of the supernatural, as it appeared in Christ himself. For it is all one and the same life or constitution. The church must have a true theanthropic character throughout. The union of the divine and human in her constitution, must be inward and real, a continuous revelation of God in the flesh, exalting this last continuously into the sphere of the Spirit (p. 247).[19]

---

15. [Ibid., 155—ed.]

16. [Ibid., 176—ed.]

17. [Hodge] Schleiermacher says, in his second *Sendschreiben* to Lucke, 'Wo *Übernatureliches bei in ir vorkommt, da ist es immer ein Erstes; es wird aber hernach ein Natüerliches als Sweites. So ist die Schoepfung uebernaturlich; aber sie wird hernach Naturzusammenhang; so ist Christus uebernaturlich seinem Angang, nach, aber er wird natuerlich als rein menschliche Person, und ebenso ist es mit dem heiligen Geiste und der christlichen Kirche.*' [Trans. Schleiermacher says, in his Second Letter to Lucke, "Where the supernatural occurs there is always a primary cause and this will turn into a second, natural cause. So if the creation is supernatural, hence she will thereafter have a natural cause. In the way that Christ is supernatural in his beginning, thereafter he becomes natural as a pure human person. And this is the same as it is with the Holy Spirit and the Christian Church."—ed.] Somewhat to the same effect, Dr. Nevin somewhere says, "The supernatural has become natural." [MTSS vol. 1, 213—ed.]

18. [Ibid., 184—ed.]

19. [Ibid., 214—ed.]

The incarnation is therefore still present and progressive, in way of actual human development, in the church.

There are two remarks, however to be made. First, according to this system, the mystical union implies a participation of the entire humanity of Christ, for if we are joined in *real* life- unity with the Logos, we should be exalted to the level of the Son of God. Still it is not with his soul alone, or his body alone, but with his whole person, for the life of Christ is one. Second, this union of Christ and his people, implies no ubiquity of his body, and no fusion of his proper personality with theirs. We must distinguish between the simple man and the universal man here joined in the same person, much as in the case of Adam. He was at once an individual and the whole race. So we distinguish between Christ's universal humanity in the church, and his humanity as a particular man, whom the heavens must receive until the restitution of all things. (p. 173).[20]

The incarnation being thus progressive, the church is in very deed, the depository and continuation of the Savior's theanthropic life itself, in which powers and resources are continually at hand, involving a real intercommunion and interpenetration of the human and divine (p. 248).[21] It follows also from this view of the case that the sacraments of the church, have real objective force. "The force of the sacrament is in the sacrament itself. Our faith is needed only to make room for it in our souls" (p. 183).[22] "The things signified are bound to the signs by the force of a divine appointment; so that the grace goes inseparably along with the signs, and is truly present for all who are prepared to make it their own" (p. 62).[23]

In the fourth place, as to the mode of union with Christ, it is by regeneration. But this regeneration is by the church. If the church is the depository of the theanthropic life of Christ, if the progress of the church takes place in the way of history, growth, living development, it would seem as unreasonable that a man should be united to Christ and made partaker of his nature, otherwise than by union with this external, historical church, as that he should possess the nature of Adam by immediate creation, instead of regular descent. It is by the ministrations of this living church, in which the incarnation of God is progressive, and by her grace-bearing sacraments, that the church life, which is the same as that of Christ, is continually carried over to new individuals. The life of the single Christian can be real only as born and sustained to the end by the life of the church, which is the living and life-giving body of Christ. The effect of the sacraments, therefore, is thus to convey and sustain the life of Christ, his whole divine-human life. We partake not of his divinity only, but also of his true and proper humanity; not of his humanity in a separate form, nor of his flesh and blood alone, but of his whole life, as a single undivided form of existence. In the Lord's Supper consequently Christ is present in a peculiar and mysterious way; present as to his body, soul and divinity, not locally as included under the elements, but really; the sign and thing signified, the

20. [Ibid., 155—ed.]
21. [Ibid., 215—ed.]
22. [Ibid., 162—ed.]
23. [Ibid., 51—ed.]

inward and outward, the visible and invisible, constitute one inseparable presence. Unbelievers indeed receive only the outward, because they lack the organ of reception for the inward grace. Still the latter is there, and the believer receives both, the outward sign and the one undivided theanthropic life of Christ, his body, soul and divinity.[24] The Eucharist has therefore "a peculiar and altogether extraordinary power."[25] It is, as Maurice is quoted as asserting, the bond of an universal life and the means whereby men become partakers of it.

Such, as we understand it, is the theory unfolded in this book. It is in all its essential features Schleiermacher's theory. We almost venture to hope that Dr. Nevin will consider it a fair exhibition, not so satisfactory of course, as he himself could make, but as good as could well be expected from the uninitiated. It is at least honestly done, and to the best of our ability.

CRITICISM [NEVIN]

I have no doubt whatever that the exhibition here given of my system by Dr. Hodge is "honestly made and to the best of his ability." In the nature of the case however, it cannot be supposed to be very complete or satisfactory. Those who take an interest in the subject, would do better to consult the *Mystical Presence* itself. This is not the place moreover, for any formal vindication of its contents on my part. That would carry us beyond all proper bounds. The leading objections of Dr. Hodge will come in our way hereafter. In the mean time, I may find no more suitable place perhaps than at the present point, to say what needs to be said on my supposed vassalage to *Schleiermacher*.

I have read Schleiermacher some; hope to read him still more; acknowledge the mighty force of his learning and genius; and trust I shall not soon cease to cherish his memory with affectionate respect. It is a mistake however to suppose, that I have copied him directly in my theory of Christianity and the Church. So far as his influence has entered into my thinking, it has been mainly in an indirect way, through the medium of the general German theology under its best form. My obligations to this theology, I have no wish to conceal or deny. But to be in living connection with it at all at the present time, is to feel necessarily to some extent the force of Schleiermacher's mind. Not as though all came from him; for that is by no means the case. The German evangelical theology includes various conflicting tendencies, and appears in broad opposition at many points to the views of Schleiermacher. But still it is admitted on all hands, that the influence of his genial spirit is felt in its whole constitution, beyond that probably of any single mind besides. He formed indeed, as is well known, no school, and left behind him no fixed system of philosophy. His power was shown rather in the way of exciting and stimulating others, by throwing out ideas of a deeply comprehensive and productive character. In this way, though dead, he still continues to speak

---

24. [Gerrish confirms Nevin's judgment on this point, stating that Calvin taught that "the gift is given to all who communicate, pious and impious, believers and unbelievers." See *Grace and Gratitude*, 138.—ed.]

25. [MTSS vol. 1, 104—ed.]

in the theology of Germany, and will do so hereafter also, no doubt, for a long time to come. Such men as *Neander, Tholuck, Julius Mueller, Nitzsch, Twesten, Ullmann, Dorner, Rothe,*[26] &c., all own his influence, and speak reverently of his character and name. If I am to be reckoned among his disciples, it can be at best only in the general way in which these, and many others of like character, with all their acknowledged theological independence, may be distinguished with the same title. I do not know, that this should be considered any very serious reproach.

Schleiermacher however, we are told, held very serious errors. This I have no wish to deny. It is admitted generally, by those who have most respect for his memory. But what then? Are his errors such as to exclude from his writings *all* wisdom and truth? Or is it only of the infallible and immaculate we may expect to learn anything, in the sphere of religion? Alas then, at whose feet should we ever find it safe to sit, though it should be only in the most transient way? Plato abounds with errors; and what philosopher, ancient or modern, can be named, who may be considered throughout a safe guide in the paths of intellectual and moral inquiry? Must we refuse all converse with Bacon[27] and Locke,[28] and eschew in full the pages of Hegel, Schelling,[29] and Kant,[30]

26. [August Neander (1789–1850), Friedrich August Tholuck (1799–1877), Julius Müller (1801–78), Karl Immanuel Nitzsch (1787–1868), August Twesten (1789–1876), Karl Ullmann (1796–1865), Isaak August Dorner (1809–84), Richard Rothe (1799–1867). All members of the loosely allied and unquestionably diverse "Mediating school" of German theology, committed to restoring orthodoxy in the face of growing rationalism while benefiting from as well as improving on the work of Schleiermacher and Hegel, as well as Kant and the rest of those we now refer to as German idealists—ed.]

27. [Francis Bacon (1561–1626), philosopher, scientist, lawyer, and politician. Noted as the great empiricist of his time. Bacon surmised that we only gain knowledge as we rise by way of induction from the experience of simple facts to fundamental principles. These ideas were published in his *Novum Organum* (1620). Ultimately he applied his methodology to the field of ethics where he attracted much attention if not entirely enthusiastic devotion. Baconian empiricism was behind Hodge's system to some extent. So it is not surprising that Nevin respected Bacon but felt his system was deeply flawed. —ed.]

28. [John Locke (1632–1704), English philosopher most admired in America by Princeton and the host of evangelicals of that day. At Oxford he became intimately familiar with the works of Descartes and Shaftesbury. His system was a blend of rationalism and empiricism and while he remained a Puritan of sorts, he was considered unorthodox in his views. His contribution to the Princeton theology was enormous, such that Hodge referred to him as the "immortal Locke."—ed.]

29. [Friedrich Wilhelm Joseph von Schelling (1775–1854), colleague of Hegel (Jena) in the early years where their critique of Fichte was widely heralded. Later they parted company especially over Hegel's great work, *The Phenomenology of Mind*, which was circulated as proof sheets in 1806 (where Hegel departed from his and Schelling's *Identitätsphilosophie* to embrace his own speculative approach), and was later published in his *Encyclopedia* of 1894. Schelling's career took a new twist later in life, which many refer to as Schelling's second period of philosophy where he became the darling of many in the Roman Catholic Church in Prussia. German Catholics embraced Schelling's new philosophy as their modern apologetic, and Philip Schaff (Nevin's colleague at Mercersburg) heard Schelling's lectures in 1841 and became convinced of his theory of historical development in the church. See Andrew Bowie, *Schelling and Modern European Philosophy.*—ed.]

30. [Immanuel Kant (1724–1804), eminent German philosopher whose reaction to Hume revolutionized philosophy throughout Europe. His form of critical idealism became the departure point for an entirely new generation of thinkers. In many ways Kant brought about (or certainly began) the demise of rationalism (not without the help of Romanticism) that held sway in Germany and to a greater or lesser extent throughout the Western world. His application of reason, but moreover his description of reason's limits, opened the way to understand theology by way of intuition, thereby freeing it from the skepticism

lest we become contaminated with their wrong doctrines and views? Surely there may be valuable truth, even in the midst of much that is false and wrong. Coleridge[31] may deserve to be studied, notwithstanding his faults. Hundreds have in fact been acted upon in a salutary way by the power of his ideas, who stand in no feeling whatever with his *system* as a whole, and know not indeed what his system was. And so it is also in the case of Schleiermacher.

It is possible however, for a "system" to be so logically compacted together in all its parts, that to have anything to do with it at all is to be entangled necessarily in its connections and consequences as a whole, if not knowingly at least in a blind way. Is the thinking of Schleiermacher of this order? So Dr. Hodge would appear to suppose. He is careful not to charge *me* with having adopted consciously Schleiermacher's worst heresies; and for this caution he has my thanks; but he still assumes throughout that my thinking with this great man in *any* respect, involves me ignorantly in these consequences of his *system*, as he calls it; and in this way contrives so to mix me up with my supposed master, that the benefit just noticed is in a great degree lost, and for most of his readers no doubt the errors charged on the "system" are taken as though they were laid at once to my account. *This* deserves no thanks. It is besides a gross mistake on the part of Dr. Hodge, in regard to Schleiermacher's posture; and might seem to show indeed, that he is by no means so fully at home in this subject as his article tacitly assumes. Schleiermacher is just one of the last men, of whom any conception of such bondage to system may be supposed to hold good. He left no fixed system, and founded no regular school. His merit is, as before said, that he stimulated others to thought, by the deep suggestive power of his ideas.[32] Hence we find very different tendencies among those who acknowledge his influence. Few such profess to agree with his own scheme of theology. His own thoughts indeed, in many cases, have carried others quite beyond his position, requiring evidently for their full development a more healthy form of Christian faith. He stood on the confines of the old rationalism, and could not be expected to clear himself, at a single leap, of its dreary power; but he was a great organ at the same time in God's hands, for breaking up the way of new and higher theological life, by which in due time he has been himself happily thrown into the rear. It is indeed ridiculous to speak of the ideas of *Schleiermacher*, as necessarily bound throughout to his scheme of theology. Every scholar knows, that in the minds of such men as Ullmann, Dorner, Rothe, Mueller, &c., some of them at least have

that had so weakened it before. Mercersburg recognized Kant as the philosopher who could be credited (among others) with initiating Christianity's recovery from rationalism.—ed]

31. [Samuel Taylor Coleridge (1772–1834), English poet and part-time philosopher. His study of Schiller and Kant made him a true disciple of the German approach. But the early appeal of Nevin for Coleridge was of his poetry and as he says above his "ideas," and he was an avid reader (while despising his personal habits). Later (as we see here) Nevin would recognize Coleridge's dependence on the Germans, whom he would ultimately rely on for a more thorough philosophical system. See Monika Class, *Coleridge and Kantian Ideas in England, 1796–1817*.—ed.]

32. [For excellent overviews of Schleiermacher's thought, see Karl Barth, *The Theology of Schleiermacher*; Brian Gerrish, *A Prince of the Church: Schleiermacher and the Beginnings of Modern Theology*; Richard Crouter, *Friedrich Schleiermacher: Between Enlightenment and Romanticism*.—ed.]

been brought into other theological connections entirely, and appear incorporated with the old Athanasian orthodoxy in its most strict form. Every scholar knows, that this is the case in particular with the very ideas, on which Dr. Hodge lays stress in this review, as borrowed from Schleiermacher and indicating the dangerous power of his *system*. They are held by German divines of the better sort generally, who are able probably at the same time to repeat the *Apostles Creed*, with quite as full mind and good conscience as the same thing can be done by Dr. Hodge himself. The truth is, that this article, in taxing me with the heresies it scrapes together as the legitimate product of these ideas, virtually taxes all the evangelical theology of Germany with the like blame. It amounts just to this, that all German theology, even in the hands of such men as Tholuck, Neander, Julius Mueller, Dorner, &c., is inwardly rotten and unsafe, as comprehending in itself consequences at least that tend directly to subvert the gospel. The only charitable supposition in their case, as we have here in mind, is that they *know not what they are about*, and cannot see fully to the end of their own system. If Dorner, for instance, and Rothe only understood Schleiermacher as well as Dr. Hodge, and were capable of seeing as he can the end of his system from the beginning, they would not be so foolish as to think of associating any of his cardinal thought with their professed belief in the proper divinity of our Lord Jesus Christ, or in the doctrine of the Trinity as heretofore held by the Church. Their orthodoxy in such circumstances must be viewed as safe, only at the expense of their learning and common sense. To this it comes necessarily at last, with this summary process of Dr. Hodge.

I have no wish or concern to make myself the apologist of Schleiermacher; just as little as I would think of making myself the apologist of Origen—whose great merits and great faults theologically, exhibit a somewhat parallel case for our contemplation. I admit his errors freely, condemn them, renounce them, make no common cause with them whatever. It may not be uninteresting here however to present the following judgment in regard to him on the part of a distinguished English scholar, whose authority may be expected to be of more force for some than any amount of *German* testimony arrayed on the same side. The extract is from MORELL'S *Historical and Critical View of the Speculative Philosophy of Europe in the Nineteenth Century*; a work that has commanded very respectful attention on both sides of the Atlantic, and that seems to be in all respects worthy of such favorable regard.

> Schleiermacher was *par excellence* a theologian. Religion had been the friend and companion of his childhood; and he never deserted his first love. The instruction of religion formed the great purpose of his life; the reformation and spread of religion the object of his most earnest endeavors; and his last words, after receiving the holy communion, were "In *this* faith I die!" Had we to portray the influence which Schleiermacher exerted upon theology of his age, we should fill many pages ere we could do justice to his long and laborious life. We should have, for example, to describe the startling effect of his "Discourses on Religion" (*Reden ueber die Religion*),[33] where he attacked infidelity in its last resource, namely that

33. [Friedrich Schleiermacher, *Über die Religion: Reden an die Gebildeten unter ihren Verächtern. (On Religion: Speeches to its cultured despisers.)*—ed.]

of indifference; to recall the solemn accents with which his "Monologues"[34] fell upon the ear of his countrymen; to picture the mighty power of his eloquence, as felt by those who listened to his Sabbath day labors, or perused them after they were immortalized by his pen; most of all should we have to trace the entrance of his great production on the Doctrine of Faith (*Glaubenslehre*),[35] into the abodes of the learned, and the halls of theology and science, to see it wrestling there with the cold hearted rationalism of the age, or recalling the common soul of humanity back to its better nature and its final rest. *Vol. II.* p. 434, 43[36]

To deduce a complete and connected system of philosophy from the miscellaneous writings of Schleiermacher would be impossible; in fact it was part of his very doctrine that no philosophical system should be propounded for universal reception, and that no school should be formed. Whilst therefore he lectured much upon philosophy, and took many original views upon most questions which it brings before us, he has left no followers behind him, to associate his name with any peculiar class of metaphysical opinions. p. 435.

His system of theology

has had more influence upon the theological thinking in the present day, than perhaps any other production of our whole European literature.—We would earnestly recommend the reader who wishes to understand somewhat of the best, the most spiritual, the most religious of the German theological literature, to peruse these noble writings of Schleiermacher; where amidst much that he may perchance reject, he will find no few materials of instruction and delight. p. 444

I have said that there has been no consciousness or design on my part of copying Schleiermacher; if any of my thoughts belong to him originally, they have come to me indirectly, rather than in an immediate and direct way. But more than this; it needs no great discernment to see that my general theological tendency is quite different from that involved in his "system." No man was less bound than Schleiermacher by the authority of the outward and objective; he is in one sense the very apostle of individualism; among all Protestants it would be hard to find one whose protestantism may be taken as more absolute and free as his. The great object of the *Mystical Presence*, on the other hand, is to assert the claims of an objective, historical, sacramental, churchly religion, over against the subjectivity of mere private judgment and private will. One great ground of complaint against it with Dr. Hodge himself, is found notoriously just in this, that it is regarded as too little Protestant and too much catholic. Nobody ever thought of bringing such a charge against the system of Schleiermacher. That some of his ideas may be applied in the end to the support of sound church views, I have no doubt; as it is certain, that some of the ideas of Schelling & Hegel also carry in themselves still more a powerful tendency in the same direction. But to speak of Schleiermacher's general system as churchly, or in any sort of affinity with Rome,

34. [Friedrich Schleiermacher, *Friedrich Schleiermachers Monologen.*—ed.]

35. [Friedrich Schleiermacher, *Der christiche Glaube.*—ed.]

36. [John Daniel Morell, *An Historical and Critical View of the Speculative Philosophy of Europe in the Nineteenth Century* (London: John Johnstone, 1847).—ed.]

would be absolutely ridiculous. Dr. Hodge does indeed refer to him, in his review of Bushnell, as the founder of some sort of Puseyism in Berlin and the great representative of what he describes as the German form of substituting the outward in religion for the spiritual and inward. But who that knows anything about Schleiermacher's spirit; can admit such an idea as this? Schleiermacher a ritualist, disposed to make undue account of forms, or to give the letter at any point a place higher than the spirit! Never surely was there a judgment more fully aside from its proper mark. Alas, it is the great fault of his theology, that it is so entirely inward and makes so little account of history and the outward church. In this respect the *Mystical Presence* moves quite in another order of thought. Altogether indeed my sense of the CHURCH, which has become to be very active and deep, has not been borrowed in any direct and immediate way from German theology. I know no writer there, whose views in full I would be willing to accept on this subject. So far as a churchly influence has been exerted upon me from this quarter, it has been mainly through the force of theological ideas, that have served to bring my mind into a right position, for perceiving and appreciating what is due to this whole side of Christianity in its own nature. The later German theology has done much undoubtedly to promote right views of history, deeper apprehensions of the christological questions, more realistic conceptions altogether of the new creation introduced into the world by Jesus Christ. Its tendency is in this way to break up the force of our common modern spiritualistic abstractions, and thus to restore at the same time old catholic ideas to their proper force. It is well adapted accordingly to make the necessity of an objective, sacramental religion felt, even *beyond* the measure of its own positive teaching. Only in this way can it be said to have anything to do, with my particular church tendency. Rothe's work[37] for instance on the early Church seems to me powerfully adapted to promote sound church feeling, although the object of the author is to find a desperate apology for the present state of our Protestant Christianity, in the idea the Catholic Church as such has nearly finished its mission, and is soon to be superseded altogether by a new order of the Christian life in the form of the state. Nay for a seriously religious mind capable of understanding it fully, and apprehending its true force, the *Leben Jesu* of Strauss[38] might be recommended perhaps as one of the best helps to be found, towards a proper sense of the necessity and significance of the Church.

37. [Richard Rothe, *Die Anfänge der Christlichen Kirche und ihrer Verfassung* (Wittemberg: Zimmermann, 1837).—ed.]

38. [This remarkable statement attests to Nevin's distance from Schleiermacher, as Strauss's *Life* was a bitter attack on same (although Strauss was the bridge between Schleiermacher and Hegel, and his ideas share a great deal in common with Schleiermacher). Despite the heterodoxy of the *Leben Jesu*, Nevin may have appreciated Strauss's critique of Schleiermacher for what Strauss believed was Schleiermacher's mythologizing the role of the church, or perhaps his subjectivizing of the community of faith. Strauss insisted on taking seriously the real, historical church in the formation of faith.—ed.]

10

Departures from Chalcedonian Orthodoxy[1]

[NEVIN]

W E COME NOW TO Dr. Hodge's list of heresies. He seems to have gone on the principle of stringing together as many as he conveniently could, with little or no regard to their coherency as a whole. My brain must be somewhat peculiarly constructed, of a truth, to admit quietly the contradictory affinities and tendencies, here laid to my charge. There is something nevertheless at times in calling *names*. I am charged with speaking reproachfully of my brethren; and the idea would seem to be that I deserve to be paid effectually in the same coin. I may ask here however, to what after all has my offence in this view amounted? In the beginning of this controversy a few harsh personalities escaped my pen, which have long since been sincerely regretted, acknowledged, and in the proper quarter *pardoned*.[2] But beyond this, it has been characterized by patience certainly far more than passion. If there be any severity in the *Mystical Presence*, it is such only as disagreeable truth must ever carry, where it is earnestly felt and clearly and firmly spoken. Modern Puritanism, the reigning character of our American religion at this time, is charged with having fallen away from the sacramental doctrine of the old Reformed Church; and the charge is supported by full historical evidence; respectfully always, though of course with such sharp decision as

1. ["Dr. Hodge on the *Mystical Presence*, Article from the *Repertory*, Continued, No. 10," *Weekly Messenger*, New Series, vol. 13, no. 46. Wednesday, July 26, 1848. Published by the Board of the Synod of the German Reformed Church: Chambersburg, PA.—ed.]

2. [Nevin is likely referring to his bitter exchange with Joseph Berg, who represented to Nevin the model of modern Puritan theological thinking, and this even in his own denomination. Berg accused Nevin of heresy in his journal the *Protestant Quarterly* and branded him there with "Romanizing Tendencies." Nevin replied in kind with a series of articles under the title *Pseudo-Protestantism*, in which he argued that Berg and modern Puritanism was not truly of the Reformed family of faith; that most of Protestant America has succumbed to this aberration of Protestant theology. He became even more caustic when the *Lutheran Observer* came out against him and he wrote another series on "Pseudo-Lutheranism." In his installment to the *Messenger* (Vol. 10. No. 52, September 1845), Nevin accused Berg of "libel." The two continued to exchanged angry letters in the *Weekly Messenger*, but seemed to have regretted the rancor and said so in print. Nevertheless, Berg would eventually leave the denomination.—ed.]

it was necessary to use, in order to be at all heard or understood. Has the charge been met and set aside as false, by fair historical proof? Never, to this day. There has been abundance of abuse and scorn heaped on the book, in various quarters; it has been grossly misrepresented, and burdened with statements and consequences which are most plainly and solemnly disclaimed on its own pages; and there might seem to have been almost a sort of conspiracy with a certain portion of our *evangelical* press, to prevent the real issue it involves from coming fairly and distinctly into view. But it has not been answered. The first respectable *attempt* to meet it in such way, is this article of Dr. Hodge; and to what this comes on the field of history, we have already seen. Dr. Hodge makes a show indeed of warding off the accusation, of which he here complains. But has he done so in fact? Every unsophisticated reader must see, that his effort has proved a most significant failure; nay, that it goes signally to confirm the truth and force of the accusation itself. Indeed the fundamental point of it is conceded by Dr. Hodge himself; though he affects to make a mere circumstance of it, and covers it with no small quantity of fog. He confines the force of the holy Eucharist to its monumental side simply, while he acknowledges at the same time that the Calvinistic view included the idea besides of a participation by means of it in the power of Christ's life. This second aspect then of the old doctrine, its proper catholic and churchly side, the entire *mystical* sense of it in one word, has been suffered to fall out of the system to which it once belonged as an "uncongenial element" that had not business ever to be there. But now what else is this, than the very change ("apostasy" or wholesome "growth," as we may choose to take it) which is laid to the charge of our modern Puritan theology in the *Mystical Presence*? And why then should it be counted either reproachful or contemptuous to give it loud, distinct expression? The fact is palpable. Puritanism itself, as here represented by Dr. Hodge, glories in it as an ornament of its faith, that it is *not* bound by the *mystical* view of Calvin, and sets down openly as a badge rather of popish superstition. We take it then, at his own word, and say to it respectfully again, what we have said to it respectfully before: This is a defection from the sacramental creed of the original Reformed Church; and it is a very serious defection, which is well entitled to earnest consideration; for the sacramental question is of central interest for all theology and church life; and if it be right for us to give up in this way the very core and marrow of the old doctrine, we should at least stand ready to give a fair and open answer, in the case, to any that may ask of us a reason for what is thus done.

It will be borne in mind, in the meantime, that the point of view from which Dr. Hodge's observations of heresy are here made, is *not* the old faith of the Reformed Church itself, but the materially different position now noticed, in which the sacramental MYSTERY, as once held, has come to be regarded as a relic only of Roman superstition.

REVIEW FROM THE REPERTORY, CONTINUED [HODGE]

It is not the truth of this system that we propose to examine, but simply its relation to the theology of the Reformed church. Dr. Nevin is loud, frequent, often, apparently at least, contemptuous, in his reproaches of his brethren for their apostasy from the doctrines of the Reformation. We propose very briefly to assign our reasons for regarding his system, as unfolded in this book, as an entire rejection not only of the peculiar doctrines of the Reformed church, on the points concerned, but of some of the leading principles of Protestant, and even Catholic, theology in general.

First, in reference to the person of Christ. Dr. Nevin denies any dualism in the constitution of man. Soul and body, in their ground, are but one life. So in the case of Christ, in virtue of the hypostatical union, his life is one. The divine and human are so united in him as to constitute one indivisible life. "It is in all respects a true human life" (p. 167).[3] "His divine nature is at the same time *human*, in the fullest sense" (p. 174).[4]

That this is a departure not only from the doctrine of the Reformed church, but of the church universal, seems to us very plain. In one view it is the Eutychian doctrine, and in another something worse. Eutyches and afterwards Monothelites[5] taught, that after the hypostatical union, there was in Christ but one nature and operation. Substitute the word "life" for its equivalent, "nature," and we have the precise statement of Dr. Nevin's. He warns us against the error of Nestorius, just as Eutychians called all who held to the existence of the two natures in Christ, Nestorians. Eutyches admitted that this one nature or life in our Lord, was theanthropic. He was constituted of two natures, but after their union, had but one. 'Omologo, he says, *ek duo phuseon gegennesthai ton kurion 'emon pro tes 'enoseos; meta de ten 'enosin, mian phusin 'omologo.*[6] And therefore, there was in Christ, as the Monothelites say, but *mia theandrike energeia.*[7] What is the difference between one theanthropic life, and one theanthropic operation? We are confirmed in the correctness of this view of the matter, from the fact, that Schleiermacher, the father of this system, strenuously objects to the use of the word *nature* in this whole connection, especially in its application to the divinity, and opposes also the adoption of the terms which the council of Chalcedon employed in the condemnation of Eutychianism.[8] This however, is a small matter. Dr. Nevin has a right to speak for himself. It is his own language, which, as it seems to us, distinctly conveys

---

3. [See MTSS edition, 149.—ed.]

4. [Ibid., 155.—ed.]

5. [Monothelitism was a christological heresy that emerged in the seventh century as an attempted compromise between the Chalcedonian teaching on Christ's two natures and the continuing monophysite dissent that insisted on only one nature. Promulgated by the Patriarch of Constantinople and the Byzantine emperor, the monothelite formula posited that while possessing two natures, Christ had but one divine-human will. Despite strong official support, the new teaching was strongly opposed by many within the Western Church and most famously by Maximus the Confessor. Ultimately, it was condemned by the Third Council of Constantinople (680–81), which ruled that the Chalcedonian formula required that Christ has two wills, one fully human will and one fully divine.—ed.]

6. [Trans. "I confess that the Lord came from two natures before the union, but after the union, I confess one nature."—ed.]

7. ["One theanthropic energy, or operation."—ed.]

8. [Hodge] Schleiermacher's *Glaubenslehre*, § 97. [Friedrich D. E. Schleiermacher, *Der christliche Glaube nach den Grundsätzen der evangelischen Kirche im Zusammemhang dargestellt* (Berlin: G. Reimer, 1821). For a modern translation, see H. R. MacKintosh and J. S. Stewart, eds., *The Christian Faith* (Edinburgh: T & T Clark, 1999).—ed.]

the Eutychian doctrine, that after the hypostatical union there was but one *phusis* ["nature"—ed.], or as he expresses it, one life, in Christ. He attributes to Calvin a wrong psychology in reference to Christ's person. What is that but to attribute to him wrong views of that person? And what is that but saying his own views differ from those of Calvin on the person of Christ? No one, however, has ever pretended that Calvin had any peculiar views on that subject. He says himself that he held all the decisions, as to such points, of the first six ecumenical counsels. In differing from Calvin, on this point, therefore, Dr. Nevin differs from the whole church.

CRITICISM [NEVIN]

This closing ratiocination is precious. How easy to retort: Dr. Hodge allows that Calvin ascribed a life power to the holy Eucharist which *he* rejects; this involves necessarily a different christology; but Calvin always professed to agree with the first six general councils; therefore Dr. Hodge, in differing from Calvin, differs from the universal church. Q. E. D. Seriously, can Dr. Hodge suppose that every variation in the science of psychology, involves necessarily a corresponding alteration in the *substance* of the Christian faith? Is his own psychology at all like that of Tertullian,[9] or of the ancient church fathers generally? Such changes necessarily affect always more or less the *form* of all doctrines for the understanding; but the truth itself may be the same under different forms; whence precisely the idea of dogmatic history. In the *Mystical Presence*, Calvin's theory is said to labor, under this view only, as exhibited through the medium of a defective psychology; and the better form of our present science is employed accordingly, not to subvert its material substance, but only to place it if possible in a light more suitable to the wants of the understanding at this time. Dr. Hodge employs a psychology too in the case; not Calvin's by any means; but his object with it is to kill the very substance of the old doctrine, which it has been my endeavor all along to preserve alive.

I owe it here however both to Calvin and myself to say publicly, that the renewed investigations into which I have been led by this article of Dr. Hodge, assisted in particular by the keen analysis of Professor Ebrard, have satisfied me that there is in reality much less need than I before supposed, for the qualifications I have taken pains to make on this subject in the *Mystical Presence*. The truth is, both Calvin and Ursinus were ahead of their own age in their ideas of nature and life generally, and show throughout a wonderful depth here, as compared with the crass and superficial thinking that still too commonly prevails. This is allowed indeed, as regards Calvin, in the *Mystical Presence*; he is charged with some unsteady confusion only in his psychology, rather than with absolute error; but even in this form, the charge is too strong. And particularly in regard to the point here before us, it is abundantly plain that he never falls at all into any such dualistic view of life as we find involved in the psychology of

---

9. [Quintus Septimius Tertullian (c. 160–c. 225), Christian convert and polemicist who became among the most renowned church fathers. He eventually joined the Montanist sect. See Geoffrey G. Dunn, *Tertullian*; Eric Osborn, *Tertullian, First Theologian of the West*.—ed.]

Dr. Hodge. With him, mind and body are always a real unity, in such sense that the new nature introduced into the *soul,* as he terms it, necessarily extends out from this to the corporeal and spiritual sides of our being alike, as the power of a single undivided fact. Evidence enough of this has been already quoted. And just as little is there any Nestorian dualism in his idea of the person of Christ. Anything so monstrous as the conception of two lives in Christ, is in full contradiction to his christological theory from beginning to end.

Dr. Hodge charges me here with *Eutychianism.* There are two ways in which this error may hold; either as confounding the two natures into a third form of existence that is neither one nor the other; or as allowing the divine side of the mystery so to prevail, that the human is reduced to a merely phenomenal unreality—which seems to have been the form of it as held by Eutyches himself. Now both of these conceptions are very distinctly repudiated in the *Mystical Presence*; and I solemnly repudiate them also in this place. I believe with the Westminster Catechism, that "Christ the eternal Son of God, became man, by taking to himself a true body, and a reasonable soul, and so was and continues to be both God and man, *in two distinct natures and one person, forever.*"[10] But I attribute to him, it is said, one indivisible life; and we have only to substitute the word nature for this, which Dr. Hodge assures us is just of equivalent force, to have the Eutychian formula in full! I confess I could hardly believe my own eyes, when I first read this specimen of theological argument, as flowing from the mind and pen of so accomplished a scholar as Dr. Hodge. I can only say, I have never dreamed of using the word life as the equivalent of nature; and have yet to learn by what *usus loquendi,*[11] philosophical or biblical, it is pretended in the present case to identify the terms in such confident and summary style. The New Testament idea of life as applied to Christ especially in the deep pregnant sense of St. John, is certainly something of a widely different character.

With me, the term life, in the case of man, is synonymous not at all with nature in Dr. Hodge's sense, but with personality.[12] It is the central consciousness of the subject, the indivisible *Ichheit* or "ME" from which his whole existence springs and to which continually it returns. It is that to which we refer both body and soul, when we say *my* body and *my* soul, requiring both to meet thus in the power of an indivisible unity, which is as such neither the one nor the other separately taken. Body and soul in this view are not the same, in their nature, but separate and distinct; and yet in their ground, they form assuredly but one life. To say the opposite of this, must involve plainly such a dualism as would in the end subvert the conception of humanity altogether.

And who may not see, that a christology constructed on any similar view must with equal certainty, when carried out to its legitimate consequences, subvert the mystery of the incarnation? If the Word became flesh actually and truly, and not merely in the way of show as pretended by the old Gnostics; if the incarnation were more than such an

---

10. [Westminster Shorter Catechism, Q. 21; although the opening phrase here is that of Q. 22, substituting for the more ponderous opening of Q. 21.—ed.]

11. ["manner of speaking."—ed.]

12. [Nevin was indebted to Frederick Rauch for his modern concept of personality.—ed.]

outward avatar only, as is presented to us in the Hindu mythology; the person of our glorious Redeemer, in whose mysterious constitution our human nature has been assumed into the union with the divine *must* be regarded as the organic comprehension of both in the power of a single undivided life. How could the union be *hypostatical* (not the blending of two persons of course into one, but still the real incorporation of our human nature into the very person of the everlasting Word) under any other view? For what is personality, if it be not the absolute centralization of its subject at last in the power of a single consciousness, that pervades and rules at every point the entire compass of his life as a whole? *How* this can be, in the case before us, we may not be able to see or say. Great is the *mystery* of godliness, God manifest in the flesh. But our faith is required here to go before our understanding. Not as we are able to construct in the first place a satisfactory theory of the incarnation, but only as we are overwhelmed through the person of Jesus Christ himself with a living sense of the fact, is the mystery which it involves to be admitted in our creed. As such a FACT, felt and apprehended by faith, we may know what it comprehends, without being able to say at all how this can have place. In this view, the mystery of the incarnation involves necessarily for our faith such a union of the two natures in Christ as makes them to be one life, one personal consciousness, as truly as the same thing can be affirmed of body and soul in our common human existence. Short of this the union cannot be regarded as hypostatical; and in no other view is it possible to retain firm hold of the Redeemer's personality, as a *real* and not merely an imaginary revelation of God in the flesh. This much, and nothing less than this, is involved in the historical fact of Christ's person. He stands before us as one life. He claims such character, when he applies to himself the pronoun *I* or *Me*; and it is allowed in every address which approaches him as *Thou*. In any different view the personal pronouns could not rightly extend to him; and so his whole life was different from what it seemed; his history was a fallacy throughout; all runs out at last into a theophany, in which the mystery of mysteries is wrecked for our faith entirely and forever. No; let the intellect labor as it may, we are bound to hold fast the fact or a real, historical, *organic* incarnation, in which God and man are ONE. Two natures, but still a single personal being. Why should the idea of such unity here necessarily overthrow the difference of the two sides embraced in it, more than in the case of our common life?

Not to admit such an organic unity in Christ's life, is the error of Nestorius. I should be sorry to have it thought, that I would charge Dr. Hodge with this in the way of offset simply to his charge of Eutychianism preferred against the *Mystical Presence*; although the facility with which he brings this charge, does constitute undoubtedly, in the circumstances, a presumption of some undue leaning to the other side on his own part. It needs a Nestorian tendency, to find Eutychianism where it is thus found by Dr. Hodge. I should be sorry moreover to make the mere name of an ancient heresy, in this case, the vehicle of any particular odium. A large part of our modern Protestantism probably, respectable and orthodox in other respects, stands on precisely the same ground, without having at all reflected on the fact. It is with the thing, of course, rather than the name, that we are here principally concerned. In such a view, I feel authorized to pronounce the christology of this entire article in the *Princeton Repertory* decidedly *Nestorian*.

It would seem to be so indeed, almost in positive and direct terms. For does not Dr. Hodge, by plain implication, assert the presence of two lives in the constitution of Christ's person? The idea of any such centralization of the Redeemer's being into a single indivisible consciousness, as is always implied by the use of the personal pronouns in other cases, he holds to be a fusion of the two natures into one, the error formerly taught by Eutyches. He must suppose then two centers in Christ; two forms of self-consciousness; two Christs in a word, one heavenly and the other earthly, joined together, not in the way of inward vital organization, but by a sort of outward partnership only under the *form* of a common person, for the accomplishment of a certain end that could not easily be reached in a different way.

But terms are always more or less of uncertain, precarious force, in the case of this awfully mysterious subject, and I have no wish to build much upon them in a separate view. The Nestorianism of Dr. Hodge is shown by other, and still more conclusive evidence. It runs through his entire theology; as it is not possible indeed, in any case, that our christological theory should not affect at last our whole scheme of religion, both theoretically and practically. It lies at the root of every objection, I may say, which he brings against the *Mystical Presence*, and stands out more or less clearly to view in every position he takes on the contrary side.

This indeed is the very sense ultimately of that divorce of "sacrifice" and "life," in the sacramental transaction, by which Dr. Hodge himself admits his system to be distinguished from that of Calvin. The sacrifice, in this view, however it may have needed the life once for its accomplishment is no longer bound to this in any way for its abiding value and force; its value lies rather in the death of Christ as something past and left behind; it is thus the intelligible import simply of that event; the thought of it, *abstracted* from its original concrete ground, and now of force only *as a thought* in the Divine Mind. The atonement, as such an abstraction, becomes a mere doctrine, a thing to be apprehended in the way of thought only and memory. The incarnation then stands related to it as a temporary transient basis simply, and not as its necessary everlasting foundation; if the person of Christ could now be dissolved, the satisfaction made for sin as a thing past would still hold good; made "once and for all," why should it be supposed to hang any longer upon the mediatorial mystery originally *contrived* for its accomplishment? But who may not see, that this is to turn the incarnation itself into a transient phenomenon, an outward divine scheme, in which the two sides of Christ's person come at last to no truly organic and permanent union? Let it be felt, on the other hand, that the everlasting Word has really become flesh in the person of Jesus Christ, and it must be felt in the same proportion that a like everlasting character belongs of necessity to all his mediatorial functions and acts. In other words, they cannot be sundered from the power of his indissoluble life (Heb. vii. 16), in the presence of which only they carry along with them their full original force, to the end of time. Thus it is that Christ "by one offering hath perfected *forever* them that are sanctified";[13] not in virtue of it as an event only, to be remembered in subsequent time; but by the

13. [Heb 10:14.—ed.]

enduring character that belongs to it as a part of his own glorified life. Thus it is, that we "have boldness to enter into the holiest by the blood of Jesus" (Heb x. 19), not as something long since separated from his person; but as the propitiatory force of an offering, whose all prevalent worth still springs from this perpetually as its ground and fountain. This is the deep idea, which we find caricatured in the perpetual sacrifice, as it is called, of the Roman mass. The sacrifice of Christ is indeed perpetual; not an event or occurrence only in past time; but an eternal fact, in which *once and always* are the same thing, in virtue of the personal presence of Christ's life, "the same yesterday, today and forever."[14] The sense of all this, as now said, goes necessarily along with the catholic idea of the incarnation as involving a real organic union of the human nature with the divine in the Savior's person; and so it follows, that where this sense is wanting, there will be a corresponding defect in the view taken of the hypostatical mystery. An abstract atonement implies an abstract Christ. To sunder the sacrifice of Christ from his life, is virtually in the end to bring in a dualistic Nestorian christology, and to place the whole weight of the Christian salvation thus on a wrong foundation.

So much is involved (*not designed*) in the sacramental theory of Dr. Hodge. It divides what God has joined together. To abstract the merit and righteousness of Christ from his life in the mystery of the Lord's Supper, is to put them asunder in their general nature; and this brings with it such an apprehension of the Savior's *person*, in its relation to his *work*, as must necessarily entangle us at last in Nestorianism. Hence the earnestness with which the Church catholic has always insisted on the opposite view. Hence the zeal evinced in its behalf, by the immortal Calvin. Dr. Hodge may affect to make small account of his acknowledged departure here from the old faith; as though Calvin and the early Reformed Church had no reason whatever for holding fast to this point but were led to so only through accident or caprice; but in reality the variation is serious and broad. It involves ultimately a rupture with the christological consciousness of the ancient Church. To the mind of Calvin a deep catholic truth was staked on this very question, going to the ground of Christianity itself; and this it is precisely the *catholic* idea embraced in the holy sacraments, which our modern Protestantism, as represented by Dr. Hodge, is urged by its whole nature continually to thrust out of sight.

We shall have occasion to notice the Nestorian complexion of Dr. Hodge's theology still farther, as we follow him in the subsequent part of his review.

REVIEW, CONTINUED [HODGE]

But in the other view of this matter. What was this one life (or nature) of Christ? Dr. Nevin says: "It was in all respects a true human life" (p. 167).[15] "Christ is the archetypal man, in whom the true idea of humanity is brought to view." He "is the true ideal man." Our nature is complete only in him (p. 201).[16] But is a perfect, or ideal man, anything more than a mere man after all? If all that was in Christ pertains to the perfection of

---

14. [Heb 13:8.—ed.]

15. [MTSS edition, p. 149.—ed.]

16. [Ibid., 176.—ed.]

our nature, he was at best, but a perfect man. The only way to escape Socinianism, on this theory, is by deifying man, identifying the divine and human, and making all the glory, wisdom and power, which belong to Christ the proper attributes of humanity. Christ is a perfect man? But what is a perfect man? We may give a pantheistic, or a Socinian answer to that question, and not really help the matter—for the real and infinite hiatus between us and Christ, is in either case closed. Thus it is that mysticism falls back on rationalism. They are but different phases of the same spirit. In Germany, it has long been a matter of dispute, to which class Schleiermacher belongs. He was accustomed to smile at the controversy as a mere logomachy. Steudel objects to Schleiermacher's Christology, that according to him "Christ is a finished man." Albert Knapp says: "He deifies the human and renders human the divine."[17] We, therefore, do not stand alone in thinking that to represent Christ's life as in all respects human, to say he was the ideal man, that human nature found its completion in him, admits naturally only of a pantheistic or Socinian interpretation. We of course do not attribute to Dr. Nevin either of these forms of doctrine. We do not believe that he adopts either. But we object both to his language and doctrine that one or the other of those heresies, is their legitimate consequence.

CRITICISM [NEVIN]

Here are two new heresies, *Socinianism* and *Pantheism*, one or the other of which, we are told, is the legitimate consequences of my doctrine. Why? Let the reader fix his eye steadily now on the point, which is made to bear the weight of this momentous charge. I make Christ the perfect idea of humanity, and say of his mediatorial person that it was in all respects truly human, and not so merely in semblance or outward show. But, says Dr. Hodge, this is either to make him a mere man, or else to deify humanity. I deny the consequences. Is a perfect, or ideal man, it is asked, anything more than a mere man after all? Without any regard to Schleiermacher's theory, I answer unhesitatingly: Yes, the true idea of humanity involves such a union with the divine nature, as we have exhibited in the SON OF MAN, Jesus Christ. Mark well; the true idea of *humanity*, not the conception of a single man separately taken. Dr. Hodge imagines plainly that the idea of man as a whole, is something proper full to the nature of each man as a solitary unit. But this is not the true force of the word *humanity*. It expresses the universal life of our race, *as a whole*, which for this very reason can never be fully at hand in any ordinary single man separately considered. And now of such a whole, we say, humanity cannot be complete save in living union with God; and to this union it comes fully only in the person of Christ, who on this very account is the central, universal, archetypal MAN; not a copy of what should have place in all as dreamed by Hegel; but the actual bearer of a fact or reality in which all are required to participate through Him, and through Him alone. Does this imply any such deification of others,

---

17. [Hodge:] F. W. Gess: *Uebersich uber Schleier. System.* p. 225. [Friedrich Wilhelm Gess, *Deutliche und möglichst vollständige Uebersicht über das theologische System Dr. Friedrich Schleiermachers* (Reutlingen: Ensslin und Laiblin, 1837). The reference to Knapp suggests a quote of a quote.—ed.]

as is admitted to hold in this case? Just the reverse. It makes him the universal center, for the very purpose of placing the whole world over against him, as a moral planetarium that can have no meaning or force, except as it revolves with perpetual free consciousness around HIM, the Sun of Righteousness, in this character. In this way we are all called to be "partakers of the divine nature,"[18] and so to have part in the true *ideal* of humanity, though it is reserved for our glorious Head alone to be at once, in his single separate personality, all that the perfection of humanity requires in this view. Is this Socianism? Or does it land us in Pantheism? Is it not rather the only right sense of the Eighth Psalm, as interpreted Heb. 2:5–9?

But turn now to Dr. Hodge's theory, as we have it here by plain implication. For him, the constitution of Christ is *not* perfectly human; the divine Word has not so become flesh as to be itself, in this form, the legitimate expression of what belongs to the idea of humanity; it has not entered inwardly, organically, really, into union with our human nature, in any such way as to be itself human as well as divine. The mystery of the incarnation, according to Dr. Hodge, is not any such process as can be said to bring the supernatural side of Christ's life, into historical and abiding marriage with the natural. Divinity and humanity cannot, with him, be so married into a single personal consciousness. They are two worlds that necessarily stand out of each other; and if they *seem* to meet and to become one in Christ, it can only be after all in the way of outward bond; the higher nature remains still always beyond the precincts of the lower; they never become concentric circles around a single ME or I.

But this is Nestorianism again almost without disguise. To say that the divine has not become human, and that the supernatural has not entered into organic union with the natural, in the person of Jesus Christ, what is it less at last than to say in other terms: The WORD has *not* become FLESH!

REVIEW, CONTINUED [HODGE]

In the second place, we think the system under consideration, is justly chargeable with a departure from the doctrine of the Reformed church and the church universal as to the nature of our union with Christ. According to the Reformed church that union is not merely moral, nor is it merely legal or federal, nor does it arise simply from Christ having assumed our nature, it is at the same time real and vital. But the bond of that union, however intimate or extensive, is the indwelling of the Holy Spirit, the third person of the Godhead, in Christ and in his people. We receive Christ himself, when we receive the Holy Spirit, who is the Spirit of Christ; we receive the life of Christ when we receive his Spirit, who is the Spirit of life. Such we believe to be the true doctrine of the Reformed church on this subject. But if to this be added, as some of the Reformed taught, there was a mysterious power emanating from the glorified body of Christ, in heaven, it falls very short, or rather is something entirely different from the doctrine of this book. Dr. Nevin's theory of the mystical union is of course determined by his view of the constitution of Christ's person. If divinity and humanity

18. [2 Pt 1:4.—ed.]

are united in him as one life; if that life is in all respects human, then it is this divine human life, humanity raised to the power of deity, that is communicated to his people. It is communicated too, in the form of a new organic principle, working in the way of history and growth. "The supernatural has become natural" (p. 246).[19] A new divine element has been introduced into our nature by the incarnation. "Humanity itself has been quickened into full correspondence with the vivific principle it has been made to enshrine."[20] Believers, therefore, receive, or take part in the entire humanity of Christ. From Adam they receive humanity as he had it, after the fall; from Christ, they receive the theanthropic life, humanity with deity enshrined in it, or rather made one with it, one undivided life.

That this is not the old view of the mystical union between Christ and his people, can hardly be a matter of dispute. Dr. Nevin says Calvin was wrong not only in the psychology of Christ, but of his people. Ullmann, in the essay prefixed to this volume, tells us Schleiermacher introduced an epoch by teaching this doctrine. This is declared to be the doctrine of the Church of the Future. It is denied to be that of the Church of the Past.[21] There is one consideration, if there were no other, which determines this question beyond appeal. It follows of necessity from Dr. Nevin's doctrine that the relation of believers to God and Christ, is essentially different, since the incarnation, from that of believers before the event. The union between the divine and human began with Christ, and from him this theanthropic life passes over to the church. There neither was nor could there be any such thing before. This he admits. He therefore teaches that the saints of old were, as to the mystical union, in a very different condition, from that of the saints of now. Hear what he says on the subject. In arguing against the doctrine that the indwelling of Christ, is by the Spirit, he says:

> Let the church know that she is no nearer God now in fact in the way of actual life, than she was under the Old Testament; that the indwelling of Christ in believers, is only parallel with the divine presence enjoyed by the Jewish saints, who all died in the faith "not having received the promises;" that the mystical union

19. [Actually Nevin wrote, "The supernatural has become itself the natural." MTSS edition, 213.—ed.]

20. [Ibid., 197.—ed.]

21. [Nevin:] Here again we have something unworthy of Dr. Hodge, a mere pun or quibble put forward as an argument. As if one should say of Wordsworth; 'The child is father of the man;' and some dry critic would retort: How then can they be the same! Can Dr. Hodge honestly believe, that the Church of the Present, in the good Presbyterian part of it to which he belongs, is a facsimile of the Church as it stood in the days of Augustine or Tertullian? If not, to what does his play upon words amount? J. W. N. [This is important because it illustrates the way the two understood change in the church. Hodge believed the Bible (in the original manuscripts) contained the Christian faith as the full, complete, and infallible factual record of God's will and dealings with people. The historic church changed for Hodge in the sense that through aeons of committed study a better understanding of those facts "developed." That is to say, the church improved upon its doctrines in light of the facts of Scripture and its history and character was reflected in those changes. That is what Hodge meant by "development." Nevin in contrast believed that changes in the church occurred systemically; that it was not simply a matter of the better understanding of the texts, but the maturing experience of the church that allowed it to think differently and, in Nevin's mind, more fruitfully about the texts and what they meant for the world. There is no question that Schleiermacher made this a banner of his historical theology and thinking, and in some sense launched the era of liberal theology.—ed.]

> in the case of Paul and John was nothing more intimate and vital and real than the relation sustained by Abraham, or Daniel, or Isaiah (p. 195).[22]

> In the religion of the Old Testament, God descends towards man, and holds out to his view in this way the promise of a real union of the divine nature with the human, as the end of the gracious economy thus introduced. To such a *real* union it is true, the dispensation itself never came. . . . The wall of partition that separated the divine from the human, was never fully broken down (p. 203).[23]

It was, he says, "a revelation of God in man." Again, "That which forms the full *reality* of religion, the union of the divine nature with the human, the revelation of God in man, and not simply to him, was wanting in the Old Testament altogether."[24] Let us now hear how Calvin, who is quoted by Dr. Nevin as the greatest representative of the Reformed church, says on this subject. He devotes the whole of chapters 10 and 11 of the Second Book of his *Institutes*, to the refutation of the doctrine that the Old Testament economy in its promises, blessings and effects, differed essentially from that of the New. The difference he declared to be merely circumstantial, relating to the mode, the clearness, and extent of its instructions, and the number embraced under its influence. He tells us he was led to the discussion of this subject by what that "*prodigiousus nebulo Servitus, et furiosi nonnuli ex Anabaptistarum secta*" (rather bad company) taught on this point; who thought of the Jews no better, "*quam de aliquo porcurum grege.*"[25][26] In opposition to them, and all like them, Calvin undertakes to prove, that the old covenant "differed in substance and reality nothing from ours, but was entirely one and the same; the administration alone being different" (10:2).[27] "What more absurd," he asks §10, "than that Abraham should be the father of all the faithful and yet not have a corner among them? But he can be cast down neither from the number, nor from his high rank among believers, without destroying the whole church."[28] He reminds Christians that Christ has promised them no higher heaven

22. [MTSS edition, 171.—ed.]

23. [Ibid., 178.—ed.]

24. [Ibid., 182.—ed.]

25. [Trans. "That wonderful rascal Servetus and certain madmen of the Anabaptist sect"; "as nothing but a herd of swine." Calvin, *Institutes*, II.10.1; ed. McNeill, 1:429.—ed.]

26. [Nevin:] Servetus and the Anabaptists here referred to are represented by Calvin as sundering the old economy entirely from the new, sinking the Jewish religion to a mere worldly character, as though all its promises and blessings were temporal only, and in no respect spiritual. A very different position of course from that taken in the *Mystical Presence*, where the Old Testament is exhibited always as the New's embryo, the glorious Advent of the still more glorious Christmas in which it came finally to its end. My bad company here quoted is no nearer to me at worst, than the contact in which Dr. Hodge accidentally stands with Mohammed and the sect of the Socinians, who, it will be borne in mind, are quite as orthodox in their view of the Old Testament saints as he claims to be himself. I am besides not altogether without some good company; the whole ancient catholic church for instance, and the Lutheran confession with Luther himself at its head. J. W. N.

27. [See *Institutes*, ed. McNeill, 1:429.—ed.]

28. [Nevin seems to mis-cite, as this passage is in fact found in chapter 11, not 10. See *Institutes*, ed. McNeill, 1:437.—ed.]

than to sit down with Abraham, Isaac and Jacob. Dr. Nevin ought surely to stop quoting Calvin as in any way abetting the monstrous doctrine, that under the old dispensation, God was only revealed to his people, while under the new, the divine nature is united in them with the human nature, as in Christ ("the same life or constitution")[29] in the way of a progressive incarnation.

What however still more clearly shows the radical differences between Dr. Nevin's theory and that of the Reformed Church, as to that point, is what he says in reference to the sacraments of the two dispensations. Romanists teach that the sacraments of the Old Testament merely prefigure grace, those of the New actually confer it. This doctrine Calvin, as we have already seen, strenuously denies, and calls its advocates miserable sophists. He asserts that "whatever is exhibited in our sacraments, the Jews formerly received in theirs, to wit, Christ and his benefits,"[30] that baptism has no higher efficacy than circumcision. He quotes the authority of Augustin for saying, *Sacramenta Judaeorum in signis fuisse diversa; in re quae significatur, paria; diversa specie visibili, paria virtute spirituali.*[31] Dr. Nevin, however, is constrained by his view of the nature of the union between Christ and his people, since the incarnation, to make the greatest possible difference between the sacraments of the two dispensations. He even goes further than the Romanists, teaching that the Passover, e. g. was properly no sacrament at all. "Not a sacrament at all indeed," in his language, "in the full New Testament sense, but a sacrament simply in the prefiguration and type" (p. 251).[32] In the same connection, he says: "The sacraments of the Old Testament are no proper measure by which to graduate directly the force that belongs to the sacraments of the New . . . To make baptism no more than circumcision, or the Lord's Supper no more than the Passover, is to wrong the new dispensation as really"[33] as by making Christ no more than a levitical priest. Systems which lead to such opposite conclusions must be radically different. The lowest Puritan, ultra Protestant, or sectary in the land, who truly believes Christ, is nearer Calvin than Dr. Nevin; and has more of the true spirit and theology of the Reformed Church, than is to be found in his book.

CRITICISM [NEVIN]

Dr. Hodge here again admits a mystical union of believers with Christ; not moral nor merely legal; not simply from the assumption of our nature by Christ; but real at the same time and *vital.* So far, we are told, the old Reformed doctrine reached. A very important concession certainly; but, alas, retracted, or turned into wind, almost as soon as made. We receive Christ, when we receive his Spirit. Granted; if this Spirit be taken

29. [MTSS edition, 214.—ed.]

30. [See *Institutes*, ed. McNeill, 2:1299.—ed.]

31. [Hodge:] *Institutes* IV.14: 23–26. [Trans. "The sacraments of the Jews were different in their signs, but equal in the thing signified; different in visible appearance, but equal in spiritual power." *Institutes,* ed. McNeill, 2:1302.—ed.]

32. [MTSS edition, 217.—ed.]

33. [Ibid.—ed.]

as the medium by which he dwells in us personally under the power of his higher life. But this is not what Dr. Hodge means. The Spirit, with him, is a third party that passes *between* Christ and his people, and so joins them together, as a river connects two cities by flowing through them both. Dr. Hodge will not admit, that the very substance of Christ's life itself, is made to pass over by the Holy Ghost into the persons of his people. Only an influence of the Spirit has place in the mystery, by which the same mind which belongs to Christ is wrought also in them. But is not this a *moral* union, when all is done? Is there more mystery in it, than what belongs to our union with Moses, or David, Peter or Paul? It is easy to *call* it a "vital" union; but we must be puzzled surely, if we think at all, to see the force of the expression. It ought to mean union with Christ's *life*. But this precisely is what Dr. Hodge will not allow it to mean. Surely he is bound, in such a case, to show how an influence of the Holy Ghost, on the outside of this life and in no dependence upon it whatever, is to stand for it notwithstanding as though it were the very thing itself; or in what *other* sense, if any, the mystical union as he holds it is to be regarded as either vital or real.

He allows that "some of the Reformed" went farther, and attributed a "mysterious power" to the glorified body of Christ in heaven. We have seen that the whole Reformed Church did so in fact, as represented by Calvin and the five standard national confessions. But this is still something "entirely different from the doctrine of this book," says Dr. Hodge. It would be so of course, if the "Mysterious power emanating from Christ's body" be conceived of as anything less than his veritable divine human life. This Dr. Hodge always takes for granted; the mysterious power resolves itself for him into some sort of magical quasi-mesmeric influence, which he finds it easy in this view to set aside as a mere unintelligible conceit, that added nothing in reality to the doctrine in question. But now, as we have seen, the old doctrine had no *such* emanation in view. Calvin says expressly that by the virtue of Christ's body, he meant the very substance of its life. Let this be felt and allowed, and the difference from the *Mystical Presence* will be found at once to be only formal and circumstantial. A difference of that sort is admitted in the work itself; but the substance of the old doctrine it professes to accept; and it does so in truth, if that be what is now said.

The case of the Old Testament saints has already been noticed. We have seen that, be the difficulty as it may, it was not allowed to set aside the doctrine here under consideration; and that it is perfectly idle to argue from it, in the way of Dr. Hodge, against the overwhelming evidence of clear historical fact. Calvin had it full before him, and still in spite of it asserts only the more strongly and distinctly, the mystery of our participation in Christ's real incarnate life. He even goes so far as to say, that the flesh of Christ, though not yet created, was made efficacious in the Old Testament saints by the mysterious power of the Holy Ghost; while he allows also however, that our participation now is of a different order, as extending directly to the substance of the historical body as such, in a way not possible before. This representation is by no means satisfactory; but it only serves all the more forcibly to confirm the point, which is here in debate. As before said, two things are plain; Calvin did not make so little difference as Dr. Hodge pretends between the old and new dispensations, and his view affected not at all his general creed in regard to the mystical union and sacramental grace.

I have no wish however, to conceal the fact of a real difference, between the old Calvinistic view of the Jewish dispensation and my own. The only material question in the case is, whether this difference be such as to show a want of agreement as regards the substance of the doctrine here under consideration. Historically, as we have seen, it is of no such force. With Dr. Hodge however, I believe that the case is not free from inward contradiction. The old Reformed doctrine labors in some respects under difficulty, as to its form; and this is one of the points precisely, where it needs to be corrected into a shape more consonant with its main character, in order to be upheld at all in its true original force. In strict logical consequence, it is not easy to reconcile the Calvinistic view of the Old Testament saints with the Calvinistic view of the mystical union; Dr. Hodge chooses to sacrifice the second in favor of the first; in the *Mystical Presence* the order is reversed, by requiring the first to do homage, as a mere accident, to the vastly more central and substantial authority of the second. This is one of the points, in which the Reformed doctrine needs to be completed by borrowing from the Lutheran, and where it is possible for it to do so without forsaking still in the least its own distinctive character and principle. For Dr. Hodge however, Lutheranism is a *heresy*, on common ground here with Servetus and the Anabaptists, from which it is desirable to be sundered by as broad a chasm as possible.

I have never questioned the identity of the old and new dispensations, in any such way as would imply two different systems of redemption. They are related as widely different stages only (Calvin also severs them as *grades*) of one and the same salvation, wrought out by Christ, and made complete at last, in the case of *every* saint, through the believing and conscious apprehension of his person. They are related as the morning dawn to the presence of the risen sun, or as the life of childhood and early youth to the consciousness of the full grown man. Together they form a single process; but they are different parts of this process, as really and broadly as the sprouting and flowering of the same life in the summer plant. Judaism is Christ *coming*; the premise of what had not yet appeared; the shadow of good things in prospect. Christianity is Christ *come*; the promise verified; the shadow turned into substance. Heb. ix. 8–15, x. 1–10, xi. 13, 39, 40. The Old Testament saints received *not* the promise, it is said; they had it indeed *as promise*, and rested on it accordingly, but the reality was not yet at hand. Their sacraments certify the presence of the promise, but not the presence of the thing promised, and thus were shadows only and types (as all besides) of *good things to come*.

Dr. Hodge allows no such relation; and the reason is simply, that he sees in Christ no such NEW CREATION literally, as is implied by a real entrance of the divine life, into organic, historical, inward and abiding, union with the life of the world, as it stood in man previously. We have before us thus a new aspect simply of the *Nestorian* flaw, that runs like a bad crack through his whole theology.

So much for the fourth and fifth heresies, *Romanism* and *Lutheranism*, here virtually laid at my door, if not precisely on my shoulders and head.

11

Departures from Reformed Orthodoxy[1]

REVIEW, CONTINUED [HODGE]

IN THE THIRD PLACE, Dr. Nevin's theory, differing so seriously from that of the Reformed Church, as to the person of Christ and his union with his people, may be expected to differ from it as to the nature of Christ's work, and method of salvation. According to him, human nature, the generic life of humanity, being corrupted by the fall, was healed by being taken into a life-union with the Logos. This union so elevated it, raised it to such a higher character, and filled it with such new meaning and power, that it was more than restored to its original state. This however could not be done without a struggle. Being the bearer of a fallen humanity, there was a necessity for suffering in order that life should triumph over the law of sin and death. This was the atonement (see p. 166).[2]

The first remark that suggests itself here, is the query, what is meant by a "fallen humanity?" Can it mean any thing else than a corrupted nature; i.e. our nature in the state to which it was reduced by the fall? How else could its assumption involve the necessity of suffering? It is however hard to see how the assumption of a corrupt nature, is consistent with the perfect sinlessness of the Redeemer. Dr. Nevin, as far as we see, does not touch this point. With Schleiermacher, according to whom absolute freedom from sin was the distinguishing prerogative of the Savior, this was secured, though clothed with our nature, by all the acts or determinations of that nature, being governed in his case, by "the God-consciousness" in him or the divine principle. This is far from being satisfactory; but we pass that point. What however are we to say to this view of the atonement? It was vicarious suffering indeed, for the Logos assumed, and by the painful process of his life and death, healed our nature, not for himself but for our sakes. But there is here no atonement, that is, no satisfaction; no propitiation of God; no reference to divine justice. All this is necessarily excluded. All these ideas

---

1. ["Dr. Hodge on the *Mystical Presence*, Article from the *Repertory*, Continued, No. 10," *Weekly Messenger*, New Series, vol. 13, no. 47. Wednesday, August 2, 1848. Published by the Board of the Synod of the German Reformed Church: Chambersburg, PA.—ed.]

2. [MTSS edition, 196–97.—ed.]

are passed over in silence by Dr. Nevin; by Schleiermacher they are openly rejected. The atonement is the painfully accomplished triumph of the new divine principle introduced into our nature, over the law of sin introduced into it by Adam. Is this the doctrine of the Reformed Church?

CRITICISM [NEVIN]

The corruption of our nature is not something essential and *necessary* in its constitution. Were that the case, it could not be redeemed. The redemption of humanity turns on its capacity of being so united with a higher principle of life, as to throw off sin entirely. This requires of course two things; a sinless development of our nature from the point in which such process may start, and power at the same time to meet and surmount the consequences of sin as found already at hand in the human mass. All this is secured in Christ. *How* the mystery is effected, we may not be able to comprehend; but the *fact* of it is before us in his person, challenging our faith on the ground of its own divine reality. The Word became flesh; truly, really, historically; actually incorporated our life, as before fallen, into union with the divine life; in such a way of course as to admit no sin; and of the fulness of the new creation thus gloriously accomplished, we are all made to receive (John 1:14, 16). This we are to *believe*, as we may see it before us, and feel it, in the person of Christ. To call it in question, is to question the truth of Christianity itself. Does not Christ come before us *always* as one bearing our nature, of the seed of Abraham and David, born of woman and made under the law, in all respects as we ourselves are, only without sin? The HOW of all this is the very mystery of the incarnation itself; the miraculous conception secured a sinless ground, and the guaranty for a holy development subsequently was found in the power of the new life thus introduced into the world. To be the bearer of a fallen humanity, it was not necessary that Christ should admit it under this form into the sphere of his own life; but only that he should so link himself to its being and destiny, as to fulfill in himself truly and really the problem of its redemption; just as a sound heart, for instance, in a sickly body, might be viewed as the organ and medium of restoration for the whole, not as admitting the disease into itself, but on the contrary as asserting continually its own vigorous health, and gradually diffusing it on all sides.

Dr. Hodge thinks this subversive of the doctrine of the atonement. But what is the proper sense of satisfaction for sin, if it be not such painful sacrifice and service as may avail to place the sinner on friendly terms with God and his own conscience? The case implies a suspension of the divine favor, a state of condemnation and curse; and the removal of all this is the idea of *atonement*. Different views may be taken of what precisely the idea involves; there are, as we all know, different theories of the atonement; but I cannot see that the conception, under any form, is absolutely excluded by the view here taken of the Christian redemption. All it affirms is, that *whatever* was required to raise our human life to righteousness and glory, Christ by the assumption of our nature laid himself under the necessity of accomplishing; and his sufferings grew naturally and unavoidably *out of this necessity*. Admit the most bald conception of a strictly commercial justice in the case, and it still comes at last to the same thing. Whatever the race needed to extricate itself from the ruin of the fall and lift it to heaven, whether the want might be in its own constitution or in its relation to God; whether the difficulty to be surmounted might be subjective or objective; all is included in its actual redemption by Christ, and goes to make up the painful process of his life and death, as accomplished for us men and our salvation. In any view, "the passion of the Son of God was the world's spiritual *crisis*, in which the principle of health came to its last struggle with the principle of disease, and burst forth from the very bosom of the grave itself in the form of immortality."[3] I really do not see any sort of reason whatever in the objection here urged by Dr. Hodge; unless the idea of the atonement be turned into sheer abstraction, in the way of absolute and complete divorce from the idea of real life. *Then* indeed there may be some difficulty.

REVIEW, CONTINUED [HODGE]

Again, the whole method of salvation is necessarily changed by this system. We become partakers of the sin of Adam, by partaking in his nature.[4] There can be no imputation of either sin or righteousness to us, except they belong to us, are inherently our own.

> Our participation in the actual unrighteousness of his (Adam's) life, forms the ground of our participation in his guilt and liability to punishment. And in no other way, we affirm, can the idea of imputation be satisfactorily sustained in the case of the second Adam.

> Righteousness, like guilt, is an attribute which supposes a subject in which it inheres, and from which it cannot be abstracted without ceasing to exist altogether. In the case before us, that subject is the mediatorial nature or life of the Savior himself. Whatever there may be of merit, virtue, efficacy, or moral value in any way, in the mediatorial work of Christ, it is all lodged in the *life*, by the power of which alone this work has been accomplished, and in the presence of which only it can have either reality or stability (p. 191).[5]

This is very plain, we receive the theanthropic nature or life of Christ; that nature is of a high character, righteous, holy, conformed to God; in receiving that life we receive its merit, its virtues and efficacy. On p. 189, he is still more explicit: "How can that be imputed or reckoned to any man on the part of God, which does not belong to him in reality?" "This objection," he says,

> is insurmountable, according to the form in which the doctrine of imputation is too generally held. The judgment of God must ever be according to truth. He cannot reckon to anyone an attribute or quality which does not belong to him in fact. He cannot declare him to be in a relation or state, which is not actually his

3. [MTSS vol. 1, 148.—ed.]

4. [The difference between Nevin and Hodge on the doctrine of imputation, and the background of earlier Reformed debate on this subject, is excellently analyzed in Bill Evans, *Imputation and Impartation*.—ed.]

5. [Ibid., 167–68.—ed.]

own, but the position merely of another. A simple external imputation here, the pleasure or purpose of God to the account of one what has been done by another, will not answer.[6]

"The Bible knows nothing of a simple outward imputation, by which something is reckoned to a man that does not belong to him in fact" (p. 190).[7] "The ground of our justification is a righteousness that *was* foreign to us before, but is *now* made to lodge itself in the inmost constitution of our being" (p. 180).[8] God's act in justification "is necessarily more than a mere declaration or form of thought. It makes us to be in fact, what it declares us to be in Christ" (*Ib.*).[9] Here we reach the very life-spot of the Reformation. Is justification a declaring just, or a making just inherently? This was the real battleground on which the blood of so many martyrs was spilt. Are we justified for something done for us, or something wrought in us, actually our own? It is a mere playing with words, to make a distinction, as Mr. Newman did, between what it is that thus makes us inherently righteous. Whether it is infused grace, a new heart, the indwelling Spirit, the humanity of Christ, his life, his theanthropic nature; it is all one. It is subjective justification after all, and nothing more. We consider Dr. Nevin's theory as impugning here, the vital doctrine of Protestantism. His doctrine is not, of course, the Romish, *teres atque rotundus;*[10] he may distinguish here, and discriminate there. But as to the main point it is a denial of the Protestant doctrine of justification. He knows as well as any man that all the churches of the 16th century, held the imputation not only of what was our own, but of what though not ours inherently, was on some adequate ground set to our account; that the sin of Adam is imputed to us, not because of our having his corrupted nature, but because of the imputation of his sin, we are involved in his corruption. He knows that when the doctrine of mediate imputation, as he teaches it, was introduced by Placaeus,[11] it was universally rejected. He knows moreover, that, with regard to justification, the main question was, whether it was a declaratory or an effective act, whether it was a declaring just on the ground of righteousness not in us, or a making just by communicating righteousness to us. Romanists were as ready as Protestants to admit that the act by which men are rendered just actually, was a gracious act, and for Christ's sake, but they denied that justification is a forensic or declaratory act founded on the imputation of the righteousness of Christ, which is neither in us, nor by that imputation communicated as a quality to our souls. It was what Romanists thus denied, Protestants asserted, and made a matter of so much importance. And it is in fact the real keystone of the arch which sustains our peace and hope towards God; for if we are no further righteous

6. [Ibid., 166. Hodge has modified the quote slightly, but he has not altered its meaning.—ed.]

7. [Ibid., 167.—ed.]

8. [Ibid., 160.—ed.]

9. [Ibid.—ed.]

10. ["polished and complete."—ed.]

11. [Joshua Placaeus (LaPlace), circa 1663. Of the French Reformed School of Saumur. He was interpreted to reject direct imputation and resolved original sin into hereditary depravity.—ed.]

than we are actually and inherent so, what have we to expect in the presence of a righteous God, but indignation and wrath?

CRITICISM [NEVIN]

Here the position taken by Dr. Hodge, that our participation in Adam's sin is not grounded upon our participation in his nature. This is consistent. To rest our relation to Christ on such an abstract decree or fiat of the Almighty, involves necessarily the same thing in the other case. Men are sinners then not because all have sinned and fallen IN ADAM, as the Westminster Catechism has it; but because God of his sovereign pleasure, has seen proper to make Adam the type and copy representatively, after which all others are called into being. To see the full force of this, we have only to suppose that one of the fallen angels had been originally made to carry in himself the spiritual fortunes of our world (still unborn), in the same way, by an act of the divine Mind; and that men in consequence of *that* arrangement come now into existence such as they are in fact. On whom must the authorship of our sin in reality fall, under any such horrible and monstrous supposition as this? And yet what difference is it at bottom, to make all turn on the case of Adam, if his *life* be in truth as distinct from ours as that of the fallen angels, and the fundamental bond of our union with him stand at last only in an outward abstract thought or purpose of God's mind?[12]

No wonder that the New School divinity, as it is called, and the divinity of New England, should break with the system of Princeton as it does at this point. *Such* an imputation of Adam's sin to his posterity—an imputation that runs ahead of the fact, and actually originates the thing it reckons—can never satisfy any theology, that is not content to take its doctrines on mere outward authority and trust. This is one of the points embraced in the controversy of the Rev. Albert Barnes[13] with this same

---

12. [Had it been a debate over predestination and the decrees of God rather than over sacramental theology, a good deal more would need to be said about these comments of Nevin and, indeed, the heat of the debate itself would be even more intense and caustic. Nevin never hid his disdain for the decretal theology that came ultimately from the second generation of Reformed schoolmen, nor was he comfortable with the milder version that came from Calvin. Hodge on the other hand was America's preeminent Calvinist who used Turretin as a textbook until his own *Systematic Theology* was published. Gerrish writes that Nevin showed his Lutheran sympathies with his view that Calvin's doctrine of predestination was at odds with his sacramental position. (The debate does not reference "predestination" but it is mentioned several times in Nevin's "Doctrine of the Reformed Church on the Lord's Supper.") Indeed, Lutherans went so far as to say it "undermined" Calvin's sacramental position. This was in spite of the fact that almost nothing that Calvin said about predestination wasn't said by Luther. But later, Lutherans pulled back from Luther's position and they accused Calvin of a fundamental inconsistency: If the reality of the sacrament is only for the elect, how can the sign and reality be inexorably linked? After all, while Calvin's doctrine does not "negate" sacramental efficacy—it clearly "limits" it by restricting it to the elect. What then, if the elect eat unworthily? Is the sign severed from the reality? Calvin says no, since although the exhibition of faith is weak here, it still exists. Gerrish observes that Nevin shared with Schleiermacher, and later Barth, a doctrine of election without accepting Calvin's specific views on predestination. See Gerrish, *Grace and Gratitude*, 169–73.—ed.]

13. [Albert Barnes (1798–1870), graduate of Princeton Seminary. Tried but not convicted of heresy in 1836. Barnes held what was considered an unorthodox view on the question of the imputation of Adam's sin to the human race. He was a prominent figure in the Presbyterian New School movement.

Princeton theology twelve years since, which may be found handled at length in his "Defence and other Documents" as published in 1836.[14] According to Mr. Barnes, there are three principal theories of our relation to Adam: 1st That of Calvin and the abler Calvinistic writers (President Edwards among them), by which imputation is made to rest on the fact that of a common life—the race "sinned *in him* and fell with him in his first transgression:" 2nd The Princeton view, which resolves all into a mere outward reckoning: and 3rd The doctrine accepted by Mr. Barnes himself, and generally allowed in New England, which requires us to take the facts as they stand without any attempt at explanation. Mr. Barnes prefers the first view decidedly to the second, while of course he rejects both.[15] It is to be regretted that he should stand where he does; his own position is such as to entangle him necessarily in new difficulties, and is only the reverse side in truth of the very same abstraction from which he seeks to make his escape; still as directed against *this* the protest is valuable, and it is encouraging always to know that Princeton, and the ecclesiastical interest represented by it, stand

Charges had previously been brought against the Reverend Albert Barnes by the Reverend George Junkin, later referred to as "the great divider of Presbyterians." There were several charges, but the one Nevin refers to here was that Barnes denied what Hodge and Princeton taught, that the original sin of Adam was imputed to his posterity. Barnes replied that neither he nor the church teaches that, therefore he is being accused of something he does not teach. He observed furthermore that the historical church holds that the "guilt" of Adam's sin is imputed to his descendants. Even there Barnes was hesitant, ultimately claiming that Scripture simply states that human beings are sinful through Adam. Beyond that Barnes was reluctant to venture. (See Marsden, *Evangelical Mind*.) His "New Testament notes" were extremely popular and widely circulated. See *Notes, Explanatory and Practical, on the Gospels* (New York: Harper & Brothers, 1861); and Robert Frew, ed., *Notes on the New Testament* (Grand Rapids, MI: Baker, 1983).—ed.]

14. [Nevin probably refers to A. J. Stansbury, *Trial of the Rev. Albert Barnes, before the Synod of Philadelphia* (New York: Van Nostrand and Dwight, 1836), to which was appended Barnes's *Defence*.—ed.]

15. [Nevin:] "It [the Princeton theory] is an abandonment of the old system, which system was at least *consistent* in its use of language. The theory has retained the *fragments* of a system and its *language*, but without retaining the *at least* CONSISTENT theory of the scholastic theology in which it was founded. When the old divines used the word *impute*, they understood its scripture sense, and its common usage, as denoting *charging on a man that which properly belonged to him*. Hence they invented the theory of the strict and proper *oneness* or *identity* with Adam, and said that his sin is truly and properly *ours*, and THEREFORE is charged on us. There the theory was consistent, and the language scriptural—whatever may be said of the theory. When they talked of *guilt*, they meant obligation to *punishment*, they used the word in its common signification as denoting a just suffering of penal evils, for sin of which they were *justly* charged because it was their own.

But in the theory now under consideration, we have the *fragments* only of a system; we have words dissevered from their proper signification; and doctrines, the absurdity of which were seen as clearly by the older divines as they can be now. We hear in this system of God's imputing to men sins which in no proper sense belong to them—thus departing wholly from the scripture use of language; we hear of God's *punishing* them for sin, when the sin is not strictly their own, and when they are not "ill-deserving;" we hear of their being bound to punishment, or guilty, when they are not "blame worthy;" we hear of *representation*, in a sense contrary to that which is used in agencies, without the consent or knowledge of those represented; and all this by an arbitrary arrangement of God, unlike any thing which actually occurs elsewhere on earth. Now whatever may be the defects of the old system, it has manifestly many advantages over this. It has the merit of consistency. It retains the scripture use of language. It uses words as they are employed in common life. So the profound mind of Edwards saw; and greatly as I dislike the system, it has so many *consistencies* over that now under notice, that I should greatly prefer it to that which in our time has supplanted it." *Barnes' Defence, p. 212, 213.*

here to a great extent solitary and alone. The only effectual way however of reaching a better theology, is offered to us in the conception of a strictly *organic* Christianity, as something different from mere abstraction. Let it be seen and felt that the new creation is a real historical constitution, having its *principle* in the person of Christ and not in an outward doctrine or decree, and we shall soon have the antithesis of Old and New School, at the point now before us, completely surmounted and left behind in the true church view, as a form of thinking higher and more comprehensive of both.

Our relation to Adam determines our relation to Christ. If life and guilt go together in the first case, life and righteousness must go together also in the second. We are made sinners *in Adam*; we become righteous *in Christ*. Even Dr. Hodge says, p. 255, "the soul, first regenerated; receives Christ, and is united with him by faith, and on this *follows* the imputation of righteousness and all-saving benefits;" language that sounds more like mediate justification, in the false sense, than any to be found in the *Mystical Presence*. Here however he would seem to insist on nothing less than a justification, which not only goes before all union with Christ, but is also of no force whatever to secure any such result. This looks like contradiction. It is plain moreover, that he misses the idea on which he tries to fix the charge of error in my book. He makes it to be *subjective* justification, inherent righteousness of some sort opening the way for God's declarative act. But this is not said in the *Mystical Presence*.

To be set to our account, it is there said, the atonement must be immanent to humanity, something that holds in the actual life of our nature; not as the inherent property of those who are justified; but as a result fully reached in Christ, in whom is comprised potentially all that our nature through him is destined to become. It is thus the attribute of humanity under its new form, just as guilt and condemnation go with our life under its first form. In justification, it is made to reach over by God's act to the believing sinner. Still it has force only as it holds in the life of Christ, and not as abstracted from this in the way of mere thought. To take effect then upon the sinner, it must bring him within the sphere of this life. He cannot be justified *out* of Christ. This is not to make what is in him in any way the cause of his justification; for all comes from the force of the act itself. In the very act of pronouncing a sinner just for Christ's sake, God sets him truly and really in Christ, the ground of this righteousness; not so as to make him at once personally holy; but in such a way that the principle of a new creation is lodged in his life. Objective and subjective flow together thus as a single fact. Justification does not make its subject inherently righteous, but it cannot leave him where he stood before. The righteousness which it sets to his account has its root in Christ's life, and becomes his only as God *thinks* him into union with this life at the same time.[16]

So Calvin always. "We look not away out of ourselves," he says, "that the righteousness of Christ may be imputed to us; but because we put him on, and are inserted into his body, and he condescends to make us one with himself, we glory in his

---

16. [Nevin:] In the act of declaring or thinking the sinner just where does God in thought plant him, in Christ or out of Christ? And can such a divine thought be less ever than the thing it thinks? He speaks, and it is DONE.

righteousness also as ours" (*Inst.* III.11.10.)[17] Justification with him is no abstraction, but something that holds ever in Christ's life. Christ ours, and so only his merits and benefits placed to our account, is the invariable order of his soteriology. "Truly I see not," he tells us, "how any one can trust that he has redemption and righteousness by the cross of Christ, if he have not in the first place a true communion with Christ himself."[18] So in the Heidelberg Catechism (Qu. 20), those only are said to be saved by Christ "who are *ingrafted* into him, and receive all his benefits by a true faith." No justification save such as *ingrafts* into Christ's life. In this sense of course must be understood Questions 60 and 61; where we are said to be made righteous by the imputation of the "satisfaction, righteousness and holiness of Christ" accounted ours through *faith*—which in this case lays hold not of an abstraction only, but of Christ himself. How indeed could we speak, with any intelligible sense, of the imputation of the Savior's *active* obedience, no less than his passive, as all the old confessions do, in any other view? Can his positive fulfillment of the law, Christ's personal holiness we may say, be set over to our credit in any other way else than as we are so joined to his very life, that what belongs to it becomes ours also, *as if* we had brought it to pass in our own persons?

The mystery of the holy Eucharist here represents the general character of the Christian salvation. "The sacramental signs certify our participation in the body and blood of Christ (Heid. Cat. Quest. 79), and so that all his sufferings and obedience are as certainly ours, as if we had in our own persons suffered and made satisfaction for our sins to God." And such also is the relation of life and merit throughout. They go together, the second borne perpetually in the bosom of the first. Dr. Hodge, however, as we have seen, sunders them in the sacramental mystery; and it is only a sort of necessary consequence, that he should here do the same thing, in the case of our general salvation. The atonement becomes thus, in his view, a mere abstraction, a passive thought in God's mind, in which it is the privilege of the believer by a like act of mere thought to confide, as the guarantee of pardon and life. The principle of the new creation accordingly is not life, but doctrine or report. The person of Christ is shorn of its true central significance, and we are landed as before in the bleak latitude of Nestorianism.

REVIEW, CONTINUED [HODGE]

In the fourth place, the obvious departure of Dr. Nevin's system from that of the Reformed Church, is seen in what he teaches concerning the church and the sacraments. The evidence here is not easy to present. As he very correctly remarks with regard to certain doctrines of the Bible, they rest far less on distinct passages which admit of quotation, than on the spirit, tenor, implications and assumptions which pervade the sacred volume. It is so with this book. Its whole spirit is churchy. It makes religion to be a church life, its manifestations a liturgical service, its support sacramental

17. [McNeill, ed., 1:737.—ed.]
18. [Ibid., 2:1372.—ed.]

grace. It is the form, the spirit, the predominance of these things, which give his book a character as different as can be from the healthful, evangelical free spirit of Luther or Calvin. The main question whether we come to Christ, and then to the church; whether we by a personal act of faith receive him, and by union with him become a member of his mystical body; or whether all our access to Christ is through a mediating church, Dr. Nevin decides against the evangelical system.

It follows of necessity, as he himself says, from his doctrine of a progressive incarnation, "that the church is the depository and continuation of the Saviour's theanthropic life itself, and as such, a truly supernatural constitution, in which powers and resources are constantly at hand, involving a real intercommunication and interpenetration of the human and divine" (p. 248).[19] The church with him, being "historical must be visible."[20] "An outward church is the necessary form of the new creation in Christ Jesus, in its very nature" (p. 5).[21] With Protestants the true church is "the communion of saints," the "*congregatio sanctorum*," "the company of faithful men;" not the "company or organization of professing men." It would be difficult to frame a proposition more subversive of the very foundation of all protestantism, than the assertion that the description above given, or anything like it belongs to the church visible as such. It is the fundamental error of Romanism, the source of her power and of her corruption, to ascribe to the outward church, the attributes and prerogatives of the mystical body of Christ.

CRITICISM [NEVIN]

No wonder Dr. Hodge should think so poorly of the holy sacraments, with so poor a conception of the Holy Catholic Church. Does he accept all this article of the Apostle's Creed? Most certainly *not*, in the old sense of the venerable symbol itself. The Church of the Creed is an object of faith, a mystery growing out of the incarnation; the Church of Dr. Hodge is an object of mere intellection, deriving its nature in no real way whatever from the living person of Christ, but simply from the thinking of men. The attributes of the old Church all sprang, with inward necessity, from its *idea*, as furnished in Christ, and were necessarily as such included in the apprehension of it by faith. It must be, in its very constitution, holy, universal, apostolic, the revelation of invisible powers under a visible form; all this at least in the way of constant inward nisus and endeavor, as the last and only full sense of the divine mystery. But with Dr. Hodge, it is the fundamental error of Romanism to ascribe the attributes and prerogative of the mystical body of Christ, to the Church in any outward view! What is this, but to translate the Church from the visible and historical world, into the world of mere abstraction and incorporeal thought; to deny to it every sort of organic connection with the old creation; and in this way to turn into ghostly phantasm the whole substance of it, as itself the new creation in Christ Jesus. Alas for the "*evangelical system*," that must needs

19. [MTSS edition, 215.—ed.]

20. [Ibid., 12.—ed.]

21. [Ibid.—ed.]

sustain itself at such costly sacrifice as this? Must we strip the Church of all its native, inborn attributes, murder in one word its real life, in order to show it honor afterwards as the spectre of our own brain? What mockery, to place it first in full parallel with the constitution of Islamism, and then say: I believe in the Holy Catholic Church! As though a thing so poor as that deserved to take such dignity upon it, among the high and solemn *mysteries* of the ancient CREED! We might just as well say, with mock pomp: I believe *in* the *Common Law* of England.

REVIEW, CONTINUED [HODGE]

We must however pass to Dr. Nevin's doctrine of the sacraments, and specify at least some of the points in which he departs from the doctrine of the Reformed Church. And in the first place, he ascribes to them a specific and "altogether extraordinary power" (p. 116).[22] There is a presence and of course a receiving of the body and blood of Christ, in the Lord's Supper, "to be had nowhere else" (p. 75).[23] This idea is presented in various forms. It is, however, in direct contravention of the confessions of the Reformed churches, as we have already seen. They make a circumstantial distinction between spiritual and sacramental manducation, but as to any specific difference, any difference as to what is there received from what is received elsewhere, they expressly deny it. In the [Second] Helv. Conf. already quoted, it is said, that the eating and drinking of Christ's body and blood takes place, even elsewhere than in the Lord's Supper, whenever and wherever a man believes in Christ. Calvin, in the *Consensus Tigurinus*, Art. xix. says: What is figured in the sacraments is granted to believers *extra eorum usum* ["outside their use"]. This he applies and proves, first in reference to baptism, and then in reference to the Lord's Supper. In the explanation of that Consensus he vindicates this doctrine against the objections of the Lutherans. "*Quod deinde prosequimur,*" he begins, "*fidelibus spiritualium bonorum effectum quae figurant sacramenta, extra eorum usum constare, quando et quotidie verum esse experimur et probatur scripturae testimoniis, mirum est si cui displiceat.*"[24] The same thing is expressly taught in this *Institutes* IV.14.14.[25]

22. [MTSS edition, 104.—ed.]

23. [Ibid., 291.—ed.]

24. [Trans. "We next proceed to say, that the effect of the spiritual blessings which the sacraments figure, is given to believers without the use of the sacraments. As this is daily experienced to be true, and is proved by passages of Scripture. It is not strange if any are displeased with it." "Exposition of the Heads of Agreement," in Torrance, ed., *Tracts and Treatises*, 2:236.—ed.]

25. [Calvin writes here that assurance and justification do not come by way of the physical sign, as justification comes by way of Christ alone, and is communicated as much by the preaching of the word as by the "seal of the sacrament." But for Calvin this Christ-infused justification comes from both Word and sacrament, while Hodge (as we shall see) says that the Lutherans maintain that it is the Word that is the source of the sacrament's effectiveness, while the Reformed make it "the attending power of the Holy Spirit." Moreover, as Nevin has been passionate to insist, Calvin writes (IV.17.5.) "no one should think that the life that we receive from him is received by mere knowledge. As it is not the seeing but the eating of bread that suffices to feed the body, so the soul must truly and deeply become partaker of Christ that it may be quickened to spiritual life by his power." This appears to go a long way in making Nevin's case

The second point on which Dr. Nevin differs from the Reformed Church relates to their efficacy. All agree that they have an objective force; that they no more owe their power to the faith of the recipient than the word of God does. But the question is what is the source to which the influence of the sacraments as means of grace, is to be referred? We have already stated that Romanists, say it is to be referred to the sacraments themselves as containing the grace they convey; Lutherans, to the supernatural power of the word, inseparably joined with the signs; the Reformed, to the attending power of the Spirit which is in no manner inseparable from the signs or the service. Dr. Nevin's doctrine seems to lie somewhere between the Romish and the Lutheran view. He agrees with the Romanists in referring the efficacy to the service itself, and the Lutherans in making faith necessary in order to the sacrament taking effect. Some of his expressions on the subject are the following:

> Faith is the condition of its (the sacrament's) efficacy for the communicant, but not the principle of the power itself. This belongs to the institution in its own nature. The signs are bound to what they represent, not subjectively simply in the thought of the worshipper, but objectively, by the force of a divine appointment. . . . The grace goes inseparably along with the sign, and is truly present for all who are prepared to make it their own (p. 61).[26]

> The invisible grace enters as a necessary constituent element into the idea of a sacrament; and must be of course objectively present with it wherever it is administered under a true form. . . . It belongs to the ordinance in its own nature. . . . The sign and the thing signified are by Christ's institution, mysteriously tied together. . . . The two form one presence (p. 178).[27]

In the case of the Lord's Supper, the grace, or thing signified, is according to his book, the divine-human nature of Christ, "his whole person," his body, soul and divinity, constituting one life. This, or these, are objectively present and inseparably joined with the signs, constituting with them one presence. The power inseparable from the theanthropic life of Christ, is inseparable from these signs, and is conveyed with them. "Where the way is open for it to take effect, it (the sacrament) *serves in itself* to convey the life of Christ into our persons" (p. 182). We know nothing in Bellarmine[28] that goes beyond that. Dr. Nevin refers for illustration, as Lutherans do, to the case

---

against Hodge, that although Hodge insists that the power of the sacrament is objective, it is really subjective—an intellectual acquiescence to the signs and that which they signify, and that what Hodge really means by "objective" is not the sacramental power itself but its source, i.e., the real, objective existence of God, his Word, Christ, and the Holy Spirit. Hodge makes it objective by the accompanying operation of the Holy Spirit. Nevin's comment is that Hodge makes the Supper effective only in the sense that, for example, a law is effective (objective). But Nevin makes it objective as in the way electricity is objective. Calvin follows the above quote with his famous line, "But here the difference between my words and theirs: for them to eat is only to believe; I say that we eat Christ's flesh believing, because it is made ours by faith, and that this eating is the result and effect of faith."—ed.]

26. [MTSS edition, 51.—ed.]

27. [Ibid., 158. Hodge has slightly changed the words in this quote but he did not change their meaning.—ed.]

28. [Robert Bellarmine (1542–1621), Jesuit priest and cardinal. He was a tireless opponent of Protestants, but by way of argument and theology rather than by papal authority and violence.—ed.]

of the woman who touched Christ's garment. As there was mysterious supernatural power ever present in Christ, so there is in the sacraments. "The virtue of Christ's mystical presence," he says, "is comprehended in the sacrament itself."[29] According to the Reformed Church, Christ is present in the sacraments in no other sense than he is present in the word.[30] Both serve to hold him up for our acceptance. Neither has any virtue in itself. Both are used by the Spirit, as means of communicating Christ & his benefits to believers. "*Spiritualiter*," says Calvin, "*per sacramenta fidem alit (Deus) QUORUM UNICUM OFFICIUM EST, EJUS PROMISSIONES OCULIS NOSTRIS SPECTANDAS SUBJICERE, IMO NOBIS EARUM ESSE PIGNORA*" (*Inst.* IV.14.12).[31]

CRITICISM [NEVIN]

It is not necessary surely to go into any formal vindication of the *Mystical Presence*, on the score of the charges *here* urged against it by the article of Dr. Hodge. That has been done most fully already, for all who have chosen to read, in the first part of my reply. We have found Dr. Hodge himself to be utterly at fault, in regard to the sacramental doctrine of the old Calvinistic or Reformed Church. The charges here made, when touched by the wand of true history, only rebound with active force upon his own head. It is he himself that has fallen away from the old doctrine of the holy sacraments; making the life side of them to be an "uncongenial foreign element" in their constitution, happily *outgrown* in later times; denying the idea of sacramental grace; stripping them of all objective force; and in one word nullifying altogether the character which belongs to them as DIVINE MYSTERIES, in plump contradiction to the faith of the holy catholic church through all ages. Calvin and the early Reformed Church did most assuredly ascribe to the holy sacraments a *special* and *extraordinary* grace; and it is just as certain, that this was supposed to stand in the actual dynamic presence, by the mystic action of the Holy Ghost, of the very realities themselves pictured and indicated by the outward signs.[32] To question this is to strike all history in the face. Only

29. [MTSS edition, 162.—ed.]

30. [This is clearly the issue between the men. As to the Reformed, both men hold that Calvin and the Reformed taught that Christ is present in the Word. Hodge insists that his presence in the Word is identical to his presence in the sacrament. Nevin, on the other hand, says Christ's presence in the sacrament is unique and that Calvin taught as much.—ed.]

31. [Trans. "He nourishes faith spiritually through the sacraments, *whose one function is to set his promises before our eyes to be looked upon, indeed, to be guarantees of them to us*" (McNeill, ed., 2:1287).—ed.]

32. [Again the combatants might be forgiven their disagreement over Calvin's teaching concerning whether there is "something extra" in the Eucharist "not found elsewhere." In the end, Hodge will say there is nothing there that is not found elsewhere. Nevin will insist there is something unique in the Lord's Supper. Yet both could, with good cause, claim Calvin in their camp. Gerrish concludes that Calvin's language surrounding the question is "ambiguous" perhaps because it is meant to be "edifying rather than exact." Gerrish goes on to say, "What Calvin does not say, however, is that this mysterious union with Christ is given exclusively in the Eucharist." On this topic Calvin wrote to his friend Peter Martyr, and he made it clear that union with Christ began with the Incarnation (Nevin would be pleased), but the reception of the benefits of union waited for the "moment we receive Christ by faith as he offers himself in the gospel" (Hodge would be satisfied). Gerrish concludes that Nevin was overconfident to declare

think of the Baptist's dove, and the tongues of fire on the day of Pentecost, employed to represent the case.

It would have been a little more fair in Dr. Hodge, to give his last capitalized quotation in connection with the rest of the sentence, of which it is only a part. Take the *whole* in English:

> Wherefore as God by bread and other food nourishes our bodies; as he illuminates the world by the sun; as he creates heat by fire; and still the bread, the sun, and the fire, are nothing save as instruments though which he dispenses to us his blessings; so spiritually he nourishes faith by the sacraments, whose only office it is to make his promises visible to our eyes, yea to be unto us their guaranty.[33]

What less can this mean, than that they are the pignoral certification of the grace they represent, not as something general, but as a *present* reality; just as the bread, sun and fire carry in themselves objectively, by divine constitution, the benefits which come to us by their instrumentality? To sustain the view of Dr. Hodge, the parallel would require that bread be taken as an outward token simply of God's general sustaining power, the sun as a pledge that there is such a thing as light in the world, and fire as the visible symbol only of what the philosophers call *latent heat*.

---

that Calvin taught something unique is offered in the Holy Supper if that something is construed as something we don't already possess by faith and the Word. Yet when Hodge dismisses Calvin's idea that in the sacrament the believer is led to grasp that Christ died personally for him while not recognizing a "continuing connection with his bodily existence," he has failed to grasp the second essential component of Calvin's sacramental theology. See Gerrish, *Grace and Gratitude*, 127–29.—ed.]

33. [*Institutes* IV.14.12; McNeill, 2:1237.—ed.]

12

Final Criticisms[1]

REVIEW, CONTINUED [HODGE]

We here leave Dr. Nevin's book; we have only one or two remarks to add not concerning him, nor his own personal belief, but concerning his system. He must excuse our saying that, in our view, it is only a specious form of rationalism. It is in its essential element a psychology. Ullmann admits that it is nearly allied to pantheistic mysticism, and to the modern speculative philosophy. In all three the main idea is, "the union of God and man through the incarnation of the first and the deification of the second."[2] It has however quite as strong an affinity for a much lower form of Rationalism. We are said to have the life of Adam. He lives in us as truly as he ever lived in his own person; we partake of his substance, are flesh of his flesh and bone of his bones. No particle of his soul or body, indeed, has come down to us. It all resolves itself into an invisible law. This and little more than this, is said of our union with Christ. What then have we to do with Christ, more than what we have to do with Adam? or than the present forests of oak have to do with the first acorn? A law is, after all, nothing but a force, a power, and the only Christ we have or need, is an inward principle. And with regard to spirits, such a law is something very ideal indeed. Christ by his excellence makes a certain impression on his disciples, which produced a new life in them. They associate to preserve and transmit that influence. A principle, belonging to the original constitution of our nature, was, by his influence, brought into governing activity, and is perpetuated in and by the church. As it owes its power to Christ, it is always referred back to him, so that it is a Christian consciousness, a consciousness of this union with Christ. We know that Schleiermacher endeavored to save the importance of an historical personal Christ; but we know also that he failed

---

1. ["Dr. Hodge on the *Mystical Presence*, Article from the *Repertory*, Continued, No. 10," *Weekly Messenger*, New Series, vol. 13, no. 48. Wednesday, August 9, 1848. Published by the Board of the Synod of the German Reformed Church: Chambersburg, PA.—ed.]

2. [Hodge:] Preliminary Essay, p. 45. [This is from Karl Ullmann's article, "The Distinctive Character of Christianity," *Theologische Studien und Kritiken* (Jan. 1845), which Nevin offered in an abridged translation as a preface to *The Mystical Presence*. See MTSS edition, p. 38.—ed.]

to prevent his system taking the low rationalist form just indicated. With some it takes the purely pantheistic form; with other a lower form, while others strive hard to give it a Christian form. But its tendency to lapse into one or the other of the two heresies just mentioned is undeniable.

CRITICISM [NEVIN]

Must a "psychology" then be something rationalistic necessarily, in the sphere of theological science? So this censure means, if it have any meaning whatever.

Because Ullmann allows a certain right element in the mysticism of the Middle Ages and the modern speculative philosophy, which he tries to save, by sundering it from its *false* connections, and exhibiting it under its true Christian form, Dr. Hodge coolly insinuates that his system must be substantially the same. As if great errors were not *always* in close proximity with great truths; and a doctrine were worthy of being trusted, only in proportion to the sterile solitariness of its character, as related to the world's life in every other view? This too towards such a man as Ullmann. Could anything well be more unreasonable or unfair?

And then again how unfair, to say of the view here opposed that it resolves our union with Christ into a mere law, parallel only with the course of nature. As if *organic and physical* must needs be always the same! This too in face of all the pains taken in the *Mystical Presence* (p. 169 and elsewhere)[3] to guard against such gross wrong. It is in the sphere of personality precisely, the sphere of thought and will, that the central character of Christ's life is represented as holding in relation to the church. Not as the power of a blind law, but as the free fountain of a free consciousness, that can be what it is only as it is borne and carried perpetually in the sense of this relation, is Christ the organic root of the new creation, in it and with it always to the end of the world.

Of Schleiermacher's theory, I have nothing to say in this place one way or another. Let it stand or fall on its own merits. But what Dr. Hodge objects to here, is the conception of *organic* Christianity in any shape. This however is not by any means bound to Schleiermacher's theology. It is in the bosom of the old catholic Creed, and under the canopy of the new heavens unfolded in the mystery of the incarnation, and here only, that it comes at last to its full significance and force. Such Christianity is not rationalistic. On the contrary, it is only here in the end, as I firmly believe, that Rationalism is made to find scientifically its proper grave.

---

3. [MTSS edition, p. 153. Here Nevin wrote, "Even in the sphere of mere nature the continuity of organic existence, as it passes from one individual to another—mounting upwards for instance from the buried seed and revealing itself at last, through leaves and flowers in a thousand new seeds after its own kind—is found to hang in the end, not on the material medium as such through which the process is effected but on the presence simply of the living force, immaterial altogether and impalpable, that imparts both form and substance to the whole."—ed.]

REVIEW, CONTINUED [HODGE]

We feel constrained to make another remark. It is obvious that his system has a strong affinity to Sabellianism.[4] According to the Bible and the creed of the church universal, the Holy Spirit has a real objective personal existence. There are three distinct persons in the Godhead, the same in substance and equal in power and glory. Being one God, where the Spirit is or dwells, there the Father and the Son are and dwell. And hence, throughout the New Testament, the current mode of representation is that the church is the temple of God and body of Christ, because of the presence and indwelling of the Holy Ghost, who is the source of knowledge, holiness and life. What the scriptures refer to the Holy Spirit, this system refers to the theanthropic nature of Christ, to a nature or life "in all respects human."—This supersedes the Holy Spirit. Every reader, therefore must be struck with the difficulty Dr. Nevin finds from this source. He does not seem to know what to do with the Spirit. His language is constrained, awkward and often unintelligible. He seems indeed sometimes to identify the Spirit with the theanthropic nature of Christ. "The Spirit of Christ," he says,

> is not his representative or surrogate simply, as some would seem to think; but *Christ himself under a certain mode of subsistence;* Christ triumphant over all the limitations of his moral [mortal?] state (*Zoopoietheis pneumatic*), received up in glory, and thus invested fully and forever with his own proper order of being in the sphere of the Holy Ghost (p. 225).[5]

The Spirit of Christ, is then Christ as exalted. On the following page, he says:

> The glorification of Christ then, was the full advancement of our human nature itself to the power of a divine life; and the Spirit for whose presence it [the glorification of Christ] made room in the world, was not the spirit as extra-anthropological simply, under such forms of sporadic and transient afflatus as had been known previously; but the Spirit as immanent now, through Jesus Christ, in the human nature itself—the form and power, in one word, of the new supernatural creation he had introduced into the world.[6]

> —Again, Christ is not sundered from the church by the intervention of the Spirit. . . . No conception can be more unbiblical, than that by which the idea of Spirit (*pneuma*) in this case, is restrained to the form of mere mind, whether as divine or human, in distinction from body. The *whole* glorified Christ subsists and acts *in the Spirit.* Under this form his nature communicates itself to his people (p. 229).[7]

---

4. [Sabellianism, named for the third-century heretic Sabellius, is a form of the trinitarian heresy of modalism which denied that the Holy Spirit was a separate person of the Trinity. Although of course Nevin will deny this, as Hodge well knows, Hodge considers it a necessary consequence of his adoption of Schleiermacher's system of theology, which many have considered to be in conflict with the Nicene doctrine of the Trinity.—ed.]

5. [MTSS edition, p. 196.—ed.]

6. [Ibid., 197.—ed.]

7. [Ibid., 199.—ed.]

But according to this book, the form in which his nature is communicated to his people, is that of "a true human life;" it is a human nature advanced to a divine power, which they receive. The Spirit is, therefore, not the third person of the Trinity, but the theanthropic nature of Christ as it dwells in the church. This seems to us the natural and unavoidable interpretation of these passages and of the general tenor of the book. We do not suppose that Dr. Nevin has consciously discarded the doctrine of the Trinity; but we fear that he has adopted a theory which destroys that doctrine. The influence of his early convictions and experience, and of his present circumstances, may constrain him to hold fast that article of faith, in some form to satisfy his conscience. But his system must banish it, just so far as it prevails. Schleiermacher, formed under different circumstances, and less inwardly trammeled, openly rejected the doctrine.[8] He wrote a system of theology, without saying a word about the Trinity.[9] It has no place in his system; he brings it in only at the conclusion of his work, and explains it as God manifested in nature, God as manifested in Christ, and God as manifested in the church. With him the Holy Spirit, is the spirit which animates the church. It had no existence before the church & has no existence beyond it. His usual expression for it is, "the common spirit" (*Gemeingeist*) of the church, which may mean either something very mystical, or nothing more than we mean by the spirit of the age, or spirit of a party, just as the reader pleases. It is a point of fact understood both ways. Burke[10] once said, he never knew what the London beggars did with their cast-off clothes, until he went to Ireland. We hope we Americans are not to be arrayed in the cast-off clothes of the German mystics, and then marshaled in bands as the "church of the future."

We said at the commencement of this article, that we had never read Dr. Nevin's book on *Mystical Presence*, until now. We have from time to time read other of his publications, and looked here and there into the work before us; and have thus been led to fear that he was allowing the German modes of thinking to get the mastery over him, but we had no idea that he had so far given himself up to their influence. If he has any faith in friendship and long continued regard, he must believe that we could not

---

8. [These two sentences reveal the personal feelings of Hodge toward Nevin, believing him to have come late to the speculative science and assume he is still constrained to some extent by the influence of Princeton and/or his former Old School Presbyterian upbringing. Hodge believed, not without good evidence, that Schleiermacher's doctrine of the Trinity was heterodox. Of course, Nevin believed that the more conservative Mediating doctrine corrected the errors of Schleiermacher.—ed.]

9. [Schleiermacher does not neglect the Trinity entirely as Hodge maintains. Although "sparse," it is nevertheless there. Schleiermacher crowns the whole development of the consciousness of grace "with a rather sparse exposition of the trinity." Here is expressed the fact that "no less than the divine being itself was in Christ and indwells the church through its common Spirit" (Barth, *The Theology of Schleiermacher*, 192). Schleiermacher published on the Trinity itself, but the work is obscure enough to have passed Hodge's and most readers' notice. See "On the Discrepancy between the Sabellian and Athanasian Method of Representing the Doctrine of the Trinity," translated into English by Moses Stuart in the *Biblical Repository and Quarterly Observer*.—ed.]

10. [Edmund Burke (1729–97), Anglo-Irish philosopher, statesman, author, and political theorist. He was a defender of the American Revolution and late critic of the French Revolution, the latter of which in part identified him among the "Old Whig" faction of the party.—ed.]

find ourselves separated from him by such serious differences without deep regret, and will therefore give us credit for sincerity of conviction and purpose.

CRITICISM [NEVIN]

Heresies make themselves *cheap*, in the hands of Dr. Hodge. Is it necessary for me to say soberly, that I am not a Sabellian? There is not a word in the *Mystical Presence*, that by fair construction can be made to carry any such sense. The book recognizes throughout the doctrine of the Trinity, in its old church form. But the *system*, says Hodge, leaves no room for the Holy Ghost. However, it may be in the case of Schleiermacher, I deny it so far as the system of *Mystical Presence* is concerned. Only for the most *outward* conception of the Trinity, can the difficulty here urged by Dr. Hodge be of any force; such a conception as has already indeed passed over into tri-theism. It is pure misrepresentation to say, that I know not what to do with the Spirit. The objection in truth is but another glimpse furnished us of the abstract Nestorian character of Dr. Hodge's theology. To sunder Christ from his Spirit, says Calvin, is to convert him into a dead image or corpse. By the Spirit, Rom. viii. 9, we are to understand, he tells us, *the mode of Christ's habitation in us.* If there be one truth clear in the New Testament it is, that the Spirit as now active in the church is the revelation of the power of Christ's mediatorial or theanthropic life, under a form that was not possible till Christ himself was glorified. But of all this Dr. Hodge would seem to have hardly a conception.

The trite and easy sarcasm about "cast-off clothes," as here applied, is unworthy of Dr. Hodge. It would not cost much trouble of course, to retort in some equally insulting style. But would it serve at all the cause of charity and truth?

Dr. Hodge regrets my *German* sympathies. Am I not however in a German church, and in conscience bound to be true and faithful to its proper historical life? Could I deserve to be regarded as anything better than a traitor to my trust, if I made it my business to overflow and overwhelm this life with foreign modes of thought, derived purely from Scotland or New England? I would say solemnly: *No man has a right to take advantage of his position in the German Church for any such purpose as this.* It is well indeed that it should be Americanized; all nationalities here require that; and the process must involve always their general approximation to a common standard. But *Americanization* in religion is not at once subjection to the one single type of thinking, that prevails in New England or the Presbyterian Church. It *should* be the result of our different nationalities, working into each other in a free and harmonious way. In such a process, the mind of Germany has rights to be respected, no less than that of England or Scotland.

But can *any* good thing come out of Germany, some may be ready to ask? Dr. Hodge would appear to think not. And yet Princeton can find it convenient too at times to make wide use of German learning under certain forms. So Andover also, and indeed all our respectable seats of education. Aye, it may be said; but only in an independent *outward* way, as the Gibeonites were made hewers of wood and drawers of water formerly to the congregation of Israel. German philosophy, lexicography, and history, may all be well enough, if properly filtrated through the good common sense of an American compiler; but it will not do to enter the real life of German thought, so as to have any sympathy whatever with its interior soul and heart. That is always dangerous, and of itself argues something wrong. So it is here assumed.

Alas for our prejudices. It is precisely this external, filtrated literature of Germany, that is most to be deprecated and feared, in its influence on our religion and theology; for it is the fruit mainly of the rationalistic period, and is animated for the most part throughout with a purely rationalistic spirit. Such literature *is* dangerous; and unfortunately we are not provided any sufficient antidote to its bad power, in our current theology. What we need is a more thoroughly scientific apprehension, not of the letter and shell of Christianity simply, but of its true divine contents; and this, I feel very sure, can never be reached by any process, in which the results of the later German theology are ignored or trampled un-inquiringly under foot. It is not necessary of course that we should follow them, in any blind slavish way; but we must at least treat them with such respect as is due, all the world over, to the earnest wrestling of earnest mind with the most solemn problems of our general human life. What philosopher can now deserve to be heard, who is altogether ignorant of Kant and Hegel? What system of ethics may be counted truly scientific, which owes *nothing* to the labors of Schleiermacher, Daub[11] or Richard Rothe?[12] Still more; can any treatise on *Sin* be now complete, which leaves out of view entirely, through ignorance or scorn, the profound investigations of Julius Mueller?[13] Can any Christology be worth reading, that makes no account whatever of the immortal work of Dorner?[14] To ask such questions is enough. Surely it is not

11. [Karl Daub (1765–1836), German philosopher and theologian. Daub was a devoted follower of Hegel and was influential in Hegel's call to Heidelberg in 1816. Hegel entrusted Daub with the correcting and revising of the second edition of Hegel's *Enzyclopädie* (1827). Daub may be numbered among the latitudinarian wing of the Mediating school of German theology, whose influence on Mercersburg is fundamental.—ed.]

12. [Richard Rothe (1799–1867), German theologian under the early influence of Schleiermacher and Neander, blending the brilliant discoveries in church history with a deep piety, which was brought to bear against the rationalism of the previous era. Rothe made valuable contributions to the German Mediating school of thought.—ed.]

13. [Julius Müller (1801–78), while a student of law he came under the influence of the outstanding Mediating theologian Tholuck, who led him to theology where he excelled. He taught dogmatics at Marburg and moved into the churchly or conservative wing of the Mediating school. Undoubtedly Müller's work on sin was a deliberate and in the eyes of many a successful attempt to restore the importance of sin for Christian theology in contrast to the minor place given it by Schleiermacher. Still, it was an unusual approach which predicated a pre- or extratemporal event brought about by the universal choice to sin by every soul. And while Nevin found Müller's work on sin important he by no means adopted his doctrine.—ed.]

14. [Isaak August Dorner (1809–84), educated at Tübingen where he studied under F. C. Baur, Hegelian of the "left." But his strong churchmanship and appreciation for and expertise in Reformed theology made him a Mediating theologian of the conservative wing. He was influential in the establishing of the United Church of Prussia, and his work on Christology was some of the best in Reformed history. Nevin would later spar with Dorner in one of the strangest disagreements in Mercersburg's history. The occasion allowed Nevin to develop his already masterful Christology. In spite of the fact that Dorner shared much of Mercersburg's theology (much more than the critics who reviled Nevin), when he was asked by the anti-Mercersburg group to speak out against Nevin, he did—most specifically on

so perfectly self-evident, as Dr. Hodge appears to suppose, that German modes of thinking must needs be false and bad, the moment they are found to fall away from the reigning tradition of America. Is our theology in truth such a *waking* Goshen, contrasted with the theological activity of the whole world besides? It may be pleasant to think so; but a man must shut his eyes, and *keep* them shut to enjoy the delectable dream.

THE TWO SYSTEMS CONTRASTED [NEVIN]

It has been already intimated, that the objections made to the *Mystical Presence* by Dr. Hodge, resolve themselves to a great extent into one. He quarrels throughout with the idea of an *organic* Christianity, and insists always on an abstract separation of the two words which are here brought into connection.

The organic character of Christianity, as represented in the *Mystical Presence*, determines in the first place the view there taken of the *Incarnation*, and in the second place the view of the *Church*.

Dr. Hodge makes both to spring from Schleiermacher, and strangely enough assumes that they cannot be sundered from his system.

But this is palpably absurd. The idea of a true historical new creation, first in Christ and then through him in the church, comes to its full force, only in the bosom of the old Athanasian creed; and tends with inward necessity, from the very start, to subvert every form of Arian, Socinian or Unitarian error. So we find it to be in fact. It is precisely the most orthodox and evangelical legacy in Germany, that is yielding itself more and more to its power.

Dr. Hodge would seem to have only a very dim conception of the organic constitution of the world, in any view. It is to his mind apparently a system of innumerable parts, brought together in an outward and mechanical way; God stands out of it and beyond it, very much as an artificer in regard to a machine which he has made; the *whole* it represents, is simply the *all* of the objects and phenomena in which it is found to consist. Nature is the platform simply, on which man is placed as another order of existence altogether, to work out the problem of his destiny beyond the grave.

But surely we have a right now to say, that every such mechanical view of the universe is left forever behind, in the progress of true philosophical thought. The world is a whole, that springs continually from the power of a single idea. The distribution it is made to undergo in space and time, can never overthrow its inward ideal unity, as one grand act of self-revelation on the part of God. Nature completes itself in man. His proper wholeness too is that of the race, extending through successive ages. History is the perpetual actualization, more and more, of the deep sense that belongs to his life.

And it is just in correspondence with all this, that we ascribe an organic character to the mystery of the incarnation. The *Word* became *Flesh*. It was not an Old Testament theophany, nor a Hindu avatar. It was not magic. It was not a mechanical, outward conjunction only of the two worlds, in any sense. There had been nothing like it before.

Nevin's rather high view of ordination, which Dorner concluded was not Reformed in character.—ed.]

It meets us as a fact without a parallel. The divine life had revealed itself in a certain way previously to Abraham, Moses and David; but *never* was there such an order of grace and glory upon the earth before. So far at least as the person of Christ himself is concerned, all must admit that an absolutely new creation was now brought into view, transcending altogether the organic life of the world as it stood under the old economy. To say less than this, would be virtually to deny the fact of the incarnation.

But this fact, thus new and original, forms no abrupt or violent chasm with the life of the world as it stood before. It falls in with it, not indeed as its product but still as its necessary and true complement, in an inward and really historical way. So much the mystery requires us to believe. To say the contrary, would be Gnosticism. The Word became flesh really; the supernatural entered into union with the natural, not fantastically, but organically, as the power of a new creation unfolding itself in the bosom of the old.

To this Dr. Hodge objects. His theory will not allow any such natural and historical character to the mystery in question. The supernatural may not overstep its ancient bounds; the divine cannot become human. *That,* we are gravely told, is Rationalism. Alas, it be so, for our reigning orthodoxy. But is not this, in very fact, the abstraction of Nestorius? If the two worlds meet not organically in the person of Christ so as to become there at least concretely one, what can the mystery mean? Who may not see that any other supposition turns it at once into magic or dream!

But now to be thus organic at all, the fact comprehended in Christ must be of universal & perennial force for the world's history. To think of our human life as something separate and distinct in him absolutely from what it is in all the world besides, is only to fall over again in a new way to the abstraction, that excludes it altogether from his person. If humanity assumed by the Word were an isolated thing, *like* our flesh indeed, but to the very power of it in a true historical view, the proper realness of the incarnation is gone. In place of the sublime reality of the Creed, we are mocked with a phenomenon or prodigy alone.

Here then follows the idea that the fact thus revealed in Christ must penetrate its force historically, as a new creation, a new order of life in the world, through all subsequent time. And thus precisely is what we are to understand by the holy catholic church. Our faith in the church is conditioned by our faith in the mystery of the incarnation. So in the old Apostles' Creed. It is a thing to be *believed*, and then understood as the case may admit. The article of the church flows out of the article of the incarnation, with inward necessity. To be fully overwhelmed with the authority of the last, is to be shut up at the same time, and to the same extent, to the authority of the fact.

But Dr. Hodge allows no such inward and organic relation again, as we have seen, between Christ and the church. This, he pretends, would be to imagine the full contents of Christ's theanthropic life passing forward continually in the church, by a sort of physical process, in such a way as to make every Christian an independent parallel with his Master! He has no idea apparently of innumerable personalities, needing to be made complete by union to a common personal center, as the *only*, but all sufficient, bond of their union with God. Hence the new creation in Christ Jesus is for him no world historical *fact*, parallel in full with the creation of man in the beginning, and going wholly beyond all that had been the world before. The Old Testament was substantially the same with the New. God was in the world as fully then as now. The incarnation is no such *act* of self-manifestation on his part, as turns all previous revelations into mere type and shadow. The church he makes an abstraction, and will hear of no divine powers permanently lodged in its constitution.

Again, it is implied by the idea of organic Christianity, as now described, that the last principle of it is the *person* of Christ, and not simply his doctrine or work. It is not a thing to be caught by every man, for his own separate use, directly from the clouds, as fanatics pretend, having relation to Christ only in the way of memory and thought. It is not a vast aggregate of new creations, spiritually educed out of *nothing* by the Holy Ghost in single Christians; but the force and power of that one new creation which has taken place in Christ himself, as a part of the world's true organic life, carried over to the souls and bodies of his people, from generation to generation. Christ is the fontal source of the entire process; the *root*, out of which strictly grows the true being of the church, to the end of time. He is himself the truth he proclaimed. His work has no value, *out of his life*. It is thus, and thus only, of perennial force, "once for all." The atonement is ever new, as standing ever in the presence of that new order of life, indissoluble, imperishable, into which "by the eternal Spirit," he is gloriously advanced.

But now see how this is shorn of its significance and force, by the Nestorian abstractions of Dr. Hodge. The person of Christ is of value for him, only as a mystery that holds beyond his doctrine and work, and not as the very act of God, we may call it, in which both are comprehended. The stupendous grandeur of the NEW CREATION, as accomplished in Christ, takes a visionary, unreal character for the eye of faith, by its being turned into the outward platform simply for the work of redemption. The sacrificial interest is divorced from the idea of life. The atonement becomes a thought, no longer bound to its original basis in the Savior's person. Justification is converted into a fiction of law. Christianity is still talked of as a religion of facts; but the facts are to a great extent dead and gone, belonging to past time, or else sublimated in full into the spirit world; things to be preached and so kept in mind; things to which our inward experience may be referred thus, as intellectual occasions of piety; while as *present* realities, in any true historical sense, it would be mysticism to dream of them as anywhere at hand. So at last Christianity resolves itself into the idea of a doctrine; and the church of course, in such view, must be content to pass for a sort of sacred school. Her sacraments include no grace. She might be extinguished altogether (was so perhaps in the middle ages), and still it would be a light thing, with the help of the bible, to make another equally as good.[15] For the church is not necessarily one, and catholic,

15. [Here we see clear evidence of Nevin's much higher regard for the Middle Ages. Hodge could envision the church becoming extinct like an ancient dinosaur during the period he referred to as the "Dark Ages." Likewise, it could be brought back to life again after the Middle Ages by a pious movement governed by Scripture. In fact, Princeton nearly said as much. Nevin, in contrast, would argue that if the church had disappeared at any point in history, it would be gone forever. As much as the extinction of natural species bars them from a future spontaneous gestation, so it is the case with the spiritual, living natural reality of the church as the spiritual new species of Christ's life in the world. For Hodge, however,

and apostolic or historical, in the sense of the old creeds; carries in its constitution no law whatever, requiring any such visible revelation; but can only hope to be all this sometime hereafter, in heaven. The old catholic *ideas* were in general wrong; their sacramental, liturgical, churchly views and feelings throughout, that seemed to aim at bringing heaven down to earth, savored more of superstition than common sense; and the longing which some have towards the same thing now, is to be set down for a secret disaffection to heart-godliness; the test of all sound Protestantism, is a disposition to get as far away as possible from all that was once held precious and dear, in the faith and worship of the catholic church.

To such broad differences does the general question before us run, when carried out on both sides to its proper consequences. And this is only a specimen of its importance in this way. It would be easy to show, that it conditions necessarily the whole science of theology.[16] But we follow it here no farther. Enough has been said, to show the deeply interesting and widely comprehensive relations of the general subject; as well as to reveal, at the same time, the vast significance of that "UNCONGENIAL FOREIGN ELEMENT," whose melancholy expulsion from the old Reformed doctrine, Dr. Hodge acknowledges with so much hearty satisfaction.

---

had the church entirely disappeared, as a purely spiritual reality it could come back to life again through the work of the Holy Spirit.—ed.]

16. [Nevin:] Take one broad illustration. Is the atonement for all, or only for a certain part, of the human race? Conceive of it as a mere expedient or device contrived to carry out a purpose of salvation in favor of a certain number of individual sinners, and we are shut up at once to the consequence that it is of force and value for these only, and carries in itself as little real relation to others as it does to the fallen angels; a result, which contradicts the New Testament throughout, and does violence to all sound religious feeling. But on the other hand, if it be for all, how can it be strictly vicarious, in any such sense as to accomplish the salvation of its objects, since *all* are not in fact saved? Thus the abstract theology before us falls into an *antinomy* of contradiction, out of which it has no power ever to effect its escape. If the principle of redemption be an outward thought simply, the atonement must be limited, or else it cannot be truly vicarious. Hence the tendency of those who shrink from the first side of the alternative, to turn the whole transaction into a mere exhibition or governmental display. But this again runs at once towards Pelagianism, and in the end Socianism. The case demands a *vicarious* atonement which shall be at the same time absolutely *universal*. This we reach by the idea of an organic, concrete Christianity, and in no way besides. The Principle of redemption is not an outward thought or decree, but a divine idea actualizing itself in and through the person of Christ. The new creation is as universal in its own nature as the old; it comprehends in itself the fullness of humanity; but all this primarily and fontally in Christ alone. The atonement then, as made in him, is at once vicarious and universal; for the *life* to which it belongs is that of the world in its highest form, the proper wholeness of humanity, in which all must come to have part in order to be saved. Be the number of the saved more or less, it cannot affect the bounds of the new creation in itself considered. This has no bounds; it is the concrete universality of the true idea of *man*, as victoriously raised above the power of sin and death in the second Adam. The two schemes turn at last on the broad difference, which holds between the conceptions of *all* and the *whole*. The first is an abstract universal; the second *concrete*. The first has limits; the second has none. Adam was potentially not merely the "all" of men actually since born (as though he had been made for this abstract election precisely and nothing beyond); but he was the "whole" of our humanity, and as such equally universal, whether the actual race might be more or less. So Christ is not simply the "all" of the actually saved, as though incarnate and crucified for these only (limited atonement in service of abstract decree of election); but he is the "whole" Church or new creation, in which alone our race is made complete. Our election is life *in Christ*, not out of him. So in the Heidelberg (Qu. 37), we have strictly vicarious propitiation asserted, which is yet declared to be *for the sins of all mankind*, not limited but universal.

CONCLUDING REMARKS [NEVIN]

My task is now done. In obedience to the Princeton challenge, I have called myself once more solemnly to account, and endeavored, in the fear of God, to review my own position as taken in the *Mystical Presence*. The Sacramental question has been examined. The objections and strictures of Dr. Hodge have been carefully tried, in the light of history, as well as by the standard of scripture. For the whole process, special assistance has been at hand besides in the masterly work of Ebrard.

The result is only a more full conviction than before, that the historical platform of the *Mystical Presence* stands sound and firm. It is not shaken in the least, by anything which Dr. Hodge has brought forward in the way of contrary criticism. My general view of the subject has indeed undergone, as already intimated, some slight modification; but this benefit is one to which the criticism in question has contributed nothing, save as an occasion for new inquiry; while it is such besides as goes only to strengthen the position previously taken. I have come to a clearer and more favorable view, than before, of Zwingli's relation to the Reformed doctrine; and I am satisfied besides, that Calvin's theory, as it stood in his own mind, calls for *less* qualification than I had supposed, to bring it into harmony with the demands of modern science. In other respects, I can only reaffirm the statement before made; and am bound consequently to reject the representation opposes to it by Dr. Hodge, as historically erroneous and unsound.

This implies of course, that Dr. Hodge is himself involved in that widespread defection from the old sacramental doctrine, which it is one great object of the *Mystical Presence* to describe and expose. The idea of *sacramental grace*, baptismal and Eucharistic, as held by the universal ancient church, he rejects. He will not allow that the sacraments carry in themselves *objective* force. The conception of any participation on the side of believers in the true *mediatorial life* of Christ, he treats as popish superstition. The holy sacraments are for him no MYSTERIES whatever, in the old church sense. Life and sacrifice, in one word, as originally bound together in the Reformed doctrine of salvation, he rends asunder, in such a way as to turn the last into a mere abstraction, leaving no room thus for the sacramental side of Christianity, as comprehended in the perpetual presence of the new creation in Christ Jesus by the church.

As for what is peculiar in the theory of the *Mystical Presence* itself, the scientific *form* in which it has been attempted to save the substance of the old doctrine, it is enough to say that it has passed unscathed through the ordeal at least of this review. The objections made to it spring either from gross misapprehension of its actual sense, or from the false relation of the reviewer himself to the old church doctrine. They are conditioned throughout by the Nestorian divorce of Christ's sacrifice from his life, which characterizes so unhappily the whole theology of Dr. Hodge. Still if the theory in question were shown to be unsatisfactory in a scientific view, the case would require only that it should be given up *as a theory*, and some better one if possible substituted in its place. Let it appear, that it is really at war with a single article of the old *Apostles' Creed*, and I stand ready to cast the first stone in the work of crushing it to death. I lay my hand upon my heart, and before heaven and earth pronounce every syllable of the Creed as MY OWN; and only wish indeed, that I had the opportunity of doing it with loud voice, in the worshipping congregation of God's people every Lord 's Day.

How does it happen, by the way, that this Creed is in such low regard practically with a large part of the modern Christian world; and with that part of it precisely which is most bent on sundering all that is objective and sacramental from the idea of the church? Puritanism (I use the term respectfully) refuses to accept it at all, in its full original sense; and after all mental qualifications, still finds it hard to utter it with hearty interest and clear sonorous voice, as the very transcript of its own inward life. It is not preached on from the pulpit, and it is not repeated in the family. And yet, why so? It is the inmost, living expression of the Christian faith, under its ancient catholic form; and it was accepted and honored in this character by the whole Protestant church, at the time of the Reformation. Why then should it be so thrust out of religious use, at the present time? The fact is strange, and deserves attention. The truth is, there runs a golden thread of catholic feeling through Creed, which cannot easily be twisted out of it; it is not a thing of abstraction, but a thing of *life*; and it is just here that our un-sacramental, un-churchly spirit, finds itself too generally at a loss, when called to join the chorus of universal Christendom in its joyful repetition. There is a chord in it, which meets in our souls no proper sympathetic response. But what is this else, than an inward separation from the life of the ancient church, which implies a falling away also to the same extent from the true life of the Reformation? It is the catholic element overwhelmed by the merely protestant, the claims of the concrete in Christianity set aside in favor of the abstract. Sympathy with the inward spirit of the old Creed, may be taken as the necessary accompaniment and sure index of church feeling, wherever it prevails; and the want of it shows just as certainly a parallel want of all lively correspondence, with the old catholic habit of thought and sentiment throughout.

It is not possible to dismiss the idea of sacramental grace, and pronounce the Creed at the same time in full unison with the ancient faith of the holy catholic church.

If any apology should seem to be needed for the length of this *Antikritik*, it may be found in the importance of the subject discussed, and the character of the occasion requiring it. There is no question before the church at this time of deeper and more vital consequence than the one here brought into view, regarded either in its theological or historical relations. The article of Dr. Hodge, at the same time, could not with any propriety be overlooked or treated in a superficial way. It is the first attempt which has yet been made to meet the *Mystical Presence*, in any sort of scientific style; and forms, in this view, the first opportunity which has been given, to come forward in its vindication and defense. Here at last is a respectable argument against it, based on some knowledge of the subject, and paying some proper tribute of respect to its intrinsic importance, by compulsion at least if not in an entirely free way. It springs from a most honorable source, it comes recommended with every advantage of outward authority, it affects to go to the bottom of the whole question, and to settle it in full and conclusive way, and it has been widely accepted, as determining thus unanswerably in fact all that it professes to determine. Such an argument, in such a case, has a right to challenge attention in some earnest and manly form. To make light of it would be disrespectful to Dr. Hodge, as well as dishonest and unfaithful to the vast religious interest which is here at stake.

The discussion might appear indeed to be more proper for the pages of a theological review, than the columns of the *Weekly Messenger*. But necessity, as we say, knows no law. Our review press, as it now stands, is not properly open for any such use. In general, it may be said, the claims of the sacramental and churchly side of Christianity, find a most step-motherly interest on the part of our religious periodicals. Most of them indeed might seem to be systematically bent on keeping even the facts of history, as connected with the subject, as much as possible out of sight. It is greatly to be wished, that we had a review in the country, capable of entering properly into the great theological problems of the age, without being bound by any merely denominational scheme of thought. Our whole theology, as a science, "groans and travels in pain together" towards some such dawn of redemption; which with all needful help besides, may God send in his own good time and way?

In addition to the necessity of the case however, as now stated, it might be regarded as due to the ministry and membership of the church to which I belong, that I should lay this defense before them in the columns of the *Messenger*. The article of Dr. Hodge amounts to this, that the German Reformed Church, whether through ignorance or otherwise, has not been properly faithful to her trust, in allowing such great errors as are here laid to the charge of my book to pass unnoticed. Either I must be a very Jesuit in art, or else our ministers no better than so many children (the people of course more dumb still), to make it possible for such a nest of heresies, Eutychianism, Rationalism, Pantheism, Romanism, Lutheranism, Pelagianism, Sabellianism, Unitarianism and Puseyism, to be kept so successfully out of sight for so long a time, till the "system" has now come to be suddenly exposed by the strong illumination here shed upon it from Princeton. The controversy is one of *popular* interest then in this view, for our own church at least, if in no other quarter; and it is reasonable that this defense should have a hearing with the people generally. Nor is there anything here so difficult or abstruse, that it may not easily enough be understood by all persons of good sense, who apply their thoughts seriously to the purpose.

There may be some possibly (I trust not many now however in the German Reformed Church) who count all theological discussion of this sort comparatively unprofitable; affecting to be so set on *practical* interests, as to have no taste for speculation or controversy in any shape. It is good certainly to make the life of religion the main thing, and to avoid vain disputations in regard to its nature. But who will pretend seriously, that the general question here in view is of this character? Who may not see, that it goes at once to the very heart of Christianity, and links itself with the most momentous practical concerns on every side? *Not* to take an interest in it, must argue in a minister especially such spiritual levity, as can hardly be reconciled with the idea of a heartfelt intelligent zeal for godliness under any other form. *What think ye of Christ?* is the searching interrogation, which lies at the bottom of this whole inquiry concerning the character of the new creation, comprehended in his church. Is he the fountain, principle, root of the whole Christian life, in a real way; or only the outward occasion of it, as a fact beyond his own person? Is the redemption of the gospel, including all the benefits of Christ's life and death, a concrete reality, that holds in the force of his living constitution as a perennial, indissoluble fact, "the *new world* which grace has made,"[17] and in this alone; or is it an abstraction, which may be applied to men and appropriated by faith, in no connection whatever with the LIFE by which originally it was brought to pass? Our inward answer to all this must ever be conditioned necessarily by our view of the church; and our view of the church finds its exact measure always, in our theory of the holy sacraments. Eviscerate these of their old catholic sense, and it is in vain to pretend any true faith in the article of a holy catholic Church, as it stood in the beginning; and without this faith again, the christological mystery is necessarily shorn of its proper significance and glory. We fall over into the arms of a Nestorian Christ; in whose constitution, the new creation becomes at best, after the similitude of Peter's vision, a great sheet-like vessel, knit at the four corners, and let down to the earth, only to be received up again soon after into heaven—since which time, "all things continue as they were from the beginning."[18]

17. [Probably an allusion to the last line of Isaac Watts's hymn, "The New Creation."—ed.]
18. [2 Pt 3:4.—ed.]

Bibliography

WORKS CONSULTED

Ahlstrom, Sydney E. "The Scottish Philosophy and American Theology." *Church History* 24 (1955): 257–72.

Appel, Theodore. *The Life and Work of John Williamson Nevin.* New York: Arno, 1969. First published in Philadelphia by the Reformed Church Publication House, 1889.

Barth, Karl. *The Theology of Schleiermacher.* Translated by Geoffrey W. Bromiley. Grand Rapids, MI: Eerdmans, 1982.

Bigler, Robert M. *The Politics of German Protestantism: The Rise of the Protestant Church Elite in Prussia 1814–1848.* Berkeley: University of California Press, 1972.

Bonomo, Jonathan G. *Incarnation and Sacrament: The Eucharistic Controversy between Charles Hodge and John Williamson Nevin.* Eugene, OR: Wipf & Stock, 2010.

Catholic Church. *Catechism of the Catholic Church.* Liguori, MO: Liguori Publications, 1994.

DeBie, Linden J. "Frederick Augustus Rauch: First American Hegelian." *New Mercersburg Review* (Spring 1996): 70–77.

———. "The Germ, Genesis and Contemporary Impact of Mercersburg Philosophy." *New Mercersburg Review*, no. 30 (2009): 5–51.

———. "German Idealism in Protestant Orthodoxy: The Mercersburg Movement, 1840–1860." PhD diss., McGill University, 1987.

———. "Real Presence or Real Absence? The Spoils of War in Nineteenth-Century American Eucharistic Controversy." *Pro Ecclesia* 4, no. 4 (1995): 431–53.

———. *Speculative Theology and Common-Sense Religion: Mercersburg and the Conservative Roots of American Religion.* Eugene, OR: Wipf & Stock, 2008.

DiPuccio, William. *The Interior Sense of Scripture: The Sacred Hermeneutics of John W. Nevin.* Macon, GA: Mercer University Press, 1998.

———. "Nevin's Idealistic Philosophy." In *Reformed Confessionalism in Nineteenth-Century America,* edited by Sam Hamstra Jr. and Arie J. Griffioen. Lanham, MD: Scarecrow, 1995.

Easton, Lloyd D. *Hegel's First American Followers: The Ohio Hegelians.* Athens: Ohio University Press, 1966.

Evans, William B. *Imputation and Impartation: Union with Christ in American Reformed Theology.* Eugene, OR: Wipf & Stock, 2008.

Fink, Roger, and Rodney Stark. *The Churching of America, 1776–1990.* New Brunswick, NJ: Rutgers University Press, 1992.

Gerrish, Brian. *Grace and Gratitude: The Eucharistic Theology of John Calvin.* Minneapolis: Fortress, 1993.

———. "John Calvin and the Reformed Doctrine of the Lord's Supper." *McCormick Quarterly* 22 (1969): 85–98.

———. *The Old Protestantism and the New: Essays on the Reformation Heritage.* Chicago: UCP; Edinburgh: T & T Clark, 1982.

———. *Tradition and the Modern World.* Chicago: UCP, 1978.

Good, James I. *History of the Reformed Church in the United States in the Nineteenth Century*. New York: The Board of Publication of the Reformed Church in America, 1911.

Graham, Stephen. "Nevin and Schaff at Mercersburg." In *Reformed Confessionalism in Nineteenth-Century America*, edited by Sam Hamstra Jr. and Arie J. Griffioen, 70–96. Lanham, MD: Scarecrow, 1995.

Hart, D. G. *John Williamson Nevin: High Church Calvinist*. Phillipsburg, NJ: P&R, 2005.

Hodge, Archibald Alexander. *The Life of Charles Hodge*. New York: Scribner's Sons, 1880.

Hodge, Charles. "Doctrine of the Reformed Church on the Lord's Supper." *Biblical Repertory and Princeton Review* 20 (1848): 227–78.

———. "Review of *The Anxious Bench*, by John W. Nevin." *Biblical Repertory and Princeton Review* 16 (1844): 137–38.

———. "Review of *Der Anglogermanismus, eine Rede u. s. w.* by Philip Schaf." *Biblical Repertory and Princeton Review* 18 (1846): 482–83.

———. "Review of John W. Nevin's 'Eulogy on the Life and Character of the Late Rev. Dr. Frederick Rauch.'" *Biblical Repertory and Princeton Review* 13 (1841): 464.

———. "Review of *The Church: A Sermon Preached on the Opening of the Synod of the German Reformed Church at Carlisle, October 15, 1846*, by John W. Nevin." *Biblical Repertory and Princeton Review* 19 (1847): 301–4.

———. "Review of *The German Language: An Address Delivered Before the Goethean Literary Society of Marshall College* by John W. Nevin." *Biblical Repertory and Princeton Review* 15 (1843): 172–73.

———. "Schaf's Protestantism. Rev. of *Principle of Protestantism as Related to the Present State of the Church*, by Philip Schaf." *Biblical Repertory and Princeton Review* 17 (1845): 626–36.

———. *Systematic Theology*. 3 vols. Reprint. Grand Rapids, MI: Eerdmans, 1999.

———. *The Way of Life*. Edited by Mark Noll. New York: Paulist, 1987.

Hoeveler, David. *James McCosh and the Scottish Intellectual Tradition*. Princeton, NJ: Princeton University Press, 1981.

Hunsinger, George. *The Eucharist and Ecumenism*. Cambridge: CUP, 2008.

Jackson, Samuel Macaulay, ed. *The New Schaff-Herzog Encyclopedia of Religious Knowledge*. 13 vols. Grand Rapids: Baker, 1949–50.

Kant, Immanuel. *Critique of Practical Reason*. New York: Cosimo, 2009.

———. *Religion within the Limits of Reason Alone*. Edited by T. M. Greene, H. H. Hudson, and J. Silber. New York: Harper & Row, 1960.

Kremer, A. R. *A Biographical Sketch of John Williamson Nevin*. Reading, PA: Daniel Miller, 1890.

Küng. Hans. *Menschwerdung Gottes*. Freiburg: Herder KG, 1970. Translated by J. R. Stevenson as *The Incarnation of God* (Edinburgh: T & T Clark, 1987).

Littlejohn, W. Bradford. *The Mercersburg Theology and the Quest for Reformed Catholicity*. Eugene, OR: Pickwick, 2009.

Mathison, Keith A. *Given for You: Reclaiming Calvin's Doctrine of the Lord's Supper*. Phillipsburg, NJ: P&R, 2002.

Maxwell, Jack. *Worship and Reformed Theology*. Pittsburgh: Pickwick, 1976.

Muller, Richard. *Dictionary of Latin and Greek Theological Terms: Drawn Principally from Protestant Scholastic Theology*. Grand Rapids, MI: Baker Book House, 1985.

Nevin, John W. "Answer to Professor Dorner." *Mercersburg Review* 15 (1869): 534–646.

———. "Catholic Unity: A Sermon." *Weekly Messenger of the German Reformed Church,* 9 (New Series), no. 49 (1844): 1861–62. Reprinted in *The Anxious Bench, Antichrist, and Catholic Unity*. Edited by Augustine Thompson. Eugene, OR: Wipf & Stock, 1999.

———. "Election Not Contrary to a Free Gospel." *Presbyterian Preacher* 1 & 2 (1832–1834): 209–24.

———. "Eulogy on the Life and Character of the Late Rev. Dr. Frederick Rauch." Chambersburg, PA: Publishing House of the German Reformed Church, 1841.

———. "The German Language." *Weekly Messenger of the German Reformed Church* 8 (New Series), no. 1 (1842).

———. "The Lutheran Confession." *Mercersburg Review* 1 (1849): 468–77.

———. *My Own Life: The Earlier Years*. Papers of the Eastern Chapter, Historical Society of the Evangelical and Reformed Church, No. 1, Lancaster, PA, 1964.

———. "Pseudo-Lutheranism." *Weekly Messenger of the German Reformed Church* 13 (New Series), no. 27 (1848).

———. "Pseudo-Protestantism." *Weekly Messenger of the German Reformed Church*, nos. 48–52, 1845.

———. "The Church: A Sermon." In *Addresses and Essays of Schaff, Nevin and etc.* Chambersburg, PA: German Reformed Church Press, 1847.

Nichols, James Hastings. *The Mercersburg Theology.* Oxford: Oxford University Press, 1966. Reprint, Eugene, OR: Wipf & Stock, 2007.

———. *Romanticism in American Theology: Nevin and Schaff at Mercersburg.* Chicago: University of Chicago Press, 1961. Reprint, Eugene, OR: Wipf & Stock, 2006.

Noll, Mark, ed. *The Princeton Theology: 1812–1921.* Grand Rapids, MI: Baker Book House, 1983.

Potter, G. R. *Zwingli.* Cambridge: Cambridge University Press, 1976.

Rahn-Clemens, Deborah. "Foundations of German Reformed Worship in the Sixteenth Century Palatinate." PhD diss., Drew University, 1995.

Rauch, Frederick Augustus. *Psychology; or, A View of the Human Soul; Including Anthropology, Adapted for the Use of Colleges.* 4th edition. New York: M. W. Dodd, 1841.

Schaff, Philip. "Princeton und Mercersburg." *Der Deutsche Kirchenfreund* 1 (1848): 154–57.

Schleiermacher, Friedrich. *The Christian Faith.* English translation of the second German edition, edited by H. R. Mackintosh and J. S. Stewart. Edinburgh: T & T Clark, 1928.

Schmidt, Leigh Eric. *Holy Fairs: Scotland and the Making of American Revivalism.* Grand Rapids, MI: Eerdmans, 2001.

Solomon, Richard C. *In the Spirit of Hegel.* Oxford: OUP, 1983.

Stepelevich, Lawrence S. "Eucharistic Theory: Hegelianism and Mercersburg Theology." *New Mercersburg Review* 20 (Autumn 1996): 3–16.

Thompson, Bard. "Melancthon and the German Reformed Church." *Bulletin of the Theological Seminary of the Evangelical and Reformed Church* 24, no.4 (1953): 162–85.

Wentz, Richard. *John Williamson Nevin, American Theologian.* New York; Oxford: OUP, 1997.

———. "Nevin and American Nationalism." In *Reformed Confessionalism in Nineteenth-Century America*, edited by Sam Hamstra Jr. and Arie J. Griffioen, 23–42. Lanham, MD: Scarecrow, 1995.

Witherspoon, John. *Lectures on Moral Philosophy.* Philadelphia: Woodward, 1822.

Yrigoyen, Charles, Jr., and George H. Bricker, eds. *Catholic and Reformed: Selected Theological Writings of John Williamson Nevin.* Pittsburgh, PA: Pickwick Press, 1978.

Ziegler, Howard J. B. *Frederick Augustus Rauch: American Hegelian.* Manheim, PA: Published by Franklin and Marshall College at the Sentinel Printing House, 1953.

WORKS CITED IN THE ORIGINAL

(where possible, the edition likely used by Nevin is provided; otherwise, either the original edition or a more modern edition is given)

Beza, Theodore. "Confessio fidei doctrinaeque de Coena Domini exhibita illustrissimo Principi Virtembergensi, authoribus Th. Beza et Guilhelmo Farello." May 14, 1557. In *Theodor Beza, nach handschriftlichen Quellen dargestellt*, edited by Johann Wilhelm Baum. Leipzig: Weidmannsche Buchhandlung, 1843.

Böckel, E. G. Adolf. *Die Bekenntniss-Schriften Der Evangelisch-Reformirten Kirche.* Leipzig: F. A. Brockhaus, 1847.

Bullinger, Heinrich. *Orthodoxa Tigurinae Ecclesiae ministrorum Confessio.* Zurich: Christoph Froschauer, 1545. Can be accessed at http://www.e-rara.ch/zuz/content/titleinfo/855784.

Calvin, John. *Commentarius ad Ephesios.* In *Ioannis Calvini noviodunensis Opera omnia : In novem tomos digesta*, vol. 7, *Commentarii in omnes Epistolis S. Pauli, atque etiam in Epistolam ad hebraeos:nec non in epistolas canonicas.* Amsterdam: John Jacob Schipper, 1667.

———. *Consensio mutua in re sacramentaria ministrorum Tigurinae Ecclesiae.* In *Opera omnia*, vol. 8, *Tractatus Theologici Omnes*, edited by Theodore Beza. Amsterdam: John Jacob Schipper, 1667.

———. *Consensionis capitum expositio.* In *Opera omnia*, vol. 8, *Tractatus Theologici Omnes*, edited by Theodore Beza. Amsterdam: John Jacob Schipper, 1667.

———. *Secunda defensio contra Westphalum.* In *Opera omnia*, vol. 8, *Tractatus Theologici Omnes*, edited by Theodore Beza. Amsterdam: John Jacob Schipper, 1667.

———. *Ultima admonition ad Westphalum.* In *Opera omnia*, vol. 8, *Tractatus Theologici Omnes*, edited by Theodore Beza. Amsterdam: John Jacob Schipper, 1667.

Dick, John. *Lectures on Theology by the Late Rev. John Dick.* Philadelphia: Wardle, 1844.

Dorner, Isaak August. *Entwicklungsgeschichte der Lehre von der Person Christi von den ältesten Zeiten bis auf die neuesten.* Stuttgart: Berlin, 1845–53. Originally printed in *Tübinger Zeitschrift*, 1835, no. 4, and 1836, no. 1. Translated by William Lindsay Alexander as *History of the Development of the Doctrine of the Person of Christ* (Edinburgh: T & T Clark, 1884).

Ebrard, August. *Das Dogma vom heiligen Abendmahl und seine Geschichte.* 2 vols. Frankfort am Main, 1846.

Gess, Friedrich Wilhelm. *Deutliche und möglichst vollständige Uebersicht über das theologische System Dr. Friedrich Schleiermachers.* Reutlingen: Ensslin und Laiblin, 1837.

Guericke, Heinrich Ernst Ferdinand. *Allgemeine christliche Symbolik.* Leipzig: K. F. Köhler, 1839.

Henry, Paul. *Das Leben Johann Calvin's.* F. und A. Perthes, 1846. English translation by Henry Stebbing as *The Life and Times of John Calvin, the Great Reformer* (London: Whittaker, 1849).

Jewel, John. *John Jewel's Apology of the Church of England.* Edited by Henry Morley. London: Cassell, 1888. May be found at http://anglicanhistory.org/jewel/apology/.

Morell, John Daniel. *An Historical and Critical View of the Speculative Philosophy of Europe in the Nineteenth Century.* London: William Pickering, 1846.

Niemeyer, H. A., ed. *Collectio Confessionum in Ecclesiis Reformatis publicatarum.* Leipzig: Klinkhardt, 1840.

Nevin, John Williamson. "Dr. Hodge on the *Mystical Presence.*" *Weekly Messenger of the German Reformed Church* 13 (New Series), nos. 37–48 (1848).

———. *History and Genius of the Heidelberg Catechism.* Chambersburg, PA: Publishing House of the German Reformed Church, 1847.

———. *The Mystical Presence: A Vindication of the Reformed or Calvinistic Doctrine of the Holy Eucharist.* Philadelphia: Lippincott, 1846.

Quick, John, ed. *Synodicon in Gallia reformata; or, The acts, decisions, decrees, and canons of those famous national councils of the Reformed churches in France [. . .].* London: T. Parkhurst and J. Robinson, 1692.

Schleiermacher, Ernst Daniel. *Der christlich Glaube nach den Grundsätzen der evangelischen Kirche im Zusammenhang dargestellt.* Berlin: Reimer, 1821. Translated and edited by H. R. Mackintosh and J. S. Stewart as *The Christian Faith* (New York: Harper & Row, 1963).

Turretini, Francois. *Institutio Theologiae Elencticae.* Geneva, 1679–1685.

Ullmann, Karl. "The Distinctive Character of Christianity." *Theologische Studien und Kritiken* (Jan. 1845). Abridged and translated by Nevin in *The Mystical Presence.*

Ursinus, Zacharias. *Commentary.* Edited and published in London by David Pareus. English translation by D. Henry Parrie. Oxford: Joseph Barnes, 1587.

———. *Gründlicher Bericht Vom Heiligen Abendmal unsers Herrn Jesu Christi, aus einhelliger Lehre der H. Schrifft, der alten Rechtglaubigen Christlichen Kirchen und auch der Augspurgischen Confession.* Neustadt, 1590. May be accessed via http://books.google.com.

Zwingli, Ulrich. *Christianae Fidei a Huldrycho Zuinglio praedicatae breuis & clara exposition.* Tiguri Zurich: Apud Christophorum Froschouerum, 1536.

———. *Huldrici Zuinglii Opera.* Edited by Melchior Schuler and Johannes Schulthess. Zurich: Friedrich Schulthess, 1829–42.

ADDITIONAL WORKS CITED IN THE ANNOTATIONS

Arminius, James. *The Private Disputations of James Arminius.* "Disputation 54: On the Lord's Supper." In *The Works of James Arminius*, Vol. 2, translated and edited by James Nichols. Public Domain: http://www.ccel.org/ccel/arminius/works2.iii.lxiv.html.

Bainton, Roland H. *Here I Stand.* Nashville: Abingdon, 1950.

Barnes, Albert. *Notes, Explanatory and Practical, on the Gospel.* New York: Harper & Brothers, 1861.

Barth, Karl. *The Theology of Schleiermacher.* Translated by Geoffrey W. Bromiley. Grand Rapids, MI: Eerdmans, 1982.

Berthoud, Jean-Marc. *Pierre Viret: A Forgotten Giant of the Reformation.* Tallahassee, FL: Zurich, 2010.

Bierman, Lyle, Charles Gunnoe, and Karin Maag. *Introduction to the Heidelberg Catechism.* Grand Rapids, MI: Baker Academic, 2005.

Booty, J. E. *John Jewel as Apologist of the Church of England.* London: Church Historical Society, S.P.C.K., 1963.

Bowie, Andrew. *Schelling and Modern European Philosophy.* London; New York: Routledge, 2001.

Bromiley, G. W. *Zwingli and Bullinger.* Philadelphia: Westminster, 1953.

Bruening, Michael W. *Calvinism's First Battleground: Conflict and Reform in the Pays de Vaud, 1528–1559.* Dordrecht: Springer, 2005.

Greschat, Martin. *Martin Bucer: A Reformer in His Times.* Translated by Stephen E. Buckwalter. Louisville, KY: Westminster John Knox Press, 2004.

Buehrer, Emil. "Zwingli's Sixty-Seven Articles." *Reformed Herald* (April 2011): 5–7.

Calvin, John. *Calvin: Theological Treatises.* Edited by J. K. S. Reid. Philadelphia: Westminster, 1977.

———. *Calvin's Commentaries.* 22 vols. Grand Rapids, MI: Baker Books, 2003.

———. *Calvin's Tracts and Treatises.* Edited by T. F. Torrance. Grand Rapids, MI: Eerdmans, 1958.

———. *Institutes of the Christian Religion.* Edited by John T. McNeill and translated by Ford Lewis Battles. Philadelphia: Westminster, 1977.

Chung-Kim, Esther. *Inventing Authority: The Use of the Church Fathers in Reformation Debates over the Eucharist.* Waco, TX: Baylor University Press, 2011.

Class, Monika. *Coleridge and Kantian Ideas in England, 1796–1817.* London; New York: Bloomsbury, 2012.

Cory, David Munroe. *Faustus Socinus.* Boston: Beacon, 1932.

Crouter, Richard. *Friedrich Schleiermacher: Between Enlightenment and Romanticism.* Cambridge: CUP, 2005.

Dennison, James T., Jr., ed. *Reformed Confessions of the 16th and 17th Centuries in English Translation:* Vol. 1, 1523–1552. Grand Rapids, MI: Reformation Heritage Books, 2008.

———. *Reformed Confessions of the 16th and 17th Centuries in English Translation:* Vol. 2, 1552–1566. Grand Rapids, MI: Reformation Heritage Books, 2010.

Dick, John. *Lectures on Theology by the Late Rev. John Dick.* 2 vols. New York: Robert Carter & Brothers, 1856. Reprint, LaVergne, TN: Kessinger Publishing Rare Reprints, 2010.

Dorner, Isaak August. *History of the Development of the Doctrine of the Person of Christ.* Translated by William Lindsay Alexander. Edinburgh: T & T Clark, 1884.

Dunlop, William, ed. *Collection of Confessions of Faith, Catechisms, Directories, Books of Discipline, etc.* Vol. 2. Edinburgh: James Watson, 1722.

Dunn, Geoffrey G. *Tertullian.* London: Routledge, 2004.

Erb, Peter. *Schwenckfeld in His Reformation Setting.* Valley Forge, PA: Judson, 1978.

Frew, Robert, ed. *Notes on the New Testament.* Grand Rapids, MI: Baker, 1983.

Gabler, Ulrich. *Huldrych Zwingli, His Life and Work.* Philadelphia: Fortress, 1986.

Gerrish, Brian. *A Prince of the Church: Schleiermacher and the Beginnings of Modern Theology.* Philadelphia: Fortress, 1984.

Gordon, Bruce, and Emidio Campi. *Architect of the Reformation: An Introduction to Heinrich Bullinger.* Grand Rapids, MI: Baker Academic, 2004.

Hartvelt, Gerrit P. *Verum Corpus: Een studie over een central hoofdstuk uit de avondmaalsleer van Calvijn.* Delft: W. D. Meinema, 1960.

Jahn, Johann. *Jahn's Biblical Archaeology.* Edited by Thomas Cogswell Upham. Andover, MA: Flagg and Gould, 1823.

Kitchen, James M. *Wolfgang Capito: From Humanist to Reformer.* Leiden: Brill, 1975.

Leibniz, Gottfried Wilhelm. *Essais de Théodicée sur la bonté de Dieu, la liberté de l'homme et l'origine du mal.* Amsterdam, 1710.

———. *Pensees sur la religion et la morale.* 2nd ed. Paris: Nyon, 1803, & (2 vols.) Brussels: Societe Nationale pour las Propagation des Bons Livres, 1838.

Maag, Karin, ed. *Melanchthon in Europe: His Work and Influence beyond Wittenberg.* Grand Rapids, MI: Baker Academic, 1999.

Malabou, Catherine. *The Future of Hegel.* New York: Routledge, 2005.

Marsden, George. *The Evangelical Mind and the New School Presbyterian Experience.* New Haven, CT: Yale University Press, 1970.

Maruyama, Tadataka. *The Ecclesiology of Theodore Beza: The Reform of the True Church.* Geneva: Librairie Droz, 1978.

McIntosh, J. R. "John Dick." In *Dictionary of Scottish Church History & Theology,* edited by Nigel Cameron. Edinburgh: T & T Clark, 1993.

McLaughlin, R. Emmet. *Caspar Schwenckfeld, Reluctant Radical.* New Haven, CT: Yale University Press, 1986.

Mosheim, J. L. von. *Institutes of Ecclesiastical History, Ancient and Modern.* Edited by James Murdock. London, 1832.

Muller, Richard A. *God, Creation and Providence in the Theology of Jacob Arminius.* Grand Rapids, MI: Baker Book House, 1991.

Nevin, John Williamson. *Antichrist; or, The Spirit of Sect and Schism.* New York: John S. Taylor, 1848. Reprinted in *The Anxious Bench, Antichrist, and Catholic Unity.* Edited by Augustine Thompson Eugene, OR: Wipf & Stock, 1999.

———. "The Anxious Bench." Chambersburg, PA: Publication Office of the German Reformed Church, 1843. Reprinted in *The Anxious Bench, Antichrist, and Catholic Unity.* Edited by Augustine Thompson Eugene, OR: Wipf & Stock, 1999

———. "The German Language." *Weekly Messenger of the German Reformed Church* 8 (New Series), no. 1 (1842): 1460.

———. *The Mystical Presence and the Doctrine of the Reformed Church on the Lord's Supper.* Edited by Linden J. DeBie. Eugene, OR: Wipf & Stock, 2012.

———. *The Mystical Presence and Other Writings on the Eucharist.* Edited by Bard Thompson and George Bricker. Philadelphia: United Church Press, 1966.

———. *Party Spirit: An Address.* Chambersburg: Publication Office of the German Reformed Church, 1840.

Nugent, Donald. *Ecumenism in the Age of the Reformation: The Colloquy of Poissy.* Cambridge, MA: Harvard University Press, 1974.

Nuzzo, Angelica. *Memory, History, Justice in Hegel.* New York: Palgrave Macmillan, 2012.

O'Donovan, Oliver. *On the Thirty-Nine Articles.* 2nd ed. London: SCM, 2011.

Olson, Roger E. *Arminian Theology: Myths and Realities.* Downers Grove, IL: IVP Academic, 2006.

Osborn, Eric. *Tertullian, First Theologian of the West.* Cambridge: CUP, 2003.

Raitt, Jill. *The Eucharistic Theology of Theodore Beza.* Atlanta: Scholars, 1998.

Rothe, Richard. *Die Anfänge der Christlichen Kirche und ihrer Verfassung.* Wittemberg: Zimmermann, 1837.

Schaff, Philip, ed. *The Creeds of Christendom.* 3 vols. New York: Harper & Brothers, 1877. Reprint, Grand Rapids, MI: Baker, 1998.

———, ed. *The History of the Christian Church.* Grand Rapids, MI: Hendrickson, 1996. First Published 1858–92 by Charles Scribner's Sons.

———, ed. *Nicene and Post-Nicene Fathers.* Translated by John Gibb. Edinburgh: T & T Clark, 1886.

———. *Principle of Protestantism: As Related to the Present State of the Church.* Chambersburg, PA: Publication Office of the German Reformed Church, 1845. Reprint, Eugene, OR: Wipf & Stock, 2004.

Schleiermacher, Friedrich Ernst Daniel. *Friedrich Schleiermachers Monologen.* Berlin: L. Heinmann, 1868.

———. "On the Discrepancy between the Sabellian and Athanasian Method of Representing the Doctrine of the Trinity." Translated by Moses Stuart. *Biblical Repository and Quarterly Observer* 5 (April 1835): 265–352, and 6 (July 1835): 1–116.

———. *Über die Religion: Reden an die Gebildeten unter ihren Verächtern.* Hamburg: F. Meiner, 1958. Translated by John Oman as *On Religion: Speeches to Its Cultured Despisers* (New York: Harper, 1958).

Stansbury, A. J. *Trial of the Rev. Albert Barnes, before the Synod of Philadelphia.* New York: Van Nostrand and Dwight, 1836.

Stupperich, Robert. *Melanchthon: The Enigma of the Reformation.* Cambridge: Lutterworth, 2005.

Sunshine, Glenn S. *Reforming French Protestantism: The Development of French Huguenot Ecclesiastical Institutions, 1557–1572.* Kirksville, MO: Truman State University Press, 2003.

Taylor, Charles. *Hegel.* New York: Cambridge: CUP, 1975.

Turretini, Francois. *Institutes of Elenctic Theology.* 3 vols. Edited by James T. Dennison and translated by George Musgrave Giger. Phillipsburg, NJ: P&R, 1992–1997.

Ursinus, Zacharias. *Commentary on the Heidelberg Catechism.* Translated by G. W. Williard. Reprint, Grand Rapids, MI: Eerdmans, 1954.

Visser, Derek. *Zacharias Ursinus: The Reluctant Reformer.* Cleveland, OH: Pilgrim, 1983.

Wright, D. F. *Martin Bucer: Reforming Church and Community.* Oxford: OUP, 1994.

Subject and Author Index